INVITATION TO Asian Religions

JEFFREY BRODD
California State University, Sacramento

LAYNE LITTLE
University of California, Berkeley

BRADLEY NYSTROM
California State University, Sacramento

ROBERT PLATZNER
California State University, Sacramento

RICHARD SHEK
California State University, Sacramento

ERIN STILES
University of Nevada, Reno

Oxford   New York
Oxford University Press

Oxford University Press is a department of the University of Oxford.
It furthers the University's objective of excellence in research,
scholarship, and education by publishing worldwide.

Oxford   New York
Auckland   Cape Town   Dar es Salaam   Hong Kong   Karachi
Kuala Lumpur   Madrid   Melbourne   Mexico City   Nairobi
New Delhi   Shanghai   Taipei   Toronto

With offices in
Argentina   Austria   Brazil   Chile   Czech Republic   France   Greece
Guatemala   Hungary   Italy   Japan   Poland   Portugal   Singapore
South Korea   Switzerland   Thailand   Turkey   Ukraine   Vietnam

For titles covered by Section 112 of the US Higher Education
Opportunity Act, please visit www.oup.com/us/he for the
latest information about pricing and alternate formats.

Published by Oxford University Press
198 Madison Avenue, New York, New York 10016
http://www.oup.com

Oxford is a registered trademark of Oxford University Press.

Library of Congress Cataloging-in-Publication Data
Brodd, Jeffrey, author.
   Invitation to Asian religions / Jeffrey Brodd, California State University, Sacramento
[and 5 others].
      pages cm
   Includes bibliographical references and index.
Summary: "Featuring a unique, consistent, and modular chapter structure--"Teachings,"
"History," and "Way of Life"--and numerous pedagogical features, Invitation to Asian
Religions invites students to explore Asia's great religions with respect and a sense of
wonder. It describes the essential features of each Asian religion and shows how they
have responded to basic human needs and to the cultural contexts in which they have
developed. The authors also encourage students to develop an appreciation of what
religious beliefs and practices actually mean to their adherents"-- Provided by publisher.
   ISBN 978-0-19-021126-4
   1. Asia--Religion. I. Title.
   BL1033.B76 2015
   200.95--dc23
                                                                        2015012252

Printing number: 9 8 7 6 5 4 3 2 1

Printed in the United States of America
on acid-free paper

BRIEF CONTENTS

CONTENTS

PREFACE

THE WORLD'S RELIGIOUS TRADITIONS have offered answers to the weightiest questions of human existence, contributed to the formation of political and social institutions, inspired masterpieces of art and literature, and provided many of the cultural values and ideals on which entire civilizations have been based. Today, religions continue to play a powerful role in shaping the ways in which people understand themselves, the world they live in, and how they should live.

Invitation to Asian Religions welcomes all students who may come to this course with concerns such as these. In these pages, we open the doors and invite the reader to explore with wonder and respect. We describe the essential features of the major Asian religions and show how they have responded to basic human needs and to the cultural settings in which they developed. We also compare the answers religions have offered us regarding some of the most essential human questions—Why are we here? What is the nature of the universe? How should we live? Our aim has been to balance concision and substance in an introductory text that is accessible, as well as challenging.

A team of authors cooperated in writing this book, each one of us bringing our particular scholarly expertise—as well as years of teaching experience—to our respective chapters. We wrote with important learning goals in mind. We want students to gain an objective understanding of the beliefs and practices associated with religions, but we also encourage an empathetic appreciation of what their beliefs and actions actually *mean* to adherents. By emphasizing the connections between religious traditions and their cultural contexts, we seek to heighten awareness of the extent to which religions have influenced, and been influenced by, politics and society, literature, the arts, and philosophy. We also examine the role of religions in our contemporary world, particularly the frequently uneasy boundaries between religion and science, urbanization, and globalization. A thoughtful reading of this book will provide a clear understanding of the characteristics that are unique to individual religions and highlight many of their shared qualities and concerns. Finally, we trust that every reader will find here a means of making sense of other ways of believing and living and of finding a solid basis for the tolerance and respect that are so critically important in times like ours.

Religions are multidimensional. Accordingly, all but the first chapter examine three primary aspects of each religion: **teachings**, **historical development**, and **way of life** (practices and experiences). These three aspects are presented in the same order in every chapter in which they appear, although we do not strive to devote equal attention to each category. To do so would be to ignore the varying nature of the religious traditions. In each case, we shape our coverage in the way that seems most natural given the characteristics of the tradition under discussion.

Teachings. Commonly found in scriptures, myths, creeds, and ethical codes, the basic teachings of a religious tradition convey its answers to fundamental questions, such as: What is the human condition? How can the human condition be improved or transcended? What is the nature of the world? What is ultimate reality, and how is it revealed? The authority on which a religion answers questions such as these is also important. Are its truths revealed? Are they the products of intellectual effort? Are they insights gained in moments of profound psychological experience? Or are they simply traditional ways of looking at reality and our place within it that have been passed down from generation to generation?

Historical Development. Every religious tradition has a history that reveals how and why it developed its distinctive features, including its system of beliefs, leadership and governance structures, social institutions, and forms of artistic expression. Sometimes the forces that generate change arise largely from within a tradition, as in the case of conflict between opposing sects or schools of thought. At other times they operate from the outside, as with the influence exerted by Western powers on foreign colonies and spheres of influence or through the expansion of a tradition into a new cultural milieu. A religion's history also functions to unite the individual with others in a shared memory of the past that helps to explain the present.

Way of Life. By way of life we mean practices—the things people *do* in making practical application of their beliefs, such as engaging in prayer, meditation, communal worship, or various other forms of ritual. Closely related to practices are modes of experience, the ways in which a religion's adherents actually experience the consequences of applying its teachings. These might include a sense of inner peace, a more acute sense of community with others, a greater awareness of the divine, or a state of profound enlightenment.

ORGANIZATION

Our survey begins with an introductory essay on the academic study of religions found in Chapter 1. After considering what religion *is*, Chapter 1 identifies some of the other important questions scholars ask: What do religions do? What issues of universal concern do they address? What do scholars mean when they speak of mystical experience or of transcendence? What are the constituent parts of religious traditions? How are religions today being affected by the forces of modernization, urbanization, globalization, and science? Finally, the chapter explains why a multidisciplinary approach is necessary in any serious attempt to understand the world's religions.

The six chapters on the religious traditions are organized according to geographical and (roughly) chronological order, as follows: first, the religions of South Asian origin (Hinduism, Buddhism, Jainism, Sikhism), followed by those of East Asian origin (Chinese religions, Japanese religions).

Invitation to Asian Religions and its companion, *Invitation to Western Religions*, are smaller, more specialized versions of *Invitation to World Religions*, Second Edition. To create *Invitation to Asian Religions*, the authors have selected and edited chapters from *Invitation to World Religions* to suit an introductory Asian religions course.

FEATURES AND PEDAGOGY

Because the concepts and contexts of the world's religions are immeasurably complex, we have worked to present a clear and accessible introductory text. Our tone throughout, while deeply informed by scholarship, is both accessible and appropriate for a wide range of undergraduate students. Consistent chapter structure also helps students to focus on *content* rather than trying to renavigate each chapter anew. With the exception of Chapter 1, every chapter in the book includes **three core modules: the teachings of the religion, the history of the religion, and the religion as a way of life**. This modular and predictable structure is also highly flexible, allowing instructors to easily create a syllabus that best reflects their own scholarly interests, as well as their students' learning needs.

The study of religions can be daunting to newcomers, who must plunge into a sea of unfamiliar words, concepts, and cultures. For this reason, we have provided a variety of ways for students to engage with important ideas, personalities, and visuals, such as:

- Voices: In personal, candid interviews, a diverse array of people share the ways they live their faith.
- Visual Guide: A key to important religious symbols, provided in an easy-to-read table for quick reference and comparison, is included in each "Way of Life" section.
- Maps and Timelines: Each chapter begins with a map to provide geographical context for a religion's development. Key features and places mentioned in the chapter are called out on the map. A Timeline at the beginning of each chapter provides social and political context to help students situate each religion and trace its development. Finally, a comprehensive Timeline of all the main religions covered in the book now appears on the inside front and back covers.
- Seeking Answers: After each chapter's Conclusion, we revisit three essential questions that religions strive to answer. This feature helps students to review the

chapter's key concepts and informs their ability to *compare* constructively the ways in which different religions address the same fundamental human questions:

1. What is ultimate reality?
2. How should we live in this world?
3. What is our ultimate purpose?

Other elements that facilitate teaching and learning include:

- Glossary: Important terms are printed in **bold type** at their first occurrence and are explained in the **Glossary** that follows each chapter. In addition, a glossary at the back of the book includes all of the key terms from the entire text.
- End-of-Chapter Questions: Each chapter concludes with two sets of questions to help students review, retain, and reflect upon chapter content. For Review questions prompt students to recall and rehearse key chapter concepts; For Further Reflection questions require students to think critically about the chapter's nuances and encourage both discussion and personal response by inviting students to engage in a more penetrating analysis of a tradition or taking a comparative approach.
- Suggestions for Further Reading: These annotated lists of some of the best and most recent works on each tradition, as well as online resources, encourage students to pursue their exploration of Asian religions.
- Rich, robust, and relevant visuals: Finally, we have filled the pages of *Invitation to Asian Religions* with an abundance of color photographs and illustrations that add visual experience to our verbal descriptions of sacred objects, buildings, art, and other material aspects of religious life.

SUPPLEMENTS

A rich set of supplemental resources is available for *Invitation to World Religions*, with which *Invitation to Asian Religions* can be paired. These supplements include an Instructor's Manual, Computerized Test Bank, PowerPoint lecture outlines, and PowerPoint art database on the Oxford University Press **Ancillary Resource Center (ARC)**; a **DVD of CNN Videos** to accompany World Religions courses; Student Resources on a **Companion Website**; integrated and automatically graded Student Resources on **Dashboard** by Oxford University Press; and **Learning Management System** Cartridges with Instructor and Student Resources.

The Oxford University Press **Ancillary Resource Center (ARC)** at oup-arc.com houses the following Instructor's Resources:

- A Computerized Test Bank, including
  - 40 multiple-choice questions per chapter
  - 30 true/false questions per chapter
  - 30 fill-in-the-blank questions per chapter
  - 10 essay/discussion questions per chapter

- An Instructor's Manual, including
  - A "pencil and paper" version of the Computerized Test Bank
  - Chapter Summaries
  - Chapter Learning Objectives
  - Suggested Weblinks and other Media Resources
  - Weblinks to Sacred Texts, accompanied by brief descriptions of their content
  - Lists of Key Terms and their definitions, from the text
- Customizable PowerPoint Lecture Outlines
- A customizable PowerPoint Art Database with images from the text

The **CNN Video DVD with Instructor's Video Guide** offers 15 recent clips on significant beliefs, practices, and places related to a variety of traditions covered in *Invitation to World Religions*. Each clip is approximately five to ten minutes in length and accompanied by a summary and series of discussion and multiple-choice questions. For a sample, please visit the Instructor's Resources page on the Companion Website at www.oup.com/us/brodd. To obtain the complete DVD, available to adopters of any OUP World Religions textbook, please contact your OUP representative or call 1-800-280-0280.

The **Companion Website** at www.oup.com/us/brodd houses links to the Instructor's Resources, as well as the following Student Resources:

- Level-one and level-two Student Quizzes taken from the Test Bank, including
  - 20 multiple-choice questions per chapter
  - 16 true/false questions per chapter
  - 16 fill-in-the-blank questions per chapter
  - 6 essay/discussion questions per chapter
- Chapter Learning Objectives
- Suggested Weblinks and other Media Resources
- Weblinks to Sacred Texts, accompanied by brief descriptions of their content
- Flashcards of Key Terms from the text
- An interactive map showing distributions of religions throughout the world

Student Resources are also available on **Dashboard**, by Oxford University Press. Dashboard delivers a wealth of activities and assessments for *Invitation to World Religions* in an intuitive, text-specific, integrated learning system. The *Invitation to World Religions* Dashboard site houses the following resources:

- Automatically graded level-one and level-two Student Quizzes from the Companion Website, with each question linked to a Chapter Learning Objective for instructor analysis of students' specific strengths and struggles
- Flashcards of Key Terms from the text
- A complete Glossary of Key Terms from the text
- An interactive map showing distributions of religions throughout the world

Access to Dashboard can be packaged with the text at a discount, stocked separately by your college bookstore, or purchased directly at www.oup.com/us/dashboard. For details, please contact your OUP representative or call 1-800-280-0280.

Learning Management System Cartridges are also available for *Invitation to World Religions,* and include the Instructor's Manual, the Computerized Test Bank, and all the Student Resources from the Companion Website. For more information on this, please contact your OUP representative or call 1-800-280-0280.

ACKNOWLEDGMENTS

This book has been a long time in the making. Along the way, family members, friends, and colleagues have supported us with love, patience, insights, and suggestions. We also are grateful to the people who kindly granted us interviews. Although there is no way we can adequately thank them here, we can at least acknowledge them: Edward Allen, Dr. Onkar Bindra, Jill Brodd, George and Kausalya Hart, Kathleen Kelly, Hari Krishnan, Ray and Marilyn Little, Watanabe Minoru, Annie Nystrom, Katherine Sei, Girish Shah, Kitty Shek, Davesh Soneji, Jason Ch'ui-hsiao Tseng, Archana Venkatesan, and Krishna and Jayashree Venkatesan.

We have also benefited immensely from the hard work and good suggestions of colleagues across the country. In particular, we would like to thank:

Marlin Adrian, Salem College

Kenneth Atkinson, University of Northern Iowa

Matthew Bingley, John Tyler Community College

Robert E. Brown, James Madison University

David Bush, Shasta College

John L. Crow, Florida State University

James Ford, Rogers State University

Matthew Hallgarth, Tarleton State University

Jon Inglett, Oklahoma City Community College

Maria Jaoudi, California State University–Sacramento

Kate S. Kelley, University of Missouri–Columbia

Mirna Lattouf, Arizona State University

Kenneth Lee, California State University, Northridge

Iain S. MacLean, James Madison University

Benjamin Murphy, Florida State University–Panama City

Arlette Poland, College of the Desert

Grant Hugh Potts, Austin Community College

Marialuce Ronconi, Marist College

John Sanders, Hendrix College

Kevin Schilbrack, Western Carolina University

Paul G. Schneider, University of
South Florida

Joshua Shelly, University of
Illinois—Urbana-Champaign

Glenn Snyder, Indiana University–
Purdue University Indianapolis

Phillip Spivey, University of Central
Arkansas

Dennis P. Tishken, Eastern Florida
State College

Mark A. Toole, High Point
University

James A. Zeller, San Joaquin
Delta College

We extend our special thanks to Ravi Gupta of Utah State University who responded so very helpfully to our request for expert advice.

Finally, we owe a debt of gratitude to the editorial staff at Oxford University Press. Our thanks go to Executive Editor Robert Miller, who originally invited us to publish with Oxford and continues to oversee the project. Editorial Assistant Kaitlin Coats helpfully managed reviews and other editorial tasks, including work with art and images and with the development and production of supplements for the book. Our thanks also go to Senior Production Editor Theresa Stockton for managing the final stages of the book's production.

An INVITATION to the STUDY of ASIAN RELIGIONS

ON AMERICAN COLLEGE CAMPUSES, indications of the world's religions are readily observable. Bulletin boards bear fliers announcing upcoming events pertaining to Buddhist meditation or Hindu sacred art or the Islamic observance of Ramadan. Campus religious groups engage in outreach activities at tables alongside walkways or in student unions, oftentimes with posters quoting scripture or displaying religious icons. Some icons even commonly adorn the students themselves—a cross necklace, for example, or a tattoo of the *yin/yang* symbol.

To study the world's religions is to progress from mere observation of things to understanding their meaning and relevance. Anyone who observes the *yin/yang* symbol can appreciate the beauty of its spiraling, interweaving symmetry, but studying Chinese religion reveals a much more complex meaning. Mysterious in their origins, *yin* and *yang* are complementary primal energies that give rise to all creation. For the human being, to maintain a perfect balance of *yin* and *yang* is to live an ideal life. The nearly ubiquitous symbol of the cross similarly takes on new depths and complexities of meaning, even for many who identify themselves as Christian, when approached through the study of world religions. To Christians, God, the creator of all things, having taken on human form in the person of Jesus Christ, willingly suffered the painful death of crucifixion on the cross to save humanity from the power of sin. We can expand on our understanding of the meaning and cultural

On many campuses, people of different religious perspectives gather for candlelight vigils to observe times of sorrow as well as celebration.

relevance of these two icons through a brief comparative study. Chinese religion, with its belief in the creative, complementary energies of *yin* and *yang,* has neither need nor room for a creator such as the Christian God. The Christian concept of sin and the corresponding need for salvation are alien to the Chinese quest for balance of *yin* and *yang.* These two icons, in other words, signify profoundly different cultural orientations.

To study the world's religions is to enhance one's understanding and appreciation of the rich variety of cultures around the globe. Limiting the scope of study to Asian religions offers similar benefits within a more focused cultural context. But whether concentrating on Asian religions or studying religions around the globe, the general approach is the same. This chapter introduces this field of study by exploring the significance, examining the foundational concepts, and describing appropriate strategies for the academic exploration of religion. ☀

APPROACHING THE STUDY OF WORLD RELIGIONS

In order to be an educated person today, one must have an awareness of world religions. To learn about this subject matter is to increase one's cultural literacy—the objective that lies at the heart of this study. The religious traditions examined in this book are foundational aspects of Asian cultures. Religion plays a crucial role in molding, transforming, and transmitting cultures. Interacting and intermeshing with other cultural aspects—politics, economics, aesthetics—religion is arguably a culture's most potent force, in ways both constructive and destructive. When people believe they are acting in a manner that is condoned by a transcendent power or is in keeping with timeless tradition, they tend to act more fervently and with greater potency. In other words, religions are powerful, sometimes even dangerous. Knowing about them is crucial for negotiating our richly complex world.

"World Religions" has been a prominent course of study in American colleges and universities for nearly a century. Recently, the category has come under scrutiny by some scholars, as has the so-called "world religions discourse" that often accompanies it.[1] Although such scrutiny sometimes tends to lose sight of the obvious—that "world religions" as an academic category, whatever its origins, is here to stay and that learning about its subject matter is vitally important—critics are correct to demand sound academic approaches to the study. A primary concern involves the fact that the study of world religions, and indeed the entire enterprise of the academic study of religion, arose within the nominally Christian European intellectual culture that tended to take for granted that Christianity was a model of what a religion ought to be and, commonly, that it was the only *true* religion. Until the late decades of the nineteenth century, theorists applied the term "world religion" (in the singular) only to Christianity. Eventually Buddhism, Judaism, and occasionally Islam were grouped with Christianity as "world religions" (or "the world's religions"). By the 1930s the list had grown to include the ten to twelve religions that still today are normally categorized as world religions.

And so, to the basic need for knowing about the world religions (however they came to be categorized), we can add another vital need: that we go about studying them appropriately through awareness of what we might call the "do's and don'ts" of religious studies, which this chapter explores in some detail. We can begin by noting that an appropriate study of world religions does not privilege any religion as being somehow exemplary or the model with which others are to be compared. On a related note, we need to avoid terms and categories that are rooted in such privileging. For example, "faith" is a natural term to use when studying Christianity, but it can hardly be applied to the study of Confucianism or Shinto. Other important issues involve underlying motives or assumptions that can too easily creep in. A common one is this: All religions ultimately say the same thing. This is an intriguing possibility, but in fact, it is impossible to prove by way of a sound academic approach—that is, well-reasoned theorizing based on careful analysis of the evidence.

The challenge of mastering the "do's" and avoiding the "don'ts" only enriches our study. We begin by considering the rise of the modern academic field of religious studies.

William James defined religion as "the feelings, acts and experiences of individual men in their solitude. . . ." Caspar David Friedrich depicted the solitary, contemplative individual in his 1818 painting, *Wanderer Above a Sea of Fog.*

Religion as a Subject of Academic Inquiry

The academic study of religion, commonly known as "religious studies" (or sometimes as "comparative religion" or "history of religions") is a relatively recent development. Prior to the European Enlightenment of the eighteenth century, it rarely occurred to anyone to think of a religion as an entity that could be separated from other aspects of culture, and therefore as something that could be defined as a distinct category and studied as such. Enlightenment thinkers, most influentially the German philosopher Immanuel Kant (1724–1804), conceived of religion as something separate from the various phenomena the human mind is capable of perceiving.[2] This impulse toward categorically separating religion, coupled with European exploration of distant lands and their unfamiliar "religions," launched efforts to understand religion that have continued to the present day. This shift means that we modern observers need to be cautious when appraising the religious aspects of other cultures, lest we make the error of assuming that all peoples have recognized religion as a distinctive category. Most cultures throughout history have had neither the conceptual category nor a term meaning "religion."

The academic study of religion is generally distinct from theology, the field of inquiry that focuses on considering the nature of the divine. Unlike religious studies, theology is an important example of *doing* and *being* religious, which naturally invites consideration of the supernatural and of the "truth" of religious claims. Religious studies, like most other academic pursuits, is to a large extent based in an approach to knowledge that depends on analysis of empirical data. The discourse and actions of human beings can be observed and studied through normal means of academic inquiry; empirical evidence can be gathered, and through rational argumentation hypotheses can be formulated and supported. Supernatural beings and events normally are held to be beyond the reach of academic inquiry. The academic study of religion,

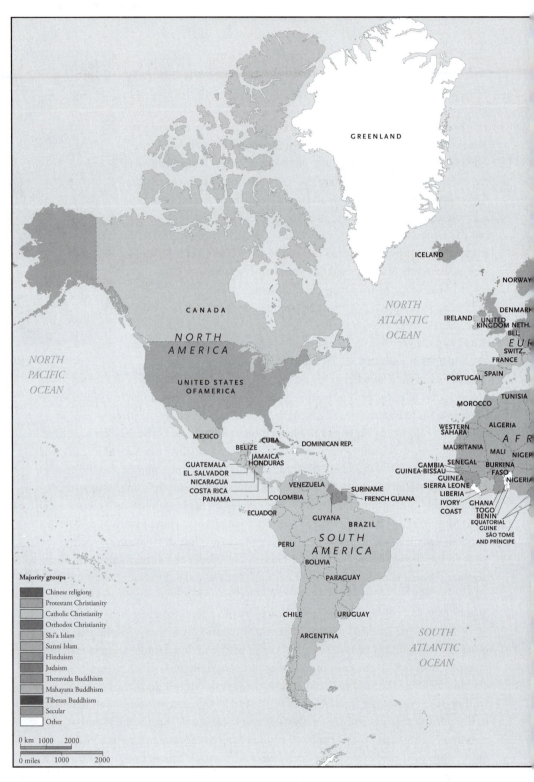

World religions today.

as understood by the authors of this book, is therefore not theology, however much we might admire theologians and enjoy studying their work, which is itself an important human enterprise and a major component of religion.

The Definitional Challenge A natural outcome of the Enlightenment impulse toward categorically separating religion from other aspects of culture has been to produce a universal definition of the term. Scholars from various academic disciplines have struggled with this challenge without having produced a single definition that pleases everyone. Many theorists today dismiss the challenge as futile, and some even go so far as to argue that use of the term "religion" in academic study should be abandoned altogether because of its ambiguity and misleading inferences. Most scholars involved in religious studies, however, agree that they are studying basically the same subject, and for lack of a better term most are content with calling it "religion."

The relevance of defining "religion" can be understood through an analogy that compares religions to houses. Embarking on a study of religions without concern over *what*, exactly, we are studying would be akin to setting off for foreign places to explore the nature of houses without first agreeing on what counts as a house. Would we include apartments? Vacation cabins? Palaces? Defining terms helps us draw clear boundaries around the subject of study. Another challenge involves our preconceived notions of things. We might assume that everyone shares a common idea of a typical "house" (like the kind we learned to draw in grade school), but such an assumption is mainly the result of preconceptions based on our own culture's norms. People from other cultures might dwell in structures that have little in common with our standard notion of a house.

Let's consider some notable attempts at conceptualizing "religion" while keeping in mind our "house" analogy. In fact, when exploring the more specific category "world religion," it will be useful to think of a similarly more specific category of house: a mansion, and more specifically, an old mansion that has undergone a long process of refurbishing. Although certainly considered a type of house, a mansion has many rooms that serve a wide variety of functions and styles. Imagine an old mansion that has kept the same foundation and basic structure over the years, but to which various inhabitants have made changes that have enabled the structure to survive into modern times. Our study of Asian religions is an invitation to explore several extraordinary "old mansions." Our tools of study—beginning with considerations of definition—are designed to help us make the most of our explorations, to take in fully the teachings, the histories, and the practices of these various world religions.

Three Classic Definitions The history of the attempt to formulate suitable definitions of "religion" is intriguing. In many instances, definitions reveal as much about the historical era and about the intentions of the individual theorist as they do about the nature of religion.

The following well-known definitions of "religion" were set forth by notable theorists in different fields:

A religion is a unified system of beliefs and practices relative to sacred things, that is to say, things set apart and forbidden—beliefs and practices which unite into one single moral community called a Church, all those who adhere to them.[3]

—Émile Durkheim

[Religion is] . . . the feelings, acts and experiences of individual men in their solitude, so far as they apprehend themselves to stand in relation to whatever they may consider the divine.[4]

—William James

[T]he religious aspect points to that which is ultimate, infinite, unconditional in man's spiritual life. Religion, in the largest and most basic sense of the word, is ultimate concern.[5]

—Paul Tillich

French sociologist Émile Durkheim (1858–1917), a founding figure of the sociological study of religion, emphasizes in his definition the *social* nature of religion. He insists on the unification brought about by "beliefs and practices," culminating in a "moral community called a Church." Durkheim surely hits on some central functions of religion, but most scholars contend that he overemphasizes this social orientation. On the other hand, American psychologist William James (1842–1910) emphasizes the *individual* nature of religion. Although this aspect is also clearly important, his definition omits any mention of religion's social nature. The definitions put forth by Durkheim and James, although provocative, are therefore problematically limiting.

Paul Tillich (1886–1965), a Protestant theologian, naturally connects religion to a focus on "man's spiritual life." His notion of religion as "ultimate concern" has been quite influential over the past several decades, probably in part because many find it true to their own experiences. But the definition is very broad, and it says nothing regarding the specific content of religious traditions. In emphasizing the existential concerns of religion, it neglects the social and institutional components of the traditions. People commonly claim to be "spiritual" while also denying that they belong to a religion. A sound definition needs to accommodate this distinction or else avoid this ambiguity altogether.

Two Prominent Definitions Let us now consider two definitions of religion that currently enjoy wide favor and that avoid these sorts of shortcomings. The *HarperCollins Dictionary of Religion*, a popular reference work, states: "One may clarify the term religion by defining it as a system of beliefs and practices that are relative to superhuman beings."[6] This definition encompasses a wide array of cultural phenomena, while at the same time restricting the category, most especially with the concept "superhuman beings."

Bruce Lincoln (b. 1948), one of the most prominent contemporary theorists of religion, asserts in his definition that a religion always consists of four "domains"—discourse, practice, community, and institution:

1. A discourse whose concerns transcend the human, temporal, and contingent, and that claims for itself a similarly transcendent status . . .
2. A set of practices whose purpose is to produce a proper world and/or proper human subjects, as defined by a religious discourse to which these practices are connected . . .
3. A community whose members construct their identity with reference to a religious discourse and its attendant practices . . .
4. An institution that regulates religious discourse, practices, and community, reproducing them over time and modifying them as necessary, while asserting their eternal validity and transcendent value.[7]

Lincoln's definition, although considerably lengthier than the *Dictionary*'s, is impressively precise. It also is helpfully inclusive. By basing religion on the notion of the "transcendent" rather than on "supernatural beings" or the like, Lincoln's definition encompasses Confucianism and forms of Buddhism, including Theravada, that do not focus on belief in supernatural beings. (Chapters 3 and 6 explore in more detail the categorization of Buddhism and Confucianism, respectively, as religions rather than "philosophies".) The religions featured in this textbook conform to Lincoln's definition. This is not to say that Lincoln, or for that matter any other theorist, has determined what religion "truly" is. In the words of sociologist Peter Berger (b. 1929), commenting on the challenge of defining religion, "a definition is not more or less true, only more or less useful."[8] For purposes of our study, Lincoln's definition provides a useful means of categorizing the subject matter. It clarifies why the traditions featured in this book qualify as religions while also, especially with its insistence that a religion involves an "institution," establishing helpful limits. The general category "spirituality," for example, would not necessarily qualify as religion based on Lincoln's definition.

We now shift our focus from what religions *are* to consider what religions *do*. In the next section, we analyze various functions of religion, concentrating especially on the fundamental questions to which religious traditions provide answers.

WHAT RELIGIONS DO

Whatever one thinks a religion *is*, this much remains certain: a religion *does*. This fact is closely related to the challenge of defining religion. Some theorists have emphasized this functional side of religion in their explanations. Underlying Durkheim's definition, for example, is a theory that reduces religion to being an effect of societal forces. Religion, in turn, serves to promote social unity. Here is a clear case in point that definitions reveal as much about the intentions of the theorist as they do about the nature of religion. As we have already noted, Durkheim is regarded as a founder of sociology;

it is not surprising that he emphasizes the social aspects of religion. Consider also this assertion from psychologist Sigmund Freud (1856–1939):

> Religion would thus be the universal obsessional neurosis of humanity; like the obsessional neurosis of children, it arose out of the Oedipus complex, out of the relation to the father.[9]

Freud was an atheist whose psychological theory held religion to be undesirable. Political philosopher Karl Marx (1818–1883), likewise an atheist, offers a similarly negative assessment, which is even more antagonistic toward religion:

> *Man makes religion*, religion does not make man. In other words, religion is the self-consciousness and self-feeling of man who has either not yet found himself or has already lost himself again. But *man* is no abstract being squatting outside the world. Man is the *world of man*, the state, society. . . . Religion is the sigh of the oppressed creature, the heart of a heartless world, just as it is the spirit of a spiritless situation. It is the *opium* of the people.[10]

At sites like this Confucian temple in Beijing, China, Confucius (Master K'ung) is honored for his enduring contributions to Chinese culture. Sound definitions of "religion" are flexible enough to include Confucianism as a religious tradition.

Marx, strongly affected by what he perceived as the economic disparities of the Industrial Revolution, was a thoroughgoing materialist who dismissed all forms of ideology as being abstractions and, to some extent, obstacles to the pursuit of true well-being. Freud similarly regarded religion as an effect of other forces, viewing it as a by-product of psychological forces. According to Freud, religion functions as an unhealthy but soothing buffer against the inner terrors of the psyche. For Marx, religion functions in a similarly unhealthy manner, as an opiate that deters the suffering individual from attending to the true cause of affliction.

These functionalist explanations, although provocative and at least somewhat insightful, are largely regarded now by scholars as being severely limited in their perspectives. Perhaps religions *do* function in these ways at certain times in certain situations; but surely religions do much more. In fact, neither Freud nor Marx ever actually tried to define religion; rather, they tried to explain it away. This does not diminish, however, the enduring relevance of these theorists for purposes of striving to understand the "big picture" of the role religion plays in the lives of individuals and in societies.

We can widen our vantage point on the functions of religion and produce a fairer and more accurate depiction by considering the variety of life's challenges that these traditions help people to face and to overcome.

Religious Questions and Challenges

It might seem disrespectful or even blasphemous to ask, Why do religions exist? But in fact this is a perfectly legitimate and instructive question. As human enterprises, religions naturally respond to human needs and readily acknowledge reasons for their doctrines and rituals. A typical reason has to do with some kind of perceived separation from the sacred or estrangement from a state of perfection or fulfillment. The human condition, as ordinarily experienced, is regarded as being disconnected from the fulfillment that lies at the end of a spiritual path. Various related questions and challenges are addressed by religions, with these three prominent questions recurring in some form in nearly every system:

1. What is ultimate reality?
2. How should we live in this world?
3. What is our ultimate purpose?

The rest of this book's chapters explore the ways major religions answer these questions. For now, let's consider these questions more broadly.

What Is Ultimate Reality? It is difficult to imagine a religion that has nothing to say about ultimate reality—even if this involves asserting that "ultimate" reality consists of no more than the natural world and we human beings who inhabit it. Religions typically assert that ultimate reality is somehow divine, and explanation of the nature and role of the divine takes center stage in a religion's belief system. But the "divine" is not necessarily thought of as God or gods. When it is, we refer to that religion as a **theistic** (from Greek *theos*, or god) belief system. When it is not, the religion is said to be **nontheistic**. Some forms of Buddhism, such as Zen, are clearly nontheistic. A helpful middle ground descriptive term is **transtheistic**, acknowledging the existence of gods—but of gods that are not vital with regard to the most crucial religious issues, such as the quest for enlightenment or salvation.[11]

Theistic religions can be further categorized. **Polytheism** (from Greek *polys*, or many) is the belief in many gods ("gods" is considered a gender-neutral term and can—and often does—include goddesses). **Monotheism** (from Greek *monos*, or only one) is the belief in only one god (and hence the term is normally capitalized—God—a proper noun referring to a specific being). Here, a kind of middle ground comes in the form of **henotheism** (from Greek *hen*, the number one), which acknowledges a plurality of gods but elevates one of them to special status. Some forms of Hindu devotion to a particular god such as Vishnu or Shiva are henotheistic.

Pantheism (from Greek *pan*, or all) is the belief that the divine is identical to nature or the material world. Although not one of the world's living religions, the ancient Greek and Roman religious philosophy known as Stoicism is an example. It is important to bear in mind, too, that the world's religions often feature entities that are supernatural and yet are not necessarily gods. These quasi-divine figures, such as angels, demons, and the monstrous characters that feature prominently in myths, are typically difficult to categorize but are important elements of religion nonetheless. To complicate matters further, scholars of non-Western religions have commonly used the term "god" to refer to supernatural beings that are more similar to angels, or even to the saints of Catholic tradition. The *theos* in the "polytheism" of such non-Western religions therefore often refers to a very different type of being than does the *theos* in "monotheism." Simplistic application of such terms is misleading.

Nontheistic belief systems include those that uphold **atheism**, which in modern parlance is a perspective that denies the existence of God or gods. In ancient times, a person could be labeled an atheist for denying the significance of deities, even while believing that they exist. Among the ancient Greeks and Romans, for example, Epicureans were considered to be atheists. Even according to the modern meaning of atheism, some atheists nevertheless could be regarded as religious—depending on how one defines "religion." The *HarperCollins Dictionary of Religion* definition, with its basis in "supernatural beings," likely would not leave room for atheism, whereas Bruce Lincoln's definition could.

Nontheistic religions (and here the term is on surer footing) also include those that conceive of the divine as an impersonal force or substratum of existence. Some nontheistic religions, such as various forms of Buddhism (Chapter 3) and Hinduism (Chapter 2), even assume the existence of divine beings while rejecting the notion that such beings can truly help humans find spiritual fulfillment. Some Hindus, for example, while believing in many gods and goddesses, hold that Brahman, impersonal and ultimately indescribable, is the essence of all. Those Hindus therefore embrace **monism** because of this primary belief that all reality is ultimately one. Monism is also described as nondualistic, because there is no distinction between the divine reality on one hand and the rest of reality, including human individuals, on the other.

Such a categorizing scheme admits to some complications. Some Hindus are monistic because they understand all reality ultimately to be one thing: Brahman. But some of those same monistic Hindus also pay homage to a variety of supernatural and divine beings, and thus might also be described as polytheists.

Along with asserting the existence of ultimate reality, religions describe how this reality is revealed to human beings. The foundational moments of **revelation** are frequently recorded in sacred texts, or scriptures. In the case of theistic religions, scriptures set forth narratives describing the role of God or the gods in history and also include pronouncements directly attributed to the divine. In the Jewish and Christian Bible, for example, God's will regarding ethical behavior is expressed directly in the Ten Commandments. The giving of the Ten Commandments is described in the long narrative about the Exodus of the Israelites from Egypt, in which God is said to have played a central role.

This painting, produced in 1810, depicts the Hindu deities Shiva and Parvati with their children, Ganesha and Kartikeya. Hindus believe in many gods and goddesses, these four—and especially Shiva—being among the most popular.

Among nontheistic religions in particular—but also among the mystical traditions that form part of every religious tradition—revelation usually combines textual transmission with a direct experience of revelation. Revelation is usually experienced by a founding figure of the religion, whose experiences are later written about; subsequent believers can then experience similar types of revelation, which requires their own participation. Buddhists, for example, have scriptural records that describe the Buddha's experience of "unbinding" or release, as well as pronouncements by various deities praising the ultimate value of that experience. Followers must then connect to such revelation through practices such as meditation.

Another helpful way of thinking about revelation is offered by historian of religions Mircea Eliade (1907–1986), who makes much descriptive use of the phenomenon he calls "hierophany," or "the *act of manifestation* of the sacred," which helps a people to establish its cosmology, or religious understanding, of the order of the world.[12] Eliade emphasizes how this concept applies to indigenous or small-scale traditions (those of "archaic man" in Eliade's terminology). But the phenomenon of the hierophany is readily apparent within the world's major religions, often, but not always, as a theophany, a manifestation of God or of gods. The role of hierophanies in establishing places of special significance can be observed in many of the sites related to the founding figures and events of the major religions: Christianity's Church of the Nativity (and other sacred sites related to the life of Christ); Islam's sacred city of Mecca; Buddhism's Bodh Gaya, site of Gautama's foundational experience of Enlightenment; and so on. Sacred moments establish sacred spatial monuments, thus establishing a sense of centrality and spatial order.

Along with often referring to other worlds, religions have much to say about *this* world. Human beings have always asked searching questions about the origin and status of our planet and of the universe. Typically these two issues—origin and status—are intertwined. If our world was intentionally fashioned by a creator god, for instance, then it bears the stamp of divine affirmation. Thus the early chapters of the Book of Genesis in the Hebrew Bible (the Christian Old Testament) describe the measured, creative activity of God, including the creation of humankind. In contrast, the creation stories of some religious traditions deemphasize the role of the divine will in bringing about the world, sometimes (as in the religion of the ancient Greeks) describing the advent of the principal deities *after* the universe itself has been created. The gods, like humans, come into a world that is already established; gods and humans are depicted as sharing the world, which naturally affects the relationship between human and divine. In other religions,

Ka'ba, Mecca.

notably those same South Asian traditions that embrace liberation as the ultimate religious objective, this world is depicted as a kind of illusion, somehow not altogether real or permanently abiding. It is thus not so surprising that liberation involves being completely freed from the confines of this world.

These are but a few examples of religious understanding of the nature of the world, a general category known as **cosmology** (from *kosmos*, the Greek term for world or universe). Along with clarifying the origin and sacred status of the world, cosmology also explains how the world is ordered. Many traditions attribute the order of the universe to the doings of divine being(s) or forces. Yet in certain respects modern scientific explanations set forth cosmologies that are intriguingly similar to some religious cosmologies taught by religious personages of the distant past,

The Andromeda Galaxy.

such as Gautama the Buddha or Epicurus, a Greek philosopher who espoused a theory of atomism, arguing that reality is composed entirely of a very large number of very small particles. (Recall that the Epicureans were labeled "atheists" because they denied the significance of the gods.)

Of course, a particular religion's cosmology strongly influences the degree to which its adherents are involved in caring for the world. Religions that are indifferent or hostile toward the natural world are not apt to encourage anything akin to environmentalism. On the other hand, a religion that teaches that the world is inherently sacred naturally encourages a sense of stewardship toward the natural world. Native American traditions, for example, are notably environmentally oriented.

How Should We Live in This World? Many religions have much to say about God or other superhuman beings and phenomena, and yet all religions are human enterprises. Their teachings are communicated in human languages, their rituals are practiced by human participants, and their histories are entwined with the development of human societies and cultures. Religions also explain what it is to be a human being.

Explanations regarding what it is to be human also figure largely into ethical or moral considerations. Are we by nature good, evil, or somewhere in between? Religions tend to recognize that human beings do not always do the right thing, and they commonly offer teachings and disciplines directed toward moral or ethical improvement. To say that we are by nature good, and at the same time to recognize moral failings, is to infer that some cause external to our nature is causing the shortcoming. If we are by nature evil, on the other hand, or at least naturally prone to doing

Sixteenth-century triptych (altar painting) depicting the creation of Eve (center), the eating of the forbidden fruit (left), and the expulsion from the Garden of Eden (right). This story of humankind's first sin sets forth basic biblical perspectives on the human condition.

wrong, then the moral challenge lies within and the means of improvement would need to be directed inwardly.

Religions typically prescribe what is right behavior and what is wrong, based on a set of ethical tenets, such as the Jewish and Christian Ten Commandments. In fact, the very prospects of improving upon the human condition and of faring well in an afterlife quite commonly are deemed to depend in some way upon right ethical behavior. The ethical teachings of many religions are notably similar. The so-called Golden Rule ("Do unto others what you would have them do unto you"[13]) set forth in the Christian New Testament is pronounced in similar forms in the scriptures of virtually all of the world's major traditions.

The religions differ, however, over the issue of the source of ethical truth. Some emphasize **revealed ethics**, asserting that God, or some other supernatural force such as Hindu *dharma* (ethical duty), has established what constitutes right behavior and has in some manner revealed this to human beings. The divine will might be conceived of as God (or gods), or it might take the form of an impersonal principle, such as *dharma*. Another common approach, in some forms of Buddhism, for example, emphasizes the role of conscience in the moral deliberations of each individual. These two emphases are not necessarily mutually exclusive. Some religions, Christianity among them, teach that both revealed ethics and individual conscience work together as means of distinguishing right from wrong.

What Is Our Ultimate Purpose?   The challenge of mortality—the fact that we are destined to die—is sometimes cited as the primary motivating force behind religion. And although it is true that all religions have at least something to say about death, the wide diversity of perspectives is quite astounding. For example, whereas Christianity, with its focus on the resurrection of Christ and the hope of eternal life, can be said to make mortality a central concern, Zen Buddhism, drawing inspiration from the classic Daoist texts, refuses to make much at all of death beyond acknowledging its natural place in the order of things.

Both the challenge of mortality and the issue of our moral nature relate to questions regarding the human condition—and what can be done about it. In many faiths, how we conduct ourselves in this world will determine our fates after we die. Most religions readily acknowledge that human beings are destined to die (although some, such as Daoism, have at times aspired to discover means of inducing physical immortality). As we have noted, some religions have little to say about the prospects of life beyond death. But most religions do provide explanations regarding the fate of the individual after death, and their explanations vary widely.

Hinduism, Buddhism, Jainism, and Sikhism all maintain belief in *samsara*, the "wheel of life" that implies a series of lives, deaths, and rebirths for every individual. The ultimate aim of each of these religions is liberation from *samsara*. Buddhist nirvana is one such form of liberation. But most of the adherents of Buddhism and these other religions anticipate that death will lead to rebirth into another life form (not necessarily human), one in a long series of rebirths. Furthermore, the reborn are destined for any one of multiple realms, including a variety of hells and heavens.

Other religions, notably Christianity and Islam, teach that individuals are destined for some sort of afterlife, usually a version of heaven or of hell. Sometimes the teachings are more complicated. The traditional Catholic doctrine of purgatory, for example, anticipates an intermediary destiny somewhere between the perfect bliss of heaven and the horrible agony of hell, where an individual can gradually be purified from sin, ultimately achieving salvation and entry to heaven.

Given what a religion says about the human condition, what ultimate purpose is the religious life intended to achieve? Is there a state of existence to which the religious person can hope to aspire that perfectly completes or even transcends the human condition, overcoming entirely its cares and shortcomings?

One such state of existence is the **numinous experience**, as described by Rudolf Otto in his classic work *The Idea of the Holy* (1923). Otto (1869–1937), a Protestant theologian and a philosopher of religion, describes the encounter with "the Holy" as "numinous," a term he coined from the Latin *numen*, meaning spirit or divinity (plural, *numina*). A genuine numinous experience, Otto asserts, is characterized by two powerful and contending forces: ***mysterium tremendum*** and ***fascinans***. *Mysterium tremendum*, which in Latin means "awe-inspiring mystery," is the feeling of awe that overwhelms a person who experiences the majestic presence of the "wholly other."[14] *Fascinans* (Latin, "fascinating"), is the contrasting feeling of overwhelming attraction. The encounter with the Holy is thus alluring (*fascinans*) even as it is frightening on account of the awe-inspiring mystery (*mysterium tremendum*). The biblical phenomenon of the "fear of God" fits this description, as the God who is being feared is at the same time recognized as the source of life and the hope for salvation.

Otto's insightful analysis of the numinous experience suffers from a significant limitation: based in his Protestant Christian outlook, it may ring true to a Protestant; from a global perspective, however, the analysis is rather limiting. For example, Otto discounts the **mystical experience**, a category that includes such phenomena as Buddhist nirvana, the complete dissolution of an individual's sense of selfhood said

Moses and the Burning Bush (1990), charcoal and pastel on paper by Hans Feibusch. In the drawing, God reveals himself to Moses in a bush that is on fire but not consumed by the flames. The event is described in Exodus, the second book of the Hebrew Bible (Old Testament).

by Buddhists to be a state of perfect bliss and ultimate fulfillment. According to Otto, nirvana involves too much *fascinans* without enough *mysterium tremendum*.

Recall that Bruce Lincoln's definition of religion is based on the notion of the transcendent. Both the numinous experience and nirvana are examples of transcendent states of existence. For Otto, the numinous experience depends on the existence of "the Holy," or God. For many Buddhists, the experience of nirvana does not depend whatsoever on belief in God or gods. Most world religions, whether they embrace belief in a supernatural being or not, assert the possibility of such a transcendent state of existence, an ultimate objective of the religious life that brings complete fulfillment of all spiritual longings. For a Buddhist who has experienced nirvana, for example, there is, paradoxically, no longer a need for Buddhism. The religious life has been lived to its fullest extent, and the ultimate objective has been reached. Because nirvana involves the complete extinction of individual existence, it is truly transcendent of the human condition. Other religions, in widely varying ways, also set forth ultimate objectives, whether or not they imply the complete transcendence of the human condition. In some cases spiritual fulfillment can be said to consist of living in harmony with nature. Others readily acknowledge the supernatural—usually God (or gods)—and the need for human beings to live in perfect relationship with it. Christianity, for example, offers salvation from the effects of sin, which otherwise estrange the individual from God. Sometimes spiritual fulfillment is thought to be achievable in this lifetime; other times it is projected into the distant future, after many lifetimes of striving and development.

Of course, improving upon the human condition does not have to involve complete transcendence or anything close to it. Day to day the world over, religious people improve upon the human condition in all sorts of ways. Belief in a loving God gives hope and fortitude in the face of life's uncertainties. Meditation and prayer bring an enhanced sense of tranquility. Religious motivations often lie behind charitable acts. Belonging to a religious group offers social benefits that can be deeply fulfilling. Even for individuals who do not participate directly in a religious tradition, sacred art, architecture, and music can bring joy to life.

DIMENSIONS OF RELIGIONS

Sound definitions strive to be universal in scope. Along with a sound definition, a means of categorizing the common, though not necessarily universal, components of a subject of study can often prove beneficial. We now explore possibilities for identifying religious phenomena, in part to bring home the important point that there is no "right" or "wrong" way to go about categorizing them. Instead, we seek the most useful means given the task at hand. This will lead naturally to clarifying how this book goes about organizing its presentation of material.

Some scholarly approaches to the world's religions feature specific categories of phenomena as the primary means of organizing information. Religious scholar Ninian Smart's (1927–2001) "dimensional" scheme, for example, divides the various aspects of religious traditions into seven dimensions:

- The mythic (or sacred narrative)
- The doctrinal (or philosophical)
- The ethical (or legal)
- The ritual (or practical)
- The experiential (or emotional)
- The social
- The material[15]

Meditating Buddha, sixth century C.E. (Thai). Sculptures of the Buddha typically depict the serene calm of the enlightened state.

Such an approach to the content of religious traditions is very useful, especially if one focuses on a comparative analysis that emphasizes particular motifs (that is, "dimensions" or aspects thereof).

In this book, we organize things into three main categories: teachings, historical development, and way of life. Although each chapter of this book is organized around these three main categories, we do not strive in all chapters to devote equal attention to each category. To do so would be to ignore the varying nature of the religious traditions and to force an inappropriately rigid structure.

Teachings

Obviously, religions tend to involve beliefs. But as long as they remain private to the individual, beliefs are problematic for the student of religion. As public elements of a religion's teachings, however, beliefs can be observed and interpreted. Such public beliefs are manifested as doctrines or creeds—sets of concepts that are *believed in.* (The term "creed" derives from the Latin verb *credo,* or "I believe.")

Religious teachings include another significant category, often referred to as **myth** (as noted in Smart's "mythic" dimension). Quite in contrast to the modern connotation of myth as a falsehood, myth as understood by the academic field of religious studies is a powerful source of sacred truth. Set forth in narrative form and originally conveyed orally, myths do not depend on empirical verifiability or rational coherence for their power. They are simply accepted by believers as true accounts, often involving events of primordial time that describe the origin of things.

As we have noted previously, religions typically include ethical instructions, whether doctrinal or mythic, among their teachings. And as Smart readily acknowledges, the various dimensions are closely interrelated; the ethical dimension, for example, extends into the doctrinal and the mythic, and so forth.

Historical Development

It almost goes without saying that the world's major religions have long and intricate histories. Thus the historical development of religious traditions incorporates a vast sweep of social, artistic, and other cultural phenomena.

The wide array of artistic, architectural, and other aspects of material culture generated within religious traditions is of course obvious to anyone who has studied art history. The ornate Hindu temple sculptures, the majestic statues of Jain *tirthankaras*, the mathematically ordered architectural features of Islamic arabesque décor—these, among countless other examples, attest to the extensive role of religion in the nurturing of material culture. Other forms of artistic creation, most prominently music and theater, also are common and significant features of religions. And, as Smart helpfully clarifies when discussing the material dimension of religion, natural entities (mountains, rivers, wooded groves) are designated as sacred by some traditions.

Devils Tower, located in northeastern Wyoming, is regarded as a sacred place by many Native Americans.

Social institutions and phenomena of various sorts—economic activities, politics, social class structures and hierarchies—have typically played highly influential roles in the historical development of religious traditions. As we have observed, Marx and

Durkheim went as far as to reduce religion to being entirely the effect of economic and societal forces, respectively. Even for theorists who opt not to go nearly as far as this, the relevance of such phenomena is obvious.

Way of Life

This main category tends to feature two general types of religious phenomena: practices and modes of experience. Recall that Smart includes the ritual (or practical) and the experiential (or emotional) among his seven dimensions of religion. Some such elements are tangible and readily observable and describable, such as a **ritual** like the exchange of marriage vows or the procession of pilgrims to a shrine. Others are highly personal and therefore hidden from the outsider's view. One of the great challenges of studying religions rests precisely in this personal, private quality. Modes of experience such as Buddhist nirvana are by definition beyond the reach of empirical observation and of description. Rudolf Otto, throughout his analysis, emphasizes the impossibility of describing the "numinous" experience fully. Even common practices such as prayer and meditation tend to involve an inner aspect that is highly personal and quite inaccessible to anyone who is not sharing the experience. A book such as this one can do its best to illustrate and to explain these experiential phenomena but cannot be expected to provide a full disclosure at certain points. Such is the nature of religion.

RELIGIONS IN THE MODERN WORLD

A sound analysis of the world's religions must pay heed to the rapid changes that characterize the modern world. Historical transformations, accelerated during the past several centuries by such diverse and powerful factors as colonialism, the scientific revolution, and economic globalization, have reshaped religious traditions. This book takes into account such factors whenever appropriate. Here we introduce four specific phenomena that will reappear frequently in the pages that follow: modernization, urbanization, globalization, and multiculturalism. We give special attention to two features of modernization that are especially noteworthy for our study: the increasingly visible place of women within religious traditions and the encounter of religion and science.

Modernization and Related Phenomena

Modernization is the general process through which societies transform economically, socially, and culturally to keep pace with an increasingly competitive global marketplace. Its net effects include increased literacy, improved education, enhanced technologies, self-sustaining economies, the increased roles of women in various aspects of society, and the greater involvement of the general populace in government (as in democracies). All these effects involve corresponding changes within religious traditions. Higher literacy rates and improved education, for example, facilitate increased access to religious texts that previously were controlled by and confined to the religious elite. Technological advances, strengthened economies, and increased participation in government all nurture greater equality for and empowerment of the common people. A general feature of modernity, moreover, is its tendency to deny the authority of tradition and the past. Traditional patriarchal modes, for example, have tended over time to be diminished. Around the globe, we are witnessing a general erosion of long-standing power structures within religions. Obviously this is not the case in all circumstances; changes have tended to occur in different societies at different times, and some religious institutions are better equipped to ward off change. But over the long haul, modernization clearly has influenced the reshaping of religious traditions.

Urbanization A significant demographic effect of modernization is **urbanization**, the shift of population centers from rural, agricultural settings to cities. A century ago, only about 10 percent of the global population lived in cities; today, more than half of us are urbanites. Many religious traditions developed within primarily rural settings, patterning their calendars of holy days and rituals around agricultural cycles. Such patterns have far less relevance today for most religious people.

Trinity Church, built in 1846, sits amidst the skyscrapers of Wall Street in New York City.

Globalization **Globalization** is the linking and intermixing of cultures. It accelerated quickly during the centuries of exploration and colonization and has been nurtured considerably by the advanced technologies brought about by modernization. The extent of this linking and intermixing is evinced in the very term "World Wide Web," and the pronounced and rapidly evolving effects of the Internet and other technologies have been extraordinary. The almost instantaneous exchange of information that this technology allows is more or less paralleled by enhanced forms of affordable transportation. In sum, we now live in a global community that could hardly have been imagined a few decades ago.

Multiculturalism The most pronounced religious effects of globalization pertain to the closely related phenomenon of **multiculturalism**, the coexistence of different peoples and their cultural ways in one time and place. Many people today live in religiously pluralistic societies, no longer sheltered from the presence of religions other than their own. This plurality increases the degree of influence exerted by one religion on another, making it difficult for many individuals to regard any one religious tradition as the *only* viable one. This circumstance, in turn, fosters general questioning and critical assessment of religion. To some extent, such questioning and critical assessment erodes the authority traditionally attributed to religion.

Globalization, then, like modernization, has nurtured the notably modern process of **secularization**, the general turning away from traditional religious authority and institutions.

The Changing Roles of Women in Religions

One of the more pronounced effects of modernization on world religions has been the increased visibility and prominence of women within many traditions. To some extent this increase also has *caused* the furtherance of modernization. As women increasingly feel themselves empowered and are afforded opportunities to effect change, their momentum propels modernizing transformations. Traditional patriarchal modes have tended to give way to more egalitarian ones, and old assumptions have gradually receded. To cite just one example, the percentage of clergy in Protestant Christian churches who are women has recently risen quite dramatically. According to a 2009 survey, in 1999 5 percent of senior pastors were female; ten years later this had doubled to 10 percent.[16]

Corresponding to the increased visibility and prominence of women in many religions has been the dramatic development over the past five decades of feminist theory and its application to the study of religion. Sometimes referred to as women's studies or as gender studies, academic approaches based in feminist theory have revealed the strong historical tendency of religious traditions to subordinate women and to enforce the perpetuation of patriarchal systems. On the one hand, these studies have revealed contributions of women through the ages that have hitherto been largely ignored, while on the other hand they have prompted changes within some religions that have expanded the roles of women and have provided opportunities for higher degrees of prominence. In other words, studies based in feminist theory have to some extent *changed* the religions themselves, along with providing new and potent means of studying them.

The Encounter of Religion and Science

Perhaps no single feature of modernization has been more challenging to traditional religious ways—and more nurturing of secularization—than the encounter of religion with science. One need only think of the impact of Charles Darwin's *Origin of Species* (1859) and its theory of evolution to note the potential for conflict between scientific and traditional religious worldviews. The question of whether the biblical account of creation should be taught alongside the theory of evolution in schools is a divisive issue in some predominantly Christian societies today. In the domain of cosmology, too, science has tended to overwhelm traditional perspectives, such as the idea that the Earth is somehow the center of the cosmos, as implied in the Bible and in the creation myths of many traditions.

Many more examples could be drawn from the history of religions and the history of science to illustrate the ongoing potential for conflict between these two domains. Of course, religions are not always hostile to science. In fact, as we have already noted, sometimes modern scientific theories seem almost to converge with ancient religious outlooks. Acquiring a more sophisticated perspective on the encounter of religion and science requires us to consider the underlying reasons for both conflict and convergence.

Fundamental to the scientific method is dependence on empirical data, the observable "facts" of any given situation. To a large extent, religions do not rely only on the observable as a source of determining truth. Religious belief is often characterized precisely by commitment to the *non*observable, such as a supernatural being. This very term, "supernatural," indicates another, related point of contention between religion and science. For whereas the latter takes for granted that the universe consistently obeys certain laws of nature, religions commonly embrace belief in beings and events that are not subject to these laws.

And yet, these issues of natural laws and of the observable versus the unobservable also lead to points of convergence between science and religion. Certain basic and extremely significant scientific questions remain unanswered. For example, what is the ground of consciousness? What causes gravity? What existed, if anything, prior to the Big Bang, and what caused *its* existence? Science and religion can perhaps generally agree over this: mystery abounds. Granted, the scientific response to a mystery is "let's solve it," whereas the religious response typically is, "this is a mystery and is meant to be." But in the meantime, mystery abides, allowing for a certain kind of convergence. It is probably no accident that the percentage of scientists in the United States who regularly attend religious services is almost the same as the percentage for the general population.[17]

AN ACADEMIC APPROACH TO THE STUDY OF RELIGIONS

Scholars approach the study of religion in a variety of ways. And although there is no such thing as *the* correct approach, it is helpful to keep some basic concepts in mind.

Balance and Empathy

One concept is the maintenance of a healthy balance between the perspective of an insider (one who practices a given religion) and the perspective of an outsider (one who studies the religion without practicing it). For, although an insider arguably has the best vantage point on the lived realities of the religion, presumably the insider is primarily concerned with *being* religious and not in explaining the religion in a manner most effective for those who hold other religious (or nonreligious) perspectives. It is quite natural for an insider to feel bias in favor of his or her own religion. The outsider, on the other hand, would have no reason to feel such bias. But the outsider would not have the benefit of experiencing the religion firsthand. It is analogous to trying to understand a goldfish in a pond. An outsider can describe the fish's color, its movements, its eating habits. But the outsider can say very little about what it is actually like to be a goldfish.[18]

The academic approach to the study of religions attempts to balance the perspectives of insider and outsider, thereby drawing upon the benefits of each. It is not an intentionally religious enterprise. As we have noted previously, it is not *doing* religion or *being* religious, unlike theology. Instead, it strives to analyze and describe religions in a way that is accurate and fair for all concerned—insiders and outsiders alike. An instructive parallel can be drawn from the discipline of political science. Rather than advocating a particular political point of view, and rather than *being* a politician, a political scientist strives to analyze and describe political viewpoints and phenomena in a fair, neutral manner. A good political scientist could, for instance, belong to the Democratic Party but still produce a fair article about a Republican politician—without ever betraying personal Democratic convictions. A good scholar of religion, of whatever religious (or nonreligious) persuasion, attends to religious matters with a similarly neutral stance.

A miniature illustration from the "Automata of al-Jazari," a Muslim scholar, inventor, engineer, mathematician, and astronomer who lived from 1136 to 1206.

Another basic concept for the academic approach to religion is **empathy**, the capacity for seeing things from another's perspective. Empathy works in tandem with the usual tools of scholarship—the observation and rational assessment of empirical data—to yield an effective academic approach to the study of religions. The sometimes cold, impersonal procedures of scholarship are enlivened by the personal insights afforded by empathy.

Comparative and Multidisciplinary Approaches

A sound study of the world's religions also features a comparative approach. The chief benefit of this was emphasized by the nineteenth-century scholar Friedrich Max Müller (1823–1900), who is generally regarded as the founder of the modern field of religious studies. He frequently asserted that to know just one religion is to know none. In other words, in order to understand the phenomena of any given tradition, it is necessary to study other traditions, observing such phenomena as they occur in a wide variety of situations. This naturally requires that the study of world religions be cross-cultural in scope. As we proceed from chapter to chapter, the usefulness of comparison will become more and more evident.

This is not to say that comparison should be undertaken haphazardly or with intention only to discover similarities while ignoring differences. Those critics mentioned earlier who deride the "world religions discourse" tend to be suspicious of attempts at comparison, claiming that too often similarities are indeed valued over differences and that the categories used to make comparisons tend to privilege Christianity over other traditions. Sometimes the results of the comparison of religion differentiate religions into groups that are too sweepingly general. Still, the benefits of comparative analysis outweigh the risks, and the potential pitfalls that these critics appropriately warn against can indeed be avoided through a conscientious approach.

Along with being cross-cultural, religious studies is multidisciplinary, or poly-methodic, drawing on the contributions of anthropology, history, sociology, psychology, philosophy, feminist theory, and other disciplines and fields of study.

This chapter on many occasions has made use of the term *culture*, the study of which is the domain of anthropology. We have noted that religion plays a crucial role in molding, transforming, and transmitting cultures and that it interacts and inter-meshes with other cultural aspects. A sound study of the world's religions requires careful consideration of the interrelationship between religion and culture; in other words, it requires a healthy dose of cultural anthropology.

The need for involvement of the other disciplines should be likewise apparent. Given their historical and social aspects, the appropriateness of the disciplines of history and sociology for the study of religions is to be expected. And especially when trying to make sense of the modes of religious experience, psychology offers important inroads to understanding that the other disciplines are not equipped to provide. Along with Freud and James, whose definitions we have considered, Swiss psychologist Carl Jung (1875–1961) deserves mention for his vital contributions to the study of religious symbolism and of the general role of the unconscious mind in the religious life. The philosophy of religion, in certain respects the closest to actually *doing* religion (or theology), endeavors to assess critically the truth claims and arguments set forth by religions. Questions involving the existence of God, for example, are among those taken up by philosophers. Feminist theory, as noted previously, has contributed substantially toward advancing the study of world religions. Theories and methods of the natural sciences also have contributed substantially, at a pace that is accelerating rapidly. The widest array of innovations has come from cognitive science, which studies both the physical capacity for thinking (i.e., the "brain"—although this category can also include computers and other systems of artificial intelligence) and mental functions (i.e., the "mind"). Cognitive science is itself a multidisciplinary field with contributors who include neuroscientists, evolutionary biologists, and computer scientists, along with specialists from the social sciences.

Suffice it to say that the multidisciplinary nature of religious studies accounts for its very *existence* as an academic discipline. Without the involvement and contributions of its many subdisciplines, there could be no academic field of religious studies.

CONCLUSION

In this chapter, we have explored the nature of religion and how to study it from an academic perspective. The main objective is to prepare for the study that follows, a chapter-by-chapter examination of the major Asian religions. But the relatively theoretical and methodological content of this introductory chapter is relevant and challenging in its own right. Indeed, some readers might be surprised to learn that the search for an adequate definition has posed a daunting challenge or that the study of religion requires special means of approach. Hopefully these same readers have come to recognize the complexity of the ideas and the challenge of the task without feeling daunted about going forward with our study.

We have noted that the rest of this book's chapters feature a threefold organizational scheme consisting of teachings, historical development, and way of life. Although these chapters, with their focus on the religious traditions themselves, naturally are quite different from this introduction, it is worth noticing that in this chapter, too, we have featured historical development—of both the attempts to explain or define religion and the approaches to studying it—and teachings, most especially the theories of various notable contributors to religious studies. The "way of life" aspect perhaps has been less obvious, but in fact it is important and deserves consideration as we end the chapter. On more than one occasion we have drawn a distinction between the academic study of religion and *doing* religion or *being* religious. Where, then, does this leave the individual who wants to do (and be) both? Ultimately, this is a question to be left for the individual reader to ponder. But it might prove helpful to know that the degree of *being* religious among scholars of religion spans the spectrum of possibilities, from not religious at all to highly devout. Either way (or someplace in between), one thing is true for all who venture forth to study the world's religions: we are investigating important and enduring aspects of human cultures, down through the millennia and around the globe. Our understanding of things that matter is sure to be enriched.

REVIEW QUESTIONS

For Review

1. Who is Émile Durkheim, and what is notable about his definition of religion?
2. Bruce Lincoln, in his definition of religion, identifies four "domains." What are they?
3. What is "revelation," and how is it pertinent to the question: What is ultimate reality?
4. Identify and briefly describe Ninian Smart's seven "dimensions" of religion.
5. What is "empathy," and how is it relevant for the academic study of religion?

For Further Reflection

1. Sigmund Freud and Karl Marx, while tending to be dismissive of the enduring importance of religion, asserted explanations that continue to provoke and to enrich academic consideration of the role of religion. Based on their statements included in this chapter, how might their perspectives be provocative and enriching in this respect?
2. This chapter and book pose three prominent questions with regard to the challenges addressed by the world's religions: What is ultimate reality? How should we live in this world? What is our ultimate purpose? Drawing on examples and ideas presented in this chapter, discuss to what extent and in what ways these three questions are interrelated.
3. Explore the interrelationship of these features of religions in the modern world: globalization, secularization, and multiculturalism.

GLOSSARY

atheism Perspective that denies the existence of God or gods.

cosmology Understanding of the nature of the world that typically explains its origin and how it is ordered.

empathy The capacity for seeing things from another's perspective, and an important methodological approach for studying religions.

globalization The linking and intermixing of cultures.

henotheism The belief that acknowledges a plurality of gods but elevates one of them to special status.

modernization The general process through which societies transform economically, socially, and culturally to become more industrial, urban, and secular.

monism The belief that all reality is ultimately one.

monotheism The belief in only one god.

multiculturalism The coexistence of different peoples and their cultural ways in one time and place.

mysterium tremendum* and *fascinans The contrasting feelings of awe-inspiring mystery and of overwhelming attraction that are said by Rudolf Otto to characterize the numinous experience.

mystical experience A general category of religious experience characterized in various ways, for example, as the uniting with the divine through inward contemplation or as the dissolution of the sense of individual selfhood.

myth A story or narrative, originally conveyed orally, that sets forth basic truths of a religious tradition; myths often involve events of primordial time that describe the origins of things.

nontheistic Term denoting a religion that does not maintain belief in God or gods.

numinous experience Rudolf Otto's term for describing an encounter with "the Holy"; it is characterized by two powerful and contending forces, *mysterium tremendum* and *fascinans*.

pantheism The belief that the divine reality is identical to nature or the material world.

polytheism The belief in many gods.

revealed ethics Truth regarding right behavior believed to be divinely established and intentionally made known to human beings.

revelation The expression of the divine will, commonly recorded in sacred texts.

ritual Formal worship practice.

secularization The general turning away from traditional religious authority and institutions.

theistic Term denoting a religion that maintains belief in God or gods.

transtheistic Term denoting a theological perspective that acknowledges the existence of gods while denying that the gods are vital with regard to the most crucial religious issues, such as the quest for salvation.

urbanization The shift of population centers from rural, agricultural settings to cities.

SUGGESTIONS FOR FURTHER READING

Eliade, Mircea. *The Sacred and the Profane: The Nature of Religion*. Translated by Willard R. Trask. New York: Harper and Row, 1961. Eliade's most accessible work, offering a rich analysis of sacred space and time.

Hinnels, John, ed. *The Routledge Companion to the Study of Religion*. 2nd ed. Oxford: Routledge, 2010. Coverage of significant issues in religious studies by leading scholars.

(*continued*)

Masuzawa, Tomoko. *The Invention of World Religions: Or, How European Universalism Was Preserved in the Language of Pluralism*. Chicago: University of Chicago Press, 2005. Careful historical analysis of the term and category "world religions."

Pals, Daniel. *Nine Theories of Religion*. 3rd ed. New York: Oxford University Press, 2014. The best introduction to the history of religious studies as an academic field, including chapters on Karl Marx, William James, Sigmund Freud, Émile Durkheim, and Mircea Eliade.

Smart, Ninian. *Dimensions of the Sacred: An Anatomy of the World's Beliefs*. Berkeley and Los Angeles: University of California Press, 1996. An engaging presentation of Smart's "dimensions."

Smith, Jonathan Z. *Imagining Religion: From Babylon to Jonestown*. Chicago Studies in the History of Judaism. Chicago and London: University of Chicago Press, 1982. A collection of essays that exemplify Smith's impressively wide-ranging and astute approach to the study of religion.

Taylor, Mark C., ed. *Critical Terms for Religious Studies*. Chicago: University of Chicago Press, 1998. Articles on various central topics for the study of religions, written by leading scholars in the field.

ONLINE RESOURCES

American Academy of Religion

aarweb.org

The largest and most influential North American academic society for the study of religion.

Pew Research Religion and Public Life Project

pewforum.org

Excellent source of information on issues involving social and political aspects of religion.

The Pluralism Project at Harvard University

pluralism.org

Offers an impressive array of helpful resources, especially with regard to the world's religions in North America.

HINDUISM

ON A SPRING MORNING in the Salt Lake Valley, Indra Neelameggham and her husband Neale join a gaily dressed crowd, many of whom clutch offerings of flowers, fresh fruits, and coconuts. Indra and Neale have watched friends and the community work to create a beautiful place for worship in this stark region of Utah.

This is the third of three days of rituals celebrating the temple's opening, during which nearly 1,000 people have passed the temple threshold, gathering to attend the intricate consecration ceremony.

A week ago a three-foot-tall icon of Ganesha had been moved from Indra's house, where she had hosted him as an honored guest for eight years while the temple was being constructed, to his new home in the temple.

With his elephant head and human body, Ganesha is one of Hinduism's most easily recognized deities. As the patron deity of arts and sciences and the god of wisdom, new beginnings, and commerce, he is especially venerated by students, writers, travelers, and businessmen. Ganesha is worshipped at the beginning of every new undertaking, and he is the first deity invoked in almost any Hindu ritual context. He is often depicted as carrying objects in his four arms (including an axe, a noose, and an elephant goad) that he uses to destroy, subdue, or control the obstacles of life. He also often holds a bowl of sweets, symbolizing his benevolent and loving nature.

Ganesha appears adorned for worship in the sanctum of the Sri Ganesha Hindu Temple of Utah. Because Hindu deities are often associated with the land in which they are worshipped, he is affectionately called "Uppu Vinayaka" or the "Salt" Ganesha, by some of the local devotees.

The previous day, at midnight, the statue of Ganesha had been permanently affixed to its base in the temple's innermost sanctum. Now, the priest conducts a ritual that invites the actual divine spirit into the icon, transforming a simple stone image into a deity. The final step of the ritual requires that the priest awaken the gaze of the deity. While the priest outlines the icon's eyes with a golden needle, a sculptor pierces the pupils with a diamond-tipped chisel. The deity is now awake, and Ganesha's initial powerful gaze must first fall on things that represent good fortune: a cow with its calf, young children, mounds of rice, and bountiful offerings of food that will be distributed to the devotees.

Like the other devotees at the temple, Neale and Indra are overcome by reverence and exuberance. They realize that they have helped to build not just a temple, but a community. And at the center of it all is their Ganesha of Salt Lake. They step forward to have **darshan**—that is, to see and to be seen by the divine—and feel the immense presence of a living being. ☀

Unlike many other religions discussed in this book, Hinduism has neither a single founder nor a single sacred book. There is no single historical event that marks its birth. The history of Hinduism embodies both continuity and change. Having never had a sole central authority, Hinduism's fluid character has always allowed it to adapt to a variety of social and cultural contexts. This diversity has led many scholars to argue that Hinduism is not one religion at all but a constellation of many religious sects that share some common aspects. Others see enough by way of common beliefs and practices to regard Hinduism as a single religious tradition. In this chapter, we will explore Hinduism's variety of sects, beliefs, and practices and seek to understand what unites a religious tradition capable of thriving as far away from its homeland of India as Salt Lake Valley.

THE TEACHINGS OF HINDUISM

Prior to the nineteenth century, the word "Hinduism" did not exist. Most Hindus identified themselves by their sectarian orientation and their communal or caste affiliations. The word *Hindu* was initially a term used by the ancient Persians to describe the people who lived beyond the Indus River in the northwestern corner of the Indian subcontinent. By 325 B.C.E., Alexander the Great had crossed the Indus; the Greek conquerors adopted the Persian convention of calling the river the "Indos" and the land beyond it "India." In the centuries that followed, the term "Indu" or "Hindu" became a territorial, as well as a racial, social, and cultural, designation for the people of India. After the sixteenth century C.E., the word appeared occasionally in Indian literature to distinguish "Hindus" from Muslims or other "foreigners." Although the "-ism" was added to "Hindu" in the early 1800s, only toward the end of the nineteenth century did the word "Hinduism" become widely used by Hindus themselves.

A photograph taken of a Hindu temple in Trinidad in 1931. The presence of Hindus in the Caribbean and South America can be traced back to the nineteenth century, when Hindus came as indentured workers on sugar cane plantations.

Some Hindus look to the authority of a group of texts known as the **Vedas** and may rely on **brahmin** priests to officiate at various rituals. Others reject the centrality of the *Vedas* and *brahmins*. Some Hindus join organizations built around saints or sages. Others seek solitude to practice contemplation, meditation, or yoga. Some Hindus believe that God is a divine person with identifiable attributes. Others say that divine reality is so expansive as to be beyond all description.

Despite Hinduism's diversity, it is possible to identify common core concepts in which most every Hindu believes. For instance, the law of **karma** determines the nature of one's incarnations in **samsara**, the continuing cycle of death and rebirth. At the end of this cycle is **moksha**, or liberation, the final release from the trials and tribulations of *samsara*.

For the sake of simplicity, in this chapter we have organized our investigation of Hindu teachings around four main topics. First, we examine beliefs about God or divine reality. Next, we explore Hinduism's key doctrines and social concepts. We then take up a discussion of Hinduism's foundational texts. We conclude with a brief survey of *Vedanta*, a philosophical school, and Hinduism's three major sects.

Hindu Beliefs about Divine Reality

In keeping with Hinduism's general diversity, Hindu beliefs about divine reality are wide ranging. Indeed, one of the most fundamental differences in Hinduism is the split between monistic and dualistic (or devotional) viewpoints. Monism, as explained in this book's introductory chapter, is the doctrine that all reality is ultimately one. It is nondualistic in that there is no distinction between the divine reality and the rest

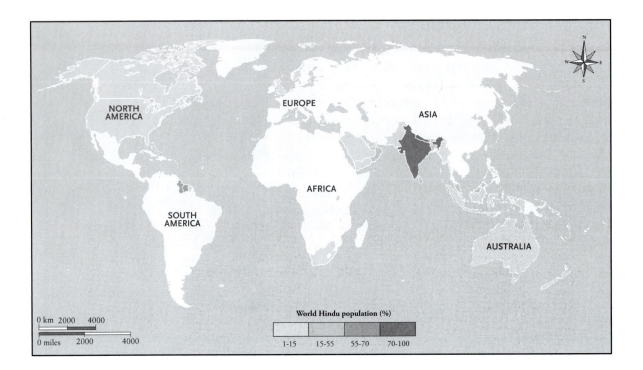

World Hindu population (%)

1-15   15-55   55-70   70-100

World Hindu population.

of reality. The Hindu dualistic viewpoint, on the other hand, understands divine reality as God, a personal being separate from the rest of reality. This means that God is separate from the individual, and therefore devotion to God is possible. Devotional practice of this sort is a primary religious activity of Hindus who hold this dualistic viewpoint. The majority of Hindus understand divine reality in this dualistic manner.

Names of the Divine Reality   Hindus refer to divine reality in a variety of ways. In this chapter, in order to maintain clarity between references to the monistic and the dualistic viewpoints, we use two distinct terms. When referencing monism, we use the term **Brahman** (lit. "expansive") to denote the divine reality, which monistic Hindus believe is the supreme, unitary reality that is the source of all being and all knowing. When referencing dualistic or devotional Hinduism, we use either "God" or the name of the specific deity under consideration.

In actual Hindu practice, conventions of naming the divine are often not so simple as our chapter's use of these two distinct terms might imply. Sometimes monistic Hindus, for example, refer to *Brahman* as "God." Many dualist Hindus use "God" to denote a universal being that encompasses all the various deities worshipped in Hinduism, and sometimes they use the term *Brahman*. When dualistic Hindus refer to a particular deity, they often use the specific name, such as Krishna, Rama, or Shiva. Devotees of the goddess traditions refer to God as *Mahadevi* ("Great Goddess") or *Mataji* ("mother"). Sometimes Hindus use Sanskrit terms such as *Bhagavan* (lit.

"Magnanimous One;" also an epithet for Vishnu) and *Svami* (or Swami, lit. "Master"; also denoting an initiate of a monastic order).

One Divine Reality, Many Gods The monistic viewpoint does not preclude belief in gods and goddesses. In a famous passage from the **Upanishads** (a collection of early philosophical texts), a sage is asked how many gods there are. Initially, he says there are "three hundred and three, and three thousand and three," but, upon reflection, he ultimately concludes that there is only one.[1] The sage explains that the various powers of the divine manifest as countless deities. In later times, the traditional number grew to 330 million. The passage from the *Upanishads* concludes with the sage giving the name of the one god: *Brahman*, which is the supreme, unitary reality, the ground of all Being.

Although *Brahman* is the true nature of all that exists, including ourselves, it is indescribable from the ordinary human perspective. *Brahman* can be described only by way of some general attributes: infinite being (*sat*), infinite awareness (*chit*), and infinite bliss (*ananda*). A passage from the *Upanishads* states that *Brahman* is *neti, neti*: "not this, not this."[2] When all of the identifiable particulars of the universe are subtracted away, what remains is *Brahman*, the essential substratum of all existence. This is monism, the belief that all reality is ultimately one.

These passages from the *Upanishads* influence how later monistic Hinduism forms its understanding of the mystery and majesty of Being. Many monistic Hindus believe that God is simultaneously one—as *Brahman*, the ground of all Being—and many. Given the worship of many deities, along with affirmation of the ultimate singularity of the divine, and indeed of *all* reality, this form of Hinduism can be described as both polytheistic and monistic. Unlike polytheistic religions that see the various gods as limited, Hinduism regards each god as a manifestation of *Brahman*.

Divine Reality as Sound The primordial sound **OM** (or, more literally, *AUM*), is constituted of three sounds of the Sanskrit language: *A, U,* and *M*—the first two, vowels, and the last, a consonant, respectively. *OM* therefore encompasses all words and all things they represent. *OM* is the sound through which the universe is manifested and thus is the very expression of *Brahman*. Some *Upanishads* also identify it with four states of consciousness: *A* is waking consciousness, *U* is dreaming consciousness, *M* is deep sleep without dreaming consciousness, and *AUM* in its entirety is the fourth and final state, oneness with *Brahman*. In later Hinduism, the sounds are identified with the gods Brahma, Vishnu, and Shiva and their functions of creating, preserving, and dissolving the universe.

God as Image Paradoxically, given the difficulty of comprehending the nature of divine reality, Hinduism is an intensely imagistic religious tradition. This is especially true of dualistic Hinduism, as imagistic representations of God are naturally well suited for devotional practices.

Ringed by cosmic time represented by a fiery ring, Shiva as Lord of the Dance (Nataraja) performs his Five Activities: creation (represented by the drum in his upper right hand), preservation (signified by the positions of his lower right and left hands), destruction (symbolized by the fire in his upraised left hand), illusion (personified by the tiny Demon of Forgetfulness crushed beneath his right leg), and liberation (offered by surrendering to his upraised left foot). Chola period, c. eleventh century. India, Tamil Nadu.

Images of supernatural beings and mythical beasts decorate Hindu temples, as well as Hindu homes. This love for the divine form emerges from Hindu notions of the simultaneous immanence and transcendence of God. An image of a deity is a symbolic representation meant to aid devotees in contemplating the deity's divine attributes, but the image is also believed to be suffused with divine presence, as we saw in the opening narrative about the Ganesha temple. Thus, Hindus believe that God becomes accessible to devotees through images. For Hindus, an image of a god *is* God.

Some images feature multiple limbs and faces that represent the deity's many aspects (such as compassion, serenity, or ferocity). The multiple hands of a deity depict gestures or hold objects that reveal his or her activities, such as providing protection, granting wishes, or holding a book of wisdom. Images can be richly adorned stationary icons enshrined in temples or beautifully crafted bronze icons carried in religious processions. Some images are quite large, such as the statue of Ganesha we encountered at the beginning of this chapter. Icons in personal shrines in Hindu homes tend to be small. Today, some Hindus revere print and online images of the divine. Because of the emphasis on divine images and their worship, Hindus sometimes have been falsely characterized as idolatrous. For Hindus, however, images of God are imbued with the divine essence. It is this essence that is worshiped and invoked through ritual action.

The Divine in Nature If *Brahman* is everywhere and everything, it follows that the natural world is an expression of the divine. This belief is held by most Hindus, whether inclined toward the monistic or the dualistic viewpoint. The worship of such natural entities as rivers, the earth, mountains, and the sun, as well as a reverence for certain trees and animals, can be traced back to the roots of Hinduism.

Many sacred sites arose in conjunction with the worship of rivers and mountains. Rivers in particular are worshipped as embodying the creative energy that generates the universe, as well as being powerful places of crossing between the divine and terrestrial worlds. It is for all of these reasons that many Hindus bathe in rivers—of which the Ganges in India is the most important—believing that they wash away one's sins. The renowned classical Sanskrit writer Kalidasa (fifth century c.e.) described the Himalayas as a *devatatma,* a great spiritual presence. For centuries, the awe-inspiring peaks of the Himalayas have attracted monks, yogis, and pilgrims seeking an experience of the divine. Mount Kailasha, believed to be the home of the god Shiva, draws devotees who perform a ritual circumambulation of the mountain over the course of several days, reaching elevations of greater than 18,000 feet on the trek. Hindu mythology portrays the sun, planets, and other celestial bodies as gods.

For Hindus, all living things are sacred, and some especially so. For example, the Pipal (*ficus religiosa*), the type of fig tree under which Gautama the Buddha attained enlightenment (Chapter 3), is sacred to the god Vishnu. As is well known, a special place is given to the cow in Hindu society, a practice that has deep historical roots in the various pastoral, cattle-tending communities found throughout India. Because a child, once weaned from its mother's breast, is frequently given cow's milk, the cow is revered by Hindus as a second mother. Cows are worshipped on the first day of the important Hindu festival of *Diwali,* as well as on the first day of a harvest festival observed in southern India. For Hindus, the worship of cows is an expression of respect for creatures that help humanity.

Although Hinduism has a long history of reverence for natural entities, this has not always translated into ecological awareness and activism. The worship of rivers does not mean that India's sacred waterways are pristine. Because rivers are divine, they are said to be able to absorb the sins of worshippers and still remain unaffected. Thus, for many Hindus, rivers remain pure even if they are polluted by waste. In recent years, Hindu environmental activists have begun to challenge these assumptions by employing Hindu beliefs about the divinity of the natural world to promote more informed ecological awareness.

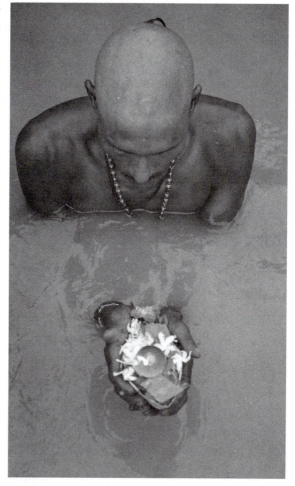

A Hindu devotee performs rituals dedicated to the Sun God as he takes a holy dip in Allahabad, India, at the confluence of the Ganges and Yamuna Rivers, one of Hinduism's important centers.

God Comes Down: Avatars Two of the most popular deities in Hinduism are Krishna and Rama. Each is an **avatar**, a "descent" (Sanskrit, *avatara*) of God to earth in a physical form with the specific goal of aiding the world. Like most avatars, they are manifestations of Vishnu, whose primary function is the preservation of order in the world. Vishnu is believed to have ten such forms, of which nine have already appeared. As noted, the most popular of the avatars are Rama, Vishnu's seventh form, and Krishna, his eighth. It is said that Vishnu's final avatar, Kalki, will arrive at the end of the present age to usher in an era of peace.

We have seen that Hindus often use the names of particular gods as a way of referring to divine reality. This is the case with avatars. For example, Hinduism's best-known sacred text, the *Bhagavad Gita* (*The Song of the Lord*), presents Krishna as a manifestation of the supreme Being.

In the *Bhagavad Gita*, Krishna asserts the principle that although God's essential nature is unchangeable, God chooses to descend into the world in the form of an avatar when intervention is necessary to reinstate peace and harmony. Krishna says:

> Although I am unborn,
> an imperishable self,
> and the Lord
> of all Beings,
> I govern my own
> earthly nature,
> and come into being
> by my own creative force.
> Son of Bharata,
> whenever there is
> a decline
> in *dharma*,
> and the absence
> of *dharma*
> increases,
> I create myself.
> I come into being
> from age to age
> with the purpose
> of fixing *dharma*—
> as a refuge for
> those who do good
> and as a doom
> for those who do evil.
> (*Bhagavad Gita*, 4:6–8)[3]

We will learn more about the *Bhagavad Gita* later in this chapter.

The Individual and the Quest for Liberation

Having explored Hindu perspectives on divine reality, we turn now to basic concepts that form the framework of the Hindu outlook on the individual and the quest for liberation. Some of these concepts, such as *samsara* and karma, are shared by other religions (Buddhism, Jainism, and Sikhism), although each treats these concepts in different ways.

Atman   All Hindus believe in an undying soul or self, the **atman**, whose nature is neither limited by the physical body nor defined by its relationship to the world. It is the *atman* that moves from body to body through successive incarnations.

The task of recognizing the true nature of the essential self is understood to be arduous and rarely achieved. Most Hindus assume that this will require many lifetimes.

One's life ordinarily revolves around a sense of selfhood that is limited, constrained by desires and by ignorance of the true nature of *atman*. Life, therefore, ordinarily is lived by the egoistic "self" that is by nature (as the term suggests) selfish and stuck with the false identification of the self with the physical body. This leads to suffering, as the body undergoes painful changes brought on by disease, old age, and death.

Monistic Hinduism, true to its basic premise that all reality is ultimately one, teaches that the *atman is Brahman*. In a famous passage from the *Upanishads*, a young man named Svetaketu receives instruction from his father on the true nature of the *atman*. Using a number of analogies, the father explains that despite the appearance of multiplicity, all reality is one. The father emphatically declares: *Tat tvam asi svetakato iti* ("*You* are that, Svetaketu!").[4] *Atman* is *Brahman*.

Karma The course of the *atman* through successive incarnations is determined by karma. In its original, most basic sense, karma means "action," but for Hindus it means the consequences of action as well. Karma functions in accordance with the law of cause and effect: good actions produce good effects, bad actions produce bad effects. Karma encompasses all kinds of action, physical as well as mental. A person's situation in any given moment has been shaped by all previous actions. Consider, for example, being a college student. This situation is no accident, but rather the effect of certain kinds of thought and behavior during high school years that put the person on this course. Similarly, the karmic forces that we set in motion in our present lives will determine the nature of our future incarnations. To ensure that the future will be good, our actions now must be good—and that means living in conformity with *dharma*.

Dharma For Hinduism, the term **dharma** can mean law, duty, righteousness, or even "religion," all of which have to do with living in a way that upholds cosmic and social order. *Dharma* is traditionally believed to have been divinely revealed to the *rishis*, the poet-sages who composed the *Vedas*.

Through the centuries, Hindu texts have set forth ritual and social obligations that define a good life. The *Laws of Manu*, for example, a classic juridical text from the period 200 B.C.E. to 200 C.E., contains detailed prescriptions for correct behavior in all aspects of life. The two ancient and enormously influential Indian epic poems, the *Ramayana* and the *Mahabharata*, depict the simultaneous particularity and universality of *dharma*. As we will consider in more detail in a later section, both poems present epic heroes who must resolve conflicts between social or family obligations and their own personal sense of what duty demands from them.

Samsara Hindus use the term *samsara* in two closely related ways. *Samsara* is the continuing cycle of birth, death, and rebirth. *Samsara* is also the this-worldly realm in which birth, death, and rebirth recur. When the physical body dies, the eternal self or soul, the *atman*, moves on to another body. This process continues until the true nature of the *atman* is recognized. As noted previously, the nature of each rebirth is determined by karma. Virtuous acts of kindness and generosity over lifetimes ensure favorable rebirths, perhaps even in the blissful heavens of the gods. Selfish action and meanness lead to undesirable rebirths.

Hindus believe in a multitude of heavens and hells, as well as other regions in between. A rebirth in a heaven or hell could last for thousands of years but is still only temporary. The most desirable rebirth of all is as a human being in a situation that offers the greatest opportunity for realizing liberation from *samsara*; for example, as a sage or an ascetic.

The concept of *samsara* presents some basic questions. What gives rise to *samsara*? And why are human beings so prone to remain stuck in this *samsaric* realm? Through the ages, Hindus have offered various answers to these questions. Some of these answers have involved the concept **maya**, which in the *Vedas* refers to the magical power the gods used to create this world. Is the world an illusion, as is often the case

A *sannyasi*, or Hindu ascetic. His sectarian affiliation is indicated by his forehead marking, which demonstrates that he is a worshipper of Vishnu.

with magic, or real? Hindus are divided on this issue. In either case, they agree that human beings are powerfully attracted to this world, with its many particulars—our egoistic selves, our relationships, our possessions, and the seemingly countless objects of our desires. Our attachment to such things in all that we think and do and the karma it generates steer us after each lifetime back into the *samsaric* realm of particulars.

All of this leads to another basic question: Why should anyone *want* to escape from *samsara*? After all, the prospect of a future filled with numerous lifetimes would seem to be appealing. Hinduism's answer is simple: beyond the *samsaric* realm lies something inexpressibly better.

Moksha Freedom from the bondage of *samsara* is achieved through *moksha*, "release" or "liberation." Having overcome attachments to this world, the *atman* realizes its true nature. For monistic Hindus, *moksha* is the union of the *atman* with *Brahman*, such that no sense of individuality any longer exists. For dualistic or devotional Hindus, for whom the divine reality is identified with their supreme God (be it Vishnu, Shiva, or another), *moksha* involves the eternal existence of the *atman* in the company of God. Hindus also have differing opinions on whether *moksha* can occur for a living person or whether it must await death of the physical body. For all Hindus, however, *moksha* marks the end of the *samsaric* cycle of rebirth and the end of the effects of karma. Like *Brahman*, *moksha* is virtually impossible to describe, beyond being characterized—also like *Brahman*—as infinite awareness and eternal bliss.

It almost goes without saying that the quest for *moksha*, for liberating oneself from *samsara* even while constrained to the limits of this world, is extremely challenging.

Hinduism offers three main paths to *moksha*, each one providing means of eradicating ignorance and egoistic attachment and thus freeing the *atman*.

Three Paths to Liberation

Typical of the diverse nature of Hinduism, there are a variety of approaches to the goal of liberation. Traditionally they have been categorized as three paths, or *margas* (also called *yogas*), each one featuring its own set of practices and being suited to certain personality traits and life situations. **Karma marga**, for those engaged in the activities of family and career, emphasizes ritual and ethical works. **Bhakti marga**, for the vast majority of Hindus who regularly worship in temples and in their homes, is devotion to a deity. **Jnana marga**, for those privileged to devote time and energy on study and contemplation, focuses on spiritual insight. The paths are by no means exclusive of one another: Hindus commonly engage in more than one. Almost all Hindus, for example, practice some form of *bhakti marga*, and *karma marga* is a natural way to approach life's everyday tasks. All three *margas* function to diminish the ignorance, attachment, and false identification of the self with the physical body that characterize life in the *samsaric* realm.

Typical of its synthesizing nature, the *Bhagavad Gita*, which was composed in about the first century of the Common Era, sets forth all three *margas*, explaining characteristics common to all three and making clear their mutual compatibility. Of fundamental concern is the need to eradicate the ignorance and attachment born of an egoistic sense of selfhood. One passage puts it this way: "He who abandons all desires and acts free from longing, without any sense of mineness or egotism—he attains to peace."[5]

Karma Marga As noted previously, all Hindus are required to act in conformity with *dharma*, the duty to live in a manner that upholds cosmic and social order. *Karma marga* combines focus on *dharma* with an attitude of detachment with regard to acting and to the results of action. In the words of the *Bhagavad Gita*:

> Relinquishing attachment,
> men of discipline perform action
> with body, mind, understanding, and senses
> for the purification of the self.
> Relinquishing the fruit of action
> the disciplined man attains perfect peace;
> the undisciplined man is in bondage,
> attached to the fruit of desire.[6]

When the self, or *atman*, is devoid of attachment to the results of action, the problems of egotism, and the suffering brought about by birth, disease, old age, and death, are resolved.

Bhakti Marga The path of devotion, *bhakti marga*, is the most widely practiced of the three paths to liberation. This chapter's survey of the history of Hinduism includes a section detailing the rise of the *bhakti* tradition. In an important manner, the tradition is grounded in the *Bhagavad Gita*, which, along with prescribing the other two *margas*, gives pride of place to *bhakti*. In the *Bhagavad Gita*, the featured deity is Krishna. *Bhakti*, however, can be directed toward whatever deity one chooses. Hindus typically worship more than one deity, depending on personal preference and on the occasion; for instance, during the festival in honor of Saraswati, goddess of education, Hindu schoolchildren offer devotion to her. There are numerous such festivals of the gods in the Hindu year.

In the *Bhagavad Gita*, Krishna makes clear to his devotee Arjuna the great benefits of *bhakti*:

> But men intent on me
> renounce all actions to me
> and worship me, meditating
> with singular discipline.
> When they entrust reason to me,
> Arjuna, I soon arise
> to rescue them from the ocean
> of death and rebirth.
> Focus your mind on me,
> let your understanding enter me;
> then you will dwell
> in me without doubt.[7]

Like *karma marga* and *jnana marga*, *bhakti marga* functions to eradicate egotism, ignorance, and attachment to the objects of desire. By devoting one's time and energy to a deity rather than to one's individualistic yearnings and concerns, the true nature of reality is realized, the effects of karma are neutralized, and liberation from *samsara* is achieved.

Jnana Marga   Generally agreed to be the steepest ascent to liberation, *jnana* ("knowledge") *marga* requires disciplined study of sacred texts and intensive contemplation, typically through the practice of meditation. This is the path of wisdom, the special pursuit of philosophers. The *Bhagavad Gita* says:

> There is nothing on earth equal in purity to wisdom. He who becomes perfected by *yoga* finds this of himself, in his self [*atman*] in course of time.
> He who has faith, who is absorbed in it [i.e., wisdom], and who has subdued his senses, gains wisdom, and having gained wisdom he attains quickly the supreme peace.[8]

The wisdom gained through *jnana marga* is spiritual knowledge or insight of a special kind. To attain this wisdom is to become aware of the true nature of *atman*. For monistic

Hindus, this is to become aware that the *atman* is none other than *Brahman*, the ultimate, unitary reality.

In a later section of this chapter we explore Yoga, one of the most important of Hinduism's six philosophical schools. The Yoga school teaches specific physical and mental exercises designed to promote *jnana*. It is this form of *jnana marga*, with its meditative practices often performed in the lotus position, that is commonly envisioned by non-Hindus when pondering the spiritual life of India.

Here, we turn our attention to *Vedanta*, the most influential of Hinduism's philosophical schools and a primary example of *jnana marga*.

Vedanta: The Predominant School of Hindu Philosophy

The philosophical system that emerged out of the *Upanishads* is called **Vedanta,** which in Sanskrit means "the end of the *Vedas*"—"end" not only as conclusion but also as culmination. The *Vedanta* school asserts that the *Upanishads* reveal the truth about the fundamental questions of existence. The *Upanishads* are both profound and challenging and are open to a variety of interpretations. Following the composition of the early *Upanishads,* philosophy became a very important part of Hinduism. Predictably, there even arose a number of different schools within *Vedanta*. Each school of *Vedanta* sought to understand the precise nature of the relationships between *Brahman, atman,* and the world.

The impact of *Vedanta* on the development of Hinduism cannot be overestimated. As different Hindu sects emerged, their distinctive understandings of *Vedanta* shaped their philosophical orientations. Of the many schools of *Vedanta*, the three most important are *Advaita*, *Vishishta-Advaita*, and *Dvaita*.

Advaita Vedanta Known as Hinduism's uncompromisingly monistic school of philosophy, *Advaita* ("Non-dualist") *Vedanta* teaches that the *atman* is identical to *Brahman* and denies any distinction whatsoever between *Brahman* and everything else. This school of thought grew directly out of the *Upanishads* but was further developed in the eighth century C.E. by Shankara, its most famous proponent. Shankara posited that the world is *maya,* "illusion." Earlier in this chapter we noted that the *Vedas* present *maya* as the magical power the gods used to create this world. For Shankara, *maya* veils the mind, such that it does not discern the true nature of the self (*atman*). According to Shankara, it is this lack of discernment, or ignorance, manifesting as attachment and desire, that keeps one bound to the cycle of death and rebirth (*samsara*). When one uses wisdom and discernment, one can cut through ignorance and recognize the inherent unity of all things, including the oneness of *Brahman* and *atman*. This in turn results in *moksha* and the complete dissolution of one's sense of individual selfhood.

Vishishta-Advaita Many of the sects that worship Vishnu differ on the subtler aspects of the relationship between *Brahman* and *atman*. For *Vaishnavas, Brahman* is identified with Vishnu. The school of *Vishishta-Advaita*, founded by the twelfth-century C.E.

philosopher Ramanuja, declared that all is *Brahman* and that the material world and individual souls also are real. The world is not illusion (*maya*); rather, it is the body of God. All beings are a part of God, eternally connected to Vishnu but not the same as him. We are more like cells in the divine body. Unlike Shankara, Ramanuja interpreted the ignorance that obscures true knowledge as forgetfulness—in particular, the devotee's forgetfulness of our eternal relationship with Vishnu. In this manner, Ramanuja's *Vedanta* marries philosophy to the devotional, sectarian traditions of Vaishnavism.

Dvaita Vedanta The school of *Dvaita* ("Dualist") *Vedanta*, founded by the thirteenth-century theologian Madhva, advocates a complete distinction between *Brahman* and *atman*. It posits that there are five acknowledged aspects of complete separateness or difference: between the *atman* and *Brahman*, between *Brahman* and matter, between the various souls, between the souls and matter, and between various forms of matter. This philosophical strain, too, is associated with the worship of Vishnu, particularly in his avatar as Krishna.

The Individual and Society

The Hindu individual's quest for liberation is played out in a life situation that is defined to a large extent for that particular person depending on factors such as gender, caste status, and age. Like all aspects of the religion, the rules governing these factors admit to diversity even while conforming to basic patterns that have persisted through the centuries. Collectively, these rules are known as *varnashrama dharma*: the religious law regulating caste (*varna*) and stage of life (*ashrama*). Traditionally, all Hindus are required to comply with *varnashrama dharma*.

The Caste System The Sanskrit term **varna** (literally, "color"), commonly translated as "caste," refers to a system of hierarchical social organization. A more accurate way of expressing the meaning of *varna* in this context is through the English term "class." There are four main classes in Hindu society: *brahmin*, the priestly class; **kshatriya**, the warrior and administrator class; **vaishya**, the producer class (farmers and merchants); and **shudra**, the servant class. *Varna* is determined by birth and is propagated through endogamy, or marriage only within a particular group. The caste system, and *varnashrama dharma* generally, has traditionally been most important for males of the three higher classes, the so-called "twice-born" castes.

We encounter the first mention of *varna* in a poem known as the *Purusha Sukta*, an early Sanskrit poem found in the tenth book of the *Rig Veda* (c. 1200 B.C.E.). The poem, which describes the primordial sacrifice of the cosmic man, ascribes a mythical origin to the *varna* system. From the various parts of the cosmic man emerge the component parts of the universe—the sun, the moon, the breath, and fire among them. At the very end, people emerge. From his mouth emerge the *brahmins*, from his arms the *kshatriyas*, from his thighs the *vaishyas*, and from his feet the *shudras*.

The *varnas* are organized along a continuum of purity and pollution. A person's state of purity or pollution is determined by the degree of contact with substances that are considered polluting (corpses, for example). Although it might appear from the *varna* system and from the *Purusha Sukta* that *brahmins* are at the top of the hierarchy, we know that from the earliest period *brahmins* and *kshatriyas* (and to some extent *vaishyas* as well) existed in close, mutually dependent relationships. The *brahmins*, with their ritual knowledge, gave legitimacy to kings and ambitious chieftains who might come to power. In turn, kings supported the priestly class with gifts of wealth and land, while merchants and landlords paid taxes and sponsored priestly activities.

A fifth group below the *shudras*, called the "untouchables" or "outcastes," was later added. Today, this lowest group constitutes nearly 20 percent of the population of India. During the Indian Independence movement of the early twentieth century, Mohandas (Mahatma) Gandhi (whom we will discuss later in the chapter) sought to uplift this class socially, referring to them as *Harijans*, "Children of God." Many people of this class now refer to themselves as **dalit**, a word that means "oppressed." In modern India, educational institutions and government jobs have been opened to the *dalits* and have helped many with social and economic mobility. Nevertheless, *dalits* continue to suffer terrible oppression, especially in rural communities in India.

The caste system is further classified through thousands of subcastes called *jatis*. **Jati** literally means "birth group." The term is often used to describe different orders of plants and animals, implying that the difference between human groups is similar to that between different species. Usually, a *jati* is composed of an endogamous group. One can marry within *jati* communities that are equal in social and ritual status, but not into a *jati* above or below one's own position. Marriage across *jatis* is usually undertaken to widen communal alliances. Over time, the *jati* system has made social hierarchy more fluid.

In modern times, the strictures of caste have broken down. Many Hindus have embraced a more utilitarian and even egalitarian outlook formulated by nineteenth-century Hindu reformers. These reformers regarded intercaste marriage as essential to bringing about social equality and the development of the Indian nation. In urban areas, caste status has often given way to a modern class-based system in which one's marriageability is based on education, current employment, and financial status, rather than solely on caste. But caste remains a challenging issue for many Hindus, particularly those living in rural settings.

The Hampi Bazaar in Karnataka, India, a sacred town where doorsteps and houses are decorated by *rangoli* or *kolam* ritual protective drawings.

The Four Stages of Life Another main aspect of the *varnashrama dharma* system involves the *ashrama,* or "stage of life." Traditional Hinduism describes four *ashramas*:

1. The student
2. The householder
3. The forest-dwelling hermit
4. The renouncer (the *sannyasi*)

As affirmed by the *Laws of Manu,* the repository of *dharma* discussed earlier, fulfilling the duties of these stages is said to repay three debts of life, which are:

1. To the ancient seers (by studying the revealed texts known as the *Vedas*)
2. To the gods (by making offerings as a householder)
3. To the ancestors (by having a son—again, as a householder—who will continue to perform ancestral rites)

The specific regulations pertaining to each stage of life are meticulously spelled out in Hindu texts. For example, the *Laws of Manu* prescribes the ritual of initiation for boys who are about to enter the student stage:

> In the eighth year after conception, one should perform the initiation (*upanāyana*) of a *brāhmin,* in the eleventh [year] after conception (that) of a *kṣatriya,* but in the twelfth that of a *vaiśya.*[9]

The student's main duty is to acquire a sufficient understanding of the *Vedas*. Upon getting married, he enters the stage of the householder, whose duties include supporting those in the other three stages of life. Hindus in the last two stages focus primarily on seeking *moksha* or liberation, first by detaching themselves from the worldly concerns of the householder and then, once this detachment has been achieved, by entering the fourth stage of the renouncer, or **sannyasi**.

Renunciation is understood to be the most effective life situation for working to achieve *moksha*. As we have seen, attachment to objects of desire binds one to *samsara*. Renouncing, or no longer clinging to, such objects is empowering. By not indulging one's desires for the impermanent things of this world, the true nature of the self (the *atman*) can be realized. Most renouncers are ascetics, celibate wanderers who engage in meditation and yoga. Some take formal vows and join a monastic order. Although estimates of the number of *sannyasis* vary, there may be as many as 15 million in India.

The four stages define the ideal life for men. Women participate primarily in vaguely defined supporting roles through the last three stages and thereby assist in repaying the three debts. Some Hindu texts, including the *Laws of Manu,* emphasize that women hold a place of honor because of these roles. In general, however, Hindu society has been highly patriarchal. (The place of women in Hinduism is explored in more detail a later section.)

The Four Aims of Life   Whereas the four stages of life describe an individual's social and familial responsibilities from birth to death, the four aims of life set forth Hinduism's primary spiritual purposes and goals. The four are: *dharma*, duty or righteousness; *kama*, sensual enjoyment; *artha*, material wealth and social prestige; and *moksha*, liberation. A Hindu is meant to diligently pursue all four of these goals.

As we have seen, *dharma* applies throughout life. Along with taking care to observe regulations governing everyday routines, some Hindus may take vows to practice nonviolence, perhaps maintaining a vegetarian diet as part of that goal. Others have strict rules for maintaining ritual purity or observe a complex ritual regimen each day to ensure the harmony and well-being of their household and family members.

The next two aims of life—*kama* and *artha*—apply especially to the second stage of life, that of the householder. *Kama* is directed at the fulfillment of desire. It encourages Hindus to enjoy the human experience and celebrate the sensual aspects of life. *Artha,* the pursuit of wealth and social prestige, is also encouraged. It is a Hindu's duty to provide security for loved ones but also to savor and share life's bounty. Of course, *kama* and *artha* must conform to *dharma*.

Moksha, the ultimate aim of human existence, is the special focus of the last two stages of life (the forest-dwelling hermit and the renouncer). Having fulfilled the duties and obligations of student and householder, one is ready to turn inward, to contemplate the nature of the *atman*.

The four stages and the four aims of life represent traditional ideals intended primarily for upper-caste men. We do not know the extent to which the prescriptions of the stages and aims have been followed in the long history of Hinduism. These ideals, while to some extent impractical in today's contemporary society, still inform the beliefs and practices of many Hindus.

VOICES: An Interview with Jayashree Venkatesan

Jayashree Venkatesan is a wife, a mother, and a retired accountant who lives in Chennai, India. She is a devotee of the goddess Sharada (a form of Saraswati, Goddess of Wisdom), whose most important temple is in the town of Shringeri, South India.

As a Hindu, what is the most important part of human existence? What should Hindus do or focus on in life?

As a Hindu, I believe that God is in all things, in every aspect of creation and in every aspect of life. Consequently, one must practice compassion and nonviolence towards all things. It is how we learn to see and experience the divine presence all around us. I also believe in the tenet that work is worship. It is an act of surrender. You don't shirk your responsibilities, whatever they may be— whether as a mother, a student, a professional—but do not cling to the fruits of work. As a Hindu I trust that when you surrender fully, God will provide you with the solution and guide you through both the happy and difficult moments of life.

What aspect of your day-to-day life as a Hindu would you characterize as being most spiritually gratifying?

Every morning and evening, I light an oil lamp in my puja room (home shrine) before the image of the Supreme Mother, Sharada Ambal. I see Sringeri Sharada Ambal as my mother, as one who takes care of everyone in this world. In these moments of quiet peace, I feel Her presence and Her guidance. I begin my day by surrendering myself into Her loving care.

What is your favorite Hindu holiday, and why?

I would not say I have a favorite Hindu festival. I like them all, as they are all so different. However, one of the most important festivals for me is Navaratri, which celebrates the Great Goddess. The festival falls sometime between September and October. We worship the goddess in Her three forms as Durga, Lakshmi, and Saraswati over nine nights and ten days. During this festival, I recite the *Lalita Sahasranama*, the one thousand names of Devi, several times a day. I do more elaborate puja (home rituals) to the goddess. Most importantly, it gives me the opportunity to invite several women of all ages to my home to feed them and give them clothes as I honor them as aspects of the Great Goddess.

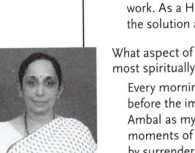

Jayashree
Venkatesan

Hindu Sacred Texts

The great diversity within Hinduism is reflected in its astonishing array of texts, composed in many different languages over the course of centuries. Down to present times, Hindu texts have facilitated the asserting of new ideas, the overturning of old ones, and the reasserting of the dominance of fading traditions. In this next section, we undertake a brief survey of Hinduism's main texts and their continued relevance.

The *Vedas*   The term *Veda* ("knowledge") is used in two ways when categorizing Hindu texts. In the broader sense, the *Vedas* refers to all of Vedic literature. These texts are regarded by most Hindus as revealed. That is, they are believed not to have been composed by man but rather "heard" by the *rishis*, the poet-sages of ancient times who were divinely inspired. Vedic literature thus belongs to the category of Hindu texts known as **shruti** ("that which is heard"), as opposed to the other category, **smriti** ("tradition").

In the more narrow sense of the term, *Vedas* refers to four collections (Sanskrit, *samhitas*) of texts. Composed in Sanskrit between 1200 and 900 B.C.E. and drawing on centuries of oral tradition, these are the earliest Hindu texts and are generally considered to be the world's oldest scriptures. The four *Vedas* are: the *Rig Veda,* a collection of hymns to the gods; the *Sama Veda,* melodic renditions of hymns from the *Rig Veda;* the *Yajur Veda,* ritual formulas; and the *Atharva Veda,* hymns, spells, and incantations.

Following upon the four *samhitas*, the *Brahmanas* set forth instructions for *brahmin* priests. The next collection of texts, the *Aranyakas* (or "forest treatises," so-named because they record esoteric teachings conveyed to students in secret), form a bridge from the *samhitas* to the *Upanishads* by exploring hidden meanings of rituals. The *Upanishads* are speculations with regard to the deeper truths of the *samhitas*, especially the *Rig Veda*.

The 1,028 hymns of the *Rig Veda*, the oldest and by far the most important of the *samhitas*, praise the gods and ask for their blessings. The gods include Indra, God of Rain and Thunder and King of the Gods; Agni, God of Fire and Messenger of the Gods; and Varuna, the God of Law and Order (who later becomes the God of the Sea). New deities emerged in the later portions of the *Rig Veda*. One that has enduring influence is the *Purusha* (literally, "Man"), who is praised and described in the famous Vedic hymn known as the *Purusha Sukta,* which was discussed earlier in connection to the caste system. This later Vedic hymn is also significant for the ways in which it asserts the centrality of sacrifice, and it continues to be recited in Hindu rituals even today. The *Purusha Sukta* describes the sacrifice of a primordial, cosmic man out of whose body the universe is created. As a creation myth, it has parallels in numerous Indo-European traditions. As we have seen, the *Purusha Sukta* not only details the first sacrifice but also delineates the structuring of society.

The *Upanishads* (900–200 B.C.E.) The *Upanishads*, also known as *Vedanta* ("end of the *Vedas*"), are so distinctive from the earlier Vedic texts and so important as to deserve their own treatment here. The term *Upanishad* means "sitting down near [a teacher]." The term *Vedanta*, while identifying these texts as the concluding portion of Vedic

HINDU SACRED TEXTS

SHRUTI ("THAT WHICH IS HEARD")
Samhitas ("Collections")

Rig Veda
Yajur Veda
Sama Veda
Atharva Veda

Brahmanas
Aranyakas
Upanishads

SMRITI ("TRADITION")
Dharma Shastras (including *Laws of Manu*)
Epics and Puranas

Ramayana
Mahabharata
Bhagavata Purana
Markandeya Purana

Darshanas (treatises of the philosophical schools)
Tantras (scriptures of the various sects)
Writings of Hindu gurus

literature, implies for some Hindus—for example, followers of the *Vedanta* philosophical school—that the *Upanishads* contain the culmination of the wisdom of the *Vedas*.

Departing from the Vedic focus on ritual, and especially sacrifice, the *Upanishads* feature philosophical speculation on the nature of the divine, the self, the world, and the relationships between them. These texts signal a significant shift away from emphasis on the external performance of sacrifice characteristic of the Vedic era. The *Upanishads* also mark a new stage in the development of religious texts, having been composed in part by people of non-*brahmin* backgrounds. The newfound emphasis on philosophical speculation, no longer the sole domain of the *brahmin* class, had an enormous impact on the development of Hinduism. It propelled the development of the contemplative disciplines of yoga and meditation and influenced the philosophical concepts found later in the *Bhagavad Gita*.

The *Upanishads* are also significant for describing for the first time the concepts of karma, *samsara*, reincarnation of the soul, and the soul's immortality, which were initially closely guarded secrets. We had occasion earlier in the chapter, when discussing *Brahman* and the monistic concept that *atman* is *Brahman*, to draw from the *Brhadaranyaka* and *Chandogya Upanishads*. They are two among the thirteen so-called "principal *Upanishads*" (some scholars set this number at ten). Traditionally there are 108 *Upanishads*, although the term has been applied to some 200 texts, some of which were written in recent times.

Ramayana   For most Hindus, belief and practice are informed by and disseminated through storytelling traditions and narrative texts. Two of the most significant of these are the Sanskrit epics the *Ramayana* and the *Mahabharata*, both of which are categorized as *smriti* rather than *shruti*—although this in no way diminishes their relevance as Hindu sacred texts. Both epics are among the most important sources of Hindu notions of duty, or *dharma*.

The *Ramayana* ("The Journey of Rama"), composed between 200 B.C.E. and 200 C.E., is a compelling tale of political intrigue, romance, and philosophical speculation. It tells the story of a ten-headed demon King named Ravana, who was rewarded for his austerities with the granting of a wish by Brahma. Ravana asks for protection from gods, celestial beings, and other members of his own demon race. Protected in this way, he and his demon hordes dominate the earth and eventually even enslave the gods of heaven. But in his arrogance, Ravana neglects to ask for protection from humans and animals.

In the meantime, King Dasharatha of Ayodhya and his three queens, desiring an heir, perform

What advantages and disadvantages can you think of when comparing the flexibility of Hindu beliefs with that of other religions?

Hindu priests perform *arati*, waving a lamp of burning camphor before an image of Hanuman (the monkey god of the *Ramayana*) at a temple in Kuala Lumpur, Malaysia, during the festival of Diwali.

a sacrifice in hopes that the gods will grant their wish. The king is blessed with four sons—Rama, Lakshmana, Bharata, and Shatrughna. Rama, as we have noted earlier (p. 37), is an avatar of Vishnu. Rama eventually marries a princess, Sita. As Rama is beloved by all for his righteousness and virtue, King Dasharatha, wishing to step down from the throne, announces that Rama's coronation will soon be held. Then Kaikeyi, Dasharatha's favorite wife, suddenly calls in two wishes that the king had once granted her. She demands that Rama be banished to the forest for fourteen years and that her own son, Bharata, ascend to the throne of Ayodhya instead. Distraught, King Dasharatha dutifully grants Kaikeyi's wish but dies of a broken heart.

Rama accepts his exile without protest and is accompanied by his brother Lakshmana and his wife Sita into the forest, where they spend many years, until one day Ravana kidnaps Sita and carries her off to his demon stronghold on the island of Lanka.

A despairing Rama and Lakshmana wander in search of Sita. They eventually meet Hanuman, a messenger from a kingdom of monkeys. Hanuman, along with the support of the kingdom of bears, helps to search for Sita. At the citadel of Ravana on Lanka, Hanuman finds Sita held prisoner in a garden. He tells her not to lose hope, promising that Rama will soon come to free her.

Upon hearing Hanuman's news, Rama and his army march to Lanka. During the fierce battle that ensues, Rama kills Ravana and is united with Sita. However, after spending a year in another man's house, Sita must publicly prove her chastity through a trial by fire. With the fire-god Agni as her witness, she passes through the flames and into Rama's embrace. Their exile concluded, Rama, Sita, and Lakshmana return to Ayodhya, where Rama is reinstated as the rightful king. All are happy for a time, but later, because of rumors circulating about Sita's chastity, Rama is compelled to abandon Sita in the forest. He doesn't know she is pregnant with their two sons, who are raised by the hermit Valmiki. Valmiki, who, while meditating, has seen all that has come to pass, composes the *Ramayana* and teaches it to the two boys, who eventually sing it before their father. Rama dies shortly thereafter, sadly pining for Sita.

For many Hindus, the characters in the *Ramayana* serve as exemplary social role models. Sita is the faithful wife, Rama is the ideal man and perfect king, Lakshmana is the loyal brother, and Hanuman is the selfless devotee. The text grapples with issues involving *dharma*, both in the public, political realm and in the private, familial realm. The characters of the *Ramayana*, however, are also understood to be divine. Thus the *Ramayana* is as much a text that imparts religious and ethical knowledge as one that reinforces Hindu beliefs about the accessibility and immanence of God.

Rama and Lakshmana, with their army of monkeys and bears, are camped outside the palace of the demon-king Ravana on the isle of Lanka, while the demons try to rouse Kumbhakarna, the giant brother of Ravana. India, Mughal period, c. 1595–1605.

Mahabharata The other great Hindu epic, the *Mahabharata*, is composed of over 100,000 verses and is the longest epic poem in the world. Like the *Ramayana*, this work is deeply concerned with issues of *dharma*. The epic also introduces Krishna, the beloved avatar of Vishnu.

The main storyline of the *Mahabharata* concerns a dynastic conflict between two groups of royal cousins. These are the *Pandavas* (the five sons of King Pandu), the heroes of the epic who are all descendants of the gods, and their antagonists, the *Kauravas* (the hundred sons of the blind king, Dhritarashtra). Their dispute ultimately results in a terrible war that marks the end of an epoch for humanity.

On the eve of the great battle, as the two armies face each other across the battlefield, the great Pandava warrior Arjuna experiences crippling doubt. When Arjuna asks his charioteer, Krishna (an avatar of Vishnu), to pull the chariot into the middle of the battlefield, he sees his friends and relatives on both sides clamoring for war. He does not want to commit the sin of killing his kinsmen; and overcome with sorrow, he refuses to fight. It is at this key point in the story that the profound philosophical discourse known as the *Bhagavad Gita* ("Song of the Lord") begins. Many Hindus regard this conversation between Krishna and Arjuna as the most significant philosophical work in Hinduism.

Krishna, in the guise of Arjuna's charioteer, counsels the warrior on the verge of battle against his kinsmen. The battle scene in the Mahabharata is the setting of the *Bhagavad Gita.*

The *Bhagavad Gita* (The Song of the Lord)

The *Bhagavad Gita*, the conversation between Krishna and Arjuna, was probably composed around the first century C.E. The text, which seeks to reconcile the tension between renunciation and worldly life, also presents radical new ideas about the pursuit of *moksha*, including the three *margas* or paths to liberation that we explored in an earlier section.

The *Gita* begins with Arjuna refusing to act on his *dharma*, as is demanded of a member of the *kshatriya*, or warrior class, out of fear of the consequences of killing his kinsmen. Krishna responds to his dilemma by revealing that one does not need to give up action to achieve *moksha*. Rather, as we noted before, one gives up the *fruit* of action. That is, one cultivates "desireless action," or acting without attachment to the fruit or benefit of the action.

Arjuna must honor his *dharma* as a warrior and fight his own kinsmen. But he transcends the karmic repercussions of this act by relinquishing personal attachment and realizing that Krishna is the primary cause leading all the individual actors toward this inevitable outcome.

The *Gita* emphasizes the concept of *bhakti* (devotion), which later comes to dominate Hindu practice and belief. The *Gita* suggests that the path of *bhakti* is available to anyone, regardless of caste or gender, as its only requirement is devotion. By allowing people to live in this world, adhering to their *dharma*, *bhakti* offers an alternate course to *moksha*. The *Gita* teaches that it is possible to achieve *moksha* by being active in the world, provided that, through selfless devotion, one surrenders clinging to the expectation of any particular result. This contrasts with earlier philosophical systems that advocated complete detachment through renunciation as the primary means for escaping *samsara*.

The concept of *bhakti* influences the development of the dualistic or devotional Hindu traditions. *Bhakti* is intimately connected to the rise of Hinduism's various sectarian affiliations and the growth of temple cultures. *Bhakti* advocates a deep, abiding love for God and encourages the devotee to nurture an intimate and personal relationship with the divine. The devotee is free to choose a favored, personal deity, who is perceived as the supreme entity and toward whom devotion is directed. For many Hindus, *bhakti* is both a belief and a practice. That is, they cultivate *bhakti* as the most effective way out of *samsara*.

Puranas In addition to the rich storehouse of narrative material in the epics, there are equally important collections of mythic stories known as **Puranas** (Sanskrit *purana*, "ancient"). Like the epics, the *Puranas* existed in oral form before being committed to writing—in this case, between the fourth and sixteenth centuries. The *Puranas* contain useful historical data, such as the genealogies of regional kings, but they also reflect the rise of dualistic or devotional Hinduism. This is evident primarily in their narrations of the deeds of the great deities such as Shiva, Vishnu, and Devi. They also take great interest in the genealogies of gods, rules governing the proper worship of the gods, the construction of temples, the observance of festivals, the undertaking of pilgrimages, and similar topics.

There are eighteen major *Puranas*, two of the most influential of which are the *Bhagavata Purana* and the *Markandeya Purana*. The *Bhagavata Purana* focuses on Vishnu and his incarnations, most especially Krishna. It is one of the most widely recited, performed, and studied texts in contemporary Hinduism. The tenth book, which serves as the primary source for Krishna's life story, is particularly important. The *Markandeya Purana* includes within it the *Devi Mahatmya,* which is an important text of Shaktism, one among various Hindu sects that we explore in the next section.

The Sects of Hinduism

There are three primary sects in Hinduism. Each features veneration of one of the major deities at the center of Hindu cosmology. The devotees of these sects are called **Vaishnavas** (devotees of Vishnu and his avatars), **Shaivas** (devotees of Shiva), and **Shaktas** (devotees of the Great Goddess, Devi). Within each of these sects are numerous individual orders that differ in the sacred texts and saints they revere, their modes of worship, and their philosophical orientation.

Vaishnavism *Vaishnavas* worship Vishnu and his consort (wife) Lakshmi as supreme. Vishnu mercifully intervenes in the world through his avatars (such as Rama in

A contemporary painting of the inner sanctum of the famous temple at Sri Rangam. Sri Ranganatha ("Lord of the Stage") is a cosmic form of Vishnu lying on the serpent, Ananta ("Infinity"), as he floats on the Cosmic Sea of Milk. This signifies the place of primordial essence from whence he emanates all of the universe.

the *Ramayana* and Krishna in the *Mahabharata*) and is inseparable from his beloved Lakshmi, who is the goddess of auspiciousness and good fortune. For *Vaishnavas*, Vishnu is the source of all existence and, as his name denotes, "The All-Pervading One." These ideas about Vishnu's fundamental nature are expressed in myths and poems that invoke him as the lord who measured out the universe in a primordial act of creation.

Hindus worship Vishnu in a number of different forms. He is often depicted reclining with Lakshmi on a thousand-headed serpent that floats on the cosmic ocean. From his navel rises a lotus, upon which Brahma the Creator God is seated. Visually, this image asserts that the world is born from Vishnu and he is its sole originator and sustainer. Brahma, Vishnu, and Shiva constitute the so-called *trimurti*, a triad of gods whose roles are, respectively, to create, preserve, and dissolve the universe as it moves through epochal cycles. For *Vaishnavas*, Vishnu is not just the preserver but the supreme god who performs all three roles, thus incorporating the functions of the *trimurti* within his own being.

In Hindu sacred art, Vishnu typically is shown holding objects in his four hands that symbolize his powers and characteristics. In his upper right hand, he holds a flaming discus (symbolizing the sun and omniscience); his upper left hand bears a white conch shell (the moon and creativity). In his lower right hand, he holds a mace (power), and in his lower left hand, he holds a lotus (purity). Most *Vaishnavas* have special devotion for Vishnu's avatars, Rama and Krishna.

Shaivism Shiva is the destroyer while at the same time a benefactor. He embodies both the ideal of ascetic renunciation and a full and sensual participation in the material world. Beyond being the god of spiritual insight and of yogis and ascetics, Shiva is also the god who destroys the universe at the end of time before a new cycle of creation can begin. Most *Shaivas* worship Shiva as a god with no beginning or end who transcends time but also presides over its endless cycles. Some *Shaivas* emphasize that Shiva is also a family man, to be venerated with his divine queen Parvati and their two sons, the divine princes Ganesha and Skanda.

Shiva is usually depicted sitting in deep meditation on Mount Kailasha in the Himalayas, with a tiger skin wrapped about his waist and wearing serpents for jewelry. His third eye is turned inward in meditative contemplation, and he wears the crescent moon and the holy river Ganges in his matted hair. A common symbol of Shiva is the *linga*, an abstract phallic symbol that represents his creative potential. His consort Parvati is also believed by *Shaivas* to represent the creative energy of the universe.

Shaktism The cults of the Great Goddess venerate her as the supreme cause and end of the universe. Although she has many names and many forms, the Great Goddess is most often referred to as Devi, Mahadevi, or Shakti. Devotees of the Goddess are referred to as *Shaktas*.

The primacy of Devi is definitively asserted in the fifth century c.e. Sanskrit text called the *Devi Mahatmya* (*The Greatness of Devi*) which, as noted previously, is part of the *Markandeya Purana*. The *Devi Mahatmya* posits that the supreme cause of the universe is feminine. The text argues for Devi's greatness through three main myths, the most important of which tells how she killed the buffalo-headed demon, Mahisha, who threatened the world and whom even the gods Vishnu and Shiva were not able to vanquish.

To *Shaktas* the Goddess is all-powerful and pervades the entire universe. She is the one who creates, preserves, and destroys the universe in harmony with the rhythms of cosmic time. The *Devi Mahatmya* teaches that the goddess is eternal and that she manifests herself over and over again in order to protect the universe as a mother would her child.

Shaivas and *Shaktas* have much in common, as Shiva and Devi (also called Parvati) are believed by both sects to be married. So the difference between Shaivism and Shaktism is a matter of emphasis regarding the importance of each of these two primal forces. For *Shaivas*, Shiva is pure consciousness that pervades all existence, and Devi is his creative (but subordinate) power. On the other hand, *Shaktas* believe that Shiva is entirely passive, and that Shakti is the creative energy that constitutes and governs the whole of existence. Thus the *Shaktas* say that "Shiva without Shakti is *shava*" (Sanskrit, "a corpse").

This idea, iconographically represented in the form of the goddess Kali dancing upon the inert body of Shiva, is a profound metaphor for the embodied soul. Shiva represents the pure consciousness in all beings that is transfixed by Kali, who is creative energy made manifest as all form, feeling, thought, and sensation. Kali's enrapturing dance makes one forget that one's true nature is Shiva/*Brahman*. But Kali also delights in granting *moksha* by letting believers awake to the true nature of her cosmic dance and the reality that *atman* is really *Brahman*.

Accompanied by a legion of other goddesses and fierce creatures and riding a lion, Devi, in the form of the goddess Durga, protects the world by battling the buffalo demon Mahishasura. (The buffalo is associated with Yama, the God of Death.) Pallava period, seventh century, Mahishasura Mardini Cave, Mamallapuram Tamil Nadu, India.

A modern painting of the goddess Kali, whose name means both "Black" and "Time," dancing on the body of Shiva. From the Indian state of Orissa.

Gurus, Saints, and Sages Entire sects of Hinduism are constantly forming around the veneration of gurus, saints, and ascetics. The fully enlightened are regarded as being one with God and therefore the most immediate means of accessing God directly, either for material and mundane blessings or to receive spiritual teaching to quicken one's own journey toward *moksha*. Some saints are venerated not as embodiments of God but for being humble and perfectly surrendered devotees. Some gurus are powerful religious authorities and preside over well-established institutions, in which the divine authority of a guru has been passed down to his senior disciple in an unbroken lineage for many generations. Certain important gurus and saints have been responsible for the formulation of the specific philosophical orientation of various sects and monastic orders, making interpretation of sacred texts and belief more systematic and consistent.

THE HISTORY OF HINDUISM

Hinduism is a vibrant tradition that has exhibited dynamic change and a willingness to embrace innovations in thought and practice. At the same time, Hinduism has preserved many of its most ancient elements to the present day, cherishing some traditions that go back more than 3,000 years.

The history of Hinduism can be traced back to the Indus Valley Civilization (c. 2600–1700 B.C.E.) and to the Indo-Aryan peoples who composed the *Vedas* (c. 1200–900 B.C.E.).

The Indus Valley Civilization

As its name suggests, the Indus Valley Civilization developed along the river Indus, which flows through modern Pakistan. It reached its developmental peak between 2300 and 2000 B.C.E., when its thriving cities, such as Harappa and Mohenjo-Daro, enjoyed a surprisingly high standard of living. Extensive archaeological excavations at Indus Valley sites have yielded evidence of trade with regions as far away as Mesopotamia and impressive skill in metallurgy, handicrafts, and urban planning. The archaeological finds include a vast number of stone seals that were perhaps used to stamp products for trade. These are decorated with depictions of animals and people and with a script that has not yet been deciphered.

Some scholars believe that in the Indus Valley seals we can detect very early elements of Hinduism. For example, the most famous seal has been called the Proto-Shiva seal because its central image may be an archaic form of Shiva. The male figure is seated in a yoga posture, wears a buffalo-horned headdress, is surrounded by

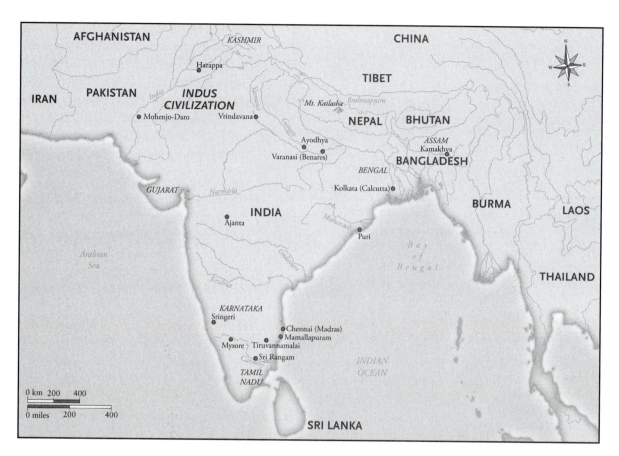

Significant sites in the history of Hinduism.

animals, and appears to have three faces. Later images of Shiva often show him in meditating in a yoga posture, being in the company of animals, and having three faces.

Of course, without a decipherment of the script it is difficult to understand fully this and other images depicted on the seals.

Archaeologists working in the Indus Valley have also discovered a number of terracotta figures depicting women. Some scholars have identified these as representations of a mother goddess. It may be that the widespread worship of goddesses in later Hinduism originated in the veneration of female deities in the ancient Indus Valley Civilization.

At some point early in the second millennium B.C.E. there was a sudden

The Proto-Shiva seal. The male figure, sometimes called the "Lord of the Animals," is surrounded by various totemic animals, such as an elephant, a tiger, a rhinoceros, a water buffalo, and two antelopes or deer.

The great bath can be seen amid the ruins of the ancient cityscape of Mohenjo-Daro, an important city of the Indus Valley Civilization. A towering granary can be viewed in the distance.

decline in the Indus Valley Civilization, which was to collapse by 1300 B.C.E. Although most scholars believe that the primary cause of the fall of the Indus Valley Civilization was climatic change that disrupted agriculture, it is possible that the migration of Aryans into the Indus Valley was a contributing factor.

Who Are the Aryans?

The brilliant English linguist Sir William "Oriental" Jones (1746–1794) described how Sanskrit, Latin, Greek, and several other ancient languages shared a common linguistic ancestor. These languages are referred to as "Indo-European" and probably stem from a lost language we call "Proto Indo-European." Jones's discoveries astounded Europeans, who soon learned that Sanskrit was closest to the original language spoken by the earliest Indo-Europeans.

The ancient speakers of Sanskrit who moved into the Indian subcontinent around 1500 B.C.E. referred to themselves as the *Arya*—that is, those who are "noble," "cultivated," and "civilized." Today, we call them Indo-Aryans or, more simply, Aryans. Skilled in handling the horse and chariot, the Aryans were a warlike and nomadic people who were well prepared to make themselves the dominant elite soon after they entered the Indian subcontinent.

Like other Indo-European peoples, the Aryans revered the horse, placed special importance on sacrifice, and organized their society into a three-part structure. For the Aryans, sacrifice was a means to maintain order in the universe. The priests (*brahmins*) who conducted sacrificial rituals occupied the top rung of the social order because of the religious power they wielded. The rulers and warriors (*kshatriyas*) were equally important. Last were the traders and farmers (*vaishyas*). As the Aryans did not place a great deal of emphasis on agriculture, one can see why the *vaishyas* would occupy a lower social position. This threefold social structure has remained fundamental to Indian society until today.

The Aryans, who eventually settled across northern India, have left us a body of texts composed in Sanskrit, of which the earliest example is the *Vedas*. It is to the era of these texts that we now turn.

The Vedic Period

Ritual was of ultimate importance in Vedic times, as rites of sacrifice were performed to sustain cosmic order and please the gods. Much of ritual sacrifice involved the pouring of offerings into a sacrificial fire as Vedic hymns were recited. Although the construction of their fire altars became quite elaborate, Indians of the Vedic period inherited from their nomadic ancestors a very "portable" religion with no fixed buildings or icons and with sacred knowledge maintained by priests.

In Vedic times, as today, fire was considered a god. Known as *Agni*, he was the mouth of the gods and the gateway to the celestial realms, so offerings were magically transported through Agni to whichever god was invoked.

In Vedic mythology it is Indra, god of thunder and lightning, and the virile god of fertility itself, who is the most powerful of the gods. More hymns in the *Vedas* are addressed to Indra than to any other god, but in later Hindu tradition and mythology he is somewhat comical: haughty, proud, and often drunk. Many of the Vedic gods continue to play a part in the later Hindu pantheon but endure only in a subordinate status.

A *yajna* or fire sacrifice, one of the most archaic of Hindu rites, is performed by priests before an image of Durga during the Durga Puja festival in Calcutta, India.

In the later Vedic period, philosophical innovations began to supplant the older Vedic emphasis on sacrifice. It is in hymns from the later period that Vedic religion begins to take a decisive turn, shifting away from an emphasis on myth, cosmology, and sacrifice to a keener interest in philosophy and introspection. In these hymns the perception of the nature of existence emerges as being more important than upholding the cosmic order through sacrifice. Late Vedic hymns mark a transition toward what would be the philosophical revolution of the speculative texts known as the *Upanishads*.

During the time of the *Upanishads* (c. 900–200 B.C.E.), contemplative and philosophical reflection became more widespread. Many philosophers moved from urban areas to the forest in order to lead simpler lives. Some lived as hermits, some lived in colonies of contemplatives, and others practiced strict ascetic disciplines in the solitude of the jungle. Still others became wanderers, going from town to town begging for food and engaging in lively philosophical debates.

The Age of the Guptas

Most scholars characterize the time of the Gupta Empire (c. 320 to 540 C.E.) as a period of remarkable creativity. The Guptas, who ruled much of northern India, patronized the arts, sciences, religion, and literature. Their reign was an era of relative peace and prosperity, often described as "the Golden Age of India." It was during this period that the epics took on their definitive forms and the first of the *Puranas* was compiled.

The Gupta rulers practiced religious tolerance and sponsored groups and institutions associated with Buddhism, Jainism, and other religions. The Guptas, who were themselves Hindus, promoted Hinduism and sought to organize society in accordance with Hindu beliefs. Thanks in part to Gupta patronage, the worship of Vishnu and Shiva became increasingly popular during this period, which also saw a shift from worship at open-air sacrificial altars to worship in temples. As temple institutions arose, so did special forms of temple art and architecture. These developments quickened the spread of *bhakti* and the emerging devotional sects.

A very significant religious development during the age of the Guptas was the rise of devotional Hinduism. The two great Sanskrit epics, the *Ramayana* and the *Mahabharata,* had been completed and were well established by this time. As we have seen, these epics are concerned with political problems, dynastic successions, duty, and obligations. But they also feature the exploits of the gods and have much to tell us about popular deities and avatars and forms of devotion to them. Composition of the *Puranas* commenced during this period, indicating the growing popularity of devotional Hinduism.

The Development of *Bhakti*

The devotional aspects of Hinduism became increasingly popular under the Guptas, but they took on new life in southern India between the sixth and ninth centuries C.E. in the form of the ecstatic movement of *bhakti*. This movement and ideology spread all over India, changing and adapting to new regional and linguistic circumstances. Like the radical innovations of the *Upanishads* and the *Bhagavad Gita*, *bhakti* changed the course of Hinduism, giving it an ecstatic dimension that expressed itself through poetry, art, architecture, and temple building. *Bhakti* was instrumental in the development of the various sectarian orientations of Hinduism and in its vibrant temple cultures. Closely linked to the most important dynasties of the time, *bhakti* was equally important for the challenge it issued to caste and gender hierarchies.

By the late fifth century C.E., Buddhism (Chapter 3) and Jainism (Chapter 4) were deeply entrenched in southern India. *Bhakti* arose as a challenge to these traditions. Over the next four centuries, wandering poets roamed the Tamil country and converted royalty and commoners alike to the devotional ethos of *bhakti*. Royal patronage for Jainism and Buddhism waned, and kings sought legitimacy through poets' songs that praised the kings as the representatives of the gods Shiva and Vishnu. The religious networks forged by the itinerant poets sometimes developed into political networks and strengthened alliances between religion and politics.

By the twelfth century, the *bhakti* movement had taken on a new role, becoming a weapon wielded against caste and gender prejudice. It often rejected ritual and temple-based worship, insisting that the body is itself a temple and that God dwells in every individual.

Caste and *Bhakti* Many scholars argue that the *bhakti* movement had such a far-reaching impact because it was egalitarian, revolutionary, and frequently anti-*brahmin*. *Bhakti* poet-saints represented a variety of caste backgrounds. Furthermore, rather than using Sanskrit, the language of the *Vedas* and of priestly authority, the *bhakti* poets used vernacular languages such as Tamil, Kannada, Marathi, and an early form of Hindi. The *bhakti* poets asserted that caste and other circumstances of one's birth did not determine one's access to God. Rather, it was the quality of one's surrender to God that mattered. Although a text such as the *Bhagavad Gita* espoused similar ideas, that text also simultaneously stressed the importance of one's duty according to caste. In defining one's sole duty as the practice of perfect surrender to God, the *bhakti* poets were revolutionary. Nonetheless, the radical ideas espoused by the poets were often blunted when absorbed into mainstream Hinduism.

Tantra

Bhakti was not the only revolutionary new idea to challenge the strictures of gender and caste. *Tantra*, another new system of thought and practice, emerged alongside it. Making use of symbols, rituals, yogic postures, breathing techniques, mantras, and other spiritual practices—sometimes in shocking or forbidden ways—*Tantra* offered the possibility of sudden liberation from *samsara*. By the seventh century it had come to influence not only Hinduism but Buddhism and Jainism as well.

Tantra (Sanskrit, "loom") assumes the interweaving and interconnectedness of all things. These include pure consciousness (identified with *Brahman* or Shiva) and material reality in its most basic state (*prakriti,* identified with Shakti), which are interwoven in a relationship of mutual interdependence and love. Similarly, *samsara* and *moksha* are not understood as two different things but as aspects of a single continuum of being. For practitioners of *Tantra,* the material world is a manifestation of the divine energy associated with pure consciousness (*Brahman*/Shiva). Their spiritual practices are said to give them the ability to manipulate or channel that energy in order to gain liberation. Unlike the ascetics who renounced the material world and its sensual pleasures as part of their spiritual quest, practitioners of *Tantra* made use of material things and the senses as means by which to transcend them. For them, *moksha* could be found in the midst of everyday experience.

Tantra likely arose among mystics in Kashmir, Nepal, and possibly Bengal and Assam. These Tantric sages and yogis asserted that the ritual transgression of social boundaries could create ideal conditions for transcending the egocentric self and achieving instantaneous *moksha*. Recognizing that people's egos are deeply embedded in caste identity and rooted in taboos regarding purity and pollution, practitioners of *Tantra* performed transgressive rituals in which they identified their bodies as deities, ritually consumed meat, fish, and wine, and engaged in ritual sex with low-caste partners. Such rituals were designed to break through the narrow confines of what one assumes the self to be.

As *Tantra* increased in popularity, it also became increasingly secretive. Many were attracted by its reputed ability to enable one to avoid the rigors of spiritual progress over the course of many lifetimes by using its rituals to achieve liberation in one's present life. But there were also allegations that some adherents exercised seductive magical powers, reports of others suffering mental breakdown, and disapproval of

How does the criticism of special knowledge and power wielded by *brahmins* compare to criticism of the power of priests and religious authorities in other religions?

rituals that violated social conventions. For these reasons, much of *Tantra* remained hidden during its later development.

Early Hindu Encounters with Islam and Rule Under the Mughal Dynasty

One of the earliest sustained encounters between Hindus and Muslims in India was initiated by the raids of Mahmud of Ghazni (Afghanistan) early in the eleventh century. Attracted by India's immense wealth and motivated by religious zeal, Mahmud repeatedly raided the subcontinent, annexed states headed by Hindu, Buddhist, and Jain kings, and left them in charge as his vassals. His most famous incursion involved the looting and destruction of the great temple of Shiva in Somnath (1025). According to Muslim sources, more than 50,000 defenders of the temple were killed, and its immense wealth taken back to Ghazni. These Muslim accounts also speak of the forced conversions of Hindus to Islam. Contemporary Hindu nationalists often point to this early encounter with Islam as the beginning of centuries of oppression and persecution under Muslim rule.

By the time the Mughal Empire was established in India, Islam had established a strong foothold there, particularly in the northern regions. The Mughals were Muslim rulers of Turkic-Mongol origin. They ruled from 1526 until the mid-eighteenth century, after which their state continued to exist but with weakened rulers incapable of exercising control over it. Under the Mughals, a complex relationship existed between Hinduism and Islam. Some Mughal emperors were hostile to religions other than their own and to Hinduism and Jainism in particular. Others, such as Akbar (1542–1605), were open to them. Akbar encouraged dialogue with representatives of different religions at a weekly salon. He even invented his own religion, the "Divine Faith" (*Din-I-Ilahi*), which incorporated elements of various religious traditions including Hinduism, Islam, and Zoroastrianism. Akbar was a clever political strategist who understood non-Muslims as subjects rather than infidels, counted Hindu kings among his closest advisors, and married the daughters of Hindu kings to cement political alliances with them. Good relationships between Mughal emperors and high-ranking Hindus helped to produce a vibrant pluralistic culture.

Under the Mughals, the conversions of Hindus to Islam do not appear to have been forced. Instead, Hindus converted for a variety of reasons, the most common being improved economic and social standing and sincere belief in the teachings of Islam. There were also conversions of Muslims to Hinduism, especially when Muslims married into Hindu families.

Some of the greatest of Hindu thinkers, poets, and philosophers lived during the time of the Mughals. The influential poet-saint Tulsidas (1532–1623), a member of Akbar's court and a devotee of Rama, wrote the *Ramcharitmanas*, an epic retelling of the original Sanskrit *Ramayana* in Hindi. The Muslim weaver-mystic Kabir (c. 1440–1518) was inspired by a Hindu teacher and composed poetry that seamlessly combined Hindu and Islamic philosophical ideas while at the same time critiquing the social policies of Hindu and Muslim rulers.

Colonial Critique and the Hindu Reformers

When employees of the British East India Company established an imperial presence in India in the late eighteenth and early nineteenth centuries, they initially adapted themselves to local customs and practices. They learned regional languages, married into local families, and even embraced local religious beliefs. One particularly colorful example is that of an Irish general in the Bengal Army, Charles Stuart (1758–1828). Stuart was such an avid admirer of Hinduism that his colleagues nicknamed him "Hindoo Stuart." His book, *Vindication of the Hindoos* (1808), was intended to discourage the ever-growing support for British missionaries who sought to convert Hindus to Christianity. When these missionaries tried to embarrass Stuart by calling attention to aspects of Hindu mythology that seemed strange to Westerners, he eloquently wrote in response: "Whenever I look around me in the vast region of Hindoo Mythology, I discover piety in the garb of allegory: and I see Morality, at every turn, blended with every tale; and, as far as I can rely on my own judgment, it appears the most complete and ample system of Moral allegory that the world has ever produced."[10]

But not everyone involved with the British East India Company admired Hindu beliefs and customs. Many felt that the "primitive backwardness" of Hindu belief was enough to warrant colonial intervention. By the middle of the nineteenth century, and certainly after the 1857 Indian Uprising (referred to as the "Mutiny" by British chroniclers, but as the "First War of Independence" by many Indian historians), the attraction to Hinduism and Indian culture represented by figures such as "Hindoo" Stuart and the linguist William "Oriental" Jones began to fade. As the commercial and administrative presence of the British East India Company gave way to the colonial control of the British Crown, critiques of Hinduism became an increasingly important means of exerting political power over the subcontinent.

By the mid-nineteenth century, English-educated Hindus took up the work of reform as a response to colonial critiques of Hinduism. They, too, began deriding Hinduism's many gods, erotic symbolism, temple worship, and rituals as crass corruptions of the purity of the authentic Hinduism embodied in the *Vedas* and *Upanishads*. They sought to transform Hinduism from within.

One of these reformers was Ram Mohan Roy (1774–1833), a member of a wealthy Bengali *brahmin* community who established the Brahmo Samaj (Community of *Brahman* Worshippers) in 1828 as a neo-Hindu religious organization open to all, regardless of religious orientation. Believing that British rule offered India considerable opportunities for progress, Roy devoted his life to religious, social, and educational reform. He was particularly concerned with issues involving the protection of women, such as child marriage, polygamy, dowry, and the practice of *sati*. *Sati* was an upper-caste practice in which a widow immolated herself on her husband's funeral pyre. This ritual suicide was believed to bring great honor to the family and raise the status of the dead widow to that of a goddess. Roy campaigned for the abolition of *sati*, arguing that there was no scriptural basis in the *Vedas* for this practice. Finally, in 1829, *sati* was made illegal in Bengal. Roy was among the first members of the Indian upper

classes to visit Europe, traveling there in 1830 to ensure that the British would not overturn the *sati* law. He died in 1833 and was buried in Bristol.

Another influential reformer was Dayananda Saraswati (1824–1883). Having become a wandering monk early in life, Dayananda studied under a blind sage who urged him to campaign for a return to what he considered the pure and original Vedic religion. Following his advice, Dayananda rejected the epics and *Puranas* as departures from the purity of the *Vedas* and spoke out against all aspects of temple tradition, image worship, and pilgrimage. In 1875 he founded the Arya Samaj (the Noble Community) as a "Vedic" religious organization whose social reform platform condemned child marriage and untouchability while promoting the equality of women. He rejected social hierarchies in the form of *jati* and thought *varna* should be decided based on one's character, which the organization would determine in a public examination. Although Dayananda Saraswati, like Ram Mohan Roy, favored a return to Vedic religion, his Arya Samaj distinguished itself from Roy's Brahmo Samaj in its encouragement of Hindu nationalism, anticipating the more extreme Hindu nationalist groups that would appear in the early twentieth century.

Other figures, less influenced by colonial and Christian critiques of Hinduism, were not as concerned as Ram Mohan Roy and Dayananda Saraswati to reform Hinduism in ways that would appeal to the West. One was the enormously popular Bengali mystic, Ramakrishna (1836–1886). A devotee and temple priest of the goddess Kali, as a young man Ramakrishna prayed for and then experienced a vision of her as an ocean of blissful light. He then devoted himself to spiritual exercises drawn from different religious traditions, including Vaishnavism, Advaita Vedanta, Tantrism, and even Islamic Sufism and Roman Catholicism. These deepened his sense of identity with the divine and served as the basis for his teaching that all religions are directed toward the experience of a God who creates religions to suit the spiritual needs and tastes of different peoples. Seen in this way, Hinduism could claim the same legitimacy as any other religion.

Among Ramakrishna's disciples was Narendranath Datta (1863–1902), a former law student who took monastic vows during Ramakrishna's last days and was thereafter known as Swami Vivekananda, founder of the Ramakrishna Math, an order of

Temple volunteers unveil a statue of Swami Vivekananda at the Hindu Temple of Greater Chicago, Saturday, July 11, 1998, in Lemont, Illinois. The statue honors Vivekananda as "the first man to bring Hindu religion and the practice of yoga to America."

monks devoted to the teachings of Ramakrishna. Swami Vivekananda had an enormous impact on the representation of Hinduism in the West, particularly in the United States. In 1893, he visited the United States to speak on behalf of Hinduism at the World Parliament of Religions in Chicago. Quoting from the *Bhagavad Gita*, he represented Hinduism as a tolerant and universal religion. Like his teacher, Ramakrishna, Vivekananda asserted that all religions are true. His stirring speech was a milestone in changing Western attitudes toward Hinduism. It also ensured his fame and popularity in America, and he went on to establish the Vedanta Society of New York. Today, Vedanta Societies throughout the world are dedicated to the study, practice, and promotion of Hinduism, emphasizing the philosophical tradition originating in the *Vedas* and *Upanishads*.

Gandhi and the Struggle for Indian Independence

Mohandas Karamchand Gandhi (1869–1948), a towering religious, political, and social reformer in India, recast many Hindu ideas in the service of the fight for Indian independence. Born into a middle-class family of merchants, Gandhi was an English-educated lawyer and a deeply religious man. As a law student in England, he had read the *Bhagavad Gita,* and it had a profound impact on him.

Gandhi's political career began in South Africa, where he worked as a lawyer. It was here, in a struggle against racial discrimination, that he began to develop his political philosophy of nonviolent resistance. He characterized nonviolent resistance as *satyagraha* (Sanskrit, "grasping the truth") and explained that its strength lay in converting wrongdoers to justice rather than striving to coerce them.

Gandhi returned to India in 1915 to join the fledgling Indian independence movement, which sought to free India from British colonial rule. Deeply influenced by the American writer Henry David Thoreau (1817 – 1862), especially his thoughts on civil disobedience, Gandhi established an *ashram* (a place of religious seclusion) to train freedom fighters. The *ashram* chose as its motto a statement from the *Upanishads*: *satyameva jayate*, "the truth alone will prevail." Like his Upanishadic forebears, Gandhi believed that truth could be sought only through selfless service and humility, which could in turn be achieved by disciplining the body through fasting and celibacy.

Gandhi did not hesitate to criticize certain Hindu beliefs and practices, particularly that of *varnashrama dharma*, the ancient system by which society was ordered into various classes or castes. He worked tirelessly to abolish untouchability, calling the untouchables *Harijans* ("Children of God"), thereby seeking to increase their respectability. Gandhi also strove to improve the status of women.

Gandhi's charisma and influence were so great that even in his lifetime he was revered as a saint or *Mahatma* (Sanskrit, "Great Soul"). A lifelong Hindu, Gandhi also advocated the universality and truth of all religions and sought throughout his life to reconcile Hinduism and Islam. Tragically, on January 30, 1948, he was assassinated by Nathuram Godse, a Hindu nationalist who thought Gandhi was too accommodating of Muslims. Godse was later executed for the crime despite the pleas of Gandhi's two sons and Jawaharlal Nehru (1889–1964), India's first prime minister, who believed that violence would dishonor everything Gandhi represented. After decades of struggle, Gandhi had lived to enjoy just five months of freedom after Great Britain had partitioned colonial India into the independent states of India and Pakistan in mid-1947.

Hindu Nationalism and *Hindutva*

Whereas reformers such as Ram Mohan Roy, Vivekananda, and Gandhi sought to build bridges with the West and other religions by calling attention to their commonalities with Hinduism, other figures, such as V. D. Savarkar (1883–1966), insisted on the distinctiveness of Hinduism. Savarkar called this concept ***hindutva*** (Sanskrit, "Hindu-ness"), a term he coined in a 1923 pamphlet. For Savarkar, *hindutva* was a force to unite Hindus in repelling all dangerous foreign influences. As president of the Hindu Mahasabha, a Hindu nationalist political party that embraced this concept, Savarkar argued that India was an exclusively "Hindu Nation."

In 1925, the Rashtriya Svayamsevak Sangh (RSS; National Volunteer Corps) was founded. Although it has presented itself as a Hindu cultural organization, its members have a long history of political actions that have intensified communal tensions, precipitated violence, and propagated religious intolerance. The founder of the RSS, K. B. Hedgewar (1889–1940), was himself inspired by V. D. Savarkar's concept of *hindutva*. The RSS was meant to be a training ground for the self-empowerment of Hindu youth who were committed to defending a Hindu nation from the perceived threat posed by the Muslim world. Gaining independence from oppressive foreign rule can often rob nationalist movements of their momentum, but this was not the case in India after 1947. Hindu nationalists continued to be a major force in that country. The political backlash following Gandhi's assassination led many Mahasabha members to leave the party and ally themselves instead with a new political organization called the Bharatiya Jana Sangh (Indian People's Alliance). Its founder, Syama Prasad Mookerjee (1901–1953), had been a member of both the Mahasabha and the RSS when he organized the Indian People's Alliance in 1951. This was a Hindu nationalist party specifically created to oppose the Indian National Congress, the more moderate party of Jawaharlal Nehru and Mahatma Gandhi. In 1981 the Indian People's Alliance became the Bharatiya Janata Party (BJP). Today, the BJP and the Indian National Congress are the two major parties in India's political system. In 2014, the BJP won a landslide victory in India's national election. Narendra Modi, India's new prime minister, has been one of the party's most visible leaders.

Today, organizations espousing Savarakar's *hindutva* ideology come under an umbrella group called the Sangh Parivar (Family of Associations). The RSS is the cultural wing, the BJP is the political wing, and the Vishwa Hindu Parishad (VHP; World Hindu Organization) is the religious wing of the Sangh Parivar. The RSS continues to attract mostly lower-middle-class male youth, who feel empowered by the strong sense of cultural identity that it advocates. The RSS has awakened a deep sense of cultural pride among Hindu youth, but some of its members have been leading participants in sectarian violence against Muslims in recent years.

In 1991 the BJP led a pilgrimage around India gathering bricks to build a temple to Rama in Ayodhya, India. This was to be no ordinary temple. The pilgrims claimed that a fifteenth-century c.e. Islamic mosque called the Babri Masjid had been erected over an older Hindu temple that marked the exact birthplace of Rama. Their purpose was to tear down the mosque and build a grand Rama temple in its place. Members of Sangh Parivar rallied around the cause, which culminated in more than 200,000 participants converging on Ayodhya and demolishing the mosque with their bare hands. RSS youth then targeted the local Muslim community, destroying other mosques, ransacking Muslim homes, raping Muslim women, and murdering Muslim men. The backlash of these events echoed throughout India and Bangladesh, resulting in more than a thousand incidents of riots and communal violence perpetrated by both Hindus and Muslims. By the time calm had been restored, more than 4,000 people had been injured and at least 1,100 had lost their lives.

The BJP has also employed less aggressive strategies in its campaign to create a thoroughly Hindu India. For example, in the 1980s and 1990s it attempted to rewrite Indian history by distributing new school textbooks throughout India. These textbooks reflected the BJP's vision of India as a Hindu nation and Hinduism as a unified, monolithic tradition. Most important, and dangerously, this historical revisionism minimized Muslim contributions to the development of India and described India's Muslim rulers as foreign invaders. The RSS also has a strong presence in the Hindu diaspora communities in Europe and North America. Many Hindu emigrants send their children to RSS youth camps to give them a sense of their Hindu identity and cultural pride.

The Future of Hinduism

Encouraged by nationalist groups and political parties in India, some of today's Hindus see Hinduism as monolithic, homogeneous, and impermeable, closed off from what they perceive as the corrupting influences of the West and foreign religions. At the same time, an emerging global movement is seeking to transcend traditional boundaries to better serve the needs of an increasingly diverse Hindu community. Hinduism has always displayed a unique ability in the face of changing conditions to sustain ancient traditions within new and ever-changing contexts. How this ability will manifest itself in the future remains to be seen, but it seems certain that the efforts of both Hindu traditionalists and progressives will ensure the continuing vibrancy of the world's oldest religions.

HINDUISM AS A WAY OF LIFE

Hindus often insist that Hinduism is more a "way of life" than a system of beliefs. Indeed, Hinduism does place greater emphasis on what one *does* rather than on what one *believes*. The emphasis on doing rather than believing might explain the disconnection

VISUAL GUIDE
Hinduism

In Hinduism, folding one's hands and offering salutations by saying *namaste* (nom-us-tay) is a simple way of giving a respectful greeting, as well as saying, "I bow to the divine in you."

OM or AUM is the most sacred syllable in Hinduism and may be traced back to the Vedas. It is regarded as the primordial sound through which the universe is manifested. It is considered sacred by Hindus, Jains, Buddhists, and Sikhs.

The word "swastika" (Sanskrit, *svastika*) is derived from the Sanskrit *su* (good) + *asti* (it is), and may be understood as "fortunate" or "auspicious." The swastika itself is an ancient solar symbol and denotes harmony, balance, and good fortune. It is venerated by Hindus, as well as Buddhists and Jains.

Hindu forehead markings: *bindi*, *tripundra*, and *namam*. *Bindi* (drop) is a decorative mark on the forehead signifying auspiciousness. An additional "dot" is often applied by married women to the top of the head where the hair is parted. The mark between the eyes is situated to signify the "third eye" (the faculty of perception beyond ordinary sight). Some forehead markings denote sectarian affiliation, such as the three horizontal lines of sacred

(continued)

between textual injunction and actual practice that one often encounters in Hinduism. Hindu texts provide many prescriptions for how to live (e.g., the aims of life and the *varnaashrama dharma* system), but these do not always translate into actual lived practice. In this section, we will explore Hinduism as a way of life.

Seeing the Divine Image: Temples and Icons

Hinduism encourages a sensory religious experience in its adherents. This experiential aspect is nowhere more evident than when a Hindu goes to a temple. As religion scholar Diana Eck observes, the devotee doesn't say, "I am going for worship." Rather, the devotee asserts, "I am going for *darshan*." The Sanskrit word *darshan* means "to see," but in the Hindu context it refers specifically to the interlocking gaze shared by the deity and the devotee. That is, *darshan* is the intimate act of both seeing the deity and being looked upon by the divine, an act which establishes a loving relationship between devotee and God.[11]

As we learned earlier in this chapter, the image of a god in a temple or a personal shrine at home is not just a representation of the deity; rather, it is imbued with the divine presence. Thus, devotees believe that to see an image of a deity is to see the deity itself. In turn, the gaze of the deity's image is believed to confer blessings on every person who comes into its presence. In many ways, the act of *darshan* is often the most meaningful experience for Hindus.

Today, most Hindus go to a local temple or on pilgrimage to a sacred site for *darshan*. For this reason, the temple is a central religious and cultural institution in Hindu religious practice.

Temples generally house two different kinds of icons. The first type is the main image (or images), which resides at the center of the temple. These images are generally made of stone and permanently fixed in the shrine. The second type of icon is the processional image, typically cast from an amalgam of five metals. Smaller and more mobile than fixed images, processional images are brought out of temples on special platforms or chariots for temple festivals and are usually adorned in elaborate costumes and jewels. Hindus gather for a *darshan* in the presence of the divine form these mobile images embody. Although both types of icons are made by human hands and are constituted of material substances, while the icon is being worshipped it is understood not to be *merely* stone or metal but the very body of God.

In temple rites, deities are treated as royal guests. Temple worship usually involves sixteen different offerings. Of these, the most significant is the eighth offering, which involves pouring various types of auspicious substances over the icon. These might include scented water, milk, and sandalwood paste. After the ritual, the deity is adorned in ornaments, textiles, and flowers. The temple rituals end with a waving of lamps before the image. For Hindus, this is the ideal moment for *darshan*.

Divine images can also directly convey religious teachings. For instance, Nataraja, Lord of the Dance, is one of the most iconic forms of Shiva. In his dance, Nataraja represents what *Shaivas* call the Five Activities of Shiva, which can also be understood as the five principal manifestations of divine energy: creation, preservation, destruction, illusion, and liberation.

Forms of Worship

The Sanskrit word **puja** is commonly used to describe worship in Hinduism. In its most simple form, *puja* involves making some offering to the deity (such as fruit, incense, or flowers). The deity is then believed to partake of the devotion inherent in the offering. The material aspect of the offerings left behind is thought to be infused with the deity's blessing.

Puja can be simple or elaborate. Along with material items, offerings can consist of such things as washing or clothing the image of the deity, greeting it, prostrating oneself before it, and similar gestures. *Puja* can be offered almost anywhere—before a home shrine, at a temple, at pilgrimage sites, by sacred trees or rivers, at roadside shrines, or within temporary structures specially made for a specific rite. Rituals may be carried out as an expression of love for the deity, in a rite of passage, in celebrating a holiday or festival, when asking for blessings, in order to create an atmosphere of

VISUAL GUIDE (*continued*)
Hinduism

ash worn by worshippers of Shiva and the vertical "V" of the worshippers of Vishnu. The red "drop" in the middle represents the descent of grace in the form of Lakshmi, the goddess of fortune.

The term *yantra* means "device," but these sacred diagrams may also be referred to by the term *mandala*, or "circle." They vary in form and function. Some are used to map cosmology, others embody deities, and still others function as talismans. These geometrical designs may be used for meditative contemplation.

Clouds of incense billow from a terracotta censer as devotees pray before a multi-armed clay icon of Durga (upper center), Ganesha (lower left), and other deities. This is the final opportunity for *darshan*, as the icon is about to be dissolved by immersion into the Ganges River at the conclusion of the festival of Durga Puja. Kolkata, India.

The majestic gate of a Shiva temple in southern India is reflected in one of the two ritual bathing tanks found within its precincts. These towers are erected in the four directions and are often covered in sculptural imagery that refers to the sacred myths of the gods venerated within. Arunachaleswar Temple, Tiruvannamalai, India, eleventh century.

peace and harmony, or to propitiate the gods in times of trouble. Ritual occasions are ideal for maintaining and strengthening community ties, as we learned at the beginning of the chapter with the consecration of the Sri Ganesha Hindu Temple of Utah.

Certain particular forms of Hindu worship are so popular as to deserve our special attention. Here we describe three of them: *arati, mantras,* and sacrifice.

Arati As a form of *puja,* **arati** involves an offering of light. *Arati* is a very common practice; in fact, some Hindus use the term *arati* rather than *puja* to refer to worship generally. A lamp fueled with *ghee* (clarified butter) or camphor is lit and waved in a clockwise direction in front of the deity. The five flames used in *arati* symbolize the five elements (earth, water, fire, air, and ether), as well as the totality of the universe. This waving of the lamp is thought to remove evil influences and to return the object or recipient of the offering to an auspicious state, regardless of any negative thoughts or desires that might have been projected onto it. At the end of the ritual, participants wave their hands over the flame and touch them to their foreheads, taking the divine light of the deity into their innermost being.

Mantra Nearly all rituals in Hinduism are accompanied by the recitation of **mantras**. These are ritual formulas used to produce a spiritual effect. *Mantras* can be used for a variety of reasons: to heighten awareness of God, to enhance the efficacy of an offering, to aid the practice of meditation, or to produce some magical effect. *Mantras* are usually—but not always—in Sanskrit.

The *mantra* that we have considered previously, *OM,* is prominent throughout Hinduism. The intonation of *OM,* the sound through which the universe is manifested, is thought to attune the mind to the essence of reality. Various Hindu sects use specific *mantras* especially suited to them. For example, the most important *mantra* for *Vaishnavas* is *Om Namo Narayanaya,* which means "obeisance to Narayana" (another name for Vishnu). For *Vaishnavas,* this *mantra* articulates the relationship between God and the devotee while also asserting the fullness and unity of Vishnu. Reciting and contemplating the *mantra* is an act of devotion that brings the devotee closer to Vishnu.

Sacrifice   Fire sacrifice has been an essential component of Hinduism since the Vedic period. Sacrifice usually involves building an altar, kindling a fire, feeding it with *ghee,* and casting auspicious offerings (milk, cereals, fruits, flowers, etc.) into the fire while chanting *mantras.* Although fire sacrifice is usually performed by a *brahmin* priest, these rites can be performed by any married upper-caste man. A fire sacrifice is a crucial component of life cycle and temple rituals.

Although sacrifice has persisted as an important feature of Hindu worship through the centuries, perspectives on the relevance and meaning of sacrifice have varied. In the Vedic period, sacrifice was seen as essential to maintaining cosmic order. This is the reason that one of the most important Vedic myths describes the universe as being born from the sacrifice of the cosmic man. The *Upanishads,* however, tend to diminish the relevance of sacrifice as an effective means of liberation from *samsara.* These texts argue that the true sacrifice takes place internally, with the breath itself fueling an inner sacrificial fire that awakens one to knowledge. The *Bhagavad Gita* follows in this line of interpretation, asserting that it is the surrender of the fruit of action (through *bhakti*) that is the true meaning and purpose of sacrifice.

In the earliest period, the sacrifice of animals was an important aspect of Hindu ritual. However, over time (and particularly under the influence of Jainism and Buddhism), animal sacrifice ceased to play a role in upper-caste sacrificial rituals. In such sacrifices, coconuts and pumpkins came to act as substitutes for the animals. Animal sacrifice continues to play a significant role in folk Hinduism.

Yoga

Yoga in its most basic sense means a "yoking" or "uniting." In religious discourse, it refers to the uniting of the self with God. Yoga is sometimes used instead of *marga* (path) to designate any one of the three great paths one can take in the pursuit of *moksha: karma, jnana,* and *bhakti.* Yoga is also used more narrowly as the name of one of the six schools of philosophy and is one form of *jnana.* Understood in this way, yoga refers to the many systems of physical and mental exercise that have developed within

A Hindu ascetic sits in the lotus position, a prominent bodily posture for the practice of yoga.

the Hindu tradition. Most of us are familiar with *hatha* yoga, which makes use of physical exercises to promote the health of the body. But there are also forms of yoga, such as Raja ("Royal") Yoga, that employ both physical and mental techniques in order to make liberation from *samsara* possible. It is this form of yoga that most concerns us here.

The origins of yoga are obscure. Most scholars see elements of yoga in the *Vedas* and *Upanishads*. It is unmistakably present in the *Ramayana* and *Mahabharata*, whose heroes perform yogic exercises. By the fourth century C.E. the principles and techniques of yoga had been systematized in the *Yoga Sutras* of Patanjali.

The *Yoga Sutras* consist of 196 instructional sayings about the moral, physical, and mental conditions and techniques that can enable the individual to achieve *moksha*. These are evident in the eight steps through which practitioners move in their quest for liberation. The first two steps have to do with moral preparation. Prohibitions against harming other beings, lying, stealing, sexual irresponsibility, and greed must be observed. In addition, the five virtues of cleanliness, contentment, discipline, studiousness, and devotion to a god must be practiced. The next three steps involve preparation of the body. The practitioner learns postures (especially the lotus position) that promote comfort and alertness and how to breathe in rhythmic patterns that calm the body. Once these ends have been achieved, it becomes possible to withdraw the senses so that they no longer demand the mind's attention. The next two steps prepare the mind for liberation. By focusing its attention on a single thing, all other particulars fade away. All that remains is to gently remove this single object of attention from the field of the mind's awareness. This brings the practitioner to the eighth step, which is also the ultimate goal: *samadhi,* a state in which one's awareness is of the self as *Brahman.*

Rites of Passage

Hindu rites of passage are intended to invoke blessings and divine favor during important times of transition. In addition, they help socialize individuals, assisting them as they move into new roles and stages of life. Some rites of passage occur very early in life. These include the naming ceremony of a child, typically held on the tenth or twelfth day after birth; a child's first haircut, usually performed between the first and third years of life; and ear piercing, which is typically done for both boys and girls before age five. The following are also major rites of passage.

A Boy's Initiation Historically, the *upanayana,* or sacred thread ceremony, was an initiatory rite for *brahmin, kshatriya,* and *vaishya* boys. (Recall the passage from *Laws of Manu,* p. 46) Today, it is performed almost exclusively for *brahmin* boys at about the age of eight, giving them permission to perform certain religious functions. Beginning with a fire sacrifice, the ritual culminates in the promotion of the initiate to the category of "twice-born." The initiate is given a sacred thread that symbolizes a kind of umbilical cord linking the boy to the sun, the source of all light and knowledge. The sacred thread lies across the chest, resting over the left shoulder and under the right arm, and consists of three cotton threads, each composed of three strands, that are joined together by a single knot. The sacred thread is a very visible sign of caste status. It is worn throughout one's life and is discarded only if a man renounces the world.

A Girl's First Menstrual Period The onset of a girl's first menstrual period, which marks the transition from childhood to adulthood, is celebrated with rituals performed for girls from all castes. Sometimes these observances include spending the first three days of her first period secluded, although friends can visit. The young woman takes a ritual bath on the fourth day, and a feast is held in her honor. This transition is a public affair because it announces her availability for marriage. Often the young woman is taken to the local temple to receive a special blessing from an older married woman in her community, who will perform an *arati* ceremony to honor her new potential to bear children. Her life radically changes afterward and, for many communities, her freedom to have unsupervised interaction with boys may be greatly curtailed.

Marriage Marriage is a very important rite of passage. It is through marriage that one enters the householder *ashrama* that provides the main support for society as a whole. Marriage was traditionally arranged by the parents between a bride and groom of the same *jati* after consulting an astrologer, who determined the couple's compatibility. In the last few decades, caste strictures have eased somewhat. As a result, marriages for love have become more commonplace.

The marriage ceremony is sanctified through a fire sacrifice in which the gods are asked for blessings and offerings are poured into the fire. A thread is tied around the bride's wrist, and she is asked to step three times on a grinding stone from the groom's family as a demonstration of her fidelity to the new household she is joining. At the high point of the rite, the bride and groom walk together seven times around the sacred fire. The bride's family then provides a sumptuous meal for all guests. After the last day of celebration, the bride goes to the home of her husband and begins her new life.

Death Hindus often liken the cremation pyre to a fire sacrifice and speak of the funerary ritual, which usually involves cremation, as "the last sacrifice." Generally, cremation takes place on the same day as death. The body is washed, smeared with sandalwood paste, wrapped in a cloth, and then carried on a litter by male relatives, who chant a holy name or phrase as they bear the body to the cremation ground. It is usually the duty of the eldest son of the deceased to conduct the last rites and light the pyre. An ancient practice that is still often observed requires him to also crack the skull of the deceased in order to release the soul from the body, a daunting task for a son to perform.

Although cremation is the usual means of disposing of the body, there are exceptions. Earth burial is practiced for babies and among some low-caste communities. Saints, yogis, and ascetics are also buried. Their bodies are placed in special tombs, around which shrines are sometimes erected and worship performed.

Following the funeral ceremony, the family and home of the deceased are considered to be polluted for a period of about ten days. The bereaved are expected to keep to themselves until rites of ancestral offerings are completed. During this period, the deceased is offered balls of rice with which he or she is believed to construct a body in the spirit world or intermediate realm. This rite, which reflects the gestation of a human embryo for ten lunar months, may very well predate the formulation of a belief in reincarnation that was developed by the time of the *Upanishads*.

Pilgrimage

In Hinduism, sacred pilgrimage sites are believed to lie at the border between this world and that of the divine. Many of the earliest pilgrimage sites were located at sacred rivers and pools, and pilgrimage specifically involved ritual bathing as a means

Hindu pilgrimage routes in India.

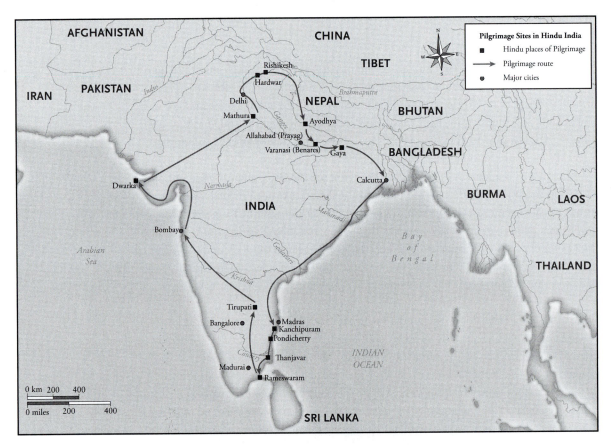

of purification. Some revered sites, marked by a shrine or temple, commemorate a sacred event or the life of a holy person. For pilgrims, these sites allow immediate, tangible access to the sacred.

One of the most important Hindu pilgrimage sites is the sacred city of Varanasi on the banks of the Ganges. Many Hindus believe that to die in Varanasi is to be immediately released from *samsara*. For this reason, many old and sick people travel to Varanasi to die. However, because the Ganges is held to be the most sacred river in India, people who are unable to go to Varanasi to die arrange to have their ashes scattered in the river. In this way, the sacred river is believed to carry the dead from this life into the divine realm.

The largest pilgrimage in India is to the sacred city of Prayag (Allahabad), where the Ganges and Yamuna Rivers (as well as the Sarasvati, a now-vanished river mentioned in sacred texts) come together. To bathe at the confluence of these three rivers is considered especially auspicious. Every twelve years, the *Kumbha Mela* festival takes place at Prayag. During the *Kumbha Mela*, the largest gathering of humans on earth takes place as pilgrims converge to bathe in the holy waters in the hope that all their sins will be washed away.

There are many other important pilgrimage sites in India. Some are dedicated to the goddess Devi and are referred to as *Shakti Peethas* ("Seats of Power"). Still others, like the city of Vrindavan in northern India, attract devotees of Krishna, who believe that it is not only the site of the god's birth and childhood but also the place where he continues to live.

How do Hindu pilgrimage practices compare to those of other religions, such as Buddhism, Islam, and Christianity? How do pilgrimage sites arise, and how do they serve the practical and spiritual needs of the visiting pilgrim?

Women in Hinduism

Hindu tradition has tended to be patriarchal, both subordinating and marginalizing women. Although there is some evidence in the Vedic literature that some women participated in early philosophical movements or dialogues, for the most part their public roles have been secondary to those of men. The role of Hindu women has been primarily domestic.

Classical Hindu texts generally give little attention to women, but there are exceptions. One example is the *Laws of Manu,* which, in the course of its extensive coverage of *varnashrama dharma*, includes some statements that confer upon women a relatively high place: "Where women are honoured, there the gods are pleased; but where they are not honoured, no sacred rite yields rewards."[12] At the same time, numerous passages subordinate and marginalize women, clearly asserting the predominance of father, husband, and even sons.

The *bhakti* movements enabled women to overturn social hierarchies. Women poets and saints such as Meera, who lived during the fifteenth century in Rajasthan, rejected marriage, devoted themselves to a spiritual life, and challenged the limits of gender, class, and caste. Today, Hindu women are increasingly assuming leadership roles in India and in the Indian diaspora. Women sometimes act as priests and are beginning to wield influence as spiritual teachers, monastics, and theologians. One of the most important contemporary female **gurus** is Mata Amritanandamayi Devi (b. 1953). Known to her followers as Ammachi ("Mother") and popularly referred to as "the hugging saint," she is believed by her devotees to be the embodiment of Devi, the divine mother.

In contemporary South Asian and Southeast Asian Hindu society, women are regarded as the custodians of traditional beliefs and ritual for the family. Generally, the social roles of men and women are expressed through clothing and other outward signs. While men wear contemporary slacks, dress shirts, and ties, women prefer traditional modes of dress. While many men eschew sectarian forehead markings except on ritual occasions, most Hindu women, especially those who are married, adorn their foreheads with the *bindi*. In addition to performing *puja* at the home shrine, observing festivals, and encouraging regular temple visits for the family, women also perform *pujas* and *vrata* for the spiritual welfare of their husbands and children on certain holidays.

Vrata   A *vrata* is a vow of temporary self-denial usually undertaken by a woman. This generally involves a short period of fasting, but a *vrata* can also be a vow of silence or a short-term renunciation of anything to which one is attached. A woman usually undertakes a *vrata* for a specific purpose, such as to ensure the health and well-being of her husband and family. There are many special *vratas* observed at specific times throughout the calendar year. One of the most popular, observed by married women throughout southern India, always falls on a Friday in early August. This *vrata* involves a period of purification and fasting, after which the woman invites the goddess Lakshmi into her home. The hope is that Lakshmi, goddess of wealth and good fortune, will bring these things to the home.

All *vratas* are vows taken by women on special festival days. Let us now examine what are the key holidays and festivals observed by all Hindus.

Festivals and Holidays

Hindus make use of both solar and lunar calendars, as well as a calendar based on twenty-seven different constellations. All three calendars are consulted to determine when festivals and holidays will be observed. Many Hindu festivals link mythic events to the agricultural cycle. There are also innumerable holidays and observances that commemorate saints and sages, historical events, and sacred sites of regional interest.

Three popular Hindu festivals that are celebrated with many regional variations serve to illustrate the diversity of observances in Hinduism.

Navaratri or Dashera   *Navaratri* ("nine nights") or *Dashera* ("ten days") is a holiday cycle celebrating the end of the monsoon season in India. In some regions, *Dashera* also commemorates the conclusion of a great war between Rama and the demon-king, Ravana. In other regions, such as southern India and in Bengal, the festival celebrates Devi's battle against the buffalo-demon, Mahisha (p. 77). To commemorate this conquest, altars are set up with images of the Goddess. For the first three days of the festival, devotees worship Devi in her manifestation as Durga. They then turn their attention to worshipping her as Lakshmi. On the concluding three days, she is worshipped as Sarasvati, the embodiment of knowledge. In Bengal, the eighth day is especially important, as it celebrates Durga slaying Mahisha and is marked with the sacrifice either of black goats or a substitute sacrifice of pumpkins. The festival culminates with street processions of large painted clay icons of Durga that are later dissolved in the nearby river or the sea. The "victorious tenth day," *Vijaya Dashami*, is celebrated all over India as Rama's final victory over the demon Ravana.

Diwali   *Diwali*, the five-day "Festival of Lights," is celebrated in October. For many Hindus, it commemorates Rama's rescue of Sita and their heroic return to Ayodhya. Other myths are invoked as an explanation for the festival in different regions of India. At Diwali, oil lamps are set out on doorsteps and window ledges, and floating lamps are placed as offerings in rivers and reservoirs to signify the triumph of good over evil. Fireworks are lit on the night of the new moon, when Lakshmi is worshipped. The third day of *Diwali* marks the end of the harvest season, and *Lakshmi Puja* is performed to thank the goddess for the abundance that she has given. New clothes are worn and gifts are exchanged. *Diwali* is also celebrated by Sikhs and Jains.

Holi   The spring festival of *Holi*, always celebrated at the vernal equinox, is Hinduism's most colorful holiday. Celebrated in either February or March, its festivities take place over two days. On the first night, bonfires are lit, and coconuts are offered as a sacrifice. The following day is a carnival celebration during which social and gender hierarchies are temporarily inverted, as crowds of young and old alike frolic in the streets, spraying colored water and staining one another with brightly colored powders.

Performance Traditions

There is a multitude of performance traditions in Hinduism, many of which cross over into the realm of ritual. Even the act of publicly reciting the *Ramayana* in Hinduism is believed to transform the performance site into sacred space. Hindu sacred performance traditions include many different genres: theater, puppetry, dance, music, storytelling, processions, and street festivals.

Ram Lila   The *Ram Lila* (*The Play of Rama*) is one of Hinduism's most popular performance traditions. During the month of September, northern Indian villages and cities host *Ram Lila* festivals to coincide with the festival of *Dashera*.

Fun and frolic characterize the spring festival of *Holi*, as participants mischievously smear colored powders or spray colored water on each other.

A performance in Mumbai, India, of *Ram Lila*, the very popular enactment of the *Ramayana*.

These festivals, lasting anywhere from ten days to a month, are costume dramas based on the *Ramayana*. The most famous and elaborate *Ram Lila* is sponsored by the Maharaja (the hereditary ruler) of Ramnagar, a city located across the Ganges from Varanasi. The Ramnagar *Ram Lila* attracts pilgrims from all over northern India who come not only to participate in this annual festival but also to have *darshan* of Rama. The roles of Rama, Lakshmana, and Sita (the three principal characters of the *Ramayana*) are played by young upper-caste boys. For the duration of the *Ram Lila*, these boys are worshipped as the embodiments of divinity. Every evening, a priest waves a lamp, illuminating the principal characters who give *darshan* to the assembled pilgrims and devotees. Just as in a temple, where God is actively present in the icon, here too the very act of performing the *Ramayana* enables the young boys to embody divinity.

Sacred Songs: *Bhajan* and *Kirtan* The term *bhajan* refers specifically to devotional songs in Hinduism and Sikhism. The *bhajan* helps the gathered community to contemplate the divine. This is usually achieved through repetition of key phrases and lines and also through a call-and-response format of singing. Often, profound mystical concepts are presented in simple language that everyone may understand.

Bhajan may be contrasted to *kirtan*, which is neither formal in form nor structure, nor is it constrained by setting. *Kirtan* may be performed in lively sing-along processionals that roam the streets. Instruments are not necessary for *kirtan* performance, although they are often used. There are two different types of *kirtan* performances: in one type, the *kirtan* leader and the chorus alternate singing the divine name; and in the other, a hymn is communally recited, usually with an opening invocation, and then the body of the composition that describes the pastimes of the deity. For Hindu devotees, *kirtan* is a key spiritual practice, and it continues to be popular today, particularly for *Vaishnava* sects.

Storytelling An important way in which Hindus learn about the content of their religion is through storytelling. Even today, as in centuries past, professional storytellers continue to travel particular routes throughout India to visit local festivals, where they sing the epics and other myths in all-night performances.

Modern Hindus enjoy sacred narratives through new and equally vibrant media, such as movies, television, and even comic books. Throughout the history of Hinduism there have been numerous versions of sacred narratives, the *Ramayana* being perhaps the most obvious example. In recent decades, sacred narratives have been invigorated through print, radio, and television, as well as the Internet, with ever-new and imaginative retellings of these ancient stories.

CONCLUSION

Throughout this chapter, we have explored the rich diversity of the Hindu tradition. The extent of this diversity has prompted some observers to remark, "There are as many Hinduisms as there are Hindus." But we also have noted aspects of Hinduism that tend to unite Hindus. For example, all seek *moksha,* the ultimate liberation from *samsara*, and the realization of the true nature of the self and its relationship to the whole of reality. Hindus traverse three main paths to liberation, *karma marga, jnana marga,* and *bhakti marga.* In these various paths, we see diversity and unity together, with three different sets of teachings and practices all leading to the same goal. We see a similar blending of diversity and unity when we consider the detailed system of *varnashrama dharma,* which assigns to each individual Hindu a specific place and stage in life, while asserting the overall duty to conform to that which upholds the cosmic and social order. The history of Hinduism, therefore, exhibits a succession of inventions and reinventions in thought and practice with respect to these teachings.

For the most part, Hinduism developed in a rural setting, in small villages, and even (as we have noted) in the forest. In recent decades, however, there has been a pronounced shift in population from rural to urban settings. Furthermore, India, the world's second largest country and its largest democracy, is fast becoming a leader in high-tech industries, with cities like Bangalore and Mumbai rapidly developing as epicenters of international corporations. Hinduism is facing significant challenges brought on by modernization and the accompanying phenomenon of globalization. The religion is being constantly reshaped. But as this chapter has shown, the diversity of the Hindu tradition is integral to its identity, in the present just as in the ancient past. Whatever shape Hinduism takes in the future, it is likely to thrive, drawing on its age-old ability to adapt and to reform with even greater diversity and vitality.

SEEKING ANSWERS

What Is Ultimate Reality?

Monistic Hindus believe that *Brahman* is the supreme, unitary reality, the ground of all Being. Understood as undifferentiated and without attributes, *Brahman* manifests itself as the world, in all its particular forms. Thus, all things are inherently divine. Humans are unable to apprehend this ultimate reality because of attachment, delusion, and identification with the limited ego-self. For dualistic or devotional Hindus, ultimate reality is typically understood to be fully embodied in a deity, such as Vishnu or Shiva.

(continued)

SEEKING ANSWERS (continued)

How Should We Live in This World?

Powerfully attracted to the *samsaric* realm of particulars—our egoistic selves, our relationships, our possessions, and the seemingly countless objects of our desires—we are caught up in the continual cycle of death and rebirth. Hinduism prescribes living in a manner that moves the self toward liberation from *samsara*. Three paths (*margas* or *yogas*) lead to *moksha*: *karma* (action), *jnana* (knowledge), and *bhakti* (devotion). All the while, Hindus are required to live in conformity with *dharma*, upholding the cosmic and social order.

What Is Our Ultimate Purpose?

Moksha is liberation from *samsara*—the continuous cycle of death and rebirth, and the this-worldly realm in which this cycle recurs. Impossible fully to describe from the perspective of this world, the experience of *moksha* is said to be one of infinite awareness and eternal bliss. For monistic Hindus, *moksha* involves the full realization of the identity of the self with *Brahman* rather than with the world. For dualistic or devotional Hindus, *moksha* is the complete realization of the soul's perpetual and deep loving relationship with God.

REVIEW QUESTIONS

For Review

1. What were the essential features of Vedic religion? How was it different from Hinduism as it is practiced by most Hindus today?
2. In what ways do Hindus seek an experience of the divine?
3. What is the relationship between the ideas of karma, *samsara*, and *dharma*?
4. Describe the three *margas*, or paths, to liberation.
5. Describe the *Vedas*, *Upanishads*, epics, and *Puranas*. What are the most important features of each?

For Further Reflection

1. What are the various ways in which Hindus understand divine reality? How do these compare with those of other religions?
2. What is an avatar? How does the concept of avatar compare with the ways in which other religions speak of God on earth?
3. How does the traditional system of *varnashrama dharma* compare to systems of social organization with which you are familiar?
4. How were Hindus and Hinduism affected by British colonialism?
5. What are the most important turning points or milestones in the history of Hinduism?

GLOSSARY

arati (aah-ra-tee; Sanskrit) Worship with light, involving the waving of a lamp in front of the deity.

atman (aat-mun; Sanskrit) The eternal self or soul that is successively reincarnated until released from *samsara* through *moksha*.

avatar (ah-vah-taahr; from Sanskrit *avatara*) A "descent" of God (usually Vishnu) to earth in a physical form with the specific goal of aiding the world.

bhakti marga (bhah-k-tee; Sanskrit) The path of devotion.

Brahman (braah-mun; Sanskrit, "expansive") For monistic Hinduism, the supreme, unitary reality, the ground of all Being; for dualistic Hinduism, *Brahman* can refer to the supreme God (e.g. Vishnu).

brahmin (braah-mun; Sanskrit) A member of the priestly class of the *varna* or caste system.

dalit (daah-lit; Sanskrit, "oppressed"; Marathi, "broken") Self-designation of people who had traditionally been classified as untouchables or outcastes.

darshan (dur-shaan; Sanskrit, "to see") Worship through simultaneously seeing and being seen by a deity in the presence of its image.

dharma (dhur-mah; Sanskrit) Duty, righteousness, "religion"; basis for living in a way that upholds cosmic and social order.

hindutva (hin-doot-vah; Sanskrit, "Hindu-ness") A modern term that encompasses the ideology of Hindu nationalism.

jati (jaah-tee; Sanskrit, "birth group") One of thousands of endogamous groups or subcastes, each equal in social and ritual status.

jnana marga (nyah-nah mar-guh) The path of knowledge.

karma (kur-mah; Sanskrit, "action") Action; also the consequences of action.

karma marga (kur-mah mar-guh) The path of ethical and ritual works, or "action."

kshatriya (kshut-ree-yuh; Sanskrit) A member of the warrior and administrator class of the *varna* or caste system.

mantra (mun-trah; Sanskrit) A ritual formula recited to produce a spiritual effect.

maya (my-yah: Sanskrit, "magic" or "illusion") In the *Vedas*, the magical power the gods used to create this world; in *Vedanta* philosophy, illusion that veils the mind.

moksha (mohk-shah; Sanskrit, "release") Liberation, the final release from *samsara*.

OM (oh-m) (from three Sanskrit letters: *A-U-M*) The primordial sound through which the universe is manifested.

puja (poo-jah; Sanskrit, "worship") Generally, worship; usually the offering before an image of the deity of fruit, incense, or flowers.

Purana (pooh-raa-nah; Sanskrit, "ancient") A compendium of myth, usually with a sectarian emphasis.

samsara (sum-saah-rah; Sanskrit) The continuing cycle of birth, death, and rebirth; also the this-worldly realm in which the cycle recurs.

sannyasi (sun-nyaah-see; Sanskrit) Renouncer in the fourth stage (*ashrama*) of life.

Shaiva (shay-vah; Sanskrit) A devotee of Shiva.

Shakta (shah-k-tah; Sanskrit) A devotee of the Great Goddess, Devi.

shruti (shroo-tee; Sanskrit, "that which is heard") Term denoting the category of Vedic literature accepted by orthodox Hindus as revealed truth.

shudra (shoo-druh; Sanskrit) A member of the servant class of the *varna* or caste system.

smriti (smree-tee; Sanskrit, "tradition") Term denoting the vast category of Hindu sacred texts that is not *shruti*.

Upanishad (ooh-pah-nee-shud; Sanskrit, "sitting down near [a teacher]") A philosophical text from the later period of Vedic literature, also called *Vedanta* ("end of the *Vedas*").

Vaishnava (vie-sh-na-vah; Sanskrit) A devotee of Vishnu and his avatars.

(*continued*)

GLOSSARY (continued)

vaishya (vie-sh-yuh; Sanskrit) A member of the producer (farmer and merchant) class of the *varna* or caste system.

varna (vaar-nah; Sanskrit, "color") Caste or class; the four main classes form the basis of the traditional hierarchical organization of Hindu society.

Vedanta (veh-daan-tah; Sanskrit, "end of the *Vedas*") Synonym for *Upanishads*; prominent Hindu philosophical school.

Vedas (veh-duh; from Sanskrit *veda*, "knowledge") Broadly, all Vedic literature; narrowly, four ancient collections (*samhitas*) of hymns and other religious material.

yoga (yoh-gah; Sanskrit, "yoking" or "uniting") Generally, uniting of the self with God; sometimes used as an alternative to *marga* when referring to the three main paths to liberation; also (normally capitalized: Yoga) one of the six philosophical schools, focusing on moral, physical, and spiritual practices leading to liberation.

SUGGESTIONS FOR FURTHER READING

Eck, Diana. *Darsan: Seeing the Divine Image in India.* New York: Columbia University Press, 1998. An excellent discussion on the significance of *darshan* and traditions of Hindu temple worship.

Flood, Gavin. *An Introduction to Hinduism.* Cambridge, UK: Cambridge University Press, 1996. A concise and in-depth study of Hinduism.

Flood, Gavin, ed. *The Blackwell Companion to Hinduism.* Oxford, UK: Blackwell, 2003. A presentation on select special topics that are key to understanding Hindu belief and practice.

Hawley, John Stratton, and Mark Juergensmeyer. *Songs of the Saints of India.* Oxford, UK: Oxford University Press, 2006. A survey of the lives of medieval *bhakti* saints, with excellent translation of some of their poetry.

Hawley, John Stratton, and Vasudha Narayanan, eds. *The Life of Hinduism.* Berkeley: University of California Press, 2006. Special topical articles that explore personal voices and perspectives on Hindu life experience.

Klostermaier, Klaus K. *Hindu Writings: A Short Introduction to the Major Sources.* Oxford, UK: One World Publications, 2000. A keen survey of excerpts from many of the important textual sources that inform Hindu belief.

Knipe, David M. *Hinduism: Experiments in the Sacred.* New York: HarperCollins, 1991. A dependable and clear study organized based on the history of the tradition; includes a helpful timeline and glossaries.

ONLINE RESOURCES

The Internet Sacred Text Archive of Hinduism
www.sacred-texts.com/hin/
The Internet Sacred Text Archive of Hinduism provides an excellent array of the many genres of Hindu sacred texts with multiple public domain translations of key works.

The University of Wyoming Hinduism Website
http://www.uwyo.edu/religionet/er/hinduism/index.htm
The University of Wyoming Hinduism website offers concise but in-depth discussions on numerous aspects of Hindu tradition, literature, and belief.

(continued)

ONLINE RESOURCES (continued)

Understanding Hinduism

www.hinduism.co.za/index.html

An informal collection of articles and information on key topics offering some range of viewpoints.

The Sri Vaishnava Homepage

www.ramanuja.org

The Sri Vaishnava homepage is a unique resource for adherents to this important sect of Hinduism, yet is accessible and informative for outsiders.

The Shaivam.org Site

www.shaivam.org/index.html

The Shaivam.org site is a unique resource in that it explores multiple sectarian views of Shaivism yet is vast in scope and rich in detail.

The Internet Sacred Text Archive on Yoga

www.sacred-texts.com/hin/yoga/index.htm

The Internet Sacred Text Archive offers an extensive array of works on yoga, including both original sacred texts in translation and modern explorations of the subject.

BUDDHISM

IN A ZEN BUDDHIST MONASTERY IN NEW MEXICO, a young Buddhist nun named Jisen has spent years preparing for her ordination as a Zen priest. For the past week, she has spent each night sleeping outdoors under a tree that her fellow monks and nuns honor as the living embodiment of an ancient monk named Jizo, a bodhisattva famed for his compassion and devotion to others. Now the day has arrived for Jisen to take her vows. It is her hope that, as a priest, she will be better able to follow in Jizo's footsteps, working to alleviate suffering in the world by helping others to understand the workings of the mind and the nature of reality.

Before dawn, Jisen walks from the tree down to the river. There, in a rite called the tonsure ceremony, a small group of monks and nuns from her monastery shaves her head, leaving only a single strand at the crown. The tonsure ceremony symbolizes the letting go of worldly attachments, a step Buddhists believe is necessary on the road to enlightenment.

Jisen next joins a procession of monks and nuns who make their way to the temple, where the ordination ceremony will be completed. As she kneels before the altar, the monastery's Preceptor, or principal teacher, invokes all the buddhas, bodhisattvas, and earlier teachers of this lineage of Zen Buddhism. Then the Preceptor turns and addresses Jisen:

"Jisen, clinging and delusion do not cease, yet your original true nature has been revealed. After entering the priesthood, heaven neither covers nor does the earth sustain. Having nothing with which to cover your round

Tonsure ceremony of a Buddhist nun in Vietnam.

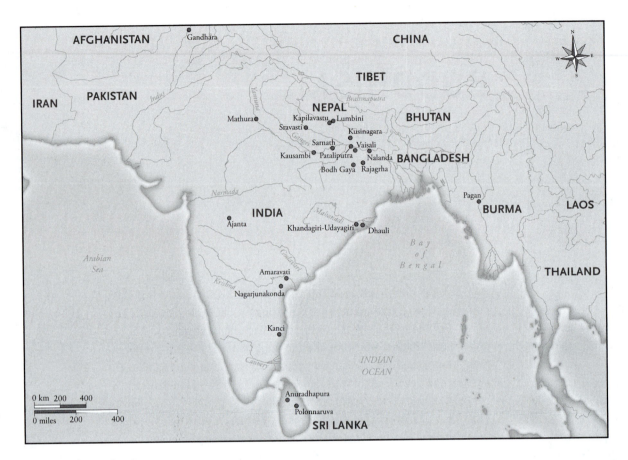

Significant sites of early Buddhism.

head and your robes embodying enlightenment, you stand out. . . . You will now be able to dedicate this life freely to the welfare and service of all beings."

An ordination robe is placed in Jisen's outstretched arms, and the elder nuns and monks help her to put it on. The Preceptor then continues, "Now, the last of your hair will be cut. Will you allow me to cut it?"

The Preceptor repeats this question three times, and each time Jisen answers "I will." Finally, as the Preceptor cuts the final strand of hair, Jisen recites her vows, pledging to let go of all attachments while helping to end the suffering of others. The Preceptor then ceremoniously invests Jisen with the begging bowl of a Zen priest and calls her to atone for any harmful actions done in both this and all of her previous lives. Having formally committed herself to observing the Buddhist precepts of her order, Jisen is now an ordained priest. ❁

Jisen is one of nearly 500 million Buddhists in the world today, about 7% of the population.[1] They belong to a vast number of Buddhist groups. Each has its distinctive characteristics, and their differences are sometimes remarkable, but all trace their origins back to the life and teachings of the Buddha, our point of departure for this chapter. We will then briefly survey the history of Buddhism and, finally, take note of the more important features of the Buddhist way of life.

THE TEACHINGS OF BUDDHISM

The **Buddha**, the "Awakened One," lived in northern India more than 2,500 years ago. It was the Buddha who set in motion the "wheel of the **Dharma**," the body of teachings about the cause and end of suffering that lies at the heart of Buddhism.

The Life of the Buddha

There is little we know with certainty about the life of the Buddha. The many accounts we have are legendary rather than historical, although their agreement on many points suggests they are based on a genuine historical figure. As much as reliable historical sources might do to satisfy our curiosity about the course of the Buddha's life, the legends about him are more helpful to us here. This is because they are didactic in character, telling the story of the Buddha in a way that educates us about the essential features of his teaching.

Because both Sanskrit and Pali (another language of ancient India) were so instrumental in the early transmission of accounts of the Buddha's life and teaching, we will make occasional use of both, aiming in each instance to provide only what is most helpful.

The Early Life of the Buddha

Siddhartha Gautama, who was to become the Buddha, was probably born in the sixth century B.C.E. Western scholars have traditionally set the dates for his life at 583–463 B.C.E., though good arguments can be made for moving them as much as a century earlier or later. According to tradition, Siddhartha's father was the ruler of a small kingdom that straddled part of what is now the border of India and Nepal. It is said that astrologers and seers observed auspicious marks on the infant Siddhartha's body, indicating that he was destined to

---

TIMELINE
Buddhism

c. 563–483 B.C.E. Traditional dates for the life of the Buddha

c. 483 B.C.E. First Buddhist Council.

c. 383 B.C.E. Second Buddhist Council.

c. 360 B.C.E. Council of King Mahapadma.

c. 272–231 B.C.E. Reign of Ashoka in India.

c. 247 B.C.E. Third Buddhist Council.

250–200 B.C.E. Buddhism arrives in Southeast Asia.

65 C.E. Buddhism arrives in China.

100–200 Composition of the *Lotus Sutra*.

300–400 Buddhism arrives in Korea.

400–450 According to tradition, Bodhidharma brings Chan (Zen) Buddhism from India to China.

552 Buddhism arrives in Japan.

775 The first Buddhist monastery in Tibet is built at Samye.

c. 800 Borobudur Stupa built in Java.

c. 1200 Destruction of Buddhist universities at Nalanda and Vikramasila.

1185–1333 Pure Land, Zen, and Nichiren flourish in Japan during the Kamakura period.

c. 1500 Virtual disappearance of Buddhism in India.

1890–1921 T. W. Rhys-Davids, professor of Pali at the Universities of London and Manchester, translates Buddhist texts into English.

1899 The Buddhist Churches of America founded in San Francisco by Japanese immigrants of the Jodo Shinshu sect.

1900 Over 40,000 Buddhist and Daoist texts are rediscovered in a cave at Dunhuang, in western China.

1956 Indian social activist B. R. Ambedkar (1891–1956) converts to Buddhism along with 400,000 others to protest Hindu oppression of "untouchables."

1959 The 14th Dalai Lama flees to India from Tibet.

conquer the world. But there was a question: Would he conquer the outer world as a victorious monarch, or the inner world as a holy sage?

Siddhartha's father was determined that his son would follow in his footsteps. Fearing that Siddhartha would be drawn to the spiritual life if he became aware of the existence of suffering in the world, the king went to great lengths to shield him from the harsh realities of life. And so Siddhartha grew up surrounded by palace walls, living an idyllic life in which every pleasure was made available to him and there was no hint of pain. In time, he married a beautiful princess, Yasodhara, whom he loved deeply and with whom he had a son. It was what many would consider a perfect life— and yet Siddhartha grew restless.

Finally, at the age of twenty-nine, Siddhartha ventured outside the sheltered world of the palace. Accompanied by his charioteer, he saw things that were to change the course of his life. Buddhists call these the "Four Sights." The first was a frail old man, bent and leaning on his staff. Siddhartha, who had never seen old age, asked if he, too, would become old and decrepit. He was dismayed when his charioteer assured him that he would. The second sight was a man afflicted by disease. Sickness, said the charioteer, is also a part of human life. The third sight, a corpse being carried off to a cremation, was terrifying. Death, too, said the charioteer, is something no one can escape. Siddhartha now saw through the illusion that his father had perpetrated. Filled with horror and disgust by the inescapable truths of old age, sickness, and death, he fell into

Siddhartha cuts his hair. Mural depicting the Life of Buddha, Jogyesa Temple, Seoul, South Korea.

despair. It was not until he witnessed the fourth sight that he found some reason to hope. Sitting by the side of a road, he saw a wandering ascetic, homeless and without possessions, who seemed to be content.

The "Great Going Forth" For Siddhartha, the ascetic pointed the way. To return to life within the palace would be to hide from the truth. He resolved instead to face it. He would renounce the life he had lived, take up the life of an ascetic, and search for the truth about suffering. One night, he arose from his bed, kissed his sleeping wife and son good-bye, and silently slipped away. As soon as he was alone in the forest, he took off his expensive clothing and used his sword to cut off his hair, symbolically severing the bonds that tied him to his old life.

At first, Siddhartha turned to ascetic sages who were acknowledged for their wisdom, becoming a disciple first of one, then another. They taught him meditation techniques and yogic disciplines, but although he mastered these, they left him unsatisfied. He then committed himself to extreme asceticism. After a time of wandering, he found a grove of trees watered by a river. Joined there by five other ascetics who wished to follow his example, he began to practice severe austerities in the hope that they would somehow clarify his thought. For five years, Siddhartha wore rags. Never cleaning himself, he allowed filth to cover his body. He slept on thorny brambles and in cemeteries strewn with half-burned corpses. Weakened by eating as little as a single grain of rice a day, he became a skeletal figure whose eyes had withdrawn into their sockets and whose distorted mind was tormented by searing pain and thunderous sound.

One day, after a long period of intense fasting, Siddhartha set out for the river. On the way, he overheard a music teacher explaining to his student that an instrument string wound too tight will break, whereas one that is too loose makes no sound at all. These words brought Siddhartha to the realization that neither sensual indulgence nor self-denial is helpful in the quest for understanding and liberation from suffering. Because both weaken the body and the mind, the best path lies between them, between attachment and aversion. This principle of the **Middle Way** was to become foundational in Buddhism. According to tradition, it was at just this moment that a young woman from a nearby village came to Siddhartha with a bowl of porridge. He accepted her offer of nourishment, ate it, and bathed himself. He then returned to his ascetic companions, but they left him when they learned he had abandoned their way of life.

Enlightenment Siddhartha's determination was now absolute. At a village in northern India now known as Bodh Gaya, he sat down beneath a fig tree and vowed to remain there in meditation until he gained the understanding he sought. Restored to health by his practice of moderation, he sat for forty-nine days, moving into ever-deeper states of awareness. Then, during his meditation in the course of a single night, his enlightenment came. In a series of psychological breakthroughs made possible by the power and clarity of his mind, Siddhartha first recalled all of his past lives. He then saw how **karma**— the law of actions and their consequences—had been at work throughout time, conditioning the existence of all beings as they took form and then passed away. Finally, Siddhartha realized that desire is the cause of suffering and that for suffering to end there must be an end to desire.

According to Buddhist tradition, Siddhartha was not the first to attain enlightenment. Buddhists believe that others before and after him became, and will become, buddhas. But it is from *this* buddha that they have received the Dharma, and so for them he is *the* Buddha, the "Awakened One." His enlightenment brought an end to the desire that causes suffering. It also brought freedom from rebirth, which results from attachment to the world. Freed from the disturbances caused by attachment, his mind came to rest in its natural state, and he was filled with joy. He had attained **nirvana**, the "extinguishing" of desire and suffering. For many days the Buddha remained close to the site of his enlightenment. Then, moved by compassion for others, he set out to teach what he had learned.

"Calling the Earth to Witness." According to tradition, the demon Mara afflicted the Buddha with powerful temptations to give up his quest for enlightenment. Ignoring them, the Buddha touched his right hand to the ground, thereby calling upon the earth to witness his unshakeable resolve. Immediately thereafter, he experienced nirvana.

Rock-cut reclining statue of the Buddha preparing to enter *parinirvana*, in a cave shrine at Ajanta, Maharashtra State, India. Fifth century C.E.

Beginnings of the Buddhist Community He went first to a deer park at Sarnath (near modern Varanasi in India), where the five ascetics who had earlier abandoned him were still practicing harsh austerities. Seeing that he had broken through to some new understanding, they gathered around the Buddha, who gave them his first teaching. This was the "Sermon in the Deer Park," in which he told them of the Middle Way and set forth the Four Noble Truths and the Noble Eightfold Path, which describe the cause and cure of suffering (pp. 93–94). Having heard him, the ascetics became followers of the Buddha, the first Buddhist monks and the first members of the Buddhist **Sangha** (Pali, "community").

From Sarnath, the Buddha began to retrace his steps back home, attracting more followers to the Sangha along the way. Many were relatives, including his father and his son, Rahula. A cousin, Ananda, became one of the Buddha's most devoted disciples and later played such an important role in remembering and transmitting his teachings that he has been called the "Guardian of the Dharma." The Buddha wandered across northern India for more than four decades, teaching, ordaining monks and nuns, accepting lay followers, and inviting doubters to test his teachings in order to see for themselves if they had merit.

The Death of the Buddha The life of the Buddha came to an end forty-five years after his enlightenment. He was eighty. He and Ananda had been on their way to Kusinara, not far from Varanasi, when they stopped to eat at the home of a blacksmith. Something in the meal was tainted—some accounts say pork, some say a nut or a mushroom—causing the Buddha to become fatally ill. In a grove on the outskirts of the village, Ananda made a bed for him between two trees. According to some accounts, as the Buddha lay down, the trees suddenly burst into bloom and showered him with their petals. At the same time, fragrant sandalwood powder fell from the sky, and the air was filled with celestial music. His monks soon began to gather at the scene, frantically seeking a final fragment of the Buddha's wisdom. When they asked what they would do without him to teach them, he responded that the Dharma would always be their guide. Then, closing his eyes, the Buddha went deep into meditation and died. Without attachments to the world, and unbound by karmic forces that would have brought another incarnation, he passed into ***parinirvana***, the complete and final entry into nirvana.

The Essentials of the Buddha's Teaching

The Buddha's motive for embarking upon the spiritual life had been to find the truth about human suffering. What was its cause? How could it be ended? His enlightenment had brought answers to these questions, and these answers constitute the core of the Dharma. We saw in Chapter 2 that in Hindu usage, the Sanskrit word *dharma* has a wide range of meanings, including "law," "duty," and "righteousness." In Buddhist contexts, *dharma* (Pali, *dhamma*) in its broader sense refers to nature and its laws, but it is more often and more narrowly used to describe the body of the Buddha's teaching, passed down through the centuries. The difference between the broader and narrower meanings of *dharma* is not as great as one might imagine. As we will see, the teachings of the Buddha are based on his observations of nature and its laws.

Interdependent Origination We will begin our investigation of the Buddha's teaching with the doctrine of **Interdependent Origination** (Pali, *Panicca-samuppada*), also known as Dependent Origination, because so much of the Dharma is based upon it.

To most of us, the world seems to be a composite system consisting of different and separate things. The chair you are sitting in certainly appears to exist on its own, apart from all other things in the room. And it is likely that you see yourself as existing independently from everyone and everything else you encounter.

Looking deeply into reality, the Buddha saw things very differently. He taught that reality is a complex of interrelated and interdependent phenomena in which nothing exists apart from anything else. Instead, all things depend on other things for their coming-into-existence—that is, for their origination. Of course, everyone recognizes at some level that this is the case. Someone built your chair, for example, and your parents had something to do with you. But the Buddha's teaching, augmented by later Buddhist thinkers, goes far beyond this in identifying a cycle of twelve causal factors (such as ignorance, desire, and rebirth) that bring about a coming-into-existence once any one of them is set in motion.

Of course, things also *remain* in existence—or at least they *seem* to. How can this be explained? And what *are* things, really? Here, again, the Buddha taught that all things are interdependent; so much so, in fact, that they have no existence whatsoever *in and of themselves*. Once again, take your chair as an example. Looking deeply, you will find that it is constituted of different elements: height, width, leather, legs, texture, firmness, color, and so on. But you will not find "chair." Instead, your chair exists only as a complex of "not chair" elements, and only for as long as these constituent parts remain together. And so it is with all things. Each thing exists as a collection of other elements, having no independent existence of its own.

The Three Marks of Existence Building on his teaching about the interrelatedness and interdependence of things, the Buddha taught that there are **Three Marks of Existence**—Impermanence, Suffering, and No-Self.

The Buddha's doctrine of **Impermanence** (Pali, *anicca*) holds that all things are always changing. Nothing remains the same, even for a moment. All things are always in a state of *becoming*. For example, imagine a blade of grass. Although it may seem static, the truth is that it is growing and therefore becoming a *different* blade of grass in every moment.

The Buddha's teaching about suffering (Pali, **dukkha**) is central to the Dharma. He once said, "I have taught one thing and one thing only, suffering and the cessation of suffering." Although *dukkha* is usually translated as "suffering," it can also mean "unease" and "dissatisfaction," as well as specific forms of unease and dissatisfaction (such as anxiety, fear, doubt, and so on).

Suffering is caused by the desire to hold on to things when, in fact, nothing can be held. Uncomfortable with constant change and the impermanence of things, we want them to remain as we want them to be. Buddhists describe this wanting in a variety of ways—as desiring, craving, clinging, and thirsting (the literal meaning of the Pali *tanha*, commonly translated as "desire"). However it is described, desire is made possible by ignorance (and, in particular, ignorance of impermanence) and can take the form of an attachment to something we want in our lives or an aversion to something we don't want. These three qualities of attachment, aversion, and ignorance (also referred to as greed, hatred, and delusion) are known as the "Three Poisons." The suffering that arises from them can take innumerable forms. Wanting is suffering. Lacking is suffering. Fearing that something you have might one day be lost is suffering. Believing that you cannot be happy unless you have something is suffering. Being averse to something is suffering. Wanting things to stay the same is suffering. Wanting things to be different is suffering. Stress and worry are suffering. Envy and jealousy are suffering. Anger, hatred, grief, loneliness, and frustration are suffering. Finally, the unhealthy effects many of these mental or psychological states have on the body constitute suffering.

The third of the Three Marks of Existence is the doctrine of **No-Self** (Sanskrit, **anatman**; Pali, *anatta*). Of all the things we desire, it is likely that our greatest attachment is to our notion of self. As we saw in Chapter 2, Hinduism includes the belief that at the core of one's self is the unchanging and eternal *atman*, which survives the death of the body through successive incarnations. The Buddha rejected this idea, teaching that just as there are no other things that remain unchanged, there is no static self that remains the same, even from moment to moment. The doctrine of No-Self does not mean that there is no "you." Clearly, you exist. You have a body, a mind, movement, interests, and other qualities. The Buddha taught that these are rooted in the **skandhas** (Sanskrit, "bundles" or "heaps"), the five basic components of every self: the body, perception, feelings, innate tendencies shaped by karma, and thought—all of which are always in flux. Thus the Buddha taught that each of us is a shifting self that is always changing in response to changes happening elsewhere in the great web of interrelated, interdependent, and impermanent phenomena that make up reality.

It can be difficult to accept this idea. After all, most of us are quite attached to our individual identities and to the notion that for as long as we live (and, perhaps, even after we die) there are some ways in which we remain the same. No-Self might seem to imply a destruction or annihilation of something we like very much—ourselves. But this is not the case. Instead, the Buddha urged only that his followers recognize that the self is not concrete, permanent, or independent of all other things. The great

THE FOUR NOBLE TRUTHS

1. Suffering is inherent in life.
2. The cause of suffering is desire.
3. There is a way to put an end to desire and suffering.
4. The way is the Noble Eightfold Path.

benefit he saw in this teaching is that it opens the way to living without the suffering that arises from a false notion of self and from clinging to things that cannot be held. The Buddha found the full realization of this ideal in his enlightenment and in the bliss of nirvana.

Compare the Buddha's teachings about the self or soul with the teachings of other religions.

The Four Noble Truths and the Noble Eightfold Path   We saw earlier that the first teaching the Buddha offered to the Sangha was the Sermon in the Deer Park, in which he told the five ascetics who had been his companions about the **Four Noble Truths** and the **Noble Eightfold Path**. Like a physician dealing with some illness—in fact, his followers often spoke of him as the *Bhisakko*, or "the Peerless Physician"—he structured his most fundamental teaching about suffering as if it were a medical diagnosis and prescription for a cure. The Four Noble Truths follow the four steps ancient Indian doctors used to diagnose and treat illness: (1) identifying a symptom, (2) discovering its cause, (3) determining if there is a way to remove the cause, and (4) prescribing a therapy to effect a cure. As a process of identifying and treating the disease of suffering, the Four Noble Truths empower those who follow them to understand the root cause of suffering and to cure themselves.

Now that we have investigated some of the Buddha's other teachings, we are in a good position to understand the Four Noble Truths. In teaching that suffering is inherent in life, the Buddha was pointing to the inevitability of suffering and its everyday presence in its many forms in people's lives. In identifying the cause of suffering as desire, the Buddha was not teaching that all forms of desire are unhealthy. Satisfying our desire for nourishment, employment, and a decent place to live certainly makes sense. But when we desire to grasp and hold on to things that cannot be held, we will always be disappointed. The good news is that there is a way to deal with desire and to minimize, even to end, the suffering it causes.

The Buddha's prescription for a cure for suffering is the Noble Eightfold Path. In treading the Eightfold Path, one follows in the footsteps of the Buddha in eradicating attachment, aversion, and ignorance, putting an end to desire, and ultimately achieving enlightenment and nirvana, just as the Buddha did.

The eight aspects of the Noble Eightfold Path are sometimes divided into three divisions, each with its own goal. The first is the *prajna* (Sanskrit, "wisdom") division,

THE NOBLE EIGHTFOLD PATH

1. **Right View**: seeing things as they are, in accordance with the Buddha's teachings.
2. **Right Intention**: cultivating an unshakeable commitment to tread the path to enlightenment in accordance with the Buddha's teachings.
3. **Right Speech**: cultivating the virtue of addressing others with kindness, while abstaining from lying, divisive or abusive speech, and idle chatter.
4. **Right Action**: abstaining from killing, stealing, and sexual misconduct.
5. **Right Livelihood**: making a living in a way that harms no one and benefits all.
6. **Right Effort**: striving to abandon all thought and action that is harmful to oneself or others and to cultivate virtues that benefit oneself and others.
7. **Right Mindfulness**: focused awareness of the body and mind and the phenomena arising within and affecting each.
8. **Right Concentration**: cultivating the four stages of concentration leading to equanimity beyond pleasure and pain.

which includes Right View and Right Intention. Here, the aim is to ensure that one understands and accepts the Buddha's teachings about Interdependent Origination, Impermanence, and Suffering and is committed to striving for goals consistent with them. The second division has the purpose of cultivating ethical conduct (Sanskrit and Pali, *sila*) through Right Speech, Right Action, and Right Livelihood. The Buddha taught that unethical conduct is an obstacle to mental clarity. For this reason, destructive speech, immoral behavior, and making a living in a way that does not benefit oneself and others are to be avoided. The third division promotes concentration (Sanskrit and Pali, *samadhi*). Through Right Effort, one seeks to eliminate all qualities of the mind that give rise to unwholesome thought and action and to encourage those that produce more positive effects. Right Mindfulness is the observation of thoughts, feelings, and all other phenomena that occur in the body and mind. Finally, Right Concentration involves progress through four stages of concentration until one achieves a state of nonattachment and equanimity.

Karma and Rebirth The Buddha taught a doctrine of rebirth that differed from the Hindu view in denying that there is an eternal and unchanging soul (*atman*) that passes through many incarnations. According to his doctrine of No-Self (*anatman*), one's sense of self arises from the interrelationship of the five *skandhas* and exists only for as long as they function together in such a way as to give rise to that sense of self. When they separate at death that sense of self ceases to exist, and so there is nothing substantial that passes from one incarnation to another. And yet there is a definite connection between one life and the next; there is a type of rebirth. The Buddha's teaching on this point is obscure and much debated. What *is* clear is that one's actions and the karma they generate bring about the conditions for the coming-into-existence of a new set of *skandhas*. This, in turn, gives rise to another sense of self. Nothing concrete passes from one life to the next; only the karmic and character-related elements of the previous life, which shape a new life in some ways consistent with the old. There are a variety of analogies Buddhists have used to illustrate this idea. According to one, rebirth is much like what happens when one candle is used to light another. A light appears where none had existed before, and yet nothing has passed over other than the energy (which we might compare to karmic energy) generated by the first candle.

Of course, these teachings about karma and rebirth do not apply to those who have found enlightenment. The Buddha taught that these individuals no longer set in motion the karma that leads to rebirth and are also freed entirely from the karma produced in earlier lives. There is no rebirth for them. Only those who continue to thirst for things and to seek to satisfy their desire through attachment to them are reborn in **samsara** (Pali, "perpetual wandering"), which, just as it is in Hinduism, has for Buddhism two closely related meanings: the continuous cycle of birth, death, and rebirth and the this-worldly realm in which this recurs.

Nirvana   The ultimate goal of Buddhist practice, nirvana is liberation from suffering in the cyclic existence of samsara. A Sanskrit word, nirvana means a "blowing out" or "extinguishing" and can refer to the extinguishing of desire and of suffering. The Buddha taught that all people have the potential to attain nirvana. Buddhists employ a variety of techniques for attaining nirvana but agree that its attainment brings perfect bliss and an end to suffering. Beyond this, any description of nirvana is uncertain. Being utterly unlike anything one might experience with ordinary awareness, no comparison is possible. For this reason, the Buddha said very little about nirvana, as it is something that must be experienced in order to be understood.

Gods in Buddhism?   It is often said that Buddhism is an atheistic religion. And indeed, some Buddhists are atheists. Many others, however, believe in a wide variety of divine beings.

The Buddha had little to say about the gods and discouraged devotion to them. He urged his followers instead to focus their attention on the Dharma and devote themselves to putting its precepts into practice. The Buddha's perspective on the gods is perhaps best described as *transtheistic*[2] (see the Introduction, p. 12), in the sense that he acknowledged the existence of gods; but when it comes to the truly crucial issues of the quest for enlightenment and nirvana, the gods are not helpful.

Later forms of Buddhism tend to acknowledge the existence of supernatural beings—celestial Buddhas and bodhisattvas—who are the objects of devotion and who are believed to bestow benefits on their followers. Whether or not these supernatural beings are "gods" depends on how one defines the term. We will explore the ideas of celestial Buddhas and bodhisattvas in more detail below.

Katherine Sei is an American Buddhist who lives in California. She is a practitioner of Vajrayana Buddhism and has been a student of Lama Lodru Rinpoche for nearly three decades. She is the facilitator of a Buddhist study center in Sacramento.

As a Buddhist, what is the most important aspect of human existence? What should Buddhists do or focus on in life?

The most important aspect of human existence, to me, is that we have an opportunity to evolve as beings. This evolution encompasses uncovering our true nature. This true nature is comprised of a spontaneous, natural compassion and a clear wisdom as to "what is really going on here." I've found through all the years of meditation that we all tend to really limit our minds, and the expression of our true wise and benevolent nature. As I uncover and begin to understand my mind's true nature, and learn to let go of my limiting definitions of self, others, and events in my life, suffering diminishes. Life becomes more joyful, more peaceful, and I feel more interconnected with everyone. Life also becomes very, very interesting as I begin to become aware of all the interconnections of karmic causes and effects, and I can relax into the "play" of events.

Katherine Sei

Does Buddhism give you a unique outlook on life? How so or why?

I'm not sure if Buddhism gives a unique outlook as much as a useful outlook on life in this culture. The teachings of Lord Buddha are not necessarily unique to Buddhism—I think many aspects of Hinduism, Christianity, Judaism, and Islam provide a framework for becoming a more loving and wise person. What may be unique in terms of Buddha's teachings is that one can examine one's mind and one's life through meditation practices. It's more like a science than a religion, analogous to a physicist learning mathematics to explore the universe. I've found through meditation that life isn't quite as rigid as we often make it out to be. Knowing that, one can learn to let go of many of the emotional habits and knee-jerk reactions. One can find many creative solutions to life's problems, big and small, from "What is death?" or "What does it all mean?" to "How do I deal with my angry boss?" "How do I deal with the stress in my life?" and so on.

What single event in your life would you characterize as your most meaningful religious experience?

It's hard to pick one single event in my life that I consider most meaningful. Three come to mind. First would be when I took refuge with Trungpa Rinpoche in the 1980s. At that time, I discovered that I could treat others and myself with more gentleness. The second event would be when I met Ven. Lama Lodru Rinpoche, my direct teacher for the past twenty-seven years. Lama Lodru has taught me the same meditation practices that Tibetan lamas go through in a formal three-year retreat, but spread out over fifteen years. In doing this, he demonstrated that anyone can learn to meditate and apply it in their day-to-day life.

One doesn't have to become a monk or nun to become liberated. The third event was having the nature of my mind pointed out by Mingyur Rinpoche. Mingyur Rinpoche is a Tibetan lama who had to overcome panic attacks when he was a teenager. He showed me how applicable Buddha's teachings on meditation are to all aspects of life.

THE HISTORY OF BUDDHISM

In this section we explore the early history of Buddhism in India, its expansion into other parts of Asia and beyond, and the developments of new forms of Buddhism, each interpreting in its own way the teachings of the Buddha. Along the way, we pause to consider in some detail each of the three main forms: **Theravada**, **Mahayana**, and **Vajrayana**.

The Period of the Buddhist Councils

According to traditional Buddhist accounts, immediately after the death of the Buddha a council was convened at the town of Rajagriha in northeast India. It was the first of a series of such councils, which would define Buddhism by addressing key doctrinal and practical issues as they arose at particular times and places in its history.

Diffusion of Buddhism across Asia.

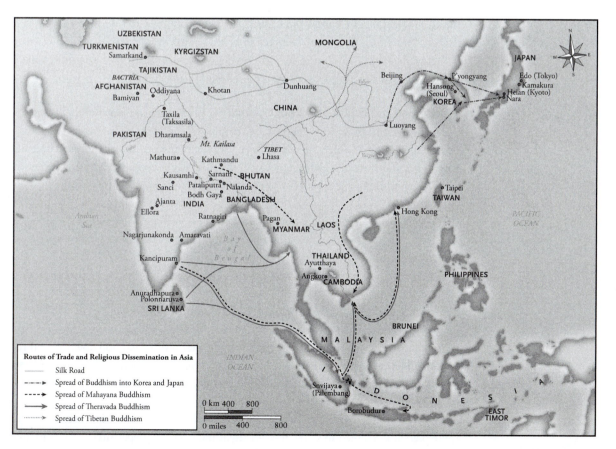

Routes of Trade and Religious Dissemination in Asia
——— Silk Road
–·–·– Spread of Buddhism into Korea and Japan
– – – Spread of Mahayana Buddhism
⟶ Spread of Theravada Buddhism
········ Spread of Tibetan Buddhism

The First and Second Buddhist Councils   The First Council, convened c. 483 B.C.E., shortly after the Buddha's death, was made up of his direct disciples, who wished to ensure that they all accurately remembered his teaching. The First Council formalized an oral canon, thereby establishing an authority for a community that had lost its teacher.

During the Buddha's lifetime, he and his *bhikkus*, or monks, had been wanderers, remaining in one place only during the annual rainy season. This changed in the centuries after his death as formerly itinerant monks and nuns began to settle in permanent monastic communities. Over time, these communities became increasingly insular and geographically dispersed. Without a unifying authority above them, there was a proliferation of variations in practice and doctrine that led in turn to sectarian splits. This tendency is apparent as early as the Second Buddhist Council (c. 383 B.C.E.), which was convened to address issues relating to discipline; some monks, for example, had begun to accept money for services they performed for their lay followers.

A few early Buddhist sources allude to another council held c. 360 B.C.E., shortly after the Second Council. On this occasion, the monks assembled to address the issue of the authority of the Buddhist canon. A majority, known as the *Mahasanghika* (Sanskrit, "Great Community"), held that the canon was not absolutely authoritative and that there were other legitimate means for the transmission of the Dharma. The minority held that the canon did indeed faithfully preserve the Buddha's teachings. This group, who called themselves the *Sthaviras* (Sanskrit, "Elders"), was a precursor of Theravada Buddhism. In the years following, subdivisions within both groups arose that foreshadow the events of Ashoka's Third Buddhist Council.

Ashoka and the Third Buddhist Council   The renowned emperor of the Mauryan Dynasty, Ashoka (r. c. 272–231 B.C.E.), embodies the ideal of Buddhist kingship. He united the subcontinent of South Asia on a scale unseen either before or after his time. It was not until the British colonized India in the eighteenth and nineteenth centuries that such a large portion of the subcontinent would again be unified under a single ruler.

Despite his success as a conqueror, Ashoka later profoundly regretted the violence involved in his conquests. According to legend, he underwent a conversion experience immediately following a military triumph over his rivals in 260 B.C.E. He abandoned his expansionist policies and began to channel his efforts into social reform grounded in Buddhist ethics.

Although Ashoka had been influenced by Buddhist ideals even before his victory, his conversion was clearly the pivotal moment of his reign. His sincerity was evident in his edicts, which promoted moral purification, self-awareness, nonviolence, and respect of all religious viewpoints. The edicts were promulgated across his empire. Often carved on stone pillars (some of which are still preserved today), these edicts are our earliest evidence for the widespread promotion of Buddhist ideals.

Ashoka convened the Third Buddhist Council in his capital at Pataliputra c. 247 B.C.E. Those present attempted to settle disputes regarding doctrinal departures of some monks

ACTIONS TAKEN DURING EACH OF THE BUDDHIST COUNCILS

First Council (c. 483 B.C.E.): preserved the teaching and created a Buddhist canon
Second Council (c. 383 B.C.E.): preserved vows and banned handling money and the selling of selling religious services
King Mahapadma's Council (c. 360 B.C.E.): according to some sources, asserted that the

Dharma teaching is not bound by canon and can be modified
Third Council (c. 247 B.C.E.): defined what the "authentic" view of the Buddha is and acknowledged the later Theravada sect as representing that view (under Ashoka's reign)

from the teachings of the Buddha. The council ultimately concluded that one sect (*Vibhajyava*), which eventually gave rise to Theravada Buddhism, represented the authentic and orthodox viewpoint of the Buddha.

Theravada is the only modern form of Buddhism that can trace its origin back to the years immediately following these disputes. The study of philosophical texts, combined with cosmological speculations and new ways of thinking about the Buddha, brought about the emergence by the first century C.E. of Mahayana Buddhism. By the seventh or eighth century C.E., new symbolism and ritual techniques contributed to the development of Vajrayana Buddhism, which gained a particularly powerful foothold in Tibet. Let us now examine the distinctive features of these three primary Buddhist paths and the sacred texts that inform them.

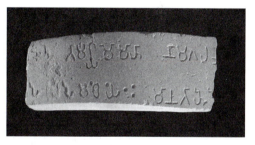

The Brahmi script is an ancestor of all modern Indian scripts. This example is from the sixth edict of Emperor Ashoka, 238 B.C.E.

Theravada Buddhism

Theravada (Sanskrit, "way of the elders") views itself as representing the original and authentic teaching of the Buddha. Theravada is also known as *Hinayana* (Sanskrit, "Lesser Vehicle"), although this name is sometimes considered to be derisive. There are over 100 million Theravada Buddhists around the world today. Theravada is the predominant Buddhist tradition in Sri Lanka, Thailand, Cambodia, Laos, and Burma.

Theravada emphasizes pursuit of nirvana through the individual's own efforts. The Buddha is revered as one who achieved nirvana and provided his teachings, the Dharma, so that others could do the same. But the Buddha himself is beyond the reach of the individual and no longer available to provide direct assistance. Theravada stays true to the Buddha's last words: "Work out your salvation with diligence."[3] The individual pursues nirvana primarily through meditation, for which the monastic lifestyle is best suited. Theravada therefore also emphasizes the central role of the monastic community, or Sangha.

With its emphasis on the monastic community, Theravada naturally incorporates a hierarchy that separates the ordained—monks and nuns—from the laity. There are at least ten times as many monks in Theravada as nuns, and monks have always tended to exert the most influence over the Sangha. Both nuns and monks, however, devote themselves through study and meditation to attaining nirvana. Those who do attain it are known as **arhats**, who represent the religious ideal for Theravada. In many countries where Theravada is dominant, the monastic body acts as an advisor to governments or rulers and provides teaching to the lay community, while its monks also serve as ritual specialists during festivals, at funerals, or in rites that confer blessings and supernatural protection. The central role of the monastic community can also be seen in the support it receives from laypeople, who seek to accumulate karmic merit by making offerings to the monastic community.

Theravada Texts Theravada lays claim to following the original teachings of the Buddha, contained within the early canonical group of Buddhist texts known as the **Pali Canon**, or *Tripitaka*. According to tradition, four centuries after the Buddha's death a group of 500 monks met in Sri Lanka to commit his teachings to writing for the first time. As there were already significant differences in reports of what the Buddha had said, these monks labored to finally fix his teaching in written form. The Sanskrit term *Tripitaka,* which means "three baskets," refers to the fact that in ancient times, manuscripts were written on palm leaves, which were then stored in baskets. Theravada's collection is the only complete version of the *Tripitaka* that has survived to the present day.

The first of the three baskets, the *Vinaya Pitaka* (Sanskrit, "Discipline Basket"), contains hundreds of monastic rules reportedly prescribed by the Buddha and stories that illustrate how these rules originated. The second basket, the *Sutra Pitaka* (Sanskrit, "Basket of Discourses"), consists of many teachings of the Buddha. The term **sutra** generally means a Buddhist text but often is used to refer specifically to the contents of the *Sutra Pitaka*. Although one cannot assume that everything recorded in the *sutras* is the literal word of the Buddha, their overall content is remarkably consistent in portraying the Buddha's teaching, suggesting to a significant extent the ideas, practices, and personality of the Buddha himself. The third basket is the *Abhidharma Pitaka*; the basket of "that which is above or about the Dharma."[4] These texts seek to reorganize and systemize the teaching in the *Sutra Pitaka* while also elaborating upon them, exploring the nature of consciousness, epistemology (the nature of knowledge), cosmology, and meditation.

The opening verses of the *Dhammapada*, a collection of aphorisms on Buddhist morals and one of the texts in the *Sutra Pitaka*, afford a glimpse into the way *sutras* are structured and how they poetically present ideas. They also illustrate a key feature of Theravada thought: we are responsible for our own happiness.

> What we are today comes from our thoughts of yesterday, and our present thoughts build our life of tomorrow: our life is the creation of our mind.

If a man speaks or acts with an impure mind, suffering follows him as the wheel of the cart follows the beast that draws the cart.

What we are today comes from our thoughts of yesterday, and our present thoughts build our life of tomorrow: our life is the creation of our mind.

If a man speaks or acts with a pure mind, joy follows him as his own shadow.[5]

Mahayana Buddhism

With origins in the early years of the Common Era, the period to which we can trace its earliest sutras, Mahayana Buddhism soon grew to become the largest of the Buddhist traditions. This is suggested by its very name—the Sanskrit word *mahayana* means "Great Vehicle"—as is its great variety of schools and sects, which make Mahayana a large and accommodating "vehicle" with room for Buddhists of all kinds. Mahayana Buddhism sees itself as a tradition that penetrates the teachings of the Buddha more deeply than does Theravada. Its careful analysis and elaboration of the many aspects of the Dharma help to explain its expansive doctrines, which are sufficiently elastic to allow for an easy coexistence among the many sects within the Mahayana tradition. Sometimes called "Buddhism for the masses," Mahayana, unlike Theravada, understands everyone as being capable of attaining nirvana, not only monks and nuns. Today, the great majority of Buddhists belong to the Mahayana tradition, which is the dominant form of Buddhism in East Asia and in parts of Southeast Asia.

As we have seen, Theravada Buddhism regards Gautama the Buddha as only a man, albeit an extraordinary man. Mahayana Buddhism understands the Buddha as something far greater: the earthly expression of ultimate reality. In the Mahayana view, reality exists at three levels called "Buddha Bodies." At the lowest level is the *Nirmanakaya*, the "earthly body," which is ultimate reality expressed rather crudely in material forms. These can be personal and are always limited by factors such as time and space. Gautama Buddha, the man who was known to other human beings as he traveled and taught across northern India, was ultimate reality expressed at this level. The second Buddha Body is the *Samboghakaya*, or "bliss body." This is ultimate reality expressed at what we might think of as a "heavenly" level, at which particulars exist but are beyond space and time. This is the level at which many bodhisattvas and "celestial buddhas" exist. At its highest level, the *Dharmakaya,* or "truth body," ultimate reality exists as it is: undifferentiated, impersonal, absolute—and completely beyond all forms and labels. Mahayana Buddhists describe ultimate reality at this level in a variety of ways: Void, Consciousness, Nirvana, Buddha Nature, and Buddha Mind.

Understood in this way, the universe is the great setting in which the Mahayana ideal of compassion makes enlightenment and freedom from suffering possible for everyone. Instead of having to "go it alone" in seeking nirvana, the Mahayana Buddhist can benefit from the compassion of others.

Indeed, one of the characteristics that distinguishes Mahayana from Theravada is its teaching that compassion for others and working to bring about their liberation is a higher goal than attaining one's own enlightenment. Many Mahayana Buddhists take a "bodhisattva vow" to subject themselves to rebirth until all other beings have been liberated from suffering. Whereas Theravada Buddhism makes the *arhat* its spiritual hero in recognition of his detachment from the world and attainment of nirvana, Mahayana recognizes as its ideal figure the compassionate and selfless bodhisattva, who remains devoted to others in the samsaric realm of suffering.

Bodhisattvas   In the early years of Buddhism, **bodhisattva** (Sanskrit, "enlightenment being") was a term used to denote Gautama the Buddha in the lives he lived prior to that in which he achieved enlightenment. It was also used to refer to future buddhas (in fact, many Buddhists today look to the bodhisattva Maitreya as the next buddha to arise in the world). Later, Mahayana Buddhists began to describe a multitude of bodhisattvas. Some were simply people who had taken a bodhisattva vow to help

Gilded bronze Sitting Maitreya icon. Maitreya ("Loving-kindness") is the future Buddha. Like Rodin's Thinker, he is seated on his throne in deep contemplation with his hand touching his chin. Three Kingdoms period, seventh century. National Museum, Seoul, Korea.

"Manjushri, Bodhisattva of Wisdom" appearing with the flaming sword of discrimination and a copy of the *Prajnaparamita Sutra* in the blooming lotus of enlightenment. Kopan monastery, Kathmandu, Nepal.

others. This was done by practicing the "Six Perfections" (generosity, morality, patience, energy, meditation, and wisdom), thereby generating merit that could be transferred to those not as advanced on the path to enlightenment. Other bodhisattvas were figures who had already attained insight and power nearly equivalent to that of a buddha. Many legends describe them intervening in the lives of both ordinary people and aspiring saints with their pithy wisdom, psychic powers, and skillful magic. Some of these legendary bodhisattvas no longer required human bodies, dwelling instead in heavenly realms and appearing to those who prayed to them.

One of the earliest and most popular bodhisattvas is Manjushri, Patron of Buddhist Scholars and Lord of Wisdom. He is often represented with his flaming sword of discriminating insight in one hand and the *Perfection of Wisdom Sutra* in the other. Without a doubt, the most widely venerated of all the bodhisattvas is the Bodhisattva of Compassion, Avalokiteshvara. A male deity in South Asia, in East Asia this bodhisattva is known as Guanyin, the Goddess of Mercy. The bodhisattva Jizo (Ksitigarbha), mentioned at the beginning of this chapter, is also popular. As guardian of the dead in the underworld, he provides a safe journey to their next incarnation.

Mahayana Texts   Mahayana schools revere a wide array of texts that build upon the Pali Canon, or *Tripitaka*. These vary widely in the subjects they address. Some investigate the profound states of consciousness reached during meditation. Others elaborate on the implications of doctrines such as Interdependent Origination. Still others analyze the qualities of bodhisattvas or explain the benefits of calling upon various buddhas. All are thought to be thoroughly grounded in the teachings of the Buddha, whose implications they identify and explain.

One of the earliest Mahayana texts is the *Perfection of Wisdom Sutra*, which probably dates from the first century B.C.E. (with longer versions appearing in the centuries that followed). Between 300 and 700 C.E., important condensed versions arose, such

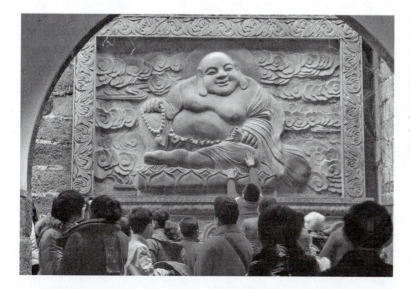

"The Laughing Buddha." This form of Maitreya is popular in China, where his fatness symbolizes prosperity and joy. It is customary for Buddhists to rub his belly for good luck. Here, people try to improve their luck by touching an image of Maitreya during the New Year fair at the Huayan Temple on the Laoshan Mountain in Qingdao, China.

Frontispiece of the Diamond Sutra of Dunhuang, 868 C.E. This manuscript is the oldest known printed book in the world; it appeared 587 years before the Gutenberg Bible.

Buddhist bodhisattvas can be understood as intermediary figures who serve others. What kinds of intermediary figures exist in other religions and what are their functions?

---

as the *Diamond Sutra* and the *Heart Sutra*. Both emphasize the cultivation of **bodhichitta** (Sanskrit, "awakened thought"), the aspiration to achieve enlightenment in order to benefit others. They also emphasize the Six Perfections, which were to become very important in relation to the ideal of compassion in the bodhisattva path.

Among the most widely venerated Buddhist works in East Asia is the *Lotus Sutra*, composed in Sanskrit in the second century C.E. While exploring the path of the bodhisattva, it places particular emphasis on skillful means, the thoughtful application of knowledge and insight in making decisions related to ethics and spiritual progress. Another interesting feature of the *Lotus Sutra* is its teaching that the death of the Buddha did not bring about his absolute dissolution. Instead, he is an eternal entity who remains in the cycle of samsara in order to benefit those who have not yet achieved liberation. Another important Mahayana text, the *Lankavatara Sutra* (fourth century C.E.), provides a detailed study of the nature of consciousness and explores how the mind has both the propensity to generate illusory, dualistic misperceptions and the potential to clearly apprehend the unity of existence. Another theological innovation appears in the *Pure Land Sutras* (second century C.E.), which describe Amitabha Buddha, "The Buddha of Boundless Light," who brings those who call upon him to rebirth in his Buddha Realm, "the Pure Land." The Pure Land is a kind of heaven where the faithful enjoy happiness and affluence. The *Pure Land Sutras* became foundational to Pure Land Buddhism (also known as Jodo Buddhism).

Two Mahayana Schools: Pure Land and Zen In fact, Pure Land Buddhism, popular throughout East Asia, is arguably the most important of all the schools within the Mahayana tradition. Based on belief in the infinite compassion of the Amitabha Buddha—known in China as Amito and in Japan as Amida—this tradition is best known for its practice of "reciting the Buddha's name" (Chinese, *nianfo*; Japanese, *nembutsu*) as a way of guaranteeing entry into his Pure Land at death. For those who join Amitabha in his Pure Land, there will be no more rebirth in the samsaric world. Instead, their reward for their devotion to him is happiness in his heavenly paradise. There is also the possibility of attaining full and complete enlightenment in Amitabha's Pure Land. Pure Land Buddhism's total reliance on the grace of Amitabha Buddha is in stark contrast to Theravada Buddhism's insistence on self-reliance and individual effort.

One of the best-known Mahayana Buddhist schools in the West is **Zen** Buddhism (known in China as **Chan**). Although Zen traces its teachings back to the Buddha himself, it traditionally holds that it became a distinct school when the South Indian sage Bodhidharma (early fifth century C.E.) brought it to China. From China, it spread throughout the rest of East Asia.

Zen emphasizes practice over doctrine, considering doctrine to be a distraction from the sudden, spontaneous experience of enlightenment called *satori*. Even devotion to the Buddha can be an obstacle to *satori*. This helps to explain the well-known Zen saying: "If you meet the Buddha on the road, kill him." Any form of attachment, even to the Buddha, is an obstacle. The Zen sayings called *koans* present the mind with paradoxes. Two well-known examples of *koans* are: "What is the sound of one hand clapping?" and "Show me your Original Face before your mother and father were born." Seeking to resolve these paradoxes through deliberate, logical thought, the impotence of rational cognition is exposed—and ultimately abandoned. What remains is direct intuition of reality, which is enlightenment.

Zen practitioners often use artistic mediums such as poetry, calligraphy, and garden design to enable the insights gained in meditation to find articulation outside the constraints of language. This creative aspect of Zen, its deeply ingrained sense of humor, and its emphasis on direct apprehension over doctrine helped to popularize this form of Buddhism in American pop culture and subculture. This is particularly evident in its influence on the 1950s "Beat" poets Gary Snyder and Allen Ginsberg.

Zen asserts the total efficacy of the mind rather than unswerving devotion to a savior figure as the only path to enlightenment and liberation. In other words, it rejects the Pure Land reliance on the Buddha's compassion for salvation in favor of gaining personal insight into the true nature of all things. Zen is the most radically self-reliant tradition among all Buddhist traditions.

Vajrayana Buddhism

Although **Vajrayana** Buddhism began in India in the sixth or seventh century C.E., it has little presence there now. Today, it is the dominant form of Buddhism in Tibet, Nepal, Bhutan, and Mongolia. Although it is generally understood as deriving from Mahayana Buddhism, Vajrayana Buddhists say their tradition can be traced back directly to the Buddha, who began expounding its teachings sixteen years after his enlightenment. Whatever position one might take on this issue, one thing is clear: Vajrayana is a unique form of Buddhism that combines elements of Mahayana—and, in particular, the bodhisattva ideal—with secret teachings found in the Tantras, ancient Indian texts that teach esoteric knowledge about special methods for attaining enlightenment and liberation.

The Tantric texts reveal Tantra as a system of thought and practice based on the idea that the material world is a manifestation of divine energy. Practitioners of Tantra seek to gain control of this energy and to channel it in ways that will allow them to break through the confines of the ego, thereby finding enlightenment and liberation. Some of the most prominent features of Tantra are its emphasis on secret knowledge, ritual use of mantras and mandalas, worship of deities, visualization of deities and identification with them, and the deliberate breaking of taboos. Taken together, these and other features of Tantra are said to give practitioners powerful and even shocking means for shattering the illusion of self. One scholar has defined Tantra as "a technique for magically storming the gates of Buddhahood."[6]

As a Buddhist tradition that combines Tantra with Mahayana Buddhism and shamanism, Vajrayana was originally conceived as a spiritual method of such intense power that it could catapult an ordinary person to the level of an advanced bodhisattva—a level of awareness that would normally take many eons to attain—in a single lifetime. Adherents of this tradition refer to it as the "Diamond Vehicle" because of the clarity of its wisdom and its ability to cut through all misperceptions of reality. It is also known as the "Thunderbolt Vehicle" because of its power and as Tantric Buddhism. Among Vajrayana's most visible features are its *lamas*, the spiritual teachers (such as the Dalai Lama) in Tibetan Buddhism; its devotion to vast arrays of buddhas and bodhisattvas and to fierce gods and goddesses; its complex rituals; and its special meditation techniques, whose purpose is to propel one to the status of bodhisattva and, ultimately, to full enlightenment and buddhahood.

The most fundamental practice in Vajrayana Buddhism is "deity yoga." This exercise, which involves visualizing oneself as a deity, ultimately leads to the experience of becoming one with the deity and attaining its heightened perspective of reality. In "guru yoga," the practitioner seeks to unite his mind with that of his guru, or teacher, thereby gaining and experiencing his wisdom. Other forms of Vajrayana practice take advantage of states in which the mind is more attuned to the true nature of things and well positioned to gain enlightenment. These can occur in meditation, while dreaming, during sex, and at death. "Death yoga," for example, is based on the belief that there are moments during the death process in which the mind's vision is especially clear. If the dying person makes skillful use of such a moment to meditate on the "emptiness" (*shunyata*) of all things—that is, the absence of any enduring identity or quality in them, as the Buddha taught—then enlightenment can be achieved.

Vajrayana Texts Tibetan Buddhism preserves two large canonical collections of sacred texts, including traditional *sutras* (such as those found in the Pali Canon and Mahayana *sutras*), as well as Buddhist Tantras. In addition, Tibetan Buddhism has also maintained a tradition (dating back to the eleventh century C.E.) of "hidden texts." Often called "hidden treasures," these texts are attributed to Padmasambhava, the tantric master who is credited with bringing Vajrayana Buddhism to Tibet in the eighth century. According to Tibetan tradition, these texts were hidden away by Padmasambhava with the intention that each would be found at the proper time. The "treasure finders" who discover them do so only when Padmasambhava's "time-lock" spells unravel—always at a time when the world is ready for a new revelation.

What general tendencies do you see in the Theravada, Mahayana, and Vajrayana forms of Buddhism? Do you see similar tendencies in divisions within other religions?

Buddhism in India

During the centuries after Ashoka, Buddhism thrived in India and expanded into Central, East, and Southeast Asia. We will soon turn to the story of Buddhism's expansion, but it is important first to say something about its early history in its Indian homeland.

The Theravada, Mahayana, and Vajrayana traditions all began their historical development in India. Of these three, Theravada, which traces its origins back to the Sthavira sect in the time of the Buddhist Councils, had the least impact in India. As we will see, its future lay instead in Sri Lanka and Southeast Asia. Mahayana and Vajrayana maintained a longer cultural presence in India.

The Mahayana tradition, which originated in the first centuries of the common era, was fortunate in receiving financial and political support from the Gupta Dynasty (320–550 C.E.) of northern India. As we saw in Chapter 2 (pp. 59–60), the Guptas succeeded in bringing about a partial restoration of the great empire of Ashoka. Many Indian monasteries adopted Mahayana ideas and practices during the Gupta period. This is made clear by records of donations made to monasteries, some of which describe the support of monastic leaders for "Great Vehicle" teachings and the praise they offered their monks for becoming Mahayana adepts. The vibrancy of Mahayana in India is also attested to by the fact that from the fifth century onward East Asian monks regularly traveled to India to study and bring home copies of Mahayana texts such as the *Lotus Sutra*. The accounts of these East Asian pilgrim monks confirm that Mahayana ideas and practices were widespread among Indian Buddhists. By the seventh century, many of India's monasteries had formally allied themselves with the growing Mahayana tradition, with the greatest concentration of these being in northern India.

By that time, some influential teachers in northeast India were promoting Vajrayana Buddhism. A number of Buddhist universities were founded in this period. From these, Vajrayana was transmitted to nearby Tibet and Nepal, and subsequently to Mongolia and Bhutan, as well as to parts of East and Southeast Asia.

The Decline of Buddhism in India
Even as Mahayana and Vajrayana were flourishing in India, the forces that were to bring about their decline had already been set in motion. The fall of the Gupta Empire in the mid-sixth century brought political fragmentation and an end to much of the royal support and protection given to Buddhists and Buddhist institutions in earlier years. At the same time, Indian Buddhism had to contend with a resurgence of Hinduism. The Hindu Brahminical establishment began making concerted efforts to regain and enforce its supremacy in Indian society and culture. In southern India, Buddhism was challenged by the flourishing *bhakti* movement (Chapter 2). By the tenth century, Hinduism had won back both royal and popular support across India, and Buddhist monasteries had fallen into a decline from which they would never recover.

The final stage in the decline of Indian Buddhism was initiated by Muslim Turks, whose raids into northern India in the eleventh and twelfth centuries disrupted all of society but were particularly damaging to Buddhist monasteries and universities. The Turkish destruction of the Buddhist universities at Nalanda and Vikramasila around 1200 delivered the final blow. When the Tibetan Buddhist monk Dharmasvamin wrote of his travels in India the mid-thirteenth century, he despaired that almost no one would openly profess to being a Buddhist. Nevertheless, small pockets of Buddhism did endure in India, particularly in its southern regions, until the seventeenth century.

Buddhism Beyond India

Even as the light of Buddhism dimmed in India, it was thriving and spreading along three major routes that took it far from its homeland: a southern transmission into Sri Lanka and Southeast Asia, a northern transmission into Central Asia and East Asia, and a western transmission in the colonial period that brought Buddhism into contact with Europe and North America.

The Southern Transmission   Sri Lankan legend recounts that King Devanampiyatissa (250–210 B.C.E.) was converted to Buddhism by Ashoka's own son, Mahinda. The newly converted king had a huge monastery complex built in his capital at Anuradhapura. Ashoka's daughter, Sanghamitta, also came to the island to plant a sapling from the Buddha's *bodhi* tree and to establish the first order of Sri Lankan nuns.

From the beginning, monastic institutions were strong in Sri Lanka. Monasteries competed with each other for royal patronage, sometimes causing disputes and schisms within the Sangha. Despite such periodic disruptions, Sri Lanka has been renowned for more than a millennium as a bastion of Theravada Buddhism.

In Burma, the pivotal moment for Buddhism occurred in 1057 when Anwar, the Bamar king of Pagan, invaded the Mon kingdom of the south to establish the first Burmese empire (1057–1287). Along with other spoils of his conquest, he carried off Buddhist relics (believed to be fragments of the Buddha's remains), Pali texts, and a retinue of monks to whom he granted control of the Sangha. As a result, Theravada became the state religion of this new empire. These events spurred the spread of Theravada Buddhism throughout Southeast Asia. In Thailand, Laos, and Cambodia between the twelfth and fifteenth centuries, an earlier mingling of various Buddhist sects, Hinduism, and indigenous traditions gave way to state-sponsored Theravada.

It is important to note that Mahayana also had a significant place in the history of these regions. In Cambodia, kings frequently identified themselves as bodhisattvas, and the worship of Lokeshvara (another name for Avalokiteshvara) was of prime importance during the latter part of the Angkor period (twelfth–fifteenth centuries C.E.). Mahayana also reigned supreme in

Lokeshwara peers out in all directions from the temple towers at the Angkor Wat temple complex in Cambodia. These colossal faces were identified both as Shiva and as Avalokiteshvara by their worshippers.

Indonesia and on the Malay Peninsula. By the seventh century, sites such as Srivijaya in Sumatra were important centers of Buddhist training and attracted monks from as far away as China. The renowned Indian monk Atisha (982–1054) came to study in Srivijaya under the great master Dharmakirti before journeying in 1042 to Tibet, where he founded the Kadampa sect of Vajrayana, from which the Gelugpa school of the Dalai Lamas eventually arose.

In Java, Mahayana Buddhism was promoted by the native Sailendra Dynasty, which ruled much of Indonesia, including Sumatra and Bali, in the eighth and ninth centuries. One of the great monuments built by the Sailendras is the Borobudur Temple (c. 800). This gigantic complex includes 540 statues of the Buddha, some of them hidden within perforated screens of stone. There are also 2,672 relief sculpture panels depicting the Buddha. Buddhism thrived alongside Hinduism in Indonesia until both were eclipsed by Islam, originally introduced by Muslim traders, in the thirteenth through fifteenth centuries.

The earliest known image of the Buddha appears on the reverse of a coin minted by the second-century Kushan king, Kanishka I. Previously, the Buddha was not ever portrayed in physical form but was depicted more as an absence than a presence, symbolized with images such as footprints or an empty chair.

The Northern Transmission Buddhist communities were also founded in Central Asia during the time of Ashoka's reign (c. 272–231 B.C.E.). Ashoka sent Buddhist missionaries to Afghanistan. Legend says that he sent his son, Kustana, to the region northwest of Tibet, where he founded the Buddhist kingdom of Khotan in 240 B.C.E. Later, the Central Asian ruler Kanishka I (r. c. 110–139 C.E.), after inheriting the portions of Bactria and northwest India conquered by his Kushan predecessors, is said to have embraced and vigorously supported Buddhist tradition in the second century C.E. Some of the earliest Buddhist images date from the period of his reign. Indeed, the oldest extant image of the Buddha appears on a coin of Kanishka.

Buddhism Comes to East Asia Buddhism may have first appeared in China as early as the first century C.E., brought by monks and missionaries from Central Asia who accompanied merchants along the Silk Road to China. When Buddhism arrived in the refined world of China's Han Dynasty (206 B.C.E.–220 C.E.), it was received as an exotic import.

China The first dated proof of Buddhism's entry into China is found in the Han chronicles, which assign this event to 65 C.E. In that year, they say, the Han emperor Ming dreamed of an encounter with a golden-robed flying figure his diviners later identified as the Buddha. The chronicles also describe imperial relatives and aristocrats making offerings to the Buddha. Three years later, the emperor built the famous White Horse Temple in his capital city of Luoyang. According to a well-known tale, he did so to honor two missionary monks from Central Asia who brought the first Buddhist texts to make their way into China on the back of a white horse. Translation of Buddhist texts into Chinese

Borobudur Temple, Java, Indonesia, c. 800 C.E. Here, one of the hidden statues of the Buddha is revealed. In order to see others, pilgrims would have to peer through holes in bell-shaped stupas, such as those visible in the background.

began as soon as they appeared in China. This was especially true of texts relating to meditation and breath control techniques. These were of great interest to Daoists (Chapter 6), who at first regarded Buddhists as like-minded seekers of physical health and immortality. Daoist interest in the new religion diminished only when Buddhism's teachings were better understood and after its differences with Daoism had become apparent.

To a great degree, Buddhism established itself in China through adaptation and accommodation to the Chinese cultural landscape. The Central Asian missionary translator An Shigao is a good example of this adjustment. He was one of the first to translate Mahayana works into Chinese in the latter half of the second century C.E. Not unexpectedly, the process of translation often produced a fair amount of deviation from the original sources. Early on, for example, Daoist equivalents stood in for Buddhist philosophical terms; only later were new Chinese words coined to better convey abstract Buddhist concepts.

After the fall of the Han Dynasty (c. 220 C.E.), the Chinese empire split into a north-south division that lasted another three and a half centuries. The north was ruled by successive groups of non-Chinese tribes, while the south was colonized by the fleeing native Chinese elites who also founded their successive dynasties there. The Chinese Buddhist community experienced a similar split. Many Buddhist clerics and their followers stayed in the north, while others followed the Chinese authorities and fled to the south, taking the Dharma into new territory, where it quickly found acceptance among locals. Confucianism (Chapter 6), which had always supported the aims of the state, had lost some of its influence in the wake of China's political upheavals, and Buddhism was primed to take its place. Moreover, Buddhism appealed to the Chinese in both the north and the south because it reflected the contemplative and mystic introversion of native Daoism. In northern China, Buddhist intellectualism had given way to an emphasis on practice. "Barbarian" kings who ruled in the vacuum created by the fleeing native Chinese rulers patronized Buddhist ascetics and magicians who had roots in Central Asian traditions. In the south, there was an intense expression of faith and piety in the plea for Buddha's compassion, as well as an incipient movement toward meditation and enlightenment.

The golden age of Buddhism in China lasted from the fifth to the eighth centuries C.E. As we have seen, many Mahayana texts were translated during this period into Chinese by eminent scholars, both native and foreign. Pilgrim monks from China also took long and often dangerous journeys to India in search of Buddhist wisdom from its point of origin. New *sutras* were authored by Chinese patriarchs to proclaim equal authority with the Indian and Central Asian texts. Of the Mahayana schools of today, many took on their definitive forms in China. In particular, the Mahayana convention of devotion to a particular text can be clearly seen as informing the primary character of these schools.

The two major schools that would eventually arise to signal the final stage in the Chinese transformation of Buddhism into a native faith were Pure Land and Chan (Japanese, Zen, Korean, Seon). Pure Land appeared at the start of the fifth century C.E. According to its own tradition, Chan was introduced to China by the legendary Bodhidharma in the fifth century C.E. It was in the eighth century, however, that it began to make its mark on the Chinese religious scene thanks to a succession of Chinese patriarchs (masters of a particular sect of Buddhism), most notably the Sixth Patriarch, named Huineng (c. 638–713 C.E.). An illiterate firewood vendor who allegedly attained enlightenment after merely hearing a neighbor's chanting of the *Diamond Sutra*, Huineng gained full patriarchal status after correctly discerning the ultimate message of the Buddha's original teaching.

Korea and Japan Buddhism arrived in Korea in the fourth century C.E. and closely emulated the text-based Chinese systems by developing the Five Doctrinal Schools. The new religion from China soon blended with native Korean shamanism, with the result that it took on a very distinctive flavor. Many Buddhist temples, for example, also became centers for the veneration of Korean mountain spirits and local deities. Moreover, Korean Buddhists eventually adopted a holistic approach to their belief by ignoring many of the sectarian differences that plagued the Indian and Chinese Buddhist establishments. Seon (Chan, Zen) has long been the dominant form of Buddhism in Korea.

In Japan, Buddhism was first introduced in 552 C.E., when the Korean king of Paekche presented Emperor Kinmei of Japan (r. 531–571) with a gift of *sutras* and an icon of the Buddha. The leader of a clan with the least vested interest in native Shinto (Chapter 7), Kinmei embraced Buddhism and promoted its adoption by the imperial family. Its success was evidenced by the accomplishment of Prince Shotoku (574–622), a prominent member of this clan. According to tradition, Prince Shotoku produced for the newly institutionalized Japanese state a constitution that stressed the ideals of the Buddhist Three Jewels as well as the Confucian virtue of harmony. By the Nara period (710–784), six schools of Buddhism had been imported directly to Japan from China. In the Heian period (794–1185), Tantric Buddhism and the Tendai sect were added, and by the Kamakura period (1185–1333), Pure Land, Zen, and the Nichiren sect came to essentially define the sectarian complexity of Buddhism in Japan. Among these, Pure Land would later have the most enduring and greatest impact on Japanese culture and values. Today, its presence is ubiquitous in almost every Japanese home. Zen Buddhism is embraced by the Japanese cultural and military elite and has influenced many Japanese art forms.

Vietnam Mahayana Buddhism also made major inroads in Vietnam. Because of Vietnam's cultural and geographical proximity to China (it was twice annexed by China and sent tribute to China for much of its premodern history), Vietnamese Buddhism shares a great deal with its Chinese counterpart. Because Vietnam served as the point of convergence between the northern and southern routes of Buddhist expansion out of India (north from China and south from Sri Lanka and Indochina), Vietnamese Buddhism displays Theravada influence as well.

Tibet Although Buddhism took root in Tibet later than in China, its transmission came directly from India. Since its arrival in Tibet (around 650 C.E.), the region has remained a stronghold of Vajrayana Buddhism. Initially, the new religion met with resistance, for the shamans and court wizards of the indigenous Tibetan *Bön* religion had strong influence over the nobility. But legend has it that when King Songtsen Gampo (c. 617–649) arranged alliances with the king of Nepal and the emperor of China through marriages to their daughters, he found that his new wives were Buddhists. Their presence began to soften Tibetan attitudes to Buddhism, and so it was not long before the king built Tibet's first Buddhist temple and made arrangements for the translation of *sutras* into Tibetan. As monks and teachers poured into Tibet, Buddhism flourished. Trisong Detsen (c. 742–798), Tibet's first Buddhist king, consecrated the Samye monastery in 775 C.E. and also ordained members of the Tibetan aristocracy.

In the early ninth century, Buddhism was again under siege in Tibet and forced underground during the reign of King Lang Darma (r. 838–842 C.E.). When the king was assassinated and his dynasty collapsed, Buddhism was blamed for instilling weakness in the military. The scholarly monk Atisa, who arrived in Tibet in 1042 C.E., provided Tibet with an effective synthesis of the Theravada, Mahayana, and Tantric forms of Buddhism and united the Tibetan *Sangha*. Atisa instituted the practice of formal initiation into lineages of tantric teachers, which still characterizes Tibetan Vajrayana today.

During the thirteenth century, Tibetan Buddhist masters entered into a "patron-priest" relationship with the Khans (descendants of Genghis Khan) who ruled an empire that extended from China to eastern Europe. In 1578 C.E. the head of the Gelugpa monastery, Sonam Gyatsho (1543–1588), converted Altan Khan, the ruler of the Mongols. The Great Khan bestowed upon Sonam Gyatsho the title *Dalai Lama* (Mongolian, "Ocean [of Wisdom] Teacher"). Because this title was later assigned to two of his predecessors, tradition calls him the third Dalai Lama. It was the fifth Dalai Lama (1617–1682) who took full advantage of Mongol patronage. Backed by Mongol troops, he took over all of Tibet and sent other sects with conflicting political aspirations fleeing to other parts of the Himalayas. By the seventeenth century, with the Dalai Lama as the primary ruler of Tibet, great efforts were made to identify and reinstate him in this role each time he died and took rebirth.

Across all of these regions and countries, Buddhism adapted to local cultures and integrated indigenous beliefs. These patterns of transformation have also extended to Buddhism's encounter with Europe and America in the modern and postmodern contexts.

The Western Transmission

It has been during only the last two centuries that Buddhist traditions have come to the attention of the West. Many of those who were among the first to understand Buddhist teachings and practices and share them with Western audiences were also among the first Western converts to Buddhism. These early Western Buddhists both anticipated and inspired the growing popularity of the religion in Europe and America today.

Some say that the story of the Western transmission begins in the early nineteenth century, when T. W. Rhys-Davids (1843–1922), a British colonial administrator, first "discovered" Buddhist teaching while stationed in Sri Lanka. His translations of Buddhist texts sparked the interest of an English-speaking audience, many of whom saw the Buddha as embodying the modern values of the era as a radically independent, rugged individual who relied only on his own introspection and insight. These early Western readers of Buddhist texts preferred to characterize Buddhism primarily as a philosophy that radically contrasted with the perceived antirational dogmas of Western religion.

In recent years, Western adherents have increasingly come to value a deeper commitment to particular lineages of Buddhist teachers and a more well-rounded understanding of the subtle complexities of specific systems of Buddhist practice.

Although Chinese and Japanese immigrants had established Buddhist institutions on American soil many years earlier, the first notable conversion of an American to Buddhism did not occur until 1893. In that year, Charles T. Strauss formally converted, following a series of lectures on Buddhism delivered at the World Parliament of Religions in Chicago. But it was the American subcultures of the 1950s and 1960s, and particularly those of the Beats and hippies, that helped catalyze a deep and abiding

In 1963, the Vietnamese Buddhist monk Thich Quang Duc, while seated in meditation, burned himself to death in Saigon's Market Square to protest his government's religious policies.

As the young Thich Nhat Hanh, a Vietnamese monk, looks on, Dr. Martin Luther King, Jr., calls for a halt to the bombing of Vietnam (May 31, 1966).

interest in Buddhism among Americans. The perception of Buddhist leaders as political dissidents and peace activists helped to inspire new generations of American Buddhists. Martin Luther King Jr.'s nonviolent approach to civil rights activism was informed in part by Buddhist thought and practice. King's admiration for the Vietnamese Buddhist monk and peace activist Thich Nhat Hanh (b. 1926), whose commitment to community service helped to heal the emotional wounds of many American veterans of the Vietnam War, led King to nominate Hanh for a Nobel Peace Prize in 1967. The ever-growing popularity of the fourteenth Dalai Lama, Tenzin Gyatso (b. 1935), who was awarded the Nobel Peace Prize in 1989, also exemplifies the identification of Buddhism with peaceful political dissidence in America.

Buddhists in the World Today

Today, teachings about the Dharma are delivered as podcasts. Apps that help Buddhists time their meditations or look up specific *sutras* are available for mobile devices. In Japan, vending machines sell pocket-sized plastic replicas of some of the most revered Buddhist icons. Chinese animated hagiographies of saints and bodhisattvas can be easily downloaded. In America, Trey Parker and Matt Stone, creators of the television show South Park, offer online versions of old Zen lectures by Alan Watts (a twentieth-century philosopher and proponent of Buddhism), accompanied by their own "cartoon commentaries."[7] In the world of American comic books, an increasing number of superheroes are turning Buddhist (such as "Xorn" of the X-Men; even Batman has been revealed to have received Buddhist training in Tibet). Even as far back as the 1930s and

World Buddhist population.

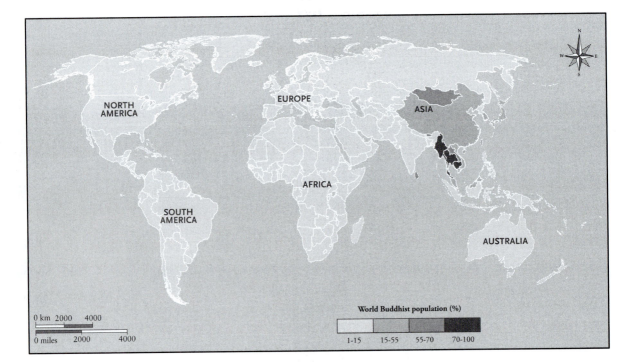

World Buddhist population (%)

| 1-15 | 15-55 | 55-70 | 70-100 |

1940s there were mystic American heroes trained in Buddhist practice, such as the Shadow and the Green Lama, who appeared in pulp magazines, radio serials, and comic books.

Today, no scribes are needed to copy *sutras,* as the vast majority of the Buddhist canon is available online. It is possible to visit virtual temples and meditation halls without stepping outside your front door. New technologies and media challenge Buddhists to adapt, expand, and explore new environments. But Buddhism has encountered a multitude of cultures in its spread throughout Asia (and beyond) over the past 2,500 years and has always found skillful ways of applying new technologies. Buddhists continue to develop innovative ways to integrate modern realities into an ancient Buddhist worldview, as they convey traditional teachings through contemporary media that preserve the sacred *sutras,* stories, and songs that comprise Buddhist traditions.

A modern Cambodian monk at work on his computer.

BUDDHISM AS A WAY OF LIFE

Buddhists put the teachings of the Buddha into practice in many ways. Seeking to observe the ethical principles he taught, they aspire to proper conduct in daily life. Seeking to observe the workings of the mind and to see reality more clearly, many make use of meditative disciplines. Some become members of monastic orders. All Buddhists participate in festivals that commemorate important events and engage in rituals that mark important transitions in life, from birth to death. In this part of our investigation, we will look at several Buddhist practices in order to gain an understanding of the meaning they have for followers of the Buddha.

Who Is a Buddhist?

You will recall that the first followers of the Buddha were the five ascetics who had once practiced severe austerities with him. Convinced by his example and by his Sermon in the Deer Park that he had found what they, too, had been looking for, they became the first members of the Sangha. Their formal conversion was solemnized by their recitation of the "Three Refuges," also known as the "Three Jewels":

> I take refuge in the Buddha.
> I take refuge in the Dharma.
> I take refuge in the Sangha.

Since then, all followers of the Buddha have affirmed their Buddhist identity by reciting this formula, Buddhism's most fundamental ritual practice and the closest thing the Buddhist tradition has to a creed. The Three Refuges are recited throughout one's

Pema Chodron is an American-born Buddhist nun whose books, such as *When Things Fall Apart: Heart Advice for Difficult Times*, address skillful ways to cope with everyday suffering and how to keep one's heart open in the face of adversity.

life, and often daily. To take refuge in the Buddha is to acknowledge the Buddha as the supreme example of the potential of human life. To take refuge in the Dharma is to recognize it as the path to enlightenment and an end to suffering. To take refuge in the Sangha is to recognize one's reliance on the Buddhist community—and, in particular, the order of monks—as the custodian of the Dharma, responsible for its preservation and transmission.

The Buddha's Teachings on Ethics and "Skillful Means"

As we have seen, the path to nirvana requires ethical conduct. This may be as simple as serving the Buddhist community and supporting its institutions. Some Buddhists formally commit themselves to observing the Five Precepts. These are (1) not killing or causing harm, (2) not stealing, (3) not committing inappropriate sexual acts, (4) not lying, and (5) not using intoxicants.

Beyond these formal precepts, the Buddha also taught a practical approach to ethical conduct in which the first and most important consideration is one's intention. Conduct intended to benefit oneself or others, or at least not to do harm, is ethical conduct. To put this another way, ethical conduct is conduct that does not arise from the Three Poisons of greed, hatred, and delusion. For the Buddha, the distinction between "ethical" and "unethical" was not something that could be discerned with reference to traditional standards of "right" and "wrong." Such standards, which often hold that an action is *always* right or wrong, do not necessarily result in ethical behavior when applied in particular circumstances. Thus, one must bring creativity and insight to every situation in order to skillfully consider one's intention in determining how to behave. In later forms of Buddhism, **upaya** (Sanskrit, "skillful means") was developed into a formal practice that encourages the individual to thoughtfully apply knowledge and insight in making decisions related to ethics and spiritual progress.

Meditation and the Cultivation of Mind

The Buddha encouraged his followers to practice meditation, which enables practitioners to identify, understand, and eliminate patterns of thought that perpetuate desire and suffering. In fact, it is sometimes said that the full implications of the Buddha's teaching cannot be understood without devoting oneself to meditative practice. Of course, most of the Buddha's followers were monks and nuns who had given up ordinary life in order to devote themselves entirely to monastic practices. For them, there was no obstacle to meditation. Others, who continued to meet their obligations in ordinary society, had to be content with offering support to monastic communities in the hope of gaining merit and a more favorable rebirth. This remains the case today. Most Buddhists do not meditate regularly. Instead, they seek to make spiritual progress by supporting Buddhist causes, including monastic orders, and by doing their best to put Buddhist principles into practice in their daily lives. They are inspired by the great achievements of monastics who have developed a remarkable range of meditative techniques, as well as an impressive body of literature on meditation, over the past 2,500 years.

Meditation: *Shamatha* and *Vipassana* From the beginning, Buddhists have made extensive use of two basic types of meditation: *shamatha* (Sanskrit, "calm abiding" or "stabilizing meditation") and *vipassana* (Sanskrit, *vipashyana*, "insight"). These are still widely practiced today and are often employed by the same practitioner. Both are practiced in a variety of forms by the many Buddhist sects.

Shamatha cultivates the ability to focus awareness upon a single object of concentration. This focal point is very often the breath, but any object or sensation is appropriate as it is concentration upon *something* that matters, not the nature of the thing itself. Focused awareness stabilizes the mind, making it less easily disturbed by the disruptive influences of thoughts and feelings.

By comparison, the object of *vipassana* meditation, often called "mindfulness meditation" or "insight meditation," is awareness itself. Typically, the practitioner begins with a focus on the breath, which brings focused concentration and a stable mind. These make it possible to move beyond the thoughts, feelings, daydreams, and other concerns that normally occupy the attention of the mind and to calmly observe, as if from a distance, the unfolding of all mental and physical phenomena—neither obsessing, reacting, nor judging, but simply allowing them to be. In doing so, the practitioner gains insight into the workings of compulsive and restless thought and the ability to move past the suffering they cause.

Walking Meditation The Buddha taught that there are four postures in which one should practice meditation: sitting, standing, walking, and lying down. Any activity, he asserted, is an opportunity for meditation. Many Buddhist traditions encourage walking meditation as a means for making the serenity and insight found in the meditation hall possible out in the everyday world as well. The foundation of this practice is simply being mindful of and content with what one is doing:

> When walking, just walk.
> When sitting, just sit.
> Above all, don't wobble.
> —Yunmen (d. 949 C.E.; Tang Dynasty founder of the Yunmen school of Chan Buddhism)[8]

According to the Vietnamese monk Thich Nhat Hanh, who has written extensively on meditation, walking meditation involves relinquishing the impulse to "get somewhere"

A large contemporary image of the Walking Buddha in Thailand. Thai images often stylistically craft his right arm to represent the graceful swaying trunk of an elephant.

and to practice instead the mindful enjoyment of each breath and each step. To emphasize the spontaneity and naturalness of walking meditation, he often alludes to the Chinese Zen master Linji (d. 866), who taught that whereas most people think it is a miracle to walk across burning hot coals, to walk on water, or to walk through the air, the real miracle is simply to be walking upon the earth.

Some forms of Buddhism, such as Zen, are quite formal in their approach to walking meditation. In most *Zendo*s, or "meditation halls," meditators execute prescribed movements very slowly and deliberately in order to be completely aware of each subtle shift in posture, breathing, and sensation.

Visualization, Deity Yoga, and Inner *Mandalas* Another important form of meditation entails the practice of visualization. Practices involving the mental contemplation of the body of the Buddha developed early in the history of Buddhism. The visualization of buddhas and bodhisattvas came to occupy a central place in the meditation practices of such Mahayana sects as Pure Land Buddhism. But undoubtedly it is in Vajrayana Buddhism that a true virtuosity in employing visualization techniques developed. By means of a combination of visualization and mantra recitation, "deity yoga" (as it in known in the West) or "actualization" (as it is called in Tibet) creates conditions in which the very substance of the practitioner's mind comes to embody the deity that is invoked.

Other visualization techniques employ the contemplation of ***mandalas***. *Mandalas* are circular cosmological diagrams that often map out how a Buddhist deity or group of deities manifests both *in* and *as* the universe. These deities embody the function and interaction of archetypal forces within the sphere of being. As with deities, mandalas are also venerated externally as *tankas* ("tapestries"), sand paintings, and three-dimensional models, such as the Borobudur Stupa in Java.

Mantra, Liturgical Ritual, and Chanting

Perhaps the most widespread of Buddhist rituals is chanting, which is practiced by almost every Buddhist group. The Three Refuges, in which Buddhists declare their reliance on the Buddha, the Dharma, and the Sangha, are often chanted. Most Buddhist services include liturgical chanting that reflects the philosophical orientation of that particular tradition. The content of the chant and its function can vary greatly. Some forms of chanting consist of entire *sutras*, whereas others focus on key passages in particular philosophical texts. Still other varieties of chant make use of ritual formulas or simple ***mantras*** (sacred sounds or syllables).

Conversion and Ordination

As noted earlier, most Buddhists consider a simple heartfelt recitation of the Three Refuges to be sufficient in declaring oneself a "Buddhist." A striking example of this occurred in 1956 at Pune, India, when thousands of protesting *dalits*, the oppressed "untouchables" of Hinduism's lowest caste, recited the Three Refuges and converted to Buddhism en masse under the leadership of the *dalit* activist Dr. B. R. Ambedkar (1891–1956).

In most cases, Buddhists seeking to make their conversion public or to be ordained as priests, monks, or nuns participate in formal rites conducted in the presence of the Sangha and a revered senior monk, lama, or spiritual teacher.

Typically, there are two different levels of ordination as a monk or nun. The first is that of the novice, which can be conferred on children as young as seven or eight in Theravada. The novice agrees to abide by ten precepts and essentially functions as a student under the direct guidance of a Preceptor. The second, higher ordination of an adult monk requires candidates to be at least twenty years of age. In both cases (but to varying degrees) the recipient of the ordination makes a commitment to embody, maintain, and transmit the Buddhist Dharma.

At the beginning of this chapter we had a glimpse into the form and structure of an ordination ceremony in which the nun Jisen became a priest. The authority conferred in this kind of ceremony is primarily transmitted through the formal acknowledgment that the initiate is part of a lineage of teachers that can be traced directly back to the Buddha. Sometimes a scroll or document tracing this spiritual genealogy is presented to the newly ordained. We can imagine how moving it must be to see one's name at the bottom of a list headed by the Buddha, indicating that one has been formally admitted into the Buddha's own "Dharma family."

Women in Buddhism

For much of its history, Buddhism's institutions were formed and controlled primarily by men. In mainstream monasteries nuns did not have much of a place in the preservation and transmission of the Dharma. But Buddhist women did take on more central roles outside of monasteries, both as lay Buddhists and as wandering ascetics, and their significance is acknowledged in many sources. Powerful political figures such as the Empress Wu Zetian of Tang Dynasty China (late seventh century C.E.) and Camadevi (seventh century C.E.), the legendary queen of Haripunjana in northern Thailand, have left an indelible mark in the history of Buddhism as patrons whose support and example helped to spread Buddhist traditions.

But beyond the historical influence of Buddhist women as powerful secular leaders, several important female spiritual leaders emerged even at the very beginnings of Buddhism. In the early formation of the Pali Canon, one collection called the *Khuddaka Nikaya* canonized a group of early saints in two collections of poems: the *Theragatha* ("Poems of Male Elders") and the *Therigatha* ("Poems of Female Elders"). Thus, even in Buddhism's very early years, the tradition acknowledged and preserved the compositions of its women saints. Later, other women saints, particularly in Vajrayana Buddhism, stood out as great virtuosos and innovators of the highest esoteric practices.

In 2003 there were approximately 125,000 Buddhist nuns worldwide. However, centuries ago lineages of Buddhists nuns in many regions either disappeared (such as in the eleventh century in Sri Lanka) or never existed in the first place (as in Thailand). Only in China, Korea, Taiwan, and Vietnam have nuns traditionally been given full ordination and regarded with the same respect as their male counterparts. In other countries, only novitiate ordination (that is a beginning or trial ordination) has been conferred on women. Elsewhere, women have not been eligible for ordination at all. In Tibet, for example, nuns were originally allowed to take only the vows prescribed for laypeople.

Resistance to women taking an active role in Buddhist monastic institutions goes all the way back to the time when Mahaprajapati, the Buddha's stepmother, petitioned for women to be allowed ordination. Though the Buddha eventually relented, he noted that allowing nuns into the order would only hasten the demise of the Buddhist teaching. Even those regions that allowed nuns placed additional constraints on female monastics.

Where there have been some nunneries attached to Theravada monasteries, the nuns have often been relegated to serving the domestic needs of monks, primarily by cooking and cleaning for them. Some women, like the *maechi* (female renunciants) of Thailand, have preferred a solitary ascetic life to the limitations of ordination in the male-dominated monastic institutions.

Recently, in most of the Theravada world, full ordination of women has begun to be revived. Women renouncers have been proactive in these regions, adopting ascetic disciplines and formal vows on their own or forming small groups of female practitioners. And there has been an explosion in the number of notable women Buddhist leaders in the West, who have profoundly influenced and empowered Buddhist women around the world. Because of their efforts, new opportunities for women to receive ordination have begun to open up in many countries as women are transforming the Buddhist institutional landscape.

One such example is that of Ayya Khema (1923–1997), who organized the First Council of Buddhist Nuns. Born to a Jewish family in Berlin, Ayya Khema was evacuated from Germany along with hundreds of other children in 1938. Her parents eventually escaped to China, where she was reunited with them in Shanghai. When the Japanese invaded Shanghai, the family was placed in a prisoner-of-war camp. Ayya Khema's father died in the camp before the Americans liberated it. After these life-altering experiences, Ayya Khema traveled extensively and spent time studying meditation in the Himalayas. The experiences that grew out of her meditation practice led to her taking ordination as a Buddhist nun in Sri Lanka in 1983. She founded an international training center for Buddhist nuns in 1983 in Sri Lanka, and in Germany she helped organize thirty-seven different meditation groups. But Ayya Khema is most widely remembered for organizing the first international council for nuns in Buddhist history. This conference led to the founding of a worldwide Buddhist women's organization called Sakyadhita ("Daughters of the Buddha"). In May 1987 Ayya Khema became the first Buddhist nun to ever address the United Nations.

Sacred Places and Objects of Veneration

Like adherents of other religions, Buddhists recognize special places and objects as having a sacred character that makes them worthy of reverence and veneration. The most important of these are places where particularly important events in the life of the Buddha occurred and that contain the relics of the Buddha.

The principal sacred sites in Buddhism are Lumbini (in modern Nepal), the site of the Buddha's birth; Bodh Gaya, the place where he attained enlightenment; Sarnath, where he preached his first sermon, the "Sermon in the Deer Park"; and Kusinara, the place of the Buddha's death and passing into *parinirvana*. These sacred places are visited by thousands of pilgrims each year.

According to the *Mahaparinibbana Sutra*, the Buddha's followers collected the relics that remained after his cremation. Apparently, they intended to keep all of the relics in a single place, but conflict arose when local kings made claims to them. In the end, they were divided into eight portions so that they could be distributed equally among the claimants. According to another account, in the time of Ashoka the relics were divided again, this time into 84,000 portions that were taken to all parts of the Indian subcontinent. Although we cannot be certain of the accuracy of every detail in these stories, there is good evidence that soon after his death the relics of the Buddha were divided and placed in reliquary mounds called **stupas**. In time, the custom arose of placing the relics of Buddhist saints in *stupas* as well. Today, most *stupas* are large and impressive hemispherical structures that resemble the original mounds built on the sites where they stand. As symbols of the achievements of others in grasping truth and bringing an end to suffering, the relics they preserve have a powerful and inspiring effect on those who venerate them.

Because the Buddha said that his teaching would serve as his Dharma-body after his passing, many Buddhists venerate the sacred texts in which the Dharma is preserved. For example, some Mahayana groups place manuscripts of sutras in images of the Buddha or in the structures of shrines, making them a part of ritual worship. The thirteenth-century Japanese teacher Nichiren advocated worship of the title of the *Lotus Sutra* in the form of a calligraphic mandala.

Early Buddhist arts and artifacts tended to represent the Buddha more as an absence than a presence. For example, the Buddha was often indicated by an empty chair, a pair of footprints, or the *bodhi* tree he sat under when he obtained enlightenment. In time, though, Buddhists began to make extensive use of images to recall more vividly the physical form of the Buddha and to visualize appearances of other buddhas and bodhisattvas. Many of these images make use of subtle iconographic cues—such as hand gestures and postures—to symbolize events and functions associated with the Buddha and other enlightened beings.

From the beginning, Buddhists also venerated images that represent important events in the life of the Buddha and aspects of his teaching. To this day, in fact, fig trees continue to be objects of reverence, as it was beneath the shade of a fig tree that the Buddha achieved enlightenment. Another commonly venerated symbol is the wheel.

The Great Stupa of Sanchi, India. Early Andhra Dynasty, first century B.C.E.

Cherry trees in front of Goju-No-To Pagoda. Built in 1407 on the island of Miyajima, this Japanese adaptation of the Indian *stupa* has a central shaft with stylized umbrellas that extends down through all five stories to a reliquary casket below.

With its eight spokes, the "Dharma Wheel" is an ancient Buddhist symbol that represents the Noble Eightfold Path. The prayer wheel, commonly used in Vajrayana ritual, is a device filled with printed scrolls believed to emit thousands of prayers and mantra recitations when they are rotated.

Holidays and Festivals

The Buddhist year is filled with holidays, festivals, and other special observances. In most countries, their dates are determined by the lunar calendar and therefore fall on different days each year. The most important occasions are commemorations of key events in the life of the Buddha, but there are also celebrations of the birthdays of bodhisattvas, remembrances of historical events, and seasonal observances that have taken on a religious significance.

Vesak By far, the most important Buddhist celebration is *Vesak*. Although it originally commemorated the day on which the Buddha was born, *Vesak* has also become a celebration of the Buddha's death and *parinirvana*. It occurs on the day of the first full moon in the month of *Vesakha*, usually in May. On *Vesak*, Theravada Buddhists decorate local shrines and light lamps to symbolize the Buddha's enlightenment and the spreading of his insight throughout the world. People send out greeting cards that depict key events in the life of the Buddha. Some lay Buddhists stay up all night in meditation as the Buddha had done on the night of his enlightenment.

In Tibet this festival is called *Saga Dawa*. Tibetan Buddhists light lamps and, like Buddhists in other countries, express their devotion by circumambulating shrines and *stupas*. They also show reverence and seek to acquire merit through repeated prostrations—lying face down in supplication before a sacred site or object. Many Tibetan Buddhists observe *Saga Dawa* by taking turns bathing an image of the infant Buddha. In Japan, *Vesak* is known as *Hana Matsuri* ("The Flower Festival"). Celebrated on April 8, when it coincides with the blooming of the cherry blossoms, *Hana Mutsuri* also involves the practice of bathing images of the infant Buddha. In some regions, this bathing ritual occurs at other times of the year, usually as a rite of purification.

Asala In Theravada Buddhism, *Asala* is a holiday that originally marked the beginning of the three-month rainy season. During this time, monks would cease their wandering and remain in a monastery for an extended period of meditation and introspection. Today, many lay Buddhists in Burma and Thailand take temporary ordinations and live as monks for this three-month period. *Asala* also commemorates the "First Turning of the Wheel of the *Dharma*," when the Buddha gave his first teaching. Many sermons are given to laypeople at this time.

Father and child bathe an image of the Buddha as a baby in a Taipei temple during the April 2001 celebration of the Buddha's birth in Taiwan.

Other Festivals The conclusion of the three-month retreat season coincides with other festival observances. During the *Kathina* ceremony, observed by Theravada Buddhists, the laity offer new robes to monks and make special requests for spiritual guidance and intervention. The Tibetan form of this holiday is called *Lhabap* and is characterized by feasting and visits to temples.

There are many important culturally specific festivals that lack corollaries in other regions. To mention just one interesting example, during the "Festival of the Hungry Ghosts" in China and Japan's "Feast of the Dead," the spirits of ancestors are placated with food offerings, and monks are called upon to recite *sutras* in order to aid the departed in securing a favorable rebirth.

Funerary Rites

When the death of a Buddhist approaches, family and friends will often come and sit in the dying person's room to offer comfort and assurances that death is a natural part of the life cycle. They may speak of the good deeds that he or she has done and note that these are likely to bring a favorable rebirth. In some cases monks may be

Prime Minister Abhisit offers Kathina robes to monks at a 2010 Kathina ceremony in Bangkok, Thailand.

invited to chant comforting *sutras*. A small statue of the Buddha is often placed near the head of the dying person.

Buddhists practice both cremation and burial. Funeral services may be held either before these events or, in the form of a memorial service, after them. Whatever form a funeral takes, it is always a solemn and dignified affair. Funerals are not appropriate occasions, as other important events might be, for displays of emotion or wealth. A photograph or other image of the deceased is usually set upon an altar at the front of the room in which the service is held, as are flowers provided by family and friends. When entering the room, mourners approach the altar, bow with their hands pressed together in a prayerful manner, spend a moment in quiet reflection, and then take their seats. It is customary for monks, family, and friends to speak, offering eulogies to honor the deceased. In most cases there is also chanting, led either by monks or family members.

VISUAL GUIDE
Buddhism

The Buddha achieved enlightenment while seated beneath a fig tree that came to be known as the Bodhi Tree ("Enlightenment Tree"). The fig tree was already considered a sacred tree long before the Buddha lived, but during his lifetime it came to symbolize his enlightenment. Here,

monks gather at Bodh Gaya in India, the site of the Buddha's enlightenment, to venerate a descendant of the original Bodhi Tree under which he sat.

Before the Buddha himself was first depicted in works of art, Buddhists venerated his footprints, which symbolized his path into nirvana. Although Buddha statues that actually depict his form later become common, the convention of

(continued)

CONCLUSION

We began this chapter by reflecting on the life of the Buddha, which offers his followers an example worthy of emulation. The life of the Buddha was a journey from the sorrow inherent in clinging to impermanent things to the ineffable joy and freedom that spring from understanding and accepting reality as it is. The Buddha's teaching is intended to dislodge the mind from clinging to the illusion of permanence and to empower each individual to find the joy and freedom this realization brings.

Through its history, Buddhism has adapted itself to diverse cultural contexts. Much of its versatility was fostered by the teaching of the Buddha, who insisted that wherever the Dharma is transplanted, local custom, convention, and religious observance should always be maintained. This allowed Buddhism to syncretize easily with regional beliefs and customs, as its predisposition was not to displace but to augment. New ways of understanding and practicing the Buddha's teachings proliferated as the Dharma took root in new settings. These sometimes created divisions within the Sangha, but Buddhists have always tended to see diversification as a natural and wholesome development in which the versatility of the Dharma was demonstrated even as its essential features were maintained. Many Buddhists believe that there are ultimately as many "Buddhisms" as there are beings in the universe. Each Buddhist must rely on his own understanding of the Dharma and make his own way. As the Buddha once said to his disciple, Ananda: "Be a lamp unto yourself."

In the modern context, Buddhism has inspired productive and progressive forms of social dissidence and political liberation, as in the mass conversion of *dalits* to Buddhism in 1956. But, as with other religions, Buddhist institutions have also at times functioned as mechanisms of social control and state-sponsored violence, as may be seen in the fact that there have often been "fighting monks" in Tibetan and East Asian monastic traditions that developed various martial arts traditions, often to enforce both sectarian and political agendas.[9] Nevertheless, many modern Buddhist leaders have come to exemplify the power of nonviolent modes of resistance and reform, such as the Burmese Buddhist dissident Aung San Suu Kyi (b. 1945), whose commitment to peaceful resistance resulted in her receiving the Nobel Peace Prize in 1991, among other awards and accolades.

A new development in the modern context—and one that has emphasized the teaching of Interdependent Origination—views ecology as a primary model for understanding and embracing the interconnectedness of all things. This trend, which sees the individual and the environment in perpetual relationship, embraces a timely and essential evolution of the Dharma.

VISUAL GUIDE (continued)
Buddhism

venerating his footprints continues today. The Buddha's footprints, which remind Buddhists of the immediacy of Buddha and the law of Impermanence, are inscribed with the sacred marks said to have been present on the body of the infant Siddhartha.

Buddhists of all sects demonstrate their reverence for the Buddha by bowing and prostrating themselves. In the Tibetan Nongdro (*sngon'gro*) or preliminary practices of Vajrayana, some Buddhists will perform 100,000 prostrations as an act of purification. Others show reverence while walking to a sacred site by bowing or prostrating themselves every step of the way.

As in Hinduism and Jainism, the lotus in Buddhism is a symbol of both purity and enlightenment. The lotus has its roots in the mud of the world but rises up as its pure blossom expands in the light of the sun.

While *mandalas* are used in Hinduism, where they also function as cosmological diagrams used for meditation, some Buddhists utilize them in other ways. In Vajrayana Buddhism, monks spend weeks constructing sand *mandalas* such as the Avalokiteshvara Mandala shown here. The sacred image will then be swept toward the center and destroyed as a reminder that art, like all other things, is impermanent.

SEEKING ANSWERS

What Is Ultimate Reality?

Buddhists often use the word *dharma* in its broader sense (that is, as nature and its laws) to refer to ultimate reality, or reality as it is (rather than as it usually perceived, or misperceived). According to the doctrine of Interdependent Origination, reality is a web of interrelated and interdependent phenomena in which nothing comes into existence independently of other things. Instead, the origination, or coming-into-existence, of things depends on all other things, as does their continued existence. All things are constituted of elements of other things. Nothing exists in and of itself. Further, according to the Buddha's doctrine of Impermanence, all things are in a constant state of flux and without any underlying or enduring essence or identity.

How Should We Live in This World?

Believing that there is stability and permanence in the world, we seek to possess what we want and to avoid what we do not want. Our inability to do so results in suffering that arises from our ignorance of the true nature of reality. Accordingly, the Buddha's guide to life, the Noble Eightfold Path, begins with the acceptance of a correct view of reality. The importance of striving for goals consistent with this understanding and living according to corresponding ethical principles follows. Finally, the Eightfold Path enjoins Buddhists to cultivate awareness and concentration that lead to enlightenment and an end to suffering.

What Is Our Ultimate Purpose?

For Buddhists, one's ultimate purpose is to break free of *samsara* and to achieve the end of suffering that is found in nirvana. But Buddhists also recognize that suffering is a condition that afflicts all sentient beings. Moved by compassion for others, they seek to live in a way that allows and encourages them to follow the path that will lead to their own enlightenment and liberation from suffering.

REVIEW QUESTIONS

For Review

1. Describe some of the distinctive ways in which Buddhism differs from other religions.
2. What are the implications of the Buddha's doctrine of Interdependent Origination?
3. What are the Three Marks of Existence? How do they relate to the doctrine of Interdependent Origination?
4. Describe some of the different ways in which adherents of various Buddhist groups put the teachings of the Buddha into practice.

5. What did the Buddha mean by "suffering" (*dukkha*)? How does following the Noble Eightfold Path bring an end to suffering?

For Further Reflection

1. It is sometimes said that Buddhism is a philosophy rather than a religion. Do you agree? Why or why not?
2. What are the most significant ways in which the teachings of the Buddha deviated from those of Hinduism?

3. In what specific ways do the teachings of Mahayana and Vajrayana Buddhism elaborate on those of Theravada?
4. Why is the principle of the Middle Way essential to Buddhism?
5. To what extent are the Buddha's teachings about the nature of reality in agreement with those of modern science?
6. Would you find it difficult to accept the Buddha's doctrine of No-Self? Why or why not?

GLOSSARY

anatman (un-aat-mun; Sanskrit) The doctrine that there is no independent, eternal self or soul underlying personal existence.

arhat (ar'hut) In Theravada Buddhism, one who has attained enlightenment.

bodhichitta (bow-dhi-chit-ta; Sanskrit, "the awakening mind or heart") In Mahayana Buddhism, the wise and compassionate intention to attain Buddhahood for the sake of all other sentient beings.

bodhisattva (bow-dhi-sut-tva; Sanskrit, "enlightenment being") One who is on the verge of enlightenment. In Mahayana Buddhism, a bodhisattva is one who has taken a "bodhisattva vow" to remain in samsara in order to work for the enlightenment of all sentient beings.

Buddha (bood-dha; Sanskrit, "the Awakened One") A fully enlightened being.

Chan or Zen (chah-aahn/Zehn) Respectively, the Chinese and Japanese names for the "meditation" school of Buddhism that values meditative experience far and above doctrine.

Dharma (dhur-mah; Sanskrit, "that which upholds") In the Buddhist context, Dharma refers both to Buddhist teaching and Buddhism as a religion.

dukkha (doo-kah; Pali, "suffering") Usually translated as "suffering," it can also be understood as the anxiety, unease, and dissatisfaction caused by desire.

Four Noble Truths The four truths that form the basis of the Dharma: Suffering is inherent in human life, suffering is caused by desire, there can be an end to desire, the way to end desire is the Noble Eightfold Path.

Impermanence According to the Buddha's doctrine of Impermanence, all phenomena are in a constant state of change.

Interdependent Origination (Sanskrit: *pratitya-samutpada*, "arising on the ground of a preceding cause") The doctrine that reality is a complex of interrelated and interdependent phenomena in which nothing exists independently; instead, the origination of all things depends on other things.

karma (kur-mah; Sanskrit, "action") Action; also, the consequences of actions.

lama (laah-mah; Tibetan) In Tibet, a teacher of the Dharma.

Mahayana (muh-haah-yaah-na; Sanskrit, "great vehicle") Also known as the "Great Vehicle," Mahayana is the form of Buddhism most prominent in China, Japan, Mongolia, Tibet, and Korea.

mandala (muhn-daah-la; Sanskrit "circle") Typically, a circular diagram representing the entire universe. Often used as an aid in meditation.   (*continued*)

GLOSSARY (continued)

mantra (mun-trah; Sanskrit) A sacred sound or syllable used as a focus for meditation, as an invocation of a deity, or as a protective spell.

Middle Way The Buddha's principle of the path between extremes of asceticism and self-indulgence that leads to enlightenment.

nirvana (nihr-vaah-nah; Sanskrit, an "extinguishing" or "blowing out") The ultimate goal of Buddhist practice, nirvana is the extinguishing of desire and the suffering it causes.

Noble Eightfold Path The Buddha's prescription for a way of life that leads to enlightenment. Based on the principle of the Middle Way, it is also defined by eight virtues.

No-Self The doctrine that there is no independent, eternal self or soul underlying personal existence. See also *anatman*.

Pali Canon Also known as the *Tripitaka* (Sanskrit, "Three Baskets"), the Pali Canon is the first canon of Buddhist texts. It consists of three "baskets" or collections of sutras.

parinirvana (pah-ree nihr-vaah-nah; Sanskrit, "supreme release") The full entry into nirvana that occurs at the death of one who has achieved nirvana in his or her lifetime.

samsara (sum-saah-ra; Sanskrit, "continuous flow") The continuing cycle of birth, death, and rebirth; also, the this-worldly realm in which the cycle recurs.

Sangha (suhn-ghaah; Sanskrit, "community") The worldwide community of Buddhists. Alternatively, the order of Buddhist monks or the membership of a particular Buddhist congregation.

skandhas (skuhn-dhaah; Sanskrit, "heaps" or "bundles") The five components (body, perceptions, feelings, innate tendencies, and thought) that give rise to a sense of self.

stupa (stooh-puh; Sanskrit, "heap") A reliquary mound in which the relics of the Buddha or a Buddhist saint are buried and venerated.

sutra (sooh-trah; Sanskrit, "a thread") Verses of text or scripture.

Theravada (thair-ah-vaah-duh; Pali, "the Way of the Elders") The form of Buddhism that is most prominent in Sri Lanka, Cambodia, Laos, and Vietnam.

Three Marks of Existence The Buddha's teachings on impermanence, suffering, and the nonexistence of an eternal unchanging self or soul.

Tripitaka (see *Pali Canon*)

upaya (ooh-paah-ya; Sanskrit, "expedient means") "Skillful Means" was developed into a form of Buddhist practice that encourages imaginatively applying wisdom to whatever circumstances one is in to assist in easing suffering or cultivating insight.

Vajrayana (vaah-jiraah-yaah-nah; Sanskrit, "Diamond Vehicle" or "Thunderbolt Vehicle") Often described as a form of Mahayana, Vajrayana is the most prominent form of Buddhism in Tibet and Nepal. It incorporates both Mahayana and tantric ideas and practices.

SUGGESTIONS FOR FURTHER READING

Byrom, Thomas. *The Dhammapada: The Sayings of the Buddha*. New York: Vintage Books, 1976. A very accessible and readable version of a key early Buddhist text.

Faure, Bernard. *Buddhism*. New York: Konecky and Konecky, 1977. A richly illustrated and descriptive introduction to Buddhism.

Lopez, Donald. *Buddhist Scriptures*. London: Penguin Books, 2004. A survey of Buddhist scriptures.

Skilton, Andrew. *A Concise History of Buddhism*. Birmingham, UK: Windhorse Publications, 1994. An excellent and accessible history of Buddhism.

(continued)

Snelling, John. *The Buddhist Handbook: The Complete Guide to Buddhist Schools, Teaching, Practice and History*. Rochester, VT: Inner Traditions, 1998. A guide to Buddhism that includes a detailed directory of contemporary institutions.

Suzuki, Shunryu. *Zen Mind, Beginner's Mind*. New York: Weatherhill, 1997. An excellent introduction to meditation practice.

Williams, Paul. *Mahayana Buddhism: The Doctrinal Foundations*. 2nd ed. New York: Routledge, 2008. A history of Mahayana that places emphasis on the veneration of certain Buddhist texts.

ONLINE RESOURCES

The Wikipedia Buddhism Portal

en.wikipedia.org/wiki/Portal:Buddhism
The collection of articles in the Wikipedia Buddhism series are generally quite reliable and extensive in scope.

Access to Insight: Readings in *Theravada* Buddhism

accesstoinsight.org/canon
Includes very helpful summaries and substantial translated portions of the Pali *Tripitaka*.

The Berzin Archives

berzinarchives.com/web/en/index.html
An excellent collection of translations, teaching, and scholarship on the Vajrayana tradition.

JAINISM

4

IN A SMALL VILLAGE in the southern Indian state of Karnataka, a middle-aged man stands silently in the main room of the home of Mr. and Mrs. Chandra, lifelong residents of the village and followers of the Jain religious tradition. Mr. Chandra carefully places small amounts of food in the cupped hands of his visitor. Other family members look on reverently, respectful and admiring both of the man who is receiving the food and of all that he represents—even though they have not met him before this day. These morsels of food—thirty-two altogether—and the small amount of water to follow are the only things he will ingest on this or any other day. His sole possessions consist of a gourd for drinking water and a broom for sweeping the path before him as he walks, lest he accidentally destroy a living being even as small as an ant. As a monk of the **Digambara** (literally, "sky-clad") sect of Jainism, this visitor does not even possess clothing. He stands naked before the Chandra family and, during his annual eight-month period of wandering about the land, goes naked before the elements.

Along with illustrating the austerities of the Jain monastic life, this ritual of giving, known as *dana*, indicates certain distinctions between ascetics (which includes both monks and nuns) and laypeople. The Chandras and the other laypeople who have gathered to participate in this *dana* represent the great majority of Jains in the world today.

Jains worship in a temple at Ranakpur, India. Splendid marble temples such as this are a common feature of the Jain tradition.

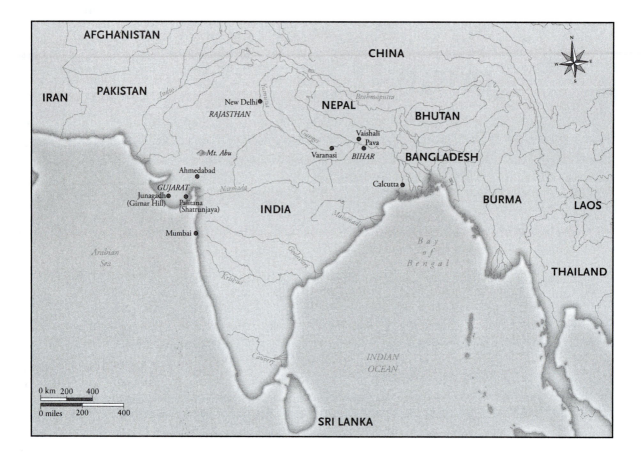

Significant sites in the development of Jainism.

As members of the laity, their religious duties differ from those of the ascetics, who exemplify Jainism's highest ideals of nonviolence and self-denial. The layperson depends on the ascetic for spiritual nourishment. But this in no way diminishes the sanctity or relevance of the lay religious life. The reverence shown by the roomful of admirers is as true to Jainism as is the monk's extraordinary self-discipline as he follows the ascetic path. Through such acts as *dana*, the lay participants can positively affect their **karma** ("action") and its consequences that determine prospects for a good rebirth. At the same time, the ascetic depends on laypeople like the Chandras for physical nourishment and support.

Viewing the scene from a more distant perspective, we can note other features of Jainism. For one thing, Mr. and Mrs. Chandra painstakingly prepared the food and carefully strained the water in preparation of the ritual, in order to avoid harming any living organism such as a tiny plant or insect in the water. They had invited the monk to partake of the food, for it would not befit one so venerated as a Digambara monk actually to have to beg for his food. The monk's accepting of the offerings was not a foregone conclusion. Had he for any reason found the circumstances objectionable and refused, the Chandras' reputation would have been damaged. In other words, the ritual of *dana* is played out within an interwoven network of religious and social ideas and forces. The fact that the monk stands naked with cupped hands is proof that he is a member of the Digambara sect, the more prevalent sect in southern India. In any number of households across India on this very morning, we could find similar scenes, but with some variations. Members of Jainism's **Shvetambara** sect, for example, don white robes and hold alms bowls for receiving their food. Or the ascetic could be a nun, in which case she would be clothed, even if of the Digambara sect.

Stepping back even further as we view this ritual of *dana*, we can observe a number of correlations with other South Asian religions. A nonviolent ethical stance, the ascetic path, karma, rebirth, and *dana* are also prominent aspects of Hinduism and Buddhism. Compared with those two religions, Jainism is a very small one, with just over 5 million adherents, the great majority of whom live in India. Because it rejects the authority of the *Vedas* (Chapter 2), Jainism (along with Buddhism) is considered to be distinctive relative to the Hindu traditions. Through the centuries, Jainism has earned a special reputation for having exemplified the ideal of nonviolence. ☀

This chapter sheds light on the main elements of Jainism, with regard to both the ascetics and the laity—and the interplay between the two groups. We have already identified some central Jain teachings: nonviolence, the need for an ascetic lifestyle, and the ultimate need to attain perfect knowledge. In the following section we explore in more detail these central elements and how they relate to the Jain understanding of the nature of the universe, the human condition, and the quest for spiritual deliverance. But first we will look to the distant past, to the foundational figures whom all Jains revere as the *jinas* (Sanskrit, "conquerors"), those the Jains believe have shown the way to spiritual deliverance.

TIMELINE
Jainism

c. Eighth century B.C.E. Probable period of Parshva, the twenty-third *tirthankara*.

Sixth or fifth centuries B.C.E. Probable period of Mahavira (Shvetambara traditional dates 599–527 B.C.E.; Digambaras date Mahavira's death at 510 B.C.E.; current scholarly opinion holds that he died in app. 425 B.C.E.).

(From antiquity through the medieval period, there is scant evidence for historical events, though there is much evidence for general involvement by Jains in the cultural life of India, through the building of temples and monuments, founding of schools and sects, and interaction with other religions.)

1313 C.E. Pillaging of Mount Shatrunjaya by Turkish invaders.

Fifteenth century Period of Lonka, precursor of Sthanakvasi and Terapanthi sects.

1526 Founding of the Mughal Empire.

1556–1605 Akbar the Great (Mughal emperor who maintained good relations with Jain leaders).

Seventeenth century Period of the founding of the Sthanakvasi sect.

1726–1803 Acarya Bhikshu, founder of the Terapanthi sect.

1867–1901 Shrimad Rajacandra (also spelled Rajchandra) teacher and mystic, friend of Mohandas (Mahatma) Gandhi.

1893 Lecture on Jainism delivered by Virchand Gandhi at the World Parliament of Religions at Chicago.

1900–2000 Period of geographical expansion of sizable Jain communities outside of India.

THE TEACHINGS OF JAINISM

Most of the world's religions look to a glorious founding figure, who is typically regarded both as an exemplar of the religious life and as the revealer of the religion's most significant teachings; the Buddha, Confucius, Jesus, and Muhammad are examples of such founding figures. Jainism looks not to just one but to a series of founding figures, the **tirthankaras**, "makers of the ford (or river crossing)." Each is considered to be a *jina*, "conqueror"—whence comes the name Jainism. Through having conquered the realm of *samsara*, the continuing cycle of death and rebirth (also a concept prominent in Hinduism and Buddhism), the *tirthankara* has, metaphorically, successfully crossed the river from the worldly realm to the beyond—the realm of the liberated.

The most recent of the *tirthankaras*, Mahavira, is especially significant. We begin this section by considering his captivating and highly influential life story.

Mahavira, the Twenty–Fourth and Last *Tirthankara* of This World Cycle

Nataputta Vardhamana, popularly known as Mahavira ("great hero"), was probably born near Vaishali (located in the northern Indian state of Bihar). He lived, according to the Shvetambara sect, from 599 to 527 B.C.E., although the Digambaras date his death at 510 (and scholars tend to date it later still, to sometime in the second half of the fifth century B.C.E.). The earliest biography of Mahavira is from the ninth century C.E. (the Sanskrit work *Vardhamanacarita*, by the poet Asaga), and so it is not possible to determine with historical certainty the details of his life. One thing, though, is agreed on by all: Mahavira was a contemporary or near-contemporary of Gautama the Buddha, who lived in the same area of northern India and preached his last sermon at Vaishali. There is no record of the two having met, but their legendary biographies are strikingly similar.

Vardhamana is said to have been born into the ruling class (the *kshatriyas*), the second son of a *rajah* or local ruler who was also a pious Jain. Vardhamana grew up amidst the luxuries of the palace, eventually marrying a princess named Yashoda (although the Digambara sect denies that he married), with whom he had a daughter. Eventually, however, he yearned for more than his princely life could offer, and so at age thirty he asked for permission to leave and become a monk. He joined a group of Jain ascetics who were followers of Parshva, the last *tirthankara* to have lived prior to Mahavira.

Vardhamana soon set off from the other ascetics and wandered about for over twelve years, naked and exposed. Fasting, going for long periods without sleep, withstanding the verbal and physical abuse of human opponents, and enduring the bites of insects rather than doing them harm, Vardhamana exemplified the ideals of nonviolence and asceticism, thereby earning his epithet "great hero," Mahavira.

In the thirteenth year of his ascetic wanderings, Mahavira is believed by Jains to have attained the state of **kevala**, or omniscience, the complete and perfect knowledge that leads at the time of death to liberation from the realm of *samsara*. The tradition recounts that Mahavira attained this enlightenment after spending two and a half days fasting in the heat of the sun, squatting near a tree but out of its shade. With these acts of extreme asceticism, his steadfastly nonviolent approach to life, and his supreme spiritual achievement of attaining *kevala*, Mahavira exemplifies Jainism's central ideals.

Now perfectly enlightened, Mahavira set about preaching the tenets of Jainism. His followers included eleven *ganadharas*, or disciples, who had been Hindu *brahmins* before hearing Mahavira's message. All of them eventually attained *kevala*, ending with Jambu, who is regarded as the last human being ever to attain *kevala* in this world cycle.

Mahavira preached for some thirty years until, at the age of seventy-two, he died in the town of Pava (like Vaishali, located in the northern Indian state of Bihar). Now liberated from his body, Mahavira's perfected soul is said to have ascended to the top of the universe in a state of eternal bliss.

Sculpture of Mahavira in the cave temples of Ellora, India.

It is helpful at this point to recall the similarities between the Buddhist accounts of Gautama's path to enlightenment (Chapter 3) and Mahavira's path to *kevala*. Both men practiced severe austerities. But whereas Mahavira continued on the path of strict asceticism to the very end of his life, Gautama, at the time of his enlightenment, rejected strict asceticism and instead embraced the Middle Way, which calls for moderation in the treatment of one's body. The distinction is highlighted during the climactic moments of each story, for while Gautama is said to have sat underneath the *bo* (or *bodhi*) tree when he experienced enlightenment, Mahavira is said to have squatted in the scorching heat of the sun, near a tree but apparently intentionally avoiding its shade.

Whatever the historical accuracy of these accounts, clearly the two traditions diverged over the question of the degree of ascetic rigor. Indeed, Buddhists typically held Jains in contempt for their extraordinary rigor, which for Jains has always been the hallmark of their religion and a mark of honor. And so, even though Buddhism and Jainism have a considerable amount in common doctrinally and even in terms of practice, the two traditions seem not to have engaged much with each other. Apparently it was this way from the beginning, for while Mahavira and Gautama the Buddha seem to have been at least near-contemporaries, none of the texts claim that they ever met.

An Eternal Succession of *Tirthankaras*

Jainism, like Hinduism and Buddhism, is categorized by scholars as being an "eternal" religion in the sense that it subscribes to an ongoing succession of world cycles, without beginning or end. Jains believe that twenty-four *tirthankaras*, or *jinas,* have appeared in this current world cycle. Mahavira is the latest in an infinite line of previous *tirthankaras*, but he is not expected to be the last.

All twenty-four *tirthankaras* of this world cycle are known by name and by their specific symbols: Mahavira by the lion, for example, and Parshva—of whom there are

Sandstone sculpture of Parshva, the *tirthankara* most commonly depicted in Jain art.

more sculptures in India than of any other *tirthankara*—by the serpent. Along with Parshva and Mahavira, however, the only additional *jinas* who play a prominent role in the scriptures and in the tradition generally are the first, Rishabha (symbolized by the bull), and the twenty-second, Nemi (symbolized by the conch shell). Rishabha, who is clearly legendary and not historical, is believed to have been the father of Bharata, whom Jains regard as the first world emperor of this world cycle. Nemi, in addition to being the predecessor to Parshva, is traditionally thought to be a relative of Krishna, whom many Hindus revere as an avatar (human incarnation) of the god Vishnu (Chapter 2). The nineteenth *tirthankara*, Malli (symbolized by the jar), is also especially notable, for according to the Shvetambara sect, Malli was a woman. The Digambaras, who in general are more conservative, deny this, regarding this *tirthankara* as a man by the name of Mallinatha.

Jainism and Hinduism

Throughout the centuries, Jainism has coexisted with Hinduism. The list of interesting and relevant points of contact between the two religious traditions is almost endless. Here we shall make note of just a few, in order to shed some light on the cultural interplay.

Jains commonly worship deities of the Hindu pantheon, and they tend to think of them in similar ways. There are, however, certain rather glaring exceptions. For example, Hindus would probably be surprised to learn from one popular Jain text that Rama and Krishna were both pious Jains. Also, the various Jain renditions of the *Mahabharata*, the great epic poem that, in its more standard form, is regarded with devotion by almost every Hindu, transform Krishna into a devious trickster. On the other hand, the *Bhagavad Gita*, which forms a very small portion of the *Mahabharata* and is typically regarded as Hinduism's most popular text, has been very favorably received by Jains. As for Hinduism's part in this cultural interplay, devotees of the god Vishnu have at times adopted the *tirthankara* Rishabha as being an avatar of their god. These few examples suffice at least to indicate the extensive interaction between Jain and Hindu religious and other cultural aspects.

Cultural interaction and similarities notwithstanding, Jainism is very much its own tradition. Among its more distinctive features is the very special status assigned to the *tirthankaras*. Jains believe them to be human—not gods or avatars of gods—but nevertheless to deserve the highest degree of veneration.

Jain reverence for twenty-four *tirthankaras*, as opposed to focusing on just one founding figure, is instructive with regard to some basic elements of the religion. Why, one might wonder, would more than one *jina* be needed? Human nature, Jainism would answer, is depraved to the point of needing repeated assistance from these spiritual masters. In a related manner, Mahavira is the last *jina* of the present world cycle because human nature has become continually *more* depraved. In the present state of affairs, *kevala* is no longer a possibility in this world, having been attained for the last time by Jambu, the disciple of Mahavira.

So, the next logical question is, what hope do human beings have if they are confined to this realm of *samsara*? What needs to happen before a *tirthankara* once again appears to show humanity how to cross the river from this shore to the beyond, the eternal realm of complete freedom and perfect bliss? Answers to such questions call for an analysis of Jain teachings.

We will now turn to a brief survey of Jain scriptures, the main source of Jain teachings. All Jains agree that, originally, there were fifty-eight books of scripture based on the preaching of Mahavira, who in turn based his views on the earlier *tirthankaras*. These books are divided into three categories: *Purva*, *Anga*, and *Angabahya*. But much is believed to have been lost. The Digambaras believe that only excerpts from one of the books of *Purva* survive; these excerpts, together with later commentaries written about them, constitute Digambara scripture. The Shvetambara sect, on the other hand, officially rejects the Digambara texts and follows instead eleven books of *Anga* and thirty-four books of *Angabahya*.

Ahimsa and Asceticism: Jainism's Ideals

We have observed how, in the ritual of *dana* ("giving") and in the ascetic practices of Mahavira, the principle of nonviolence functions as a basic ethical norm in Jainism. This principle, commonly known by its Sanskrit name **ahimsa**, is prevalent throughout the traditional religions of India. Hindus and Buddhists, for instance, all tend to favor vegetarianism because of its relative nonviolence. Jainism emphasizes the place of *ahimsa*, the "pure, unchangeable, eternal law" in this well-known passage from the *Acarangasutra*, the first book of the *Angas*:

> All breathing, existing, living, sentient creatures should not be slain,
> nor treated with violence, nor abused, nor tormented, nor driven away.
> This is the pure, unchangeable, eternal law which the clever ones, who
> understand the world, have proclaimed.[1]

All aspects of life are set in the context of avoiding injury toward "sentient creatures," an extensive category that includes not only human beings and animals but also plant life. Jain ascetics expand the category nearly to its logical extreme, striving even to avoid harming the atomic particles believed to pervade the natural elements.

The most distinctive characteristic of Jain doctrine, then, is *ahimsa*, the avoidance of doing injury to any life form. Or, put differently, Jains strive toward constant friendship with all fellow living creatures. As this striving becomes more intense, an ascetic lifestyle emerges naturally. Denying the body anything beyond what is necessary to sustain life lessens the risk of injuring other forms of life. Restricting one's diet to vegetables, for example, avoids doing violence to animals. On a more subtle level, straining one's water before drinking it (as we saw in this chapter's opening account of the Chandra household) and, indeed, drinking only as much water as is absolutely necessary further decreases violence, in this case to the small organisms that live undetected in drinking water.

Interrelated aspects of *ahimsa* are helpfully set forth by two other Jain concepts: *anekantavada* ("nonabsolutism") and *aparigraha* ("nonpossessiveness"). As stated in this introductory section of *Jain Way of Life*, a publication of the Federation of Jain Associations of North America, these three concepts—AAA—set forth the foundations of Jain teachings:

> Jainism is a religion and a way of life. For thousands of years, Jains have been practicing vegetarianism, yoga, meditation, and environmentalism. Jains have three core practices: Non-Violence, Non-Absolutism, and Non-Possessiveness (Ahimsa, Anekantvad, and Aparigraha—AAA).
>
> **Non-Violence** is compassion and forgiveness in thoughts, words, and deeds toward all living beings. For this reason, Jains are vegetarians.
> **Non-Absolutism** is respecting views of others. Jains encourage dialog and harmony with other faiths.
> **Non-Possessiveness** is the balancing of needs and desires, while staying detached from our possessions.[2]

In what ways is the teaching of nonviolence relevant for other world religions?

Another basic doctrine of Jainism is the need to diminish karma through limiting one's actions. In order to understand karma and Jain beliefs regarding spiritual fulfillment, it is best first to consider Jain cosmology, or its theory of the universe.

Theory of the Universe

According to tradition, Mahavira taught extensively and in detail about the nature of the universe, its makeup, and its functioning. He did so not merely as an intellectual exercise, but because, as he saw it, understanding the universe had sweeping implications for the spiritual quest. Thus, to understand Jain doctrine, one must understand Jain cosmology. We begin with considering the Jain concept of time, which incorporates the notion of eternally recurring cosmic or world cycles. Then we examine the makeup of the universe and all that exists within it.

Cosmic Cycles of Generation and Degeneration In keeping with the general Indian notion of *samsara*, Jainism conceives of time as cyclical and envisions the cycles as upward and downward turnings of a wheel. During the upward turning of the wheel (which proceeds through six spokes, or ages), the world is in a state of ascendancy, with all aspects of existence, notably including the moral propensity of human beings, in the process of improvement. The three upper spokes are considered to be a golden age of goodness and prosperity. Once passing the top of the wheel and entering into its downward turning, however, things begin gradually to decline, until the end of the age of the sixth spoke, at which point the universe reaches utter moral deprivation. Then the wheel once again begins its turn upward. And so it continues, eternally.

The traditional length of each of the six ages is 21,000 years. The world currently is in the age of the fifth spoke of the downward turning, called *Kali Yuga*, to be followed by the sixth, final period of degeneration. In this sixth age, the theory goes, people are more prone to immorality, and they become physically smaller. The consequences for the spiritual quest are pronounced, for human beings can no longer hope to attain *kevala* in this world until the wheel has once again begun its upward turning. Mahavira is the last of the *tirthankaras* of the turning of the wheel in which we now live, and his eleven *ganadharas*, ending with Jambu, are the last people to achieve liberation during this cycle. The wheel will need to advance considerably into its upward motion before anyone else can hope again to attain *kevala* in this world.

Notably, Rishabha, the first *tirthankara* of this downward turning of the world cycle, is believed to have appeared during the third spoke. Before that, the world was so healthy morally and spiritually that human beings did not need a *jina* to show them the way to liberation. Rishabha and the other early *tirthankaras* are understood to have been of greater physical stature than their successors.

The concept of *Kali Yuga* and the continuing downward turning of the wheel gives rise to a fundamental and serious question. If indeed *kevala* is no longer a possibility, what purpose is there in continuing to pursue the religious life? Thinking again of the *dana* ritual, why should laypeople like the Chandras go to the effort of giving so conscientiously to monks? And why would anyone opt to undergo the physical hardships of the ascetic life? Part of the answer depends on the nature of karma, which we will address next. Another part of the answer is provided through consideration of the composition of the universe, which Jains call the **loka** and regard as containing within it three distinct lands inhabited by human beings.

The Loka The *loka* is understood to be vast almost beyond description. Over the centuries, Jains have speculated as to just how vast the *loka* is, deriving a unit of measure known as the "rope," which is strikingly similar to the "light year" of modern astrophysics. According to one account, the *loka* is fourteen ropes from top to bottom. This means, according to traditional Jain calculations, that it would take a god, flying at the speed of 10 million miles per second, seven years to traverse its full span. These attempts at specifying the size of the universe are probably to be taken figuratively rather than literally. Still, a tendency toward something like scientific understanding is in keeping with the Jain belief that perfect and complete knowledge is attainable and indeed has been attained—namely, by Mahavira, his disciples, and the countless numbers of those who have achieved enlightenment before them.

The *loka*, then, is a vast and yet a finite space, within which all beings dwell. Beyond the *loka* there is nothing but strong winds. The *loka*, together with everything in it, has always existed and will continue to exist eternally. Jainism thus does not believe in a creator god.

Jains sometimes depict the *loka* as a diagram in the shape of a giant man, the *purusha*. Across the midsection runs a relatively small band known as the Middle Realm, which contains a series of oceans and continents, three of which together form the region inhabited by human beings. This region is further divided into various lands, one of which is India and another of which, Mahavideha, is not affected by the corruption of this world cycle and therefore continues to be the home of *tirthankaras* and of human beings who still can attain *kevala*. This notion is crucial when considering the quest for spiritual liberation that takes place in this corrupt world. As we shall discuss in more detail shortly, living a good life that is true to Jain ideals leads to a good rebirth, perhaps even in a land like Mahavideha, where *tirthankaras* currently reside and where *kevala* is a possibility.

Below the Middle Realm is a series of progressively darker hells, whose denizens suffer agonizing torments. At the very bottom of the *loka*, below the lowest hell, there are only clouds. Above the Middle Realm is a series of progressively brighter heavens, inhabited by deities who enjoy pleasures not unlike those of earthly rulers. For both the denizens of hell and the deities, their stays in those realms are only temporary, as they will eventually be reborn in another realm. In other words, just as in Hinduism and Buddhism, the realm of *samsara* extends well beyond the human domain. Because only humans can ever attain *kevala*, however, the Jains believe that even being reborn as a deity in one of the brightest heavens is ultimately not as fortunate as it might seem. The best rebirth is as a human being, so that the quest for spiritual fulfillment can be continued.

At the top of the *loka*, in the crown of the head of *purusha*, is a roof that is described as having the shape of an umbrella. Called the "slightly curved place," this is the eternal home of the souls that have been liberated from the realm of *samsara*.

Categories of Existence: *Jiva* and *Ajiva*   Jain scriptures spell out the categories of existing things in meticulous detail (in keeping with the belief in the omniscience of Mahavira and others who have attained *kevala*). The categories of existence can be said to begin with a simple distinction: that between the living, which is termed ***jiva***, and the nonliving, ***ajiva***. The nonliving is further divided into four: motion, rest, atoms, and space. These four basic entities plus the *jiva* are the five building blocks of all that exists in the universe. The entities interact, but forever maintain their individual existence. This view contrasts with the main form of Hindu cosmology, which envisions an ultimate union of all being. Furthermore, Jainism holds that the universe has an infinite number of atoms, forever distinct from one another, along with an infinite number of *jivas*, or souls.

Each *jiva* ("soul") is eternal, completely without form, and yet capable of interacting with the atoms of the body it inhabits in such a way that it can control the body's mechanisms. While avoiding the notion that the *jiva* is in any way dependent upon the body, Jainism does posit a complex integration of soul with body. Thus, while bodies do act, it is the soul that wills actions and therefore is held responsible for their moral quality.

All *jivas* are essentially equal, regardless of the bodies they inhabit. For example, the *jiva* of an insect is considered to be of identical quality to that of a large animal or a human being. This belief has significant implications with regard to the doctrine of *ahimsa*, as it encourages equal treatment of all living beings.

The great variety of bodies inhabited by the *jivas* produces many different life forms. Jainism's detailed classification of these life forms is among its most fascinating features, and one that shows remarkable similarities to the modern field of zoology. A simple twofold approach distinguishes life forms that are stationary, such as plants, from those that are moving. Another approach categorizes life forms based on the number of senses they have. In the words of one text:

> Up to the vegetable-bodied ones, selves have one sense [i.e., touch].
>   Worms, ants, bumblebees, and men each have one more than the one preceding.[3]

Human beings are thus categorized with life forms having five senses: deities, denizens of hell, and most animals aside from insects. Flying insects (bumblebees and the like) are thought to lack the sense of hearing, while most that crawl on legs also lack sight. Along with such insects as worms, shellfish are thought to have only the senses of touch and taste. Plants and "microbes" (a large category of the most basic life forms) are devoid of all sensations but touch.

More elaborate systems of classification abound in Jain scriptures. This fascination with the intricacies of life forms supports the religion's general concern for their welfare and for maintaining the attitude and practices that secure this welfare as best possible. To some extent, the attitude and practices of the religious life are expected of nonhuman life forms as well. Lions, for example, are said to be able to learn to fast. Even plants and the simplest microbes are believed to have some basic religious capacity that they can apply toward spiritual advancement. Ultimately, however, all *jivas* must be reborn as human beings before they have any chance of attaining *kevala* and release from the realm of *samsara*.

Liberation and Salvation

Many religions typically emphasize teachings concerning salvation or liberation, and Jainism is no exception. As our account will make clear, salvation depends on understanding the challenges of *samsara* and how to overcome them.

To begin, salvation in no way depends on the power of a deity. Just as Jainism has no creator god, neither does it have one to assist with the all-important quest for liberation. Some would thus label Jainism an atheistic religion, but this is not quite accurate. We have seen that in the Jain cosmology, deities inhabit the various heavens. Many of their names would be recognizable to the student of Hinduism, for the pantheons are similar. Thus Jainism might best be labeled *transtheistic*[4] in the sense that there are gods (in fact, a great variety of gods), but ultimately the religion moves beyond them when it comes to the truly crucial issues of salvation. To understand why this is, let us first examine Jainism's concept of karma.

Karma and the Human Condition Notwithstanding the intricate categories of existence, so far as the human condition is concerned, Jainism is best understood in terms of two categories: soul (*jiva*) and matter (*ajiva*). As noted earlier, the *jiva* is essentially pure and formless. And yet, for reasons that defy explanation, souls have become entwined with impure matter, causing them to be weighed down and bound to *samsara*. Human beings are born into this state. The religious life strives to clean away the dirt that tarnishes the *jiva*, returning it to its original state of pristine purity and releasing it from *samsara*, so it can ascend upward to the "umbrella" ceiling of the *loka*, the realm of liberated souls.

For Jains, the term karma refers to the process in which matter dirties the soul. In both Hinduism and Buddhism, karma is commonly understood as being the consequence of action per the law of cause and effect. This general definition applies to Jainism as well, but here the term's more literal meaning of "action" is stressed. Because all actions encumber the *jiva* with matter, whenever the soul wills an action, it risks tarnishing itself. Immoral actions, those that violate the principle of *ahimsa* or other Jain ethical teachings, are especially damaging because they dirty the *jiva* with heavier impurities. Highly virtuous actions, on the other hand, bring about only small quantities of light matter that neither cling to the soul nor weigh it down.

Along with this emphasis on the material aspects of karma, Jainism also emphasizes the intentions behind one's actions. That is, the immorality that tarnishes the soul with heavy matter lies mainly in the evil intention, not in the consequence of the action. Similarly, an action that might appear to have evil consequence could be considered moral if good was intended. For example, the accidental killing of microbes, provided proper means were taken to avoid it, would generally not be immoral and thus would not lead to the dirtying of the *jiva*.

***Kevala*: Omniscience That Leads to Liberation** *Kevala* is best translated as "omniscience"; one who has attained this state is a *kevalin*. Whereas Buddhist enlightenment (*bodhi*) incorporates the sort of knowledge that is vital for spiritual perfection (Chapter 3), Jain *kevala* is knowledge of everything: the nature of one's inner self, of one's past lives, and of the external world and all things, including fellow living beings (and their past lives and future lives) that inhabit it. Little wonder that Jainism so boldly sets forth cosmological explanations, based as they are on the omniscience of Mahavira and the other *tirthankaras*.

The most significant feature of *kevala* is that it frees the *jiva* completely from the tarnishing effects of karma so that it may be liberated. The final experience of liberation or release is known as *moksha* (as it is in Hinduism). *Moksha* and *kevala* are distinguishable in that one who has attained *kevala* normally goes on living in the physical body, confined to the realm of *samsara*, while one who achieves *moksha* is liberated from the body. Mahavira, like the *jinas* before him, passed many years as an enlightened one (sometimes referred to in Jainism, as in Buddhism, as *arhat*) before experiencing *moksha* at the time of his death, which finally freed him completely from any impurities that would bind him to the material world.

One might ask at this point whether omniscience leads to the purity of the soul or whether purification of soul brings about omniscience. A Jain might respond by asserting that the two work together harmoniously. This notion of religious impulses working in harmony is embodied in the Jain concept of the Three Jewels of the religion: right faith (*darshana*), right knowledge (*jnana*), and right practice (*caritra*). All three are integral to the religious quest. Right faith, which for Jainism involves a proper outlook or mindset, the correct way of "seeing" (which is the root meaning of *darshana*), nurtures right knowledge and practice. Likewise for the other Jewels; they function together like three legs of a stool.

The Quest for a Heavenly Rebirth We have noted that Jambu, the last of Mahavira's eleven disciples to attain *kevala*, is believed to be the last person of this world in the current cycle ever to achieve liberation. But this does not imply that for Jains living since Jambu's time it is meaningless to seek liberation. Every living being remains destined for rebirth, and the nature of rebirth depends on karmic status. A good rebirth, into the delights of one of the heavens or back into the human realm, therefore requires living a good life.

In contrast to Hindu and Buddhist beliefs, Jainism understands rebirth as occurring immediately after death. This has various implications that set Jainism apart from Buddhism and Hinduism, especially in regard to the need to perform rituals on behalf of the dead. For Jains, such rituals are deemed superfluous—which is not to say that Jains forgo mourning rituals or that they fail to honor their deceased loved ones. But the most crucial thing, the destiny of the deceased's soul, is determined as soon as the person dies. In fact, the soul is believed immediately to begin animating another life form.

Having examined the primary teachings of Jainism, we now turn our attention to the various ways these teachings have been manifested in Jain society and rituals.

THE HISTORY OF JAINISM

In the previous section, we have focused attention on Jain teachings. Turning now to a study of Jain history, we begin by considering the general place of Jainism in the context of Indian religions.

The Indian Historical Context

Earlier in this chapter we learned about the traditional understanding of Jainism's founding figures: the *tirthankaras* of this world cycle, most notably Mahavira. Here, our attention shifts to the scholarly understanding of Jainism's historical foundations, so we can observe some features of Indian religious culture that help situate the stories of the *tirthankaras* within a broader context.

Jains themselves do not regard Mahavira as having founded their religion. Historians, too, tend to agree with the traditional view that Mahavira himself followed an already established form of Jainism—possibly that of Parshva, the twenty-third *tirthankara* of this world cycle. Scholars situate Parshva's lifetime in the eighth century B.C.E. As noted previously, there are more sculptures in India of this *tirthankara* than of any other, Mahavira included, indicating his great popularity as an object of Jain devotion.

In the eighth century B.C.E., the probable period of Parshva, Indian civilization was beginning an important transition. The Vedic period, named for the Sanskrit texts that form the scriptural foundation of Hinduism, was ending, as was the domination of the priestly leadership of the *brahmin* caste (Chapter 2). Now began a period of religious diversity that included philosophical speculation on the *Upanishads* (themselves, technically, the last section of the Vedic corpus) and religious movements that eventually gave rise to Buddhism and the devotional forms of Hinduism that continue today. Parshva, and Mahavira after him, fit into a general category of religious movements that emphasized asceticism as a means of spiritual development.

Perhaps because of Jainism's belief in a never-ending succession of world cycles, Jains have not kept a detailed historical record of their own tradition. As we have seen, the dates for the lifespan of Mahavira are a matter of dispute, and so, too, is the place of his birth. The texts that contain the accounts were written hundreds of years after the fact. Much of the story of Jainism through its early centuries similarly does not lend itself to precise historical reckoning. With the religious changes of the period around 1000 C.E., the historical record begins to become clearer.

Jains' lack of emphasis on maintaining a detailed historical record seems to be based on religious belief—specifically, belief in a never-ending succession of world cycles. What is the relationship in other religions between religious beliefs and the relevance of history?

The Legacy of the *Tirthankaras*: Jainism through the Centuries

In the ninth century C.E., about the time that the influence of Buddhists was severely diminishing in India, the country's religious landscape was undergoing a rather sudden shift with the influx of Islam. Muslim rule was established in 1192 in the form of the Delhi Sultanate, which was succeeded in 1526 by the Mughal Empire. During the early centuries of Muslim rule, relations between Muslims and Jains were not always friendly. There are accounts of large-scale destruction of sacred Jain sites, for example, the pillaging by Muslims in 1313 of Mount Shatrunjaya, a major Jain pilgrimage site in the western state of Gujarat. But during the period of Mughal rule, and especially at its apex during the reign of Akbar the Great (1556–1605), remarkably close relations developed. Akbar himself was the close friend of a Jain leader, and he issued several decrees promoting the protection of animals, motivated apparently by learning about the Jain emphasis on *ahimsa*.

During the eighteenth and nineteenth centuries, Jainism became somewhat more diverse through the establishment of the Sthanakvasi and Terapanthi sects. In the twentieth century, immigration led to the establishment of Jain communities in various places around the globe.

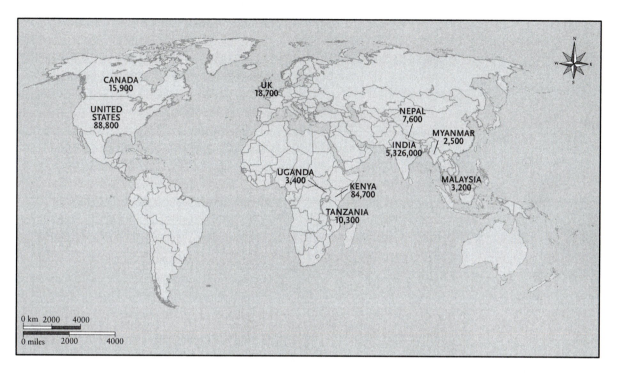

World Jain population.

Jainism in Today's World

The total number of Jains today is about 5.6 million, with all but about 275,000 living in India. Still, in India Jainism is dwarfed numerically by the Hindu population, which now numbers near 1 billion. In light of these numbers, the influence that Jainism has on Indian culture is quite remarkable. To some extent, this influence can be measured in financial terms. For centuries, Jains have been very successful in business, perhaps because of their religiously motivated focus on trade as opposed to agriculture. Also, the Jain community is highly respected for its charitable giving. In keeping with their profound emphasis on *ahimsa*, Jains commonly take in and care for animals that are maltreated or are targeted for slaughter. Although they generally do not actively seek converts to their religion, Jains tend to be outspoken advocates of universal vegetarianism, and so have exercised wide influence in this regard.

Among Jains of recent times, Shrimad Rajacandra (1867–1901; also spelled Rajchandra) is especially known outside India because of his connection to Mohandas (Mahatma) Gandhi. Both from the state of Gujarat, they met in 1891, and according to Gandhi's autobiography, Rajacandra made a strong impression and had a very positive impact on his spiritual development. Gandhi, of course, is perhaps the most famous advocate of *ahimsa* the world has ever known, even though he never overtly adopted Jainism as his religion.

Jain influence has also reached well beyond India through the Indian diaspora population. Their centuries-old focus on business has made life in the modern world a

Jain ascetics and impressive religious monuments, such as this nun on pilgrimage at Shravanabelagola, are common sights in India. Through its diaspora population of some 275,000 people, Jainism also has a significant presence outside of India.

relatively natural thing for the Jain laity. For ascetics, of course, life outside their traditional homeland is especially challenging; and indeed, it is quite rare, as only the Sthanakvasi and Terapanthi sects even allow monks and nuns to journey in the world at large. The Terapanthis are responsible, too, for having founded the first Jain university, recently established at Ladnum in the state of Rajasthan.

JAINISM AS A WAY OF LIFE

In the opening section of this chapter, we glimpsed a moment in the religious life of Jainism, the ritual of giving known as *dana*. While illustrating concern for the central Jain principles of *ahimsa* and the ascetic path, the ritual also indicates some of the diversity of the religion. For example, we noted features of the Digambara version of *dana* that are not found among Shvetambaras, and the basic distinction between the ascetics and the Jain laity was evident. In this section, we examine in greater detail these varieties of Jainism and consider other significant practices and characteristics of the Jain religious life.

Digambaras and Shvetambaras

Before highlighting those things that distinguish the Digambaras from the Shvetambaras, it is important to acknowledge the many things they share in common, including a general heritage of teachings and similar forms of practice. Still, the differences are interesting and instructive, helping to illustrate Jainism's rich diversity.

We have noted some differences at earlier points in the chapter. The two sects posit differing dates for the death of Mahavira (527 B.C.E. for Shvetambaras, 510 B.C.E. for Digambaras). The Digambaras deny that Mahavira ever married. In keeping with their generally more conservative views, Digambaras do not agree that the nineteenth *tirthankara*, whom the Shvetambaras know as Malli and the Digambaras as Mallinatha, was a woman.

The most obvious issue differentiating the two sects involves clothing. Digambara (or "sky-clad") monks, as their name infers (and as we have witnessed in the *dana* ceremony), go about naked; Digambara nuns do not, donning simple white garments like their counterparts in other Jain sects. From the Digambara perspective, wearing clothes puts monks back into the ordinary category of the laity. Nuns are not esteemed quite as highly as monks, and in general, Digambara doctrine is more severe than the other sects when it comes to spiritual deliverance of men versus women. In short, women (including nuns, even though they perform the same ascetic practices as monks) are deemed incapable of attaining *kevala;* they must await rebirth in a male body in order to reach the potential of final deliverance.

VOICES: An Interview with Girish Shah

Girish Shah was born in the Indian state of Gujarat, which is home to many Jains and to important pilgrimage destinations. He attended college in Mumbai and then left India to attend graduate school in the United States, where he now lives. A founding member and director of the Jain Center of Northern California and the Federation of Jain Associations in North America, Mr. Shah is dedicated to educating people about his religion.

What do you consider to be the most important reason for living a proper Jain religious life?

The goal is to become free of karma. To make your soul and its properties of infinite knowledge, infinite vision, infinite strength, and infinite capacity to character "clean," you have to get rid of all the karmas that are polluting it. For one to live a religious life it is important to achieve that. . . . But for me, the more important part of living the proper religious life is that it is the way you will support each other, it is the way you will serve each other. You are helping each other grow, and you are reciprocating, giving back. We need to have empathy toward everyone. Forgiveness is not for those who have done nothing to you; forgiveness is for someone who has hurt you.

Girish Shah

Do you consider Jainism to be an atheistic religion?

I think the question is what you mean by "atheistic religion." If you mean by atheistic religion god the creator and god the controller and god the sustainer; that there is an entity that created the world, that controls the world, that sustains the world, and that judges everybody, then no. We do not believe in god in that sense, but we do believe in the quality of the soul, which is godliness. Infinite compassion—that is the characteristic of soul. The knowledge, the vision, and working with and relating to everybody, comes from infinite compassion. And that has the power, that has the godlike characteristics. It doesn't control anything. Even our enlightened or *tirthankaras* cannot make me achieve *moksha*. They can show me the path, but cannot say, such as the gods will say, "I bless you." There is no blessing. There is no divine grace that anyone can give. Forgiveness has to be done by you, by your own action. The burden is on you completely, but you can achieve it. Jainism is the religion that says: "I am god" (if we call the *tirthankara* "god," which is the common word that we use). No other religion tells you that you can become god. But Jainism says everyone can become god.

How important to you are vegetarianism and other forms of *ahimsa*?

Very important. The idea is to minimize the amount of *himsa* that you are doing, and so you give up some of these things—at least for the important religious days, if not all the time. Some people will take vows to give up this or that for their entire lifetime. Increasingly I am becoming vegan, knowing that there is so much *himsa* in dairy. I have not become fully vegan, but hopefully some day I'll get there. Traditionally, milk was okay, because of the way cows were treated before. Now things have changed, and so we have to evolve and look at it. It's just sensitivity to it. Here is another example. I ask myself: "Why am I wasting natural resources?" I have a nice home. I have never felt the need to go beyond. This is my first house and my last house. I have no attachment to the house. People say, "Girish, you should be living in a beautiful big home," and I say, "What beautiful big home? Why do I need one?" It's all internalizing. I don't have the need. I have a four-bedroom house; it's big enough. That's plenty of space, 1,800 square feet. Why do I need a 7,000-square-foot house, why do I need a 10,000-square-foot house? Just because I can afford it doesn't mean that I should have it. . . . This is all part of *ahimsa*. It's all part of *ahimsa* because then you are not wasting your resources. Charity is a form of *ahimsa* because you are now using money that you made for the benefit of others, for their growth, their progress, their betterment of life. People need to have betterment of life beyond their basic needs in order for them to spiritually think. If you don't have enough even to eat and to think, you're not going to have spirituality.

You immigrated to the United States from India. What do you consider to be the most notable differences between being a Jain in India and being a Jain in the United States?

For Jains in India, things are taken for granted, whereas being a Jain here, you have to put up with a lot of issues. Every time I go shopping, it takes a half hour reading the ingredients to see how many animal products are in it. There is no green mark on food packaging here like we have in India, where you can look at it and say, green—it is vegetarian. Also, I can't walk to places here. In India, you walk to places. You don't have to use the car. To go shopping, to go to the temple, you walk. Here in California you have to drive, particularly when you drive here in summer, your car windshield is filled with all those butterflies that you're killing on the way. And so my wife refuses to travel at night. You're going to get up in the morning and go. You're not going to kill all those butterflies, just to get there at night.

Another identifying feature of the Digambara sect involves the ascetics' avoidance of alms bowls as means of collecting food, using instead only their cupped hands. The reasoning is based in the principle of *ahimsa:* washing of bowls presumably would bring about greater harm to living beings. The same reasoning supports the "sky-clad" practice of monks, for the washing of dirty clothes causes harm. Finally, as previously noted, the Digambaras have their own official collection of scriptures.

A sizable majority of Jains are Shvetambaras. Since about the thirteenth century C.E., they have followed their set of forty-five sacred texts as authoritative. Unlike the Digambaras, they use alms bowls when begging for food; they accept the possibility of a woman attaining *kevala;* and, of course, they wear clothing (monks and nuns alike), consisting of upper and lower white garments.

Interestingly, even Shvetambara texts make clear that Mahavira and his early male followers went about naked. Gradually the opinion arose among Shvetambaras that the wearing of clothes was an option. One text from the second or third century C.E. designates three specific factors making this permissible: embarrassment; causing others to feel disgust; and inability to endure hardships caused by nakedness.[5]

Sthanakvasis and Terapanthis Within Shvetambara Jainism, two distinctive sects, the Sthanakvasi and the Terapanthi, have features that distinguish them somewhat from their parent. Most significantly, they both reject the worship of images, which is a common religious practice among the majority of Shvetambaras. Ascetics of both sects constantly wear the *muhpatti* ("mouthshield"), a cloth that protects insects from accidentally being inhaled as the monks and nuns traverse the land. And both sects allow monks and nuns to travel abroad.

The Sthanakvasis trace their origins to the seventeenth century. Today there are over 3,000 Sthanakvasi ascetics, about five-sixths of whom are nuns. A relatively liberal sect, the Sthanakvasis allow nuns to travel unaccompanied by monks.

The Terapanthis revere as their founder the Shvetambara reformer Ācārya Bhikshu (1726–1803; *ācārya* is a general term in Jainism for "leader" of a group of ascetics). He implemented what is perhaps the most characteristic Terapanthi teaching: drawing a strict distinction between the worldly sphere and the religious sphere, Bhikshu declared that it is not possible to earn merit through deeds involving the worldly sphere. For example, whereas most Jains consider it highly meritorious to purchase animals from butchers in order to set them free, the Terapanthis reject this.

The Ascetic Life

Through their biographies and teachings, the *tirthankaras*, "makers of the river crossing," show the way to liberation to all Jains. However, as neither the *tirthankaras* nor any Jain deities can bestow salvation, all individuals must make their own spiritual progress and eventually attain their own deliverance. Moreover, as noted, Jains believe that the ascetic life offers the spiritual path that best replicates the lives and follows the

VISUAL GUIDE
Jainism

Jain emblem. Incorporating a variety of symbols, the Jain emblem's outline represents the *loka*, or universe. The swastika, an ancient and common symbol in Hinduism, Buddhism, and other religious traditions, is very prominent in Jainism; its four arms represent the four realms of life (heavens, human realm, animal realm, hells). The hand represents *ahimsa*.

Tirthankara. Sculptures of *tirthankaras*, like this one of Rishabha, whom Jains revere as the first of the current world cycle, are objects of Jain worship.

Whisk. Shown here with a book of Jain scripture, the whisk is used by ascetics to clear away, and thus to protect, insect life. It symbolizes *ahimsa*.

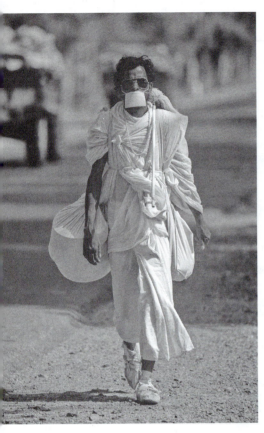

A Jain monk wearing the *muhpatti* in order to prevent unnecessary harm to airborne insects.

teachings of the *jinas*. Still, no one expects the average Jain to enter upon this arduous path. Simply having entered into the human realm does not imply that one is ready for the ascetic life. A Jain takes this life on gradually, after having become an accomplished layperson who fulfills all religious duties successfully and with a pure disposition. When the circumstances are right, whether in this lifetime or in a future lifetime, the decision to renounce the lay life and become an ascetic is made.

It almost goes without saying that the decision of renunciation is not to be made lightly. The initiation ritual, *diksha*, marks the point at which the individual becomes completely committed to the ascetic life. Through the centuries, minimum age requirements have been imposed—young adulthood for the Digambara sect, younger for the Shvetambaras (historically, as young as age 6, although today only the Terapanthi sect permits the initiation of young children). The ceremony includes a symbolic removal of hair (via the traditional method of being pulled out tuft by tuft) and presentation to the initiate of the whisk and other implements of the ascetic life, such as the alms bowl for Shvetambaras. *Diksha* is overseen by a teacher, who typically continues to provide guidance to the new ascetic. The ritual marks the symbolic rupturing of the participant's past and future lifestyles, usually involving total separation from one's family, although Shvetambara nuns are on occasion allowed to interact with family members.

Ascetics depend on the almsgiving of the Jain laity, and sometimes of Hindus, in order to eat. Usually wandering in groups, they spend eight months of the year traversing the land, and then four months, during the rainy season, with lay communities. By remaining settled during this wet period, the ascetics do not jeopardize the well-being of life forms, which tend to be on the roads in greater numbers because of the rains. So, once again, the principle of *ahimsa* underlies Jain practice.

The Five Great Vows All ascetics commit to five "Great Vows" that serve as the doctrinal groundwork of both their inner purity of intention and their outer purity of action:

1. Avoid inflicting violence (*ahimsa*) on other life forms.
2. Abstain from lying.
3. Do not take what has not been given.
4. Renounce sexual activity.
5. Renounce possessions.

Jain texts expand on these vows in great detail, elaborating on the subtleties of their content and means of satisfactorily fulfilling them. As you might expect, most attention is devoted to the first vow, as *ahimsa* is understood to be the foundation of the entire ethical outlook of Jainism. Each of the other four vows is interrelated to *ahimsa*. For example, the third vow (not to take what is not given) is interpreted to mean, in its most profound sense, not to take a life. The fifth vow is understood also to imply avoidance of violence, for to renounce possessions is to deflect the passion that arises through attachments to them. Passion is thought to be a primary cause of violence.

Ascetic Practices The basic impulse toward asceticism, so pervasive throughout the history of Jainism, is grounded in two objectives: the avoidance of further dirtying of the *jiva* with karmic matter and the eventual burning off of the matter that has already tainted it. Specific practices are prescribed in Jain texts, notably the Six Obligatory Duties, which for the Shvetambara sect are enumerated as follows (the Digambara list differs only slightly):

1. Equanimity, achieved through meditation
2. Praise of the *tirthankaras*
3. Veneration of teachers
4. Repentance
5. Laying down the body (standing or sitting motionless for varying periods of time)
6. Abandonment (renunciation of specific foods or activities for a certain period of time)

The Six Obligatory Duties are to be performed by all ascetics and, ideally, by laypeople as well. Specifics of each duty are developed in the texts. The duty of repentance, for example, involves acknowledging wrongdoings before one's teacher twice daily and ends with the recitation of a passage well known to Jains: "I ask pardon from all living creatures. May all creatures pardon me. May I have friendship for all creatures and enmity towards none."[6]

Perhaps the most startling Jain ascetic practice in the view of outsiders is *sallekhana*, the intentional fasting of oneself to death. Although this practice was quite common in earlier times and is believed to have been the form of dying adopted by Mahavira and other great ascetics of the past, today it is rare. Insistent that *sallekhana* is in no way suicidal, Jains argue that, because the act of eating generally involves the risk of harming other life forms, fasting even to the point of ending one's own life is a highly effective means of warding off karma. In general, an individual's mindset at the moment of death is considered to be a significant factor for the prospects of rebirth, and so *sallekhana*, lacking the passion and violence that regularly accompanies suicide and instead fostering a tranquil and meditative state, is thought to provide an ideal means of dying.

Jain laypeople look to monks and nuns as exemplars of Jain ideals. What similar sorts of exemplars are present in other religions?

Jainism and Women

We have observed that among Jain ascetics the places and roles of women and men vary considerably. The relatively conservative Digambaras allow only monks, not nuns, to go about naked, and they deny that women can attain *kevala*. They, unlike the Shvetambaras, also insist that the nineteenth *tirthankara* was a man. In general, there tend to be fewer distinctions between monks and nuns among Shvetambara Jains. The Sthanakvasi subsect, in which nuns outnumber monks by about five to one, can be said to be relatively liberal, even among Shvetambaras. One Sthanakvasi group has recently taken the unprecedented step of promoting a nun, Candanājī, to the rank of *ācārya*.

The long history of Jainism reveals some diversity with regard to the places and roles of women and men. One ancient text states that the original group of Mahavira's followers, both the laity and the ascetics, was composed mostly of women. It also states that during Mahavira's lifetime 1,400 women, as opposed to 700 men, attained *kevala*.[7]

For most of Jain history, however, women have tended to be regarded as less spiritually capable than men, even among the Shvetambaras. Recently, attitudes have begun to shift. For example, the long-standing assumption that women are prone to lead men away from virtuous lives by tempting them and arousing passions has gradually subsided. Today, the moral fortitude of the chaste Jain woman provides a role model for the proper behavior of women and men alike.

It almost goes without saying that Jain laywomen occupy vital roles within the family and community, roles that, especially until recently, have tended to differ from those of men, but that have been vital nonetheless. In the chapter's opening vignette we entered the home of the Chandras and observed the ritual of giving known as *dana*. It is difficult to imagine such a scene without the presence of the wife, who takes a leading role in managing the household affairs and raising the children. The fact that women tend to be less involved than men in business and other professional concerns means that they tend to have more time and energy to devote to the important lay religious practice of fasting.

The Dilwara Temple on Mount Abu in the state of Rajasthan is famous for its exquisite, delicate carvings and architectural design.

The Religious Life of the Jain Laity

Although Jainism is best known for its asceticism, a balanced understanding of the religion demands a careful look at the role of the laity. For one thing, lay adherents constitute the great majority of Jains. Also, even as the laity looks to the monks and nuns as exemplars of Jain ideals, the ascetics themselves depend on the lay community for their livelihood and support. These two components, in other words, function hand in hand. The worship activities of the Jain laity are rich and diverse and have for centuries been a vital part of the religious life of India.

Jain worship occurs on two separate levels. At the more mundane level, the objects of worship are various gods who, as we have noted, tend to be the same as those worshipped by Hindus. While having nothing to do with the ultimate religious pursuit of liberation, the gods are believed to respond to material needs, such as providing weather favorable for agriculture and cures for health maladies.

On a more sublime level, Jains worship the *tirthankaras*—even though they, like the gods, are unable actively to assist a worshipper in achieving salvation. Nevertheless, worship of the *tirthankaras* nurtures a properly devout religious attitude; its net effect is to burn off the dirtying karma that weighs down the soul. It is this second level of worship that warrants our consideration here.

Religious Places In its most visible form, Jain worship concentrates on images of the *tirthankaras*, although, as we have observed, the Sthanakvasis and Terapanthis shun this. Most of this worship takes place in temples, some of which rank among India's most impressive architectural achievements. For example, the Dharna Vihara at Ranakpur in the state of Rajasthan, which is dedicated to the *tirthankara* Rishabha, is remarkable for its unique four-directional design, four-faced image of the *tirthankara*, and 1,400 carved columns. Along with such spectacular temples as the Dharna Vihara, many temples coexist with shops and offices on city streets, indistinguishable from the neighboring buildings.

Jain sacred places also include various sites in the countryside, such as Mount Shatrunjaya in Gujarat in western India, one of five sacred mountains for Shvetambara Jains. Hundreds of shrines are located at Mount Shatrunjaya, and one textual tradition predicts that nineteen future *tirthankaras* will spend time preaching there.

Pilgrimages to places like Mount Shatrunjaya constitute an important aspect of lay worship. In fact, every Jain strives to make at least one pilgrimage in his or her lifetime. Typically undertaken at considerable expense, the pilgrimage offers each lay individual an opportunity to experience, through the interruption of normal life and the rigors of journeying to the site, an ascetic lifestyle for a temporary period. This experience allows for the concentration of effort in gaining karmic merit. Traditionally, pilgrimages were made on foot, and this is still the mode of transportation for ascetics. Today, laypeople often travel by train or other modern means. Sometimes the expenses for entire groups of pilgrims are paid for by one person, who is thought to gain much karmic merit through the act of benevolence.

Rituals and Observances In addition to the relatively rigorous periods of pilgrimage, the religious life of the Jain laity overlaps with that of the ascetics in some everyday aspects. All Jains are

Shatrunjaya, a hill near the town of Palitana, India, and for centuries an important Jain pilgrimage site, features 863 temples of various sizes and styles.

careful with regard to their eating habits. They are diligently vegetarian, and go well beyond abstaining from meat by avoiding such things as eggs, vegetables, and fruits with a large number of seeds in order not to destroy life forms unnecessarily. Fasting, a very common practice among ascetics, also is quite common among the laity, especially, as we have seen, among women.

These similarities notwithstanding, it is easy to observe that in almost every way, the ascetics' religious life demands significantly more by way of exertion and endurance of physical hardships than does the religious life of most laypeople, who strive mainly to behave morally in order to ebb the flow of harmful karma and thus to foster a good rebirth. As we observed at the outset of this chapter, the ritual of *dana* (the giving of food to monks and nuns) provides one opportunity to be a good Jain layperson and to enhance one's karmic status. A somewhat similar practice involves bidding for the right to sponsor rituals, with any extra money being donated to charitable causes and the winning bidder gaining in social esteem. Whenever a new image of a *tirthankara* is erected or installed in a temple, for example, rituals are performed to celebrate each of the "five auspicious events" of a *tirthankara's* life: conception, birth, renunciation, attainment of *kevala*, and *moksha*. The person who sponsors the building of such an image and funds the rituals is said to acquire very positive karmic merit, so that the person likely will be born into a world blessed with a living *tirthankara*.[8]

A formalized system of religious observance features the Twelve Vows for the layperson. The first of the Vows, for instance, makes clear that it is the intentionality, rather than specific action, that most matters with regard to *ahimsa*. Proper intentionality is involved, for example, in choosing the right profession, one that would not likely result in violence toward sentient life forms. As a result, Jains through the centuries have tended to engage in trade and other forms of business. Obviously harmful occupations such as hunting and fishing are strictly prohibited; farming is acceptable because it can be done without *intentionally* harming life forms. Trade and business, however, are generally considered optimal because they can be done without causing any harm at all.

CONCLUSION

In this chapter, we have learned about Jainism's teachings, historical development, and way of life. One of the world's oldest traditions, Jainism today remains relatively small, with only about 5.6 million adherents, and also relatively confined to its place of origin, with the great majority of Jains living in India. This tendency for the tradition to maintain itself demographically and geographically is natural for Jains, who do not actively seek converts to Jainism and, even when living outside of India, tend to maintain strong ties to the motherland.

Like every religion in the world today, however, Jainism has become diverse, as indicated by the differences between the sects. Some aspects of the religion are more adaptable to modernization, pluralism, and other contemporary forces, and some are less adaptable. In this regard, Jainism as a whole can perhaps best be summed up as a tradition that is both eternally constant and constantly evolving. At one extreme, a group of monks and nuns wandering the countryside, sweeping ahead of their bare feet with their whisks, hardly fit into the picture of the modern world. Paradoxically, these same ascetics carry on a tradition of cosmology that appears remarkably modern relative to most traditionally religious points of view. Moreover, the social consciousness of Jains—expressed in their advocacy of vegetarianism and other forms of nonviolence—is in step with many who are concerned over the state of the world, the environment, and humanity's plight.

SEEKING ANSWERS

What Is Ultimate Reality?

Like Hinduism and Buddhism, Jainism maintains belief in *samsara*, the wheel of life. Time is conceived of as being cyclical, such that this world is but one in an eternal sequence of worlds that have come to be. The Jain perspective on space features the *loka*, a vast expanse that includes three realms inhabited by human beings. Jainism does not emphasize the importance of deities, even to the point of appearing atheistic; it can be considered a *transtheistic* religion. Souls (*jivas*) and matter (*ajiva*) are believed to exist eternally. Ultimate reality for Jainism might best be identified as *kevala*, the supreme state in which the eternal soul is perfectly pure.

How Should We Live in This World?

Jainism bases its ethical teachings on the principle of *ahimsa* (nonviolence) and on the accompanying value of asceticism. Both are exemplified by Mahavira and the other *tirthankaras*, and Jain monks and nuns continue to act as exemplars. Jainism understands human beings—like every other sentient being—to be made up of a soul (*jiva*) combined with bodily matter (*ajiva*). This matter is believed to contaminate the soul and thus to weigh it down and to prevent it from attaining spiritual perfection. Jains explain this through their doctrine of karma, understanding the term in its literal sense as "action."

What Is Our Ultimate Purpose?

Jains believe that eventually every soul will become perfectly pure, allowing it to rise to the top of the *loka* in the transcendent state of *kevala*, the Jain equivalent of Buddhist nirvana or Hindu *moksha*. Jains also believe that the soul that does not experience *kevala* is destined for rebirth, which is understood to occur immediately after death and is determined by the adequacy of one's spiritual and moral life in this world. Death, then, does not "end it," and mortality for Jains involves the prospect of a good rebirth.

REVIEW QUESTIONS

For Review

1. What is the role of Mahavira as one of Jainism's *tirthankaras*?
2. How do Jain practices of asceticism promote the cause of *ahimsa*?
3. What is the *loka*?
4. Identify and briefly describe the various Jain sects.
5. Differentiate the main religious duties of the Jain laity from those of the ascetics, and explain what religious advantages a monk or nun might have over members of the laity.

For Further Reflection

1. Compare the biographies of Nataputta Vardhamana (Mahavira) and Siddhartha Gautama (the Buddha), focusing especially on the episodes of attaining enlightenment.
2. What is the relationship between Jain cosmology and the Jain perspective on spiritual liberation? Consider especially the classification of reality into *ajiva* and *jiva* and how this relates to the quest for spiritual liberation.
3. What is *kevala*? How does it compare to Buddhist *nirvana*? To Hindu *moksha*?

GLOSSARY

ahimsa (ah-him'suh; Sanskrit, "nonviolence," "not desiring to harm") Both the avoidance of violence toward other life forms and an active sense of compassion toward them; a basic principle of Jainism, Hinduism, and Buddhism.

ajiva (uh-jee'vuh; Sanskrit, "nonsoul") Nonliving components of the Jain universe: space, time, motion, rest, and all forms of matter.

dana (dah'nuh; Sanskrit, Pali, "giving") Ritual of giving.

Digambara (dig-ahm'buh-ruh; Sanskrit, "those whose garment is the sky") The second largest Jain sect, whose monks go about naked so as to help abolish any ties to society; generally more conservative than the Shvetambara sect.

jina (ji'nuh; Sanskrit, "conqueror") Jain title for one who has "conquered" *samsara;* synonymous with *tirthankara.*

jiva (jee'vuh; Sanskrit, "soul") The finite and eternal soul; also the category of living, as opposed to nonliving, entities of the universe.

karma (Sanskrit, "action") "Action" and the consequences of action; determines the nature of one's reincarnation; in Jainism, all activity is believed to involve various forms of matter that weigh down the soul (*jiva*) and thus hinder the quest for liberation.

kevala (kay'vuh-luh; shortened form of Sanskrit *kevalajnana,* "isolated knowledge" or "absolute knowledge") The perfect and complete knowledge or omniscience that is Jain enlightenment; marks the point at which one is free from the damaging effects of karma and is liberated from *samsara.*

loka (loh'kah; Sanskrit, "world") The Jain universe, often depicted as having the shape of a giant man.

Shvetambara (shvayt-ahm'buh-ruh; Sanskrit, "those whose garment is white") The largest Jain sect, whose monks and nuns wear white robes; generally more liberal than the Digambara sect.

tirthankaras (teert-hahn'kuhr-uhs; Sanskrit, "makers of the river crossing") The Jain spiritual heroes, such as Parshva and Mahavira, who have shown the way to salvation; synonymous with *jinas.*

SUGGESTIONS FOR FURTHER READING

Dundas, Paul. *The Jains*. 2nd ed. London: Routledge, 2002. A thorough and scholarly study that has become a standard reference work for students and academics alike.

Jain, Satish Kumar, and Kamal Chand Sogani, eds. *Perspectives in Jaina Philosophy and Culture*. New Delhi: Ahimsa International, 1985. Helpful insights from within the Jain tradition.

Jaini, Padmanabh S. *The Jaini Path of Purification*. 2nd ed. Columbia, MO: South Asia Books, 2001. The first comprehensive work in English that offers a sympathetic study of the religion, this modern-day classic has been revised and updated.

Lopez, Donald S. Jr., ed. *Religions of India in Practice*. Princeton, NJ: Princeton University Press, 1995. Offering some translations for the first time, this anthology presents a wide range of texts well beyond the usual collections of sacred writings.

Radhakrishnan, Sarvepalli, and Charles A. Moore, eds. *A Sourcebook in Indian Philosophy*. Princeton, NJ: Princeton University Press, 1957. A standard anthology of sacred texts in English translations.

ONLINE RESOURCES

The Wabash Center
wabashcenter.wabash.edu/resources
The Wabash Center, a trusted resource for all aspects of the academic study of religion, offers links to a wide variety of dependable Internet resources on Jainism.

The Jaina
jaina.org
The Jaina (Federation of Jain Associations in North America) website is especially useful for studies of Jainism in North America.

SIKHISM

MANJIT KAUR, a sixteen-year-old girl, and Sandeep Singh, a fourteen-year-old boy, stand in the **gurdwara**, the place of Sikh worship, in their small village in northwestern India. Here in the region known as the Punjab, Sikhism's ancestral homeland, Manjit and Sandeep are members of the majority religion, and *gurdwaras* are common sights in the farming villages that dot the land. Most of the village has gathered together to witness the proceedings, and Sandeep and Manjit have spent the morning preparing for this momentous event—their initiation into the Sikh **Khalsa**, or community of "Pure Ones." They have both bathed and washed their long hair carefully and have dressed especially for the occasion. Most notably, they both don the five articles of faith, known as the Five Ks: uncut hair, a comb, a steel wristlet, a short sword, and a pair of shorts.

Manjit and Sandeep join a group of five older villagers who also don the Five Ks and who for this ceremony play the part of the *Panj Piare*, or "Beloved Five." They are established members of the Khalsa and will oversee the initiation. The grouping of five recalls the founding of the Khalsa centuries ago, when Guru Gobind Singh (1675–1708 C.E.), the tenth in a line of Gurus going back to Guru Nanak (1469–1539 C.E.), chose five original initiates who had distinguished themselves for their loyalty to the Guru and for their commitment to Sikh ideals. On this day of *Amrit Sanchar*, the Khalsa initiation ceremony, the stirring memory of

The five Sikh men who participate in the *Amrit Sanchar* represent the original "Beloved Five" in commemoration of the founding of the Khalsa.

these founding figures and the ideals they embody is palpably felt. But the most vital presence of all is a large book, lying open on a special platform. It is Sri Guru Granth Sahib, or the **Adi Granth**, the sacred scripture of Sikhism, and the Sikhs' **Guru**, or spiritual teacher, from the time of Guru Gobind Singh forward.

Sandeep and Manjit stand before the *Panj Piare*, one of whom explains the basic principles of Sikhism. They agree to accept these principles by nodding, the ritual action that makes the initiation official. The new members of the Khalsa are then served **amrit** ("immortalizing fluid"), a special drink made from water and sugar crystals, which has been mixed by the *Panj Piare* in an iron bowl and stirred with a two-edged sword. Meanwhile, hymns from the Adi Granth are sung by the congregation. The *amrit* is drunk and sprinkled on the eyes and heads of the initiates, who recite the **Mul Mantra**, the summary of Sikh doctrine that comprises the opening lines of the Adi Granth. The *Panj Piare* then instruct Manjit and Sandeep about the ethical requirements of the Khalsa. These include prohibitions against the cutting of one's hair, the eating of meat that has been improperly slaughtered, extramarital sexual relations, and the use of tobacco. The initiates are also told that all Sikhs are brothers and sisters and that there should not be any distinctions made on the basis of caste.

Significant sites in the history of Sikhism.

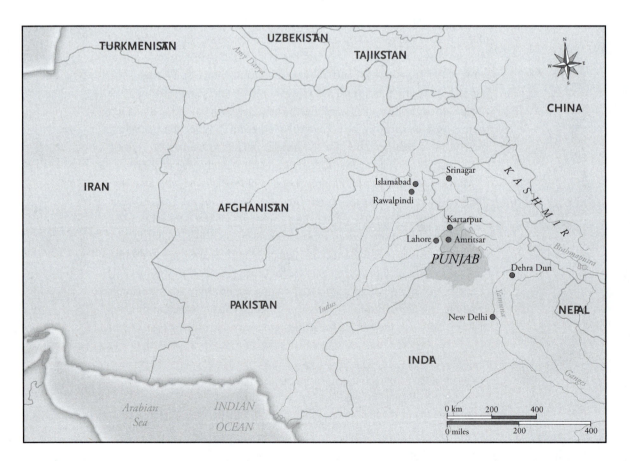

Manjit and Sandeep are among a minority of Sikhs, approximately 15 percent, who undergo the traditional ceremony of initiation into the Khalsa. Some 70 percent of the approximately 25 million Sikhs in the world,[1] however, are popularly considered to be members of the Khalsa, insofar as they observe the Five Ks, or at least the one that is generally deemed most important: not cutting one's hair.[2] And regardless of percentages or degrees of membership, the traditional ways of the Khalsa greatly influence the practices and customs of the entire **Panth**, or Sikh community. We can thus glimpse in this ceremony, with its powerful ties to tradition and its rich symbolism, key aspects that are at the heart of Sikhism. ※

TIMELINE
Sikhism

1469 C.E. Birth of Guru Nanak, founder of Sikhism.

1520s Establishment by Guru Nanak of the township of Kartarpur, the first Sikh community.

1539 Death of Guru Nanak.

1606 Death (execution?) of Guru Arjan, under Mughal emperor Jahangir.

1675 Execution of Guru Tegh Bahadur, under Mughal emperor Aurangzeb.

1699 Founding of the Khalsa by Guru Gobind Singh.

1708 Death of Guru Gobind Singh and establishment of the Adi Granth as Guru.

1799 Establishment of independent Sikh kingdom by Ranjit Singh.

1849 Annexation of Sikh kingdom by the British.

1947 Partition of Punjab with the establishment of India's independence.

1984 Indian army attacks and occupies Sikh holy sites, including the Darbar Sahib (or Golden Temple).

1999 The Panth celebrates the third centennial of the establishment of the Khalsa.

2004 Manmohan Singh elected prime minister of India, the first Sikh to attain this office.

I n this chapter we shall study these and other key aspects, attending in turn to the founding of Sikhism and its primary doctrines, its historical development, and its most prevalent rituals and worship practices. By virtue of its size alone, Sikhism is among the major religions of the world. Theologically, Sikhism's intermixing of concepts that are common to some Hindu traditions on one hand and to Islam on the other make it a very interesting subject for the comparative study of religion. And with nearly 2 million Sikhs living outside of India, and Sikh communities being found today in most of the large cities of the West, Sikhism clearly is a global tradition that has a significant impact on the world.

THE TEACHINGS OF SIKHISM

The term *Sikh* is derived from an ancient Sanskrit term that means "disciple." Sikhs are thus disciples, specifically of the ten Gurus, beginning with Guru Nanak and ending with Guru Gobind Singh, founder of the Khalsa. Since then, Sikhs have been disciples of Sri Guru Granth Sahib, the traditional name for their most important sacred text, the Adi Granth. A sound understanding of Sikhism therefore must begin with a consideration of the origins of this line of Gurus.

By the time Guru Nanak had come on the scene, the important role of the guru had long been established within Hindu traditions of northern India. A guru is a spiritual teacher. *Guru* is actually used in three slightly different ways in Sikhism. Along with being the title of Guru Nanak and his successors and of the sacred text (Sri Guru Granth Sahib), it is used as a name for God. (In fact, *Vahiguru*, "Praise to the Guru," is the most common name for God used by Sikhs today.) In each case the guru functions as the teacher of God's will. As Sikhs believe that God lovingly reveals the divine will to humans, God, too, thus functions as Guru.

We now consider the career of the guru of northern India whose extraordinary life experiences and bold spiritual leadership were to have such a profound impact that a new religion would arise.

The Life of Guru Nanak

Nanak was born in 1469 C.E. in the small village of Talvandi (modern-day Nankan Sahib, located near Lahore, Pakistan). He was born to Hindu parents of a mercantile caste who probably were worshippers of Vishnu (for more information about the caste system and the worship of Vishnu, see Chapter 2). His parents arranged for him to marry early, when he was still in his teens, as was customary at the time. Nanak and his wife, Sulakhani, moved to Sultanpur, where Nanak's older sister Nanaki lived. Soon Nanak and Sulakhani had two sons.

Sultanpur, located on the main rode between Lahore and Delhi, was a religiously diverse community, with residents and visitors who practiced varieties of Hinduism and Islam. Nanak, who is said to have been dissatisfied with traditional forms of religion, gravitated toward a religious outlook similar to Hindu *bhakti*, the path of devotion (see Chapter 2). Nanak believed in the oneness of God and in the need to move closer to God. This could best be accomplished, he believed, through meditation and singing hymns in praise of God. Eventually Nanak began composing his own hymns. With his friend Mardana, a Muslim musician, accompanying him on the *rebab* (a stringed instrument), Nanak sang his hymns at communal worship gatherings. These hymns are included in the Adi Granth and are sung in Sikh services today.

According to tradition, Nanak became recognized as a spiritual leader early in his life. He would rise before dawn and bathe in the river, meditate, and then lead others in singing hymns of praise. When Nanak was about thirty years old, he underwent a crucial experience that led to the origin of the Sikh tradition.

Sikhs pay homage to Guru Nanak, the founder of Sikhism, in a crowded room in Lahore, Pakistan.

Receiving God's Revelation One morning while Nanak was bathing in the river, he did not resurface from the water. He was presumed drowned, and yet his body was not found. Three days and three nights later, however, Nanak emerged from the river, and, returning to the village, he proclaimed: "There is neither Hindu nor Muslim so whose path shall I follow? I shall follow God's path. God is neither Hindu nor Muslim and the path which I follow is God's."[3]

When he explained what had happened, Nanak said that he had been escorted to the court of God, who gave him a cup of *amrit* (the same drink that is used in the Khalsa initiation ceremony) and said to him:

> This is the cup of the adoration of God's name. Drink it. I am with you. I bless you and raise you up. Whoever remembers you will enjoy my favor. Go, rejoice in my name and teach others to do so. I have bestowed the gift of my name upon you. Let this be your calling.[4]

The Journeys of Guru Nanak Deeply moved by this revelation, Guru Nanak spent the next stage of his life, from age thirty to about age fifty, traveling far and wide and learning about a variety of religious customs, including Hindu, Muslim, and Jain. He is said to have undertaken four long journeys: eastward to Assan; southward to Sri Lanka; northward to the Himalayas; and westward, reaching as far as Mecca and Baghdad. He visited holy sites and encountered a wide variety of religious people. He also proclaimed and practiced his own teachings, sometimes to hostile audiences.

Several incidents during Guru Nanak's travels illuminate the new message he proclaimed. On one occasion, while visiting a Hindu shrine in Haridwar, India, he found himself among *brahmins* throwing water toward the rising sun as an offering to their dead ancestors. Nanak turned and threw water the other way, explaining, "If you can send water to your dead ancestors in heaven, surely I can send it to my fields in the Punjab."[5] On another occasion, Nanak was awakened from sleep by an angry Muslim who chastised him for sleeping with his feet pointing toward the Ka'ba in Mecca, the most sacred site in Islam. (Showing the soles of one's feet is considered by many Muslims to be a grave insult.) Nanak responded: "Then turn my feet in some other direction where God does not exist."[6]

Such stories as these illustrate a general theme of Nanak's religious outlook. He consistently rejected traditional rituals and "proper" religious protocol, whether Hindu or Muslim.

Founding the Sikh Community Drawing from his revelation experience and years of journeying, Nanak continued proclaiming his own religious ideals, among them monotheism; lack of distinctions based on gender, caste, or creed (for example, whether Hindu or Muslim); and doing good deeds. Nanak attracted a large following. At about the age of fifty, he established a new settlement called Kartarpur ("abode of the creator") in what is now Pakistan. Here he and his followers formed the first Sikh community and instituted the lifestyle that has characterized Sikh society to this day.

Guru Nanak erected a special building, a *dharamsala* ("abode of faith"), for worship. In so doing, he provided the prototype of the *gurdwara*, which today is the central structure of any particular Sikh community. (The term *dharamsala* gradually was replaced in the eighteenth century with *gurdwara* to designate the Sikh place of worship.) Nanak welcomed people from all segments of society to reside in Kartarpur and to work together to maintain it. Nanak himself joined in the work, which was primarily agrarian. And though in most respects a regular member of the community, Nanak sat on a special seat when addressing the congregation. Followers recognized the nature of the Guru as merely human and yet also as very spiritually advanced.

On September 22, 1539, after leading the Kartarpur community for about twenty years, Guru Nanak died. According to the traditional account the Guru, aware of his approaching death, settled a dispute regarding the proper disposal of his body.

> Hindus and Muslims who had put their faith in the divine Name began to debate what should be done with the Guru's corpse. "We shall bury him," said the Muslims. "No, let us cremate his body," said the Hindus. "Place flowers on both sides of my body," said Baba Nanak, "flowers from the Hindus on the right side and flowers from the Muslims on the left. If tomorrow the Hindus' flowers are still fresh let my body be burned, and if the Muslims' flowers are still fresh let it be buried."
>
> Baba Nanak then commanded the congregation to sing. They sang *Kirtan Sohila* and *Arati*. . . . Baba Nanak then covered himself with a sheet and passed away. Those who had gathered around him prostrated themselves, and when the sheet was removed they found that there was nothing under it. The flowers on both sides remained fresh, and both Hindus and Muslims took their respective shares. All who were gathered there prostrated themselves again.[7]

Even with his death, Guru Nanak encouraged Hindus and Muslims to transcend their differences and to let peace prevail.

Guru Nanak's example powerfully informs the beliefs and practices of Sikhs up to the present day. We will next turn our attention briefly to Sikh scripture, the collection of texts that contains the doctrinal position as set forth by Guru Nanak and his successor Gurus.

Compare Guru Nanak to founding figures of other religious traditions, with regard to establishing teachings and way of life and to the founding figure as a role model for others to follow.

Sikh Scripture

We have previously identified the Adi Granth, commonly known as Sri Guru Granth Sahib, as Sikhism's most important sacred text. This is without question true for all Sikhs today. There are, however, other texts that most Sikhs would classify as scripture, of which the most important are the Dasam Granth and the Rahit, both of which we consider here. In addition, works by two disciples of the Gurus are granted sufficient status to be recited in the *gurdwara:* Bhai Gurda (disciple of Guru Arjan and Guru Hargobind) and Nand Lal (disciple of Guru Gobind Singh). A collection of stories about the life of Guru Nanak, called the *Janam-sakhi*, also deserves mention. The account of Guru Nanak's death cited in the previous section is from the *Janam-sakhi*.

The Adi Granth   Compiled by Guru Arjan in 1603–1604, the Adi Granth contains the works of his four predecessors, along with his own hymns and various works by poets, such as Kabir (c. 1440–1518). Through the centuries, the Adi Granth has occupied a central place in Sikhism. Whereas the Gurus once sat on a special seat amid Sikh disciples, since the time of the tenth and last historical Guru, Gobind Singh, the Adi Granth has occupied the same type of seat in the middle of any place of worship. And whereas the Gurus were once the authorities on religious matters, now Sikhs consult the Adi Granth.

The name "Adi Granth" ("the Original Volume" or "the First Book") is standard among scholars. Sikhs commonly express their reverence for the scripture by referring to it as Sri Guru Granth Sahib (*sahib* is a title of respect). Every copy is identical in both script and page number; there are 1,430 pages in every copy. It was composed using the Gurmukhi script and a variety of languages that were used in northern India at the time, most prevalently Punjabi. It also contains some words in Arabic, Persian, Prakrit, and Sanskrit. All of these factors render the Adi Granth somewhat difficult to read, as well as difficult to translate. Today, however, English and French translations are available. Many Sikh families have at least a condensed version of the Adi Granth, containing all of the works used in daily prayers, including Guru Nanak's *Japji*, which is the only portion of the entire Adi Granth that is chanted, rather than sung. For Sikhs, the Adi Granth rings with brilliance when it is set to music and proclaimed in its original language. In the words of one commentator: "The poetic excellence, the spiritual content, and the haunting, lilting melodies of the hymns of the Adi Granth are Sikhism's greatest attraction to this day."[8]

A Sikh reads from Sri Guru Granth Sahib, here occupying its customary place on a cushion within a *gurdwara*.

The Dasam Granth   The composition of the Dasam Granth ("Volume of the Tenth Master") has been traditionally attributed to Guru Gobind Singh, although many Sikhs today regard only some parts to have been authored by the Guru. The first compilation of works into the Dasam Granth is thought to have taken place in 1734 (twenty-six years after the death of Guru Gobind Singh), although in the ensuing decades variant versions appeared. In 1902, the version that is used today was officially authorized.

During the eighteenth century, the Dasam Granth was considered to be Guru alongside the Adi Granth. Today, however, only one group of Sikhs, the Nihangs, bestow equal honor on the Dasam Granth. Nevertheless, the sections of the text that all Sikhs attribute to Guru Gobind Singh can safely be categorized as Sikh scripture. These sections include the well-known *Jap Sahib* and the *Ten Savayyas;* both are recited daily in morning prayers.

The Rahit   In the chapter's opening, we observed that the *Amrit Sanchar*, the Khalsa initiation ceremony, is undertaken only by a minority of Sikhs, even though the Khalsa continues to exemplify the ideals of Sikhism. These ideals are spelled out in written form in *rahit-namas*, texts composed over the centuries and collectively referred to as the **Rahit**. Traditionally, the contents of the Rahit are believed to stem from the teachings of Guru Gobind Singh himself. In both this section on Sikh doctrinal teachings and the following section on Sikh religious life, we shall draw frequently from the contents of the Rahit.

On God, the Human Condition, and Spiritual Liberation

More than anything else, Sikhism is a religious path to spiritual liberation through devotional praise of God, most especially by way of meditation on the divine Name. This meditation is often done through prayerful recitation of sacred words. In this section, we take up in more detail three main aspects of Sikh teachings that will shed light on this religious path: the nature of God and the "divine Name"; the nature of the human condition and its need, through the aid of the Guru, to move from darkness to enlightenment; and the nature of liberation, which is release from *samsara*, the cycle of death and rebirth.

Sikhism teaches that the ultimate purpose of life is to attain **mukti** (spiritual liberation). This liberation is similar to Hindu *moksha*, "release" from *samsara*, the cycle of death and rebirth (a concept Sikhism also adopted from Hinduism). This release is believed to bring about an experience of being in the presence of God, a state of eternal bliss.

God: Formless One, Creator, True Guru Guru Nanak's understanding of the nature of God is the center from which all Sikh teachings emerge. It is fitting that the Adi Granth begins with a concise summary of Sikh theology. This summary is known as the *Mul Mantra*, the passage recited by initiates to the Khalsa (as we noted in the beginning of the chapter) and by most Sikhs daily as part of their morning prayers.

> There is one Supreme Being, the Eternal Reality, the Creator, without fear and devoid of enmity, immortal, never incarnated, self-existent, known by grace through the Guru.
> The Eternal One, from the beginning, through all time, present now, the Everlasting Reality.[9]

As this description suggests, Sikhism is similar theologically to the monotheistic religions Zoroastrianism, Judaism, Christianity, and Islam. God is one, eternal, self-existent, and "Creator." The Punjabi term that the Gurus used for God is *Akal Purakh*, "The One Beyond Time." Guru Nanak sometimes used the name *Nirankar*, "Without Form." For Sikhs, then, God is without form and beyond all attributes that humans use to describe reality. God is without gender and is referred to as "he" in Sikhism only begrudgingly and when grammatically necessary because of the limitations of language; there is no neuter pronoun in Punjabi. Sikhs actively strive to avoid assigning such human attributes to God.

For reasons beyond the grasp of human comprehension, God decided to create the world and all that is in it, including human beings. Akal Purakh (we'll use this traditional name, although modern Sikhs commonly refer to God as *Vahiguru*, "Praise to the Guru"), in addition to being the Creator, is also the Preserver and the Destroyer. Sikhism here draws from the important Hindu triad of gods and their respective functions: Brahma (Creator), Vishnu (Preserver), and Shiva (Destroyer). All Sikhs, though, insist that their God is one. These three functions are thus different aspects of the one God. For Hindu *Vaishnavas*, Vishnu similarly incorporates all three functions within his own being (Chapter 2, p. 54).

In God's primary state, to which Guru Nanak referred when he used the name *Nirankar* ("Without Form"), God is distinct from his creation in much the same way that an artist remains distinct from her or his artwork. And yet God dwells within creation—within nature and within human beings. God is thus said to be immanent, or indwelling (as opposed to transcendent, or beyond creation). In this state of immanence, Akal Purakh is personal and approachable through loving devotion. Because of God's immanence in creation, it is possible for humans to make contact with God and to come to know God. To extend our analogy, one can know something of an artist by seeing the artist's works. So too can one come to know Akal Purakh through experiencing God's creation. Indeed, part of the ongoing purpose of creation is that God, through loving grace, might reveal the divine self to human beings. It is in this capacity that God is referred to as Guru, for in this manner God delivers humans from darkness to enlightenment.

The Human Condition: Self-Centered and Bound to *Samsara*   Human beings are especially near to Akal Purakh. Though Sikhism advocates kindness to living things, it also holds that other creatures are here to provide for us. (Unlike most Hindus and all Jains, therefore, Sikhs are not opposed to eating meat—although vegetarianism is the preference of many.) More importantly, Akal Purakh is believed to dwell within all human beings and is actively concerned about their spiritual welfare. Humans, however, tend to neglect the need to center their lives on God.

Rather than being God-centered, humans are inclined to be self-centered and to depend on the powers of the mind. The Sikh term for this self-centeredness is **haumai**, which causes one to resist submitting to Akal Purakh. When life is dominated by *haumai*, its five accompanying vices—lust, anger, greed, attachment, and pride—tend to run rampant. *Haumai* and its vices increase the distance between the person and God and at the same time cause attachment to the charms of the world.

As long as *haumai* and its accompanying vices persist, humans are destined to remain in *samsara*, the ongoing cycle of death and rebirth.

Spiritual Liberation through Union with God   The quest for spiritual liberation is a constant struggle between *haumai*, the self-centeredness to which humans are naturally inclined, and the call to live in accordance with the will of God. Akal Purakh plays an essential role in determining the outcome of this struggle. God is immanent in creation through **hukam**, the divine order. It is through *hukam* that Akal Purakh asserts the divine will and communicates truth. Through Akal Purakh's grace, humans acquire the potential for perceiving this truth, and therefore for perceiving God. In the words of the *Mul Mantra* cited earlier, Akal Purakh is "known by grace through the Guru"—the Guru being either one of the historical Gurus or Sri Guru Granth Sahib. (Because the *Mul Mantra* was composed by Guru Nanak, we can assume that the original meaning was the historical Guru.) Through humbling oneself, thus denying the normally dominating powers of *haumai*, a person is opened to the power of God's grace. Having received God's grace, the task is to respond in loving devotion through meditation on the nature of God. The term most often used in the Adi Granth to denote the nature of God is *nam*, the "divine Name." Meditation on the *nam* or recitation of the *nam* is prescribed repeatedly as the path to spiritual liberation. A chapter of the *Japji* sets forth these points:

> The Eternal One whose Name is Truth speaks to us in infinite love. Insistently we beg for the gifts which are by grace bestowed. What can we offer in return for all this goodness? What gift will gain entrance to the hallowed Court? What words can we utter to attract this love? At the ambrosial hour of fragrant dawn meditate on the grandeur of the one true Name. Past actions determine the nature of our birth, but grace alone reveals the door to liberation. See the Divine Spirit, Nanak, dwelling immanent in all. Know the Divine Spirit as the One, the eternal, the changeless Truth.[10]

The significance of the *nam* for Guru Nanak, and thus for the entire Sikh tradition, can hardly be overstated. In the words of one modern commentator, "Anything that may be affirmed concerning Akal Purakh constitutes an aspect of the divine Name, and a sufficient understanding of the divine Name provides the essential means to deliverance."[11]

Mukti, spiritual liberation, brings about the eternal, infinitely blissful state of being in the presence of God. It should be noted that Sikhism's doctrine of spiritual liberation is not dependent in any way on one's caste status or gender. Also, the focus is on inward meditation and piety, rather than on outward forms of worship, such as festivals or pilgrimages—although Sikhism is not entirely without such forms of worship, as we shall consider shortly. But before we move on from this section on Sikh teachings, we next consider elements introduced with the foundation in 1699 of the Khalsa, the community of "Pure Ones," and take up the crucial question of the relationship of the Khalsa to the Panth or Sikh community at large.

Teachings of Guru Gobind Singh and the Khalsa

The teachings that Guru Gobind Singh proclaimed to the *Panj Piare*, the "Beloved Five" who became the first initiates into the Khalsa, are believed by Sikhs to make up the Rahit, the regulatory code that spells out correct belief and behavior for members of the Khalsa.

The Rahit contains vital teachings pertaining to the religious life. As we observed in the opening of the chapter, Manjit and Sandeep, as part of their initiation into the Khalsa, were taught certain norms of behavior, all of which are contained in the Rahit. Among the teachings are four cardinal prohibitions (*kurahit*): cutting one's hair, eating meat that has been improperly slaughtered (specifically, slaughtered according to Muslim regulations), engaging in extramarital sex, and using tobacco. Along with these and other prohibitions, the Rahit also sets forth requirements, including the requirement to don the Five Ks, so named because all five of the items begin in Punjabi with the letter "k." The Five Ks are:

- *Kes*, uncut hair, symbolizing Sikh belief that one should not interfere with natural, God-given form
- *Kangha*, a small comb worn in the hair, a reminder of cleanliness
- *Karā*, a steel wristlet, affirming constant connectedness with God
- *Kirpan*, a sword, a sign of devotion to truth and to the defense of just causes
- *Kachh*, a pair of shorts tied with a drawstring, symbolizing chastity.

Gurbaj Singh Multani (right) wears a ceremonial dagger, known as a *kirpan*, after a news conference on Parliament Hill in Ottawa on March 2, 2006. Multiculturalism and religious freedom trumped safety concerns in a Canadian Supreme Court decision that allows orthodox Sikh students to carry traditional daggers to school.

To some extent, both the meaning and the practical implications of the Five Ks have varied somewhat through the centuries. At the time of the founding of the Khalsa, for example, the wearing of a sword would have suggested true preparedness to fight. Today, the *kirpan* is usually only five to eight inches long and often is concealed underneath clothing in order not to appear threatening.

Study of Sikh teachings has led us naturally to a consideration of some historical aspects of the Sikh tradition. In the next section, we take up in more detail significant events from the time of Guru Nanak to the present.

THE HISTORY OF SIKHISM

Guru Nanak has remained the most prominent and revered of the ten Gurus of the Sikhs. Yet his nine successors contributed significantly to the development of the religion. Young Sikhs like Manjit and Sandeep learn about all of them as a natural part of their upbringing, celebrating their heroic life stories.

Guru Nanak's Successors

All ten Gurus are considered to have been revealers of truth and to have been linked to one another through sharing the same divine essence. This made them spiritually more adept than ordinary people. They were not, however, thought to be divine incarnations

THE TEN GURUS

The guruship of each begins with the death of his predecessor.

1. Guru Nanak (1469–1539)
2. Guru Angad (1504–1552)
3. Guru Amar Das (1479–1574)
4. Guru Ram Das (1534–1581)
5. Guru Arjan (1563–1606)
6. Guru Hargobind (1595–1644)
7. Guru Hari Rai (1630–1661)
8. Guru Hari Krishan (1656–1664)
9. Guru Tegh Bahadur (1621–1675)
10. Guru Gobind Singh (1666–1708)

of God. The Gurus thus are not to be worshipped by Sikhs, though they are greatly revered. Guru Nanak constantly stressed his human limitations, humbly referring to himself as God's slave. All the Gurus were highly prestigious persons. They were revered for their spiritual gifts and acquired much worldly prestige as well. The Mughal (therefore, Muslim) emperors who ruled northern India knew the Gurus personally and tended to respect them, in some cases developing strong friendships with them.

Nanak's successors are responsible for a wide variety of impressive accomplishments that gradually transformed the Sikh community. Arjan, the Fifth Guru (from 1581 to 1606), deserves special mention. For one thing, he compiled the scripture that would come to be known as the Adi Granth ("the Original Volume," distinguishing it from the later Dasam Granth), thus giving the Sikhs their most important sacred scripture. He included, by traditional count, 2,312 of his own compositions, beautifully melodic hymns that are considered to be among Sikhism's most impressive musical accomplishments. Arjan also constructed at the city of Amritsar the Hari Mandar ("Temple of God"), now called Darbar Sahib ("Court of the Lord") or the Golden Temple. This provided the Sikhs with a geographical center.

The Darbar Sahib remains one of the world's most impressive and important religious buildings. Along with being architecturally magnificent, it is rich in symbolic meaning, beginning with the building process itself. At Arjan's invitation, Mian Mir, a Muslim Sufi saint, laid the foundation stone. Even as the Sikh community was gaining independence from its Muslim and Hindu neighbors, Sikhism served as a bridge between religions. In contrast to Hindu temples, which typically have only one door, Arjan designed the Darbar Sahib with four doors. Traditionally this is interpreted as representing Sikhism's openness to all people—to adherents of all four of northwestern

India's major religious traditions of the time (Hinduism, Islam, Buddhism, and Sikhism); to people of all four classes of the prevalent Hindu caste system; and to people of the north, south, east, and west. In light of this, it is ironic that, in recent times, the Darbar Sahib has become associated with controversy and discord, having been the site of the bloody military action in 1984 known as Operation Blue Star, which we shall consider in more detail below.

Guru Gobind Singh and the Khalsa

The tenth Guru, Gobind Singh (1666–1708), is revered as the greatest Guru after Nanak. His strength of character and spiritual adeptness made him a successful and memorable leader. By the time he became Guru at the age of nine, he had already begun training in the art of warfare and hunting, along with the ways of religion. A modern history of the Sikhs makes note of the enduring impression made by the Guru's appearance:

> Every description of Guru Gobind Singh's person delineates him as a very handsome, sharp-featured, tall and wiry man, immaculately and richly dressed as a prince. Decked with a crest upon his lofty, cone-shaped turban with a plume suspended behind from the top, he was ever armed with various weapons, including a bow and a quiver of arrows, a sword, a discus, a shield and a spear. His choice steed was of bluish-grey color and on his left hand always perched a white hawk when he sat on the throne or went out hunting.[12]

Whereas Guru Nanak is traditionally depicted as being contemplative and the master of things spiritual, Guru Gobind Singh is depicted as a worldly prince, ever ready for battle.

Guru Gobind Singh contributed significantly to the growth of Sikh militarism and engaged in many armed conflicts during a period when revolts against the Mughals, which had been occurring periodically for about a century, were common. Due to his success in consolidating and strengthening the Panth, the Sikhs had a realistic possibility of establishing independent rule. Most notably, Guru Gobind Singh brought about two innovations that forever changed the structure of Sikhism. As we have already noted, he instituted the Khalsa, which would redefine the Panth, and he installed the Adi Granth, the sacred scripture, as Guru, which radically altered the nature of leadership.

A woman prays at the Golden Temple in Amritsar, India.

Founding the Khalsa The traditional story of this momentous event is set forth in this account by twentieth-century Sikh historians Teja Singh and Ganda Singh. Note the story's emphasis on the virtues of loyalty and unity of the Sikh community, with its details concerning various castes and livelihoods.

On the Baisakhi day, March 30 of 1699, [Guru Gobind Singh] called a big meeting at Anandpur. When all were seated, he drew out his sword and cried, "Is there anyone here who would lay down his life for dharma?" At this the whole assembly was thrown into consternation; but the Guru went on repeating his demand. At the third call, Daya Ram, a Khatri of Lahore, rose from his seat and offered himself. The Guru took him into an adjoining enclosure, where a few goats were kept tied, and seating him there cut off a goat's head. He came out with the dripping weapon and flourishing it before the multitude asked again, "Is there any other Sikh here who will offer himself as a sacrifice?" At this Dharam Das, a Jat of Delhi, came forward and was taken into the enclosure, where another goat was killed. In the same way three other men stood up one after another and offered themselves for the sacrifice. One was Muhkam Chand, a washerman of Dwarka; another was Himmat, a cook of Jagannath; and the third was Sahib Chand, a barber of Bedar. The Guru after dressing the five in handsome clothes brought them before the assembly. He baptized them with sweetened water [i.e., *amrit*] stirred with a dagger and called them his Beloved Ones.[13]

Sikh devotees celebrate the 345th birth anniversary of Guru Gobind Singh on January 1, 2011, in the northern Indian city of Jammu.

Guru Gobind Singh, after preaching to the crowd about the unity of the Sikh community, asked the *Panj Piare*, the "Beloved Ones" (or "Beloved Five"), to baptize him—a surprising request given the traditional elevated standing of the Guru. The five baptized the Guru, thus forming the original Khalsa, the community of "Pure Ones" (as we noted in the chapter's opening description of the initiation ceremony). Over the course of the next few days, some 80,000 were baptized. All the men were given the additional name Singh, which means "lion," and all the women were named Kaur, which means "princess." To this day, these names indicate a family's affiliation with the Khalsa (although they no longer imply that one has undergone initiation).

By the time of his death in 1708, Guru Gobind Singh had managed to befriend the Mughal rulership and to ease tensions between the peoples,

although his own death came at the hands of a Mughal assassin. Before dying, he is said to have declared that he was to be succeeded, not by another individual, but by the Adi Granth and by the Panth, to both of which he assigned the title "Guru."

Sikhs and Nationalism

Over the centuries, the Punjab has tended to be a volatile region, marked by political and military strife. In the century following the death of Guru Gobind Singh in 1708, the Sikhs struggled through a period of especially violent confrontations with the Mughal Empire, eventually managing to establish independent rule. Under the leadership of Ranjit Singh (1780–1839), who ascended to the throne in 1792, the Sikh community thrived as a sovereign kingdom in the Punjab. In 1849, the kingdom was annexed by the British, who had established control over India and had commenced the period known as the British Raj.

When India gained independence from the British in 1947, the Punjab was divided, with India gaining control of the east and Pakistan gaining control of the west. Most Sikhs living in the western region migrated eastward, favoring the Hindu-dominated India over the Muslim-dominated Pakistan. These Sikhs left behind their traditional homeland and many significant sites, including Nanak's birthplace.

In recent times, a new nationalist movement for independence, commonly called "Khalistan," has involved the Sikhs in conflict, both within and outside the Sikh community. The most violent tragedy of all took place in 1984 when, in an attempt to control the more radical aspects of the independence movement, the Indian government launched "Operation Blue Star," which culminated in the occupation of Sikh holy sites, most notably the Darbar Sahib (or Golden Temple), by Indian forces and the death of as many as 10,000 Sikhs. (Estimates of the death count vary widely, with various sources citing from 500 to 10,000.) This led to the assassination of Indian Prime Minister Indira Gandhi by two of her Sikh bodyguards on October 31, 1984. Today, the Khalistan movement is not nearly so prevalent as it was in the 1980s. That in 2004 a Sikh, Manmohan Singh, for the first time became India's prime minister perhaps signals a new degree of assimilation of Sikhism within Indian society.

Sikhs in the Diaspora

Sikhism clearly has become a global religion. For most Sikhs, traditional aspects of the religion as it has been practiced for centuries in its homeland, especially as defined by the Khalsa, tend to endure. At the beginning of this chapter, we noted that there are approximately 25 million Sikhs in the world,[14] of which approximately 70 percent follow at least the basic requirement of the Khalsa and do not cut their hair. Only about 15 percent of Sikhs have undergone the traditional ceremony of initiation into the Khalsa.

With nearly 2 million Sikhs now living in the diaspora[15] (that is, outside of the Punjab and of India), issues of these Sikhs have gained prominence. Many of the traditional practices taken for granted in the Punjab simply are not feasible—or, in some cases, even legal—in other lands. Consider, for example, Sikh funeral rituals.

All religious traditions feature important persons, in addition to founding figures, who have made significant contributions as innovators, institutional leaders, and so forth. Thinking of Sikhism's nine successors to Guru Nanak, compare other religions on this issue of the contributions of important persons.

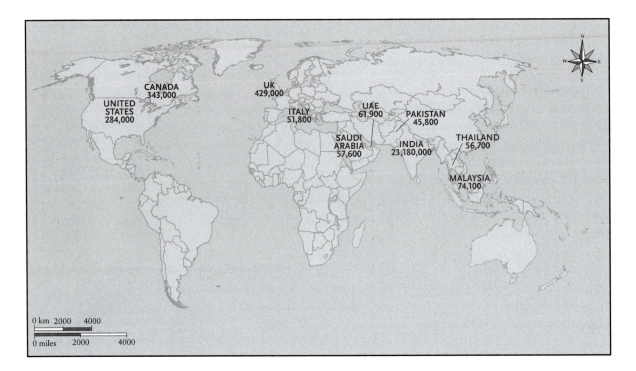

World Sikh population.

According to the Rahit, and in keeping with long-standing tradition, the body of the deceased is to be borne to the pyre on a bier, not in a coffin, and the fire is to be lit by a close relative or friend. In countries such as the United States, such a practice is not permitted; as a result, adjustments are made. The ceremonial departure for the cremation site is replaced by placing the coffin into a hearse, which then proceeds to a crematorium. (Or the ceremony is held at a funeral home that is equipped with a crematorium.) The lighting of the pyre is replaced by the chosen person pushing the button that conveys the coffin into the cremation furnace.

Other challenging situations for Sikhs in the diaspora involve the Five Ks. Wearing the turban, for example, which is based on the requirement of uncut hair and is almost universal among male Sikhs in their traditional homeland, is an important symbol of Sikh identity. But in many places in the diaspora, wearing a turban is not so easily done. In the United States, for example, there are laws requiring that helmets be worn when driving a motorcycle. A Khalsa Sikh who wishes to don the *kirpan* (the sword or knife, one of the Five Ks) when traveling by plane must be prepared for varying rules governing security practices at airport screenings.

In some cases, governments attempt to accommodate Sikhs. In the United Kingdom, for example, motorcycle helmet laws have been modified. But in many situations, such traditional practices as wearing the turban have led at least to inconvenience and sometimes even to tragedy. In the aftermath of the attacks on the World Trade Center and the Pentagon of September 11, 2001, Sikhs have been mistaken (presumably because of the wearing of the turban) for Muslims and have become targets of hate crimes, including murder.

For Sikhs living in the diaspora, this issue of identity needs to be weighed against practical concerns, sometimes even involving one's safety. Whereas most Sikhs in the Punjab continue to follow the injunction not to cut their hair, most living in Western countries do not. The Panth, as a global religious community, must contend with this complex mix of issues and concerns.

SIKHISM AS A WAY OF LIFE

One aspect of Guru Nanak's teachings was the rejection of the outward forms of religion that he found troubling in the Islam and Hinduism of his day. Focused as he was on seeking the indwelling God through meditation on the divine Name, Guru Nanak regarded the external forms of religion as useless.

A Sikh man greets Hillary Clinton, at the time a senator from New York, at the United States National Day of Prayer ceremony in 2007.

Guru Nanak's rejection of outward forms of religion, however, has not resulted in complete avoidance by Sikhs of religious observances. For one thing, Sikhs through the centuries have continued to celebrate annual festivals that are generally features of northern Indian culture. We noted previously that Guru Gobind Singh founded the Khalsa on the day of an important annual festival, Baisakhi Day, which is the first day of the Indian year (according to the Western calendar, this day occurs in March or April). For Sikhs, Baisakhi Day has the special significance of commemorating the founding of the Khalsa. Another important festival celebrated by Sikhs, as well as by Hindus and Jains, is Divali, the Festival of Lights (which takes place in October or early November). Other religious observations were instituted by the Sikh Gurus, most notably by Guru Gobind Singh, and are unique to Sikhism.

VOICES: An Interview with Onkar Singh

Onkar Singh is a Sikh who was born and raised in the Punjab; earned a Ph.D. (Entomology) from the University of California, Berkeley; and served in India, Nigeria, Sudan, Liberia, and Indonesia before immigrating to the United States and becoming a U.S. citizen. He has devoted his retirement years to educating his fellow citizens about Sikhism.

What is the significance of the Name of God, and does the fact that your name, "Onkar," is one of the Sikh names of God have special significance?

God's name is used to remember Him, to meditate on Him, to pray to Him, and to seek His blessings. People are named after different names of God (*Bhagwan, Govind, Hari, Indra, Kartar, Eshwar, Ram,* etc.) or gods and prophets (*Krishan, Shiva, Jesus, Moses, Mohamed,* etc.). I was named Onkar, after the most

Onkar Singh

common name of God in the Sikh Holy Scriptures, following the tradition of choosing a name starting with the first letter of the hymn when Sri Guru Granth Sahib is opened at random.

What is the primary purpose of prayer?

The primary purpose of Sikh prayer is to thank God (*Vahiguru*) for all His blessings thus far and to seek His blessings for the success of the task about to be started. Sikhs also ask for His continued blessings so that they submit to His Will and continue to remember Him at all times. The prayer ends with a request for their optimism and for the welfare and prosperity of the entire humanity.

How does wearing the turban relate to your religious beliefs?

In South Asia and Southwest Asia, the turban is a symbol of dignity, honor, respect, and responsibility. Guru Hargobind, the sixth Sikh Guru, asked his followers to wear turbans, carry arms, and ride horses, in opposition to a ban imposed on non-Muslims by the rulers. Further, in 1699, Guru Gobind Singh, the tenth Sikh Guru, prescribed the five articles of faith including uncut hair (and the turban) mandatory for the Khalsa. I wear a turban as per the dictates and practice of my Sikh faith.

To what extent are the Golden Temple and the Sikh homeland of Punjab in general of special meaning for you, living in the United States?

The Golden Temple, Amritsar, is the most visited Sikh shrine. More people, of different faiths, castes, etc., visit the Golden Temple than the Taj Mahal. Guru Arjan Dev, the fifth Sikh Guru, built this temple. He invited a famous Sufi saint, Mian Mir, to lay its foundation stone. Further, he compiled, edited, and installed the first edition of the Sikh Holy Book in this temple in 1604. The Golden Temple Complex houses the SGPC (Shromani Gurdwara Parbandhak Committee) and includes the Akal Takht and some historic *Gurdwaras*. Besides the Golden Temple, the Sikh homeland of Punjab has three *Takhats* and numerous historic *Gurdwaras*. Sikh Americans, irrespective of the country of their birth, look upon Punjab as the Land of their Gurus, who preached Unity of God, practiced equality of humanity, and worked lovingly to unite the populace.

What is the most important thing that non-Sikhs in the United States need to understand about your religion?

Non-Sikhs in the United States should understand that almost all who wear turbans in America are followers of Sikhism, which is not a branch of another religion (e.g., Hinduism or Islam) and has its own founder (Guru Nanak) and Holy Book (Sri Guru Granth Sahib) and worship places (*Gurdwaras*), where all are welcome.

In this section we focus on the ideals of the religious life, paying attention to the actual degree of participation among Sikhs today.

Daily Devotional Practices

Guru Nanak emphasized the importance of *nam simaran*, "remembrance of the Name." This can be done simply by repeating one of the names used to refer to God. Recall that Guru Nanak composed many hymns; *kirtan*, the singing of hymns, is another form of *nam simaran*. A third form involves meditation practices designed to contemplate the divine Name and ultimately to bring one into perfect harmony with God. On one hand, these methods are straightforward and easy to practice on one's own. On the other hand, to make significant progress normally takes years of diligence.

Daily prayers are another form of devotional practice that can (and should) be done by every Sikh. The Khalsa Rahit, which spells out the ideal regimen for much of the religious life, gives the following instructions:

> A Sikh should rise early (3 A.M. to 6 A.M.) and having bathed he should observe *nam japan* by meditating on God. Each day a Sikh should read or recite the order known as the "Daily Rule" (*nit-nem*). The Daily Rule comprises the following portions of scripture: Early morning (3 A.M.–6 A.M.): *Japji, Jap,* and the *Ten Savayyas.* . . . In the evening at sunset: *Sodar Rahiras.* . . . At night before retiring: *Sohila.* At the conclusion of the selections set down for early morning and evening (*Sodar Rahiras*) the prayer known as *Ardas* must be recited.[16]

To follow such a regimen requires much diligence and much time: altogether, these prayers cover about twenty pages in English translation. Whereas some Sikhs, especially those more advanced in age, commonly do this on a regular basis, the majority do not.

Sikh Worship in the *Gurdwara*

Gurdwara literally means "doorway of the Guru" (a variant translation is "by means of the Guru's [grace]"). Any building that contains a copy of the Adi Granth is,

Volunteers prepare food for the *langar* meal at the Golden Temple in Amritsar. Many thousands of people share meals together here daily, at no cost to the visitor.

Compare the daily ritual practices of Sikhism with those of other religions.

technically speaking, a *gurdwara*, a Sikh house of worship. There is at least one *gurdwara* in virtually every village in the Punjab. Most *gurdwaras* have a characteristic Sikh style, with minarets and chalk-white paint. Aside from the presence of the Adi Granth, which usually sits atop cushions and under a canopy, there are no specific requirements regarding the interior.

The *gurdwara* serves mainly as a place for Sikh men, women, and children to congregate for worship. This they do frequently, on no particular day of the week. Worship usually takes place in the evening, though the early morning is also a popular time. Worship in the *gurdwara* is preceded by bathing and consists of singing the Gurus' hymns, reading from the Adi Granth, or telling a story about one of the Gurus. No formal requirements govern the exact nature of worship. It generally ends, though, with a sharing of a special pudding made of wheat flour, sugar, and ghee (clarified butter), known as *karah prasad*. This act is symbolic of the unity of the Panth.

The sharing of food is an important feature of Sikhism. Each *gurdwara* typically has within it a community kitchen, called the *langar*, where Sikhs gather at various times to share in the preparation and consumption of a meal. The food served in the *langar* is strictly vegetarian; even eggs are not allowed. Again, this sharing of food symbolizes the equality of all. It also provides food for the needy.

Life Cycle Rituals

In the chapter's opening description of the *Amrit Sanchar*, the Khalsa initiation ceremony, we witnessed an example of a Sikh ritual that marks a certain point in the individual's life and does so through detailed actions and rich symbolism that are steeped in tradition. Having already considered the Khalsa initiation ceremony in some detail (and bearing in mind that only about 15 percent of Sikhs undergo initiation), we now turn to considering other important rituals of the life cycle.

Birth and Naming On the birth of a child, Khalsa Sikhs can choose to undertake a ritual that resembles an aspect of the initiation ceremony. A sweet drink is made by stirring water and sweets with a *kirpan* (the short sword, one of the Five Ks), while reciting from the *Japji*. A few drops are given to the baby, and the rest is drunk by the mother.

A short time after giving birth, the parents and child proceed to the *gurdwara*, where hymns are sung and the Adi Granth is opened randomly. The child's first name is chosen based on the first letter that appears on the left-hand page of the Adi Granth, the letter with which the name is to begin. If the child is a girl, she is also given the name Kaur; if male, he is given the name Singh. The names Singh or Kaur normally correspond to an English last name. No distinction is made between girls' and boys' first names. The "last name" of Kaur or Singh serves to make this distinction.

Tying a Turban When a boy reaches the age of ten or eleven, Sikh families often undertake a ceremonial tying of his first turban. This symbolizes the great respect that Sikhs hold for the turban. Even though wearing the turban is not technically required, it is regarded as a natural corollary of *kes*, not cutting one's hair (one of the Five Ks). Indeed, because one's hair is typically kept inside the turban, it is really the turban, not the hair, that is the most visible sign that one is a Sikh.

Traditionally, the turban is tied in a specific way that is both easy to do (once one has learned how) and effective, keeping the turban securely on the head. The style and color of the turban may sometimes indicate regional, political, or religious affiliation. The turban is generally considered to be highly practical, providing protection both from the summer sun and from the cold of winter. Women rarely wear turbans; instead, they traditionally wear a scarf or veil that can be used to cover the head.

Marriage Proper Sikh marriage, according to the traditions established by the Khalsa, is arranged by the parents of a child of marriageable age through the assistance of a relative, who seeks out a suitable spouse and sets up meetings with the families. The parents thus can become acquainted with their child's potential bride or groom. The same type of meeting takes place with the other set of parents. Once both families have agreed on a match, the marriage ceremony is planned. According to the Rahit, a Sikh woman is only to be married to a Sikh, but no account whatsoever of caste status is to be taken into consideration. In actual practice, however, there are many exceptions. Caste status commonly dictates the choice of marriage partners, and Sikhs (men more commonly than women) sometimes marry outside the tradition. As we have remarked previously, common practice by no means always complies with Khalsa ideals.

The ceremony takes place at the *gurdwara*, with Sri Guru Granth Sahib the central focal point, just as it is in everyday worship. First seated before the Adi Granth during the singing of hymns, the couple then stands and receives instruction in the teachings of the Gurus on marriage, nodding their assent to the Adi Granth, and afterward walking around it. This focus on the scripture exemplifies the central role that the Adi Granth is to play in the life of the married couple.

The ceremony concludes, like other worship services in the *gurdwara*, with the distribution of *karah prasad*, the special pudding made of wheat flour, sugar, and ghee.

Death Traditional Sikh mourning rituals center around the process of cremation. The body is washed and dressed in clean clothing and adorned with the Five Ks.

A hymn is recited, and the body is carried to the cremation grounds, which women do not enter. The funeral pyre is lit by a son or other male relative or friend, while the other mourners sing funeral hymns. The *Kirtan Sohila*, the prayer that is recited daily when retiring for the evening, is then sung.

Once the fire has burned out, the ashes are recovered and are either buried there at the cremation site or immersed in running water. Then the entire Adi Granth is read, within a period of ten days if possible. (The Rahit specifies that a full reading takes forty-eight hours, if done without interruption.)

As noted previously in the section on Sikhs in the diaspora, such traditional practices are modified today in places where laws prohibit outdoor cremations.

Worship, Work, and Charity

Like every global religion, Sikhism is continually in contact with people of other traditions. In this chapter, we have seen how Guru Nanak inspired followers who were both Muslims and Hindus. Although the common notion that Sikhism somehow resulted from the mixing of Islam and Hinduism is not an accurate one, clearly Guru Nanak and Sikhs after him helped to bridge differences among these two major religions of India. Sikhism has generally maintained peaceful relations with other religions and with other peoples, both in their homeland and abroad. Indeed, Sikhs have a well-deserved reputation for reaching out and helping to improve their communities. From its beginnings, Sikhism has been on the side of religious freedom and justice for oppressed people. Justice is carried out partly through the regular donation of one-tenth of one's income to charitable causes.

Three guiding principles of Sikh life are worship, work, and charity, as embodied in the popular Punjabi proverb, *nam japo, kirat karo, vand chhako*: "Repeat the divine Name, work, and give a share [of your earnings to the less fortunate]."[17] An outsider need only pay a visit to a Sikh *gurdwara* and witness the worship and afterward partake of the carefully prepared food in the *langar* to experience these guiding principles in action.

Women and Sikhism

Sikhism, like every religion, has both its ideals and its practical realities. Such is the case with the place of women over the centuries. The ideals are set forth straightforwardly, for instance in these words by Guru Nanak:

> From women born, shaped in the womb, to women betrothed and wed,
> We are bound to women by ties of affection; on women man's future depends.
> If a woman dies he seeks another, source of society's order and strength.
> Why then should one speak evil of women, they who give birth to kings?
> Women also are born from women, as are all who have life and breath.[18]

Sikhism has always maintained this ideal of gender equality with regard to the crucial issue of spiritual liberation (*mukti*). Sikh teachings from the beginning rejected practices such as female infanticide, which were common in the Punjab in Guru Nanak's time. The Rahit emphasizes that women are to participate fully in the religious life. But teachings alone do not always ensure equality in society, even in religious society.

Sikh society, through the centuries and up to the present day, has tended to be quite patriarchal, with positions of institutional power occupied by men. (Notably, the ten Gurus were all men.) The wedding ceremony that we have considered suggests a certain patriarchal tendency with its prescribed vows. The groom promises to be "protector" of the bride and her honor; the bride promises to accept her husband as "master of all love and respect."

On the other hand, the social history of Sikhism includes many examples of equal participation by women in religious matters and of women who serve as role models. Sulakhani, the wife of Guru Nanak, certainly is portrayed as a role model—not only in the domestic domain of the household but also as a confidant and advisor to her husband. Evidence exists showing that wives of other Gurus participated to some degree in administration of the Panth.

As is the case with all of the world's major religions, the degree of gender equality in Sikhism varies from circumstance to circumstance. Generally speaking, modern times have brought changes. In 1977, a wedding ceremony took place in a small town in the Punjab in which the bride led the groom in the final walk around the Adi Granth—a surprising incident, but no one was able to find anything in Sikh scripture to provide an objection based on doctrinal grounds. In another example of changing times, in the late 1990s women began to take on the traditionally male practice of ritual washing of the Golden Temple at midnight.[19]

The rapid growth of the Sikh diaspora in places where gender equality is held up as an ideal suggests that such changes will bring new opportunities for women to occupy roles of power in Sikh religion and society. With regard to the issue of gender equality, too, the Panth will need to continue to make adjustments as it orients its way as a global religion.

Sikh Identity

This chapter has assumed all along a rather flexible definition of who is a Sikh. On one end of the spectrum, we have considered the rigorous regimen of observance as spelled out in the Rahit, which calls for the recitation of some twenty pages of prayer every morning before six o'clock. At the other end of the spectrum, there are those who cut their hair, and yet one cannot go so far as to deny that they are Sikhs.

This flexible definition is in keeping with the Sikh perspective. Every religious tradition sets forth ideals that are not necessarily put into practice by all of its followers. Sikhism openly acknowledges this. It is also important to recognize that "Sikh" can refer broadly to an ethnic group, without necessarily implying adherence to the religion of Sikhism. For centuries, Sikhs maintained a society in the Punjab that was quite distinctive, and the vast majority of today's Sikhs are themselves descendants of Punjabi Sikhs. There is thus both a societal and a hereditary aspect of being Sikh, neither of which necessarily involves the explicitly religious aspects of belief or conduct.

CONCLUSION

In this chapter, we have learned about the teachings, the way of life, and the historical development of Sikhs and their religion. Founded by Guru Nanak (1469–1539), Sikhism is relatively young compared to other major world religions. It nevertheless is firmly rooted in tradition that is historically rich, theologically and ritually sophisticated, and adorned with impressive musical and architectural achievements. Especially because of the central role of the Khalsa, with its Five Ks and other standards for Sikh behavior and identity, the Panth tends to be a community with well-defined ideals. All of these factors contribute to the considerable holding power of Sikh tradition, even as the modern world invites—and sometimes forces—adaptations.

Sikhism today is a global religion, as vital in such places as Toronto, Canada, and the central valley of California as it is in its ancestral homeland of the Punjab. As it continues to draw upon the richness of its eventful historical tradition, Sikhism shows every sign of continuing also to adapt to modernity in the various places across the globe that it has come to call home.

SEEKING ANSWERS

What Is Ultimate Reality?

Sikhism is strictly monotheistic, emphasizing the oneness of God, while also teaching that God dwells within creation. For reasons that cannot be understood by human beings, God created the world. Knowing the divine nature can be considered as analogous to knowing the nature of an artist through contemplation of her artwork. Sikhism holds that the world is good, that God is immanent in the world, and that the world is permeated with divine order, called *hukam*. If this divine order can be recognized, it stands to reason that human beings can come to know God.

How Should We Live in This World?

Sikhs believe that God dwells within everyone. Humans tend, however, to be self-centered, rather than God-centered, a concept known as *haumai*, the self-reliance or pride that poses

(continued)

SEEKING ANSWERS *(continued)*

the primary obstacle to spiritual fulfillment. Sikhs further believe that the world is permeated with *hukam*, or divine order. To live in accord with *hukam* naturally requires proper ethical conduct. The Khalsa, though technically made up of only a minority of Sikhs, continues to be the authoritative source for ideals on the right way to live.

What Is Our Ultimate Purpose?

Immanent in creation, God is knowable to human beings. The flaws of *haumai* can be overcome through attention to the presence of the divine, most effectively through meditation on *nam*, the Name of God. As the term suggests, liberation (*mukti*), which for Sikhism is being in the presence of God, is the complete overcoming of the human condition. Sikhism teaches that the ultimate purpose of life is to attain spiritual liberation, and thereby release from *samsara*, the cycle of death and rebirth.

REVIEW QUESTIONS

For Review

1. What is the meaning of the term "guru"?
2. Identify at least three of the names for God in Sikhism. Why do you think there is more than one name? What is the relationship of the names to each other?
3. Compare the contributions of Guru Nanak and Guru Gobind Singh for the development of Sikhism.
4. What is the Khalsa? What is its ongoing relevance for Sikhism?
5. How do the "Five Ks" of Sikhism serve to strengthen Sikh identity?

For Further Reflection

1. What aspects of the Sikh God would Jews, Christians, or Muslims find familiar?
2. Describe *mukti*, spiritual liberation. How does this compare to forms of spiritual liberation in other religions—for example, to Hindu *moksha* or Buddhist *nirvana*?
3. Compare Sikh worship in the *gurdwara* with the forms of worship in religions with which you are familiar, either through studies or through personal experience. What are the notable similarities and differences? What do these comparative points regarding worship suggest about the nature of the religions, in general?

GLOSSARY

Adi Granth (ah'dee gruhnth; Punjabi, "first book") Sikhism's most important sacred text and, since the death of Guru Gobind Singh in 1708, Sikhism's primary earthly authority; traditionally known as Sri Guru Granth Sahib.

amrit (ahm-reet; Punjabi, "immortalizing fluid") A special drink made from water and sugar crystals, used in the Khalsa initiation ceremony.

gurdwara (goor'dwah-ruh; Punjabi, "doorway of the Guru" or "by means of the Guru's [grace]") A building for Sikh worship that houses a copy of the Adi Granth; the central structure of any Sikh community.

Guru (goo'roo; Sanskrit, "venerable person") A spiritual teacher and revealer of truth, common to Hinduism, Sikhism, and some forms of Buddhism. When the word *Guru* is capitalized, it refers to the ten historical leaders of Sikhism, to the sacred text (Sri Guru Granth Sahib, or Adi Granth), and to God (often as True Guru).

haumai (how'may; Punjabi, "self-reliance," "pride," or "egoism") The human inclination toward being self-centered rather than God-centered, which increases the distance between the individual and God.

hukam (huh'kahm; Punjabi, "order") The divine order of the universe.

Khalsa (khal'sah; Punjabi, "pure ones") An order within Sikhism to which the majority of Sikhs belong, founded by Guru Gobind Singh in 1699.

mukti (mook'tee; Punjabi, "liberation") Spiritual liberation bringing on the eternal and infinitely blissful state of being in the presence of God; sometimes the Sanskrit term *moksha* is used instead.

Mul Mantra The summary of Sikh doctrine that comprises the opening lines of the *Japji*, Guru Nanak's composition that in turn comprises the opening section of the Adi Granth. (See p. 166 for an English translation of the full text.)

Panth (puhnth; Punjabi, Hindi, "path") The Sikh community. In lower case, *panth* ("path") is a term applied to any number of Indian (primarily Hindu) religious traditions.

Rahit (rah-hit'; Punjabi) The *rahit-nāmā*, a collection of scripture that specifies ideals of belief and conduct for members of the Khalsa and, by extension, for Sikhism generally; the current authoritative version, the *Sikh Rahit Maryādā*, was approved in 1950.

SUGGESTIONS FOR FURTHER READING

Cole, W. Owen, and Piara Singh Sambhi. *The Sikhs: Their Religious Beliefs and Practices*. 2nd rev. ed. Brighton, UK: Sussex Academic Press, 1995. A highly readable and informative account, organized in such a way as to make easily accessible the main figures and ideas.

Mann, Gurinder Singh. *Sikhism*. Upper Saddle River, NJ: Prentice Hall, 2004. A clear and up-to-date overview, with focus on modern times.

McLeod, Hew. *Sikhism*. London: Penguin Books, 1997. A detailed yet accessible overview of the religion, with a helpful appendix of primary source material.

McLeod, W. H., ed. and trans. *Textual Sources for the Study of Sikhism*. Totowa, NJ: Barnes & Noble Books, 1984. A helpful collection of source material that goes well beyond the Adi Granth and presents texts in such a way as to clarify the identity of authors.

Singh, Khushwant. *A History of the Sikhs*. 2 vols. Princeton, NJ: Princeton University Press, 1963–1966. A detailed and authoritative resource.

ONLINE RESOURCES

Wabash Center

wabashcenter.wabash.edu/resources
The Wabash Center, a trusted resource for all aspects of the academic study of religion, offers links to a wide variety of dependable Internet resources on Sikhism.

SikhNet

sikhnet.com
SikhNet offers an extensive "insiders' view" on Sikhism, with information on many aspects of the religion.

CHINESE RELIGIONS: CONFUCIANISM and DAOISM

TODAY IS *QINGMING*, a "pure and bright" day (the literal meaning of this Chinese compound word) that arrives once a year, 105 days after the winter solstice. It is a day for all Chinese families to remember their dead relatives and ancestors in a very public way. Spring is definitely in the air. The days have been getting longer and warmer. The rice seedlings, standing in neat rows in ankle-deep water in the paddy fields, wave gracefully in the gentle breeze. Their luxuriant greenness is most pleasing to the eyes of Chen Liang,[1] a peasant from Southern China in his early fifties. He and his two sons have been working hard in the past couple of months to plow and flood the paddy fields, seed the nursery plots, and then transplant the young seedlings one at a time into their current location. It is a tedious and backbreaking job that the Chen family has been doing for generations.

But today there will be no work in the fields. *Qingming* marks the renewal of spring. It also celebrates the rekindling of the kitchen fire. Two days earlier the old fire was put out, so only cold food had been served. Chen Liang and his wife get up today at the crack of dawn to light a new fire in the kitchen. Leftovers from the previous days' cold meals are wrapped in rice pancakes and fried, making "spring rolls" that many Chinese restaurants the world over serve regularly on their appetizer menu. They prepare for an important family gathering at the ancestral graves of the Chen clan. During this annual event, family members gather at and sweep

Woman making offerings in front of her ancestor's tomb.

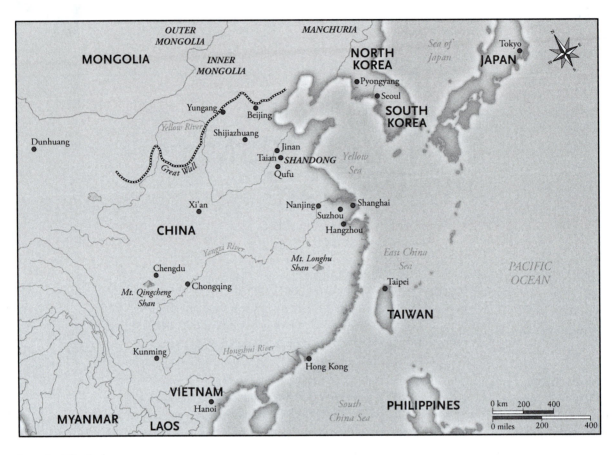

Important Confucian and Daoist sites in China.

the graves of their relatives and ancestors to renew their kinship ties with both the dead and the living. Platefuls of fruits, freshly steamed chickens, a whole roasted pig, bottles of wine, bundles of incense sticks and bright-red candles, and strings of firecrackers, as well as piles of make-believe paper money and paper clothing for the dead, are all ready to be carried to the lineage burial ground just outside the village.

At the gravesite, where several generations of the Chen clan are buried, Chen Liang meets up with his three brothers, his five cousins, and their families. The children, numbering more than twenty, are all dressed in brightly colored clothing, giggling and playing. They help remove overgrown weeds, clean the tombstones, and arrange food in front of the graves. Then, by generation and birth order, all members of the Chen clan take part in the annual ritual. They bow before their ancestors, address them in silent prayers, offer them wine and food, send them clothing and stacks of underworld money by burning paper imitations of those goods, and set off firecrackers to scare off wandering ghosts unrelated to the family.

Afterward a picture is taken of the entire gathering in front of the graves. The families divide up the fruits and the meats to be consumed later back at their respective homes. The men linger to talk about the weather and the crops, the women catch up on family news, and the children play. ✹

Era in Chinese History	Daoism	Confucianism
Shang–Zhou dynasties (c. 1600–256 B.C.E.*)	Ancient Chinese religion Shamans	Ancient Chinese religion Beginning of Ru tradition
Spring and Autumn (c. 722–481 B.C.E.)	World-escaping recluses and hermits	Confucius (551–479 B.C.E.)
Warring States (c. 480–221 B.C.E.)	Zhuangzi (365–290 B.C.E.*), *Daodejing* (earliest extant ed. c. 300 B.C.E.)	Mencius (371–289 B.C.E.*), Xunzi (c. 310–238 B.C.E.*.)
Early Han Dynasty (206 B.C.E.–9 C.E.)	Worship of Xiwangmu (Queen Mother of the West)	Confucianism declared orthodox (136 C.E.); Five Classics designated
Later Han Dynasty (25–220 C.E.)	Laozi deified as Taishang Laojun. Tianshi [Celestial Master] movement founded by Zhang Daoling (142 C.E.) *Laozi bianhua jing* (Classic of Laozi's Transformations) (170s*)	Confucian classical commentaries and Scholasticism
Period of Disunion (221–589)	Shangqing [Highest Clarity] movement (fourth century) Lingbao [Numinous Treasure] Movement (fourth century)	Confucian texts introduced to Korea, and subsequently to Japan
Tang Dynasty (618–907)	First attempt at compiling canon State patronage of Daoism Daoism merged with Chinese folk religion	First stirring of Neo-Confucianism
Song Dynasty (907–1279)	Quanzhen [Complete Perfection] movement founded by Wang Zhe (1113–1170)	Neo-Confucianism: Zhu Xi (1130–1200)
Yuan Dynasty (1279–1368)		*Four Books* designated as civil service examination curriculum (1313)
Ming Dynasty (1368–1644)	*Daozang* compiled (1445) Daoist sacrificial rituals and notions of health influenced both elites and commoners in Korea, Japan, and Southeast Asia	Wang Yangming (1472–1529), an alternative Neo-Confucian view to Zhu Xi's Confucianism became state orthodoxy in Joseon dynasty (1392–1897) Korea Confucianism also became state ideology in Tokugawa Japan (1600–1868)
Qing Dynasty (1644–1911)		Civil service examination abolished (1905) Confucianism became dominant ideology in Nguyen dynasty Vietnam (1802–1945)
Early twentieth century	Chinese intellectuals criticized Daoism as superstition	Chinese intellectuals rejected Confucianism as feudal and reactionary
Communist China (1949–present)	Cultural Revolution (1966–1976) devastated Daoism Daoism gradually recovering since 1980s	Cultural Revolution (1966–1976) devastated Confucianism Confucianism gradually recovering since 1980s

Note: Asterisks indicate contested or approximate dates.

G atherings similar to that of the Chen extended family are replicated millions of times throughout China in observance of *qingming*. It is through this activity of paying homage to the ancestors and reaffirming kinship relations that the Chinese act out one of their most basic religious assumptions. At the core of this ritual is the Confucian notion of filial piety (honoring parents and ancestors) and of the centrality of the family in Confucian teaching. Equally on display is the Daoist (Taoist) attentiveness to changes in season and in nature, as well as the practice of warding off unwelcome ghosts through thunderous explosives. From this single family ritual we see that Confucianism and Daoism can coexist quite harmoniously among the Chinese, with no sense of incompatibility or mutual exclusivity. Indeed, except for extreme partisans in each tradition, most Chinese often embrace both religions with no sense of tension or conflict. How is that possible?

In this chapter you are invited to step into the religious world of the Chinese and to see how these two native Chinese religions both rival and complement each other. (Even though Buddhism is the third main religious tradition in China, we only give passing notice to it in light of its alien origin and its totally different worldviews; see Chapter 3 for a complete treatment of Buddhism.) By focusing on the teachings, history, and practices of Confucianism and Daoism, we can appreciate the true religious nature of the two traditions as well, even though in content and expression they may differ from most other world religions.

THE TEACHINGS OF CONFUCIANISM AND DAOISM

It should be observed from the outset that before Confucianism and Daoism arose, an ancient religion already existed in China. This ancient Chinese religion took shape no later than 1600 B.C.E., fully a thousand years prior to the rise of the two traditions. In fact, both Confucianism and Daoism may be regarded as two divergent extensions or outgrowths of this ancient Chinese religion, with the former focusing on human social relationship, whereas the latter emphasizes individual physical and spiritual well-being. In order to understand the religious nature and practice of Confucianism and Daoism, therefore, this ancient Chinese religion needs to be examined first.

Ancient Chinese Religious Views

The *Book of Changes,* the *Yijing* (*I Ching,* traditionally believed to have been compiled by the end of the second millennium B.C.E.) represents the earliest expression of the Chinese religious mindset. It conveys a worldview that has been described as "organismic,"[2] meaning that every single component of the cosmos belongs to an organic whole and that all the component parts interact with one another in a continuous self-generating process. Unlike the foundational texts of most religions, the *Book of Changes* does not include a creation myth. This absence of a creation myth may be attributed to the dominance of the spirit of honoring ancestors in China since antiquity. When most of the spirits who populate the supernatural world are former human beings who share the same qualities as the living, the sense of mystery and "otherness" of a creator being may be difficult to envision. Instead, from an original state of "undifferentiated chaos" (*hundun*),[3] two polar yet complementary energies known as *qi* ("breath," "energy," or "force") emerged. One is called *yang* (literally the south-facing, sunny side of a mountain) and the other *yin* (the north-facing, shady side of a mountain). Representing all binary entities and concepts (such as day and night, male and female, hot and cold), *yang* and *yin* interact and alternate ceaselessly to form a continuum or spectrum, generating the myriad elements of the creation.

In this kind of a worldview, nothing exists outside the cosmos; therefore, everything is subject to its operating principles. This absence of a "wholly other" creator in the early Chinese cosmological myth has very significant implications. That is, the classical Chinese view uses the metaphor of procreation or giving birth, not creation or fashioning something out of nothing, for the beginning of the universe. In the Chinese view, the lack of any notion of a wholly transcendent ultimate cause makes it difficult to produce the idea of an almighty god preceding and existing outside of creation. Correspondingly, the notion of an active evil dedicated to undermining the plans of a supposedly benevolent creator is absent in the Chinese cosmological view. In other words, no frighteningly personified devil competes with a benign god to win the hearts and minds of humans. In this world without sin (at least sin as understood by the Abrahamic faiths of Judaism, Christianity, and Islam), humanity is released from an acute sense of guilt. Instead, harmony and balance are good and preferable. Disharmony and imbalance are not.

The cosmic tango of *yang* and *yin*, spontaneous and unceasing, is manifested in the *wuxing* ("five elemental phases"), the five paradigmatic states of metal, wood, fire, water, and soil. These five states or elements correlate with many categories in nature. In the human body, they correspond to the Five Viscera (heart, liver, spleen, lungs, and kidneys). In the sky they are represented by the Five Planets (Venus, Jupiter, Mercury, Mars, and Saturn), and then there are the Five Colors (red, blue, yellow, white, and black) and the Five Flavors (sour, sweet, bitter, spicy, and salty). These five states are at the same time mutually nurturing and mutually destructive. Water sustains wood, wood feeds fire, fire reduces everything back to ashes (soil), soil produces ores (metal), and ores melt into liquid (water). Conversely, water douses fire, fire melts metal, metal chops down wood, wood draws nutrients from soil, and soil blocks water. Ultimately, like the swinging of the pendulum, what drives this dynamic process is the principle of alternation: when one extreme is reached, it reverts to the other. Such is the way the cosmos operates.

Notice in the photo that the two halves of the circle are not perfectly divided right down the middle. Instead, they are interlocked and mutually penetrating. Each half also contains the seed of the other. Thus the entire cosmos is involved in a ceaseless flow of alternation and change.

Human Body and Soul   As fundamental energies of the cosmos that constantly interact with each other, *yin* and *yang* make solid matter when they coalesce and

The *yin-yang* symbol best represents the Chinese religious mentality. This worldview recognizes differences but also harmony among the differences.

remain immaterial when diffused. Thus their interplay can manifest in coarse and materialistic things, as well as in subtle and spiritual entities. It is in this context that the constitution of human beings can be understood.

All humans have a physical body, seen as the corporal manifestation of the interplay between *yin* and *yang*. But all humans also have an immaterial aspect, subdivided into *hun* and *po*. *Hun* reflects the *yang* component, being light, pure, and upward-rising. *Po*, on the other hand, indicates *yin*, being heavy, turgid, and downward-sinking. *Hun* and *po*, introduced into the physical body when the fetus is gestating, together make up the spiritual aspect of the individual. For lack of a better term, they constitute the soul matter of the individual. As long as they stay with the human body, with only short and temporary absences during the dream state or when in a coma, the individual remains alive. At death, however, *hun* departs from the body permanently, rising skyward, and *po* settles down on earth alongside the interred and decomposing body. Both *hun* and *po* eventually dissipate and become reconfigured in different proportions to form future beings.

The Spiritual World of Gods and Ghosts
After death, as long as the energy remains to keep the current identity of *hun* and *po* intact, the spirit of the deceased lingers. Though only a pale shadow of its former self, the spirit of one who dies at a ripe old age and is properly cared for by the descendants may become **shen**, a benevolent power that protects and brings benefit to the living. On the other hand, the spirit of one who dies tragically or prematurely, and one who is not given a suitable burial or sacrifice, will become **gui**, a vengeful and malevolent ghost who visits disasters on people. *Shen* is a generic term for all kindly deities and gods whose power and efficacy are sought to fulfill people's wishes for health, wealth, progeny, and status. Conversely, *gui* refers to all spiteful ghouls, demons, and ogres who wreak havoc in people's lives. Motivated both by longing and fear, the Chinese from the ancient times to the present strive to cultivate good relations with both *shen* and *gui*. This, of course, is in addition to their primary obligation in the commemorating and honoring of their ancestors. The line of demarcation between the spirits and humans thus cannot be sharply drawn. Humans can indeed possess or exhibit qualities that in other cultures or beliefs may be considered spiritual, or even divine.

The Ancient Chinese Concept of Honoring Ancestors and the Divine
To the ancient Chinese, the ancestors were not just dead, buried, and forgotten. Instead, they continued to play an active role in the lives of their living descendants. They were consulted often on matters both major and minor. From the very beginning, then, Chinese religious practice focused on kinship ties and practical living. It was not exclusively located in a separate "sacred" realm.[4] The ancestors' presence in the lives of their descendants has remained a central and characteristic aspect of Chinese civilization. It is in this sense that the depiction of *qingming* at the opening of this chapter is so demonstrative of Chinese religious behavior.

During the Shang Dynasty, the earliest verifiable historic period in China to date, whose traditional dates are 1600–1046 B.C.E., the spirits of the ancestors were sometimes asked to carry messages to a higher deity for decision and response. This higher, more authoritative deity was **Shangdi**, the Lord on High, who was the most powerful god in the Shang spiritual world and who also happened to be the ancient ancestor of the Shang imperial house. This Lord on High was the controlling power in the cosmos. Along with the spirits of the ancestors, *Shangdi* monitored the behavior of the royal descendants, dispensing rewards and meting out punishments as appropriate. It was precisely for this reason that the Shang rulers needed to maintain close contact and good relationship with *Shangdi* and the other ancestral spirits, for the spirits were their source of kingly power. This power was termed **de**, commonly translated as "virtue," but more accurately as "potency." It was through the timely and correct performance of sacrificial rites to the ancestors and to *Shangdi* that each Shang ruler could claim this power, which may be more appropriately understood as the charismatic influence he possessed. With *de* the Shang king ruled with authority and legitimacy.

But sometime near the end of the second millennium B.C.E., a former minister of the court staged a rebellion that overthrew the Shang Dynasty and founded the next regime, the Zhou Dynasty (1122–256 B.C.E.). This power shift was rationalized primarily in religious terms. The defeat of the Shang, as the victorious Zhou founders explained it, was in fact sanctioned by *Shangdi*, who turned out to have a different name and was, in fact, a different kind of deity. *Shangdi* was now known as **Tian**, literally, "the sky," but more properly "the force above." (Regrettably, most books and articles written in English on Chinese religion and philosophy translate *Tian* as "Heaven," which is both inaccurate and misleading. In this chapter we continue to use the term *Tian* rather than any English equivalent in order to avoid any mistaken notion of *Tian* being a paradise-like location.)

Tian was believed to be the source of all things in the universe (not as a creator, but rather as a procreator), the ultimate divine entity that provided order throughout the cosmos. More significantly, *Tian* was also a "will" that would support only the morally deserving as king. This made *Tian* radically different from *Shangdi*, who was understood to be partial to the Shang kings and subject to their sacrificial "bribery." *Tian* was not swayed by claimed blood ties or sacrificial offerings; instead, it insisted on the demonstration of moral uprightness as the only condition for its award of political authority and legitimacy, which was labeled **ming**, or **Tianming**. This was the "mandate" or "charge" given by *Tian* to the person and the imperial line that was to rule on *Tian*'s behalf. Moreover, this *ming* could be revoked and withdrawn and could be transferred to another person or family any time its provisional holder was found wanting in morality. This event was known as "*geming*," the revocation of the "*ming*." To this day, *geming* in Chinese means "revolution—the withdrawal of the current regime's mandate to rule."

According to the religious mindset of the Zhou, *Tian*'s workings in nature and in the human world are its **dao**, its "way" or "path." It is the *dao* of *Tian* that provides order and regularity in nature and in human society. By following and obeying this *dao*, both the natural and the human worlds would reach their optimal fulfillment. This implementation of the *dao* of *Tian* is the duty and obligation of the human ruler. Thus what had happened to the Shang regime actually validated this belief in *Tian's* mandate. Shang's last ruler, who was, according to the Zhou founders, a corrupt and immoral individual, was no longer fit to exercise *Tianming*, hence his violent removal from power.

As the chosen deputy of *Tian* in the human world, the Zhou king (and all subsequent imperial rulers in China) called himself *Tianzi* ("Son of *Tian*"), the person who had been entrusted with the power to rule *Tianxia* ("domain under *Tian*," i.e., the entire known world). The king was therefore not just a political leader exercising power over both territory and people; he was also a religious figure who served as intermediary between *Tian* and humanity, as well as the natural world. To fulfill his roles as both king and priest, the Zhou ruler had to observe a set of behavioral practices collectively referred to as ***li*** ("rituals" or "rites"). It was the correct and sincere performance of *li* that would convince *Tian* of the ruler's moral worth, ensure *Tian's* continuous favor, and guarantee the ruler's power through his *de*, his "potency." *Li* covered every aspect of kingly behavior—from matters of state to relation with ancestors to conduct on important familial occasions such as marriage and funerals and even involving military campaigns. It would in time govern all the ritual conduct of the king's ministers as well, as their proper behavior also contributed to the stability and legitimacy of the regime.

Ancient Chinese Texts Such prescribed rites for the king and his ministers would later be codified into a text known as the *Record of Rites* (*Liji*). However, the beliefs in the source of kingly power and the underlying assumptions of imperial moral obligations are fully addressed in two other texts, the *Book of Odes* (*Shijing*)[5] and the *Book of History* (*Shujing*).[6] The former is an anthology of poems and ballads expressing the sentiments of both nobles and commoners, whereas the latter consists primarily of recorded activities and pronouncements of kings and aristocrats. Another work, the previously mentioned *Book of Changes* (*Yijing*), contains early Chinese views of cosmology and the supernatural. Collectively, these texts, which existed in some form after the founding of the Zhou regime, provide most of the information on the ancient Chinese religion from which Confucianism and Daoism would evolve. The Confucians, in particular, would revere these texts as classics and as sacred texts. The four just mentioned, along with the *Spring and Autumn Annals* (*Chunqiu*), purportedly compiled by Confucius himself, would constitute the Confucian **Five Classics**. The Daoists, while fully aware of the authority of these texts, especially the *Book of Changes*, would create their own corpus of scriptural works focusing more on the constitution of the human body, the basic elements of nature and the cosmos, and the ideal human relationship with the spirits, as we shall see in later sections.

The Teachings of Confucius

In this chapter, the term Confucianism is used with reluctance. The Chinese refer to this tradition as the "Teaching of the **Ru**" (scholars and ritualists). Even though Confucius has been rightfully credited with giving this tradition prominence and profound religious meaning, he is by no means its founder, nor is he worshipped as a supernatural savior figure like Jesus Christ in Christianity or the Buddha in Mahayana Buddhism. Therefore, "Confucianism" is quite a misleading term. In fact, the name "Confucius" is equally problematic, as it is actually a Latinized way of representing the Chinese reference to "Kong Fu Zi," the honorific way of addressing "Master Kong." Master Kong's full name is Kong Qiu, whose dates are conventionally given as 551–479 B.C.E. We will take a closer look at his life and times later in this chapter; here, we turn to an examination of his teachings.

Confucius inherited the entire package of ancient Chinese religious views discussed in the preceding pages. This is made clear in the single most important work that contains his main teaching, the *Lunyu*. Literally meaning "comments and sayings" but customarily translated as the *Analects*, this text is believed to have been compiled by Confucius's leading disciples after his death. It serves as a record of statements he had made, exchanges with students he had conducted, and even remarks some of the students had offered. As such it is an authoritative source for the examination of Confucius's teaching. Despite the possibility of later interpolations and the apparent lack of organization, the extant twenty "Books" of the *Analects*, taken as a whole, reflect a coherent picture of Confucius's major concerns and aspirations. A careful analysis of the content of the *Analects* shows that, while accepting many of the preexisting cosmological notions and religious beliefs of ancient China, Confucius and his immediate followers offered many new insights and creative interpretations regarding them. In the end, these "comments and sayings" contributed to the formation of a distinct tradition with unique views on humanity and its relationship with the divine. The following are some of the most notable topics addressed in the *Analects*.

The Primacy of *Tian* Confucius lived during the last centuries of the Zhou regime, which was a period of unmistakable dynastic decline. The notion of the possible revocation and transfer of *tianming* could not be too far from the minds of the weak Zhou ruler, the ambitious feudal lords serving under him, and the "men of service" who were seeking new opportunities for social and political advancement. Confucius was no exception. What he has conveyed in the *Analects* is a reinvigorated and fresh understanding of *Tian*, *Tianming*, and their relationship to humans, especially the moral elite.

The *Tian* of early Zhou, as we have seen, was an august and aloof divine power whose interaction with human beings was largely confined to the ruler, who alone could worship it. By contrast, the *Tian* of Confucius was a far more intimate religious and ethical entity. It had a conscious will that no longer reached out to the Zhou rulers and the various feudal lords (as it had done in the past), but to moral and noble men of diverse backgrounds so that they might revive a moral order that once existed.[7] Confucius saw himself, and encouraged his followers to become, a member of this moral vanguard.

Tian's message to the moral elite is not verbal or revelatory. Unlike the biblical God or the Qur'anic Allah, *Tian* silently manifests itself in the course of the seasons and in the records of human events to allow perceptive individuals to detect the full content of its command. Once the individual moral person firmly understands that imperative, a special relationship with *Tian* becomes possible. That person feels that *Tian* "knows" him and that he in turn has direct access to *Tian*. He becomes an obedient mouthpiece through which *Tian*'s message will be spread, resulting, hopefully, in a general uplifting of society. Various passages in the *Analects* attest to this faith in the primacy of *Tian* in Confucius's life and teachings. The following are particularly illustrative.

TIAN IN THE ANALECTS

A border official from the town of Yi requested an audience with the Master. . . . After emerging from the audience, he remarked [to the Master's disciples], "The world has long been without the ideal Way. *Tian* intends to use your Master like a wooden clapper for a bell [to awaken the world]."

—*Analects 3:24*

When Huan Tui, the Minister of War of the principality of Song, tried to kill Confucius (who was visiting), Confucius exclaimed, "It is *Tian* who has endowed me with virtue. What harm can Huan Tui do to me?"

—*Analects 7:23*

When under siege in the principality of Kuang, the Master declared, "With King Wen (founder of Zhou Dynasty) dead, does not civilization rest now on me? If *Tian* intends to have civilization destroyed, those who come after me will have nothing. But if *Tian* does not intend to have civilization destroyed, then what can the men of Kuang do to me?"

—*Analects 9:5*

The Master lamented, "Alas, there is no one who understands me." Zigong said, "How is it that no one understands you?" The Master continued, "I do not complain against *Tian*, nor do I blame my fellow men. I study what is mundane to reach what is transcendent. If there is anyone who understands me, it is *Tian!*"

—*Analects 14:35*

What these passages show collectively is the centrality of *Tian* in Confucius's thinking. *Tian* is clearly the highest religious authority, as well as ultimate reality, in the *Analects*. The *Analects* suggests a conscious *Tian* who "intends" human beings to have civilization in the form of a perfect order. To that end it reaches out to a few noble individuals. It does so not by direct revelation but through the quiet natural course of nature, as well as through human events, and it charges those individuals with the mission to sustain and protect human civilization. This is *Tian*'s mandate or imperative (*ming*). *Tianming*, to Confucius, is no longer an endowment of dynastic power and legitimacy for the political power holders but a call to moral perfection and close relation with the divine ultimate for the spiritual elite.

Some scholars of Confucian studies have noted the "prophetic voice" in Confucius and his followers. William Theodore de Bary of Columbia University is a forceful advocate of this aspect of the Confucian tradition.[8]

To be sure, unlike Moses or Muhammad, Confucius did not see himself as the messenger of a personal God; nevertheless, he criticized the authorities of his time and condemned their departure from the normative ideal by appealing to *Tian*. He invoked his own power as someone who, because of his endowment with *Tian*'s command, had that right to do so. In effect Confucius changed the very nature of *Tianming*. It became the self-ascribed duty of the moral individual to serve as mouthpiece to a *Tian* that did not speak itself, to be inspired and motivated by the sense of mission, indeed of commission, by *Tian*. The men of virtue, the *Analects* insists, must be "strong and resolute, for their burden of responsibility is heavy and the journey is long. Taking upon themselves the burden of humaneness, is that not heavy? Stopping only at death, is that not long?" (*Analects* 8:7). *Tian* in the *Analects* spurned the power holders of a decadent age and instead entrusted the awesome responsibility of protecting the ideals of the human order to a nonruler like Confucius.

> How is the Confucian *Tian* different from the Judaic Yahweh, the Christian God, and the Islamic Allah?

The Content of *Tian*'s Imperative—the *Dao* Just what is this message that *Tian* seeks to convey through the spiritual elite? It is the *Dao*, the Way. Confucius often complains in the *Analects* that the "*Dao* is not in practice" (*Analects* 5:7), or the "*Dao* does not prevail in the world" (*Analects* 16:2). What he means by the *Dao* is the total normative social-political-ethical order with the prescriptions for proper ritual behavior publicly, as well as moral rectitude privately. However, when men in power were incapable or unwilling to uphold this order, as was the case during Confucius's time, men of virtue and uprightness must take it upon themselves to protect and preserve this ideal or civilization would be doomed. It is for this reason that Confucius regards the search for and embodiment of the *Dao* to be the ultimate, paramount task in life. He proclaims: "If I can hear the *Dao* in the morning, I will die contented that evening!" (*Analects* 4:8).

As *Dao* represents the entire normative human order, Confucius focuses on certain key aspects for detailed discussion: *ren* and *li*.

Ren Perhaps the single most important article of faith held by Confucius is **ren** (benevolence, humaneness, virtue)—the kernel of humanity that exists in all human beings. It is the germ of moral consciousness that enables human beings to form a perfect human order. Etymologically, it points to the interrelatedness among humans, for in writing it is a combination of the character for person (人) and the character for the number two (二), signaling that it is in a "state of person-to-person" that *ren* (仁) can be enacted. Throughout the *Analects* the importance of *ren* in Confucius's teaching is evident. Many of his leading disciples ask him about it, and he gives various answers to drive home the idea that *ren* is all-rounded and multifaceted. Indeed, *ren* is so fundamental a concept that Confucius allows the giving of one's life in order to preserve it (*Analects* 15:9), implying that a life without *ren* is meaningless.

People who can preserve and develop their *ren* can be entrusted to carry out the imperative of *Tian*. "When the root is firmly established, the *Dao* will grow. Filial piety and brotherly deference, are they not the basis of *ren*?" (*Analects* 1:2). It is the cultivation and nurturing of this root of moral propensity that constitutes the actualization of the *Dao*. Note that Confucius here is not asserting the perfection of all human beings. Rather, he is advocating their perfectibility through self-effort. This inner moral disposition needs to be expanded and developed before it can sustain the *Dao*. What is remarkable about this view is the belief that this moral potentiality is not a monopoly of those in power, or those of noble birth, but is in fact possessed by all humans. This universal accessibility makes it possible for someone like Confucius to teach others how to achieve *ren* and how to become men of virtue themselves.

Furthermore, this goodness is exemplified by filial piety (**xiao**) and brotherly deference, as well as by a sense of dutifulness (*zhong*) and reciprocity (*shu*). Filial piety honors one's indebtedness to the family elders and to the parents, and brotherly deference acknowledges the natural hierarchy in birth order among siblings. Thus it is within the family that humans first acquire their moral education. Outside the family, one should interact with other people according to the principle of exerting one's utmost effort in fulfilling one's diverse roles in society. This effort arises from one's sense of dutifulness and "not doing unto others what one does not want done unto oneself" (*Analects* 15:24), which is the height of reciprocity. *Ren* is thus the entire human moral repertoire, which, when developed and enacted, will produce harmony in the human world and in the relationship that humans maintain with *Tian*.

Li *Ren* alone, however, is not enough to enable one to preserve the *Dao*. This inner potentiality for goodness and benevolence has to be manifested by an external performance of prescribed behavior within the family, the community, the entire human society, and the spiritual world beyond. This is referred to as *li* (rites, rituals, normative behavior) in the *Analects*, a word that in ancient China meant only the sacrificial and behavioral rituals of the kings and the nobles. The ideograph for *li* shows a sacred ritual vessel, indicating that the etymological origin of the word has something to do with sacrifice to the gods or the ancestors (禮). In Confucius's understanding of the term, *li* encompasses the entirety of proper human conduct vis-à-vis other human beings, dead ancestors, and the spirits. *Li* cultivates a learned pattern of behavior that, when combined with the moral propensity present in each individual, will produce a "magical power" in human relationships, as well as in relations with the spirits. Once a ritual gesture is initiated in the proper ceremonial context and performed with grace and sincerity, the magical result of goodwill, trust, and harmony will follow. This is the irresistible and invisible power of ritual itself.

The *Analects* is most optimistic about the efficacy of *li*: In a famous response to his favorite student's question about *ren*, Confucius states: "Restraining oneself and returning to *li*, this is *ren*" (*Analects* 12:1). Only through ritualized interaction with others and with the spirits can one realize one's full potential as a human being. The mastery and performance of *li*, then, is in fact a "process of humanization."[9] *Li* is the externalization of *ren*. Conversely, *ren* is the inner source of *li*. This is why Confucius asks rhetorically: "A man who is not *ren*, what has he to do with *li*?" (*Analects* 3:3).

Junzi Confucius uses the term ***junzi*** (the noble man, the man of virtue, and the superior man) for the noble *ru* on whose shoulders rests the burden of reviving and preserving the *Dao*. This is Confucius at his most creative and revolutionary in the usage of terminology. Originally used to refer to the scions of feudal rulers, *junzi* in Confucius's refashioning comes to mean men of moral rectitude. From someone highborn, *junzi* becomes someone high-minded. From those of noble birth, *junzi* now means those of noble worth. They are the prophet-like individuals who, though holding no political office or having no privileged positions, nevertheless heed *Tian*'s call. They undertake the most arduous task of implementing *Tian*'s *Dao* in the human world. The *Analects* puts the issue most plainly: "Without knowing the imperative of *Tian*, one cannot be a *junzi*" (20:3).

The self-cultivation of the *junzi* will earn them a power (*de*) similar to that possessed by the ancient sage rulers. It is a charismatic, noncoercive, potent influence that both inspires and persuades, and coaxes and shames, people into doing what is right. In the *Analects* Confucius confidently declares: "The *de* of the *junzi* is like wind, while that of the common people is like grass. When the wind blows over the grass, the grass cannot help but bend in the direction of the wind" (*Analects* 12:19). The epitome of the *junzi* is the sage (***shengren*** or simply ***sheng*** 聖), the rarest of human beings who are perfect in their moral standing and kingly in their worldly accomplishments. The traditional Chinese character for sage contains three components: ear, mouth, and ruler (耳, 口, 王).

The sage is someone who hears or listens to the Way of *Tian*, reconveys it through the mouth, and acts in the capacity of the ancient ruler whose job it is to link up the three realms of Heaven, Earth, and Humankind. Thus the sage is decidedly a religious figure, a saintly person who is at once a messenger of *Tian* to the human world and an exemplar of human perfection in the eyes of *Tian*.

The Religious Vision of the *Analects* Taken as a whole, the vision of the *Analects* offers an amazingly clear picture of Confucius's ultimate concern. The religious aspect of this Confucian vision is unmistakable. It has been justly pointed out that, unlike many other religious figures, Confucius envisaged no escape from the world and human society, nor did he insist on ascetic self-denial as a precondition for spiritual progress. In a similar vein, Confucius did not consider concern with the afterlife or with the spirits to be of primary importance. The following exchange between him and his student Zilu on that subject is famous: "Zilu asked about serving ghosts and spirits. The Master said, 'When we are not yet able to serve fellow humans, why worry about serving the ghosts and spirits?' 'What about death?' [Zilu persisted]. 'When we do not yet know enough about life, why worry about death?' [the Master replied]" (*Analects* 11:12).

Then in what sense is the Confucian teaching religious? Confucius has an abiding faith in the transcendent ultimate *Tian*. He feels an intimate relationship with it. He has a keen awareness of its command (*ming*) given to the moral and spiritual elites (*junzi*) to create the ideal human order (*Dao*). He firmly believes in the *Tian*-endowed human capacity for perfection and genuine humanity (*ren*) through self-cultivation, and enthusiastically participates in sacrificial rituals and familial and social rites (*li*). These are all components of his religious outlook. To be sure, this religiosity does not express itself in faith in a personal God and the need for salvation through divine grace. Rather, it distinguishes itself as a form of "this-worldly transcendentalism." It treats the "secular as sacred,"[10] and it imparts deeply religious meaning to participation in the mundane. Thus it expresses a different mode of religiousness. For this reason, it has been paradoxically labeled a "humanistic religion" and a "religious humanism."[11] The distinction between the human and the divine, clearly drawn in the Abrahamic traditions, is not found here. For Confucius, the ultimate goal for humans is to heed the instruction of *Tian* by transforming themselves from potential to actual goodness. This process of transformation toward the absolute is the religious nature of the Confucian teaching, and it is right there in the *Analects*.

Admittedly, this religiousness of the Confucian *Analects* has been largely overshadowed by its familial, social, and political emphasis throughout the course of Chinese imperial history, so much so that Confucianism as a religion is not readily recognized. However, the discussion that follows should further confirm the intrinsic religiosity of the Confucian tradition as it unfolded.

The Mencius Mencius (a Latinized rendition of "Master Men") (371–289 B.C.E.?) was born a full century after Confucius's death. Claiming to be the rightful successor to Confucius, Mencius reaffirmed moral cultivation as a religious calling. He provided the moral elite with a strong sense of mission. Mencius also made one lasting contribution to the Confucian belief system with his insistence on the basic goodness of human beings, thus upholding Confucianism's optimistic view of human perfectibility.

Next to the *Analects*, the *Mencius* (likewise compiled by some of Mencius's leading disciples) is significant as a Confucian scriptural text. Unlike Confucius, who does not regard himself as a sage—a title he reserves only for the few legendary rulers in ancient China—Mencius not only boldly declares his predecessor's sageliness but also insists on his own. Indeed, he considers every human being a potential sage, as he deems that each possesses all the innate qualities to become one. It is based on that assumption that he asserts the intrinsic goodness of human nature, which he compares to the natural tendency of water to flow downward (*Mencius* 6A, 2:2). This is Mencius's fundamental article of faith.

Identifying four "sprouts of morality" in all humans—the inborn sentiments of commiseration (inability to bear to witness the suffering of others), shame, deference and yielding, and sense of right and wrong—Mencius proclaims them to be the roots of benevolence (*ren*), righteousness (*yi*), propriety (*li*), and wisdom (*zhi*), respectively. With this belief as his religious premise, he constructs a logical progression from moral cultivation to the ultimate attainment of divine spirituality. He states, "That which is sought after is called 'good.' To have it in oneself is called 'true.' To possess it fully is called 'beautiful,' while making it shine forth with brilliance is called 'great.' To be great and be able to transform others is called 'sage.' To be sage and be beyond understanding by others is called 'spiritually divine'" (*Mencius* 7B, 25). Through our moral progress, Mencius suggests, we can become not only good, true, beautiful, and great, but also sagely and ultimately divine. With utter conviction, then, he maintains, "Probing one's heart/mind to the utmost, one will know one's nature. Knowing one's nature, one will know *Tian*. To preserve one's heart/mind and nurture one's nature is to put one in the service of *Tian*" (*Mencius* 7A, 1:1). Once one has embodied the moral imperatives of *Tian*, Mencius reasons, one will find all other concerns secondary. In one of his most celebrated statements, Mencius declares: "I like fish, and I also like bear's paw. If I cannot have both, I will give up fish and keep the bear's paw. Life is what I desire, but so is righteousness. If I cannot have both, I will give up life but cling to righteousness" (*Mencius* 6A, 10:1). With morality as his ultimate concern, Mencius is willing to sacrifice his own life in order to preserve it. This is certainly reminiscent of Confucius's commitment to benevolence (*ren*), for the preservation of which he, too, is willing to suffer death. This is demonstrative of the spirit of the martyr and a deeply held religious sentiment.

The *Great Learning* and the *Doctrine of the Mean* The remaining two texts of the **Four Books**, completing the Confucian religious corpus designated by a later Confucian scholar (see the section on the history of Confucianism later in this chapter), are the *Great Learning* and the *Doctrine of the Mean*, supposedly compiled by two of Confucius's prominent students. Both are chapters from the *Book of Rituals* that have been excerpted as independent texts because of their religious significance. The former refers to learning about what is of primary importance. It prescribes a practical step-by-step road map for self-cultivation, starting with individual inquiries and ending with the transformation of humanity as a whole. Listing eight steps in personal cultivation, the *Great Learning* outlines a sequence of individual and social effort made to manifest "illustrious virtue," "love the people," and reach the "ultimate good," which is nothing short of the *Tian*-ordained perfect world order. Thus learning involves far more than the acquisition of knowledge, but is actually an ethical-religious program of personal and societal perfection.

The *Doctrine of the Mean* begins with a bold declaration: "What *Tian* has ordained is called human nature. Following this nature is called the *Dao*. Cultivating the *Dao* is called teaching" (*Doctrine of the Mean* 1:1). These three statements articulate the fundamental Confucian articles of faith, representing what Confucianism regards as self-evidently true. The text asserts that humans are born with a benign nature imparted by *Tian*, the ultimate religious authority. This nature provides them with the inner strength to reach their fullest potential as perfect beings. Furthermore, when extended beyond the individual, this human nature can bring about an ideal social-political-ethical order, the actualization of which is the purpose of education. The text further maintains that the real possibility for achieving perfect goodness exists because of the special relationship between human beings and *Tian*. There is a logical progression from self-generating moral effort to the perfection of the faithful and the world around them: "The *junzi* [noble person] cannot avoid not cultivating his person. Thinking of cultivating his person, he cannot neglect serving his parents. Thinking of serving his parents, he may not avoid knowing other humans. Thinking of knowing other humans, he cannot ignore knowledge of *Tian*" (*Doctrine of the Mean* 20:7). It is clear that human beings must fully engage themselves with others in order to actualize their genuine humanity and divine potential.

There are five cardinal human relations for such interaction—three within the family and two outside of the family: that between father and son, husband and wife, elder and younger brothers, ruler and subject, and friends. All these relations obligate individuals to perform their respective roles in society—the father has to be kind while the son is respectful; the husband has to be caring while the wife is submissive; brothers need to be mutually deferential; the ruler needs to have the people's welfare in mind while the subjects need to be obedient; and friends must maintain fidelity toward one another. It is therefore the entire human community that provides the setting for the Confucian religious quest. The *Doctrine of the Mean* offers a climactic conclusion to the process of self-cultivation:

> Only the most authentic and genuine person can fully develop his nature. Able to fully develop his nature, he can then thoroughly understand the nature of other people. Able to fully understand the nature of other people, he can develop the nature of things. Able to fully develop the nature of things, he can assist in the transforming and nourishing process of *Tian* and *Di* (earth, counterpart to *Tian*). When he assists in the transforming and nourishing process of *Tian* and *Di*, he forms a trinity with them!
>
> —*Doctrine of the Mean* 22:1

This euphoric assurance of the final outcome of human moral cultivation is breathtaking in its grandeur. Not only does the person who realizes his own nature to the full become a paradigm of genuine humanity, but also he actually becomes a "coequal" with *Tian* and *Di* through his participation in their nurture and sustenance of the myriad things. Forming a trinity with the ultimate numinous entity in the cosmos is without a doubt the highest accomplishment for any religious seeker in the Confucian mode.

In the preceding paragraphs, we have analyzed the content and the religiosity of the Four Books. These four texts neatly annotate the later Neo-Confucian goal of *neisheng waiwang*—inner moral cultivation and external skillful management of society and state (see the section on the history of Confucianism later in this chapter). This is believed to reflect the original vision of Confucius, namely, to pursue a personal relationship with the ultimate reality through moral improvement, culminating in an ordering of society and state in accordance with the Way ordained by *Tian*. This religious mission is best expressed by a famous Neo-Confucian scholar by the name of Zhang Zai (1020–1077):

> To establish the mind of *Tian* and *Di*
> To inculcate an understanding of [*Tian*'s] command (*ming*) for the multitudes
> To revive and perpetuate the teachings of the sages of the past
> To provide peace and stability for all future generations.

This is indeed the social-political, as well as religious, aspiration of Confucianism in a nutshell!

Confucianism and Women

The issue of Confucianism and sexism needs to be addressed. Despite its lofty religious teaching, Confucianism has often been criticized for its dismissive and negative attitude toward women. The single most notorious statement made by Confucius regarding women is truly incriminating: "Women and the petty men are alike, in that they are both hard to deal with" (*Analects* 17:23). In addition, one of the most prominent features of Confucianism during the Han Dynasty (206 B.C.E.–220 B.C.E.) and beyond is the submissiveness of the female to the male. Cleverly manipulating the traditional *yin-yang* belief into an argument for the priority of *yang* over *yin*, hence the male over the female, Han Confucians and their successors in later dynasties insisted that women submit to their fathers when young, their husbands when married, and their sons when old and widowed. This aspect of Confucianism in imperial China became a major cause of criticism of the tradition in the modern period. Since the beginning of the twentieth century, Confucianism has been portrayed as a sexist, patriarchal ideology responsible for the oppression of women in China. The insidious Chinese practices of foot binding (the crushing of the feet of young girls with long binding cloth to make their walking willowy and feminine), concubinage (the keeping of multiple wives by one man), disallowance of women-initiated divorce, prohibition against remarriage, and encouragement of widow suicide have all been blamed on Confucianism.

However, this view of Confucianism may be too simplistic in characterizing the two thousand years of Chinese gender history. It makes no distinction between theory and practice, as well as ideal, normative values versus actual, living experiences. Furthermore, it also overlooks the very intellectual and religious dynamism of Confucianism as a teaching of human improvement and self-cultivation with no gender specificity. Some contemporary scholars have taken note of the parallels between Confucian and feminist ethics. Confucianism as a state orthodoxy whose central purpose is social control and political manipulation is indeed incompatible with modern values. However, Confucianism as an ethical and religious teaching with an emphasis on mutual care, empathy, responsible government, and communal welfare shares many similarities with feminist care ethics.[12]

Laozi riding on the back of a water buffalo as he retires into the realm of the immortals.

The Teachings of Daoism

We have pointed out earlier that Daoism evolved out of the same ancient Chinese religious mindset as Confucianism did. But instead of regarding *Tian* as the Absolute Ultimate, as the Confucians do, Daoists from the beginning hold *Dao* to be supreme. It should be recalled that the term *Dao* is also central to the Confucian tradition. However, the Daoists articulate a very different understanding of the *Dao*. It is this alternative apprehension of the *Dao* that serves as the point of departure for their entirely different mode of religious experience from that of the Confucians.

Laozi* (Lao-tzu) and *Zhuangzi* (Chuang-tzu)** Traditionally, the best known and earliest identifiable Daoists were Laozi (Master Lao) and Zhuangzi (Master Zhuang). The former, more of a composite figure than an actual person, was the reputed author of the ***Daodejing (*Tao-te Ching*; The Scripture of the Way and Its Potent Manifestation),[13] alternatively known as the *Laozi*. The latter was an obscure individual active in the late fourth century B.C.E. who was credited with authorship of the second most influential Daoist text, the *Zhuangzi*. Both texts are more representative of certain modes of thinking than of individual thinkers, as they are actually anthologies containing different strands of thought rather than coherent and logical teachings of single authors. One thing, however, is clear: they are self-consciously non-Confucian in that they express a decidedly alternative understanding of the *dao* and of ideal human action. In addition, both the *Daodejing* and the *Zhuangzi* also contain descriptions of perfected human beings who possess amazing powers of magic and immortality. Both texts suggest that, through intense inner psychic journeying and mystical conditioning of the human body, individuals can acquire impressive powers of transformation and invulnerability to the decaying agents in nature.

The *Daodejing* The eighty-one-chapter *Daodejing* is undoubtedly the most translated and most popular Chinese text in the West. Virtually all the different movements and sectarian lineages within Daoism regard this work as the founding scripture of the tradition.

In contrast to the Confucian *Dao* being the ideal ethical-social-political order ordained by *Tian* for human beings, the *Dao* of the *Laozi* antedates *Tian* and acts as the basis of the natural order. Here *Dao* is the primordial entity that exists in an undifferentiated state prior to the coming into being of the myriad things, including *Tian* and *Di*, which now stand for nothing more than nature itself. The lofty primacy of the Confucian *Tian* is supplanted by the nebulous *Dao* of the *Daodejing*, as indicated by the following celebrated passage:

> There was something undifferentiated and yet complete, which existed
> before *Tian* and *Di*
> Soundless and formless, it depends on nothing and does not change
> It operates everywhere and does not stop
> It may be regarded as the "Mother of the world"
> I do not know its name; I call it *Dao*.
> —*Daodejing, Chap. 25*

In one broad stroke, the entire Confucian cosmological scheme is turned upside down. It is *Dao*, not *Tian*, that gives birth, like a mother, to the myriad things. It is *Dao*, not *Tian*, that serves as the primal source of the cosmos. Echoing the cosmogonic (concerning the origin of the cosmos) view of the *Book of Changes*, the *Daodejing* gives an even terser summary of the generating process of the cosmos:

> The *Dao* gives birth to the One [Being, Existence]
> The One brings forth the Two [*Yin* and *Yang*]
> The Two give rise to the Three [*Tian*, *Di*, and Humans]
> The Three engender the Ten Thousand Things [world of multiplicity
> and diversity]
> —*Daodejing, Chap. 42*

Again, the primacy of the *Dao* as the procreator of the entire universe and everything in it is unequivocally asserted here. As the ground of all beings, this *Dao* is compared to a "mysterious female," "water," "infant," and "uncarved block," all alluding to the beginning of life and form. However, unlike the Confucian *Dao*, which requires superior human beings (the *junzi* [men of virtue] and the *shengren* [sages]) to exert their utmost effort to actualize its ideal design, the *Dao* of the *Daodejing* can only maintain its pristine form when humans leave it alone. Thus the ideal course of action for insightful and wise human beings is to observe **wuwei** (actions without intention) and **ziran** (natural spontaneity) in their attempt to return to the *Dao*. These two ideal approaches to life are indicative of the *Daodejing*'s belief in the innate perfection and completeness of the *Dao*. *Wuwei* calls for a minimalist and noninterventionist attitude in human action, whereas *ziran* rejects any artificiality and contrived undertaking as detrimental to human well-being. Ultimately, the *Dao* in the *Daodejing* is indescribable, for it defies verbalization and precise definition. "The *Dao* that can be [verbally] expressed is not the constant *Dao*," insists the *Daodejing* in its first verse.

Yet the transcendent *Dao* is, at the same time, manifested in the myriad things through its presence in them as *de*—the very "potent manifestation" of each thing. In contrast to the *de* of the Confucians, which is the charismatic power of the moral elite, the *de* of the *Daodejing* points to the concrete expression of the *Dao* in all things. *De* is the "thingness" of a thing—that which makes a thing what it is. The combination of *Dao* and *de*, then, helps to bridge the gap between the transcendent and the immanent for the author(s) of the *Daodejing*. The *Dao* is the transcendent ground of being, yet through its expression in the *de* of the myriad concrete things, it is also fully immanent.

The *Zhuangzi* The extant version of the *Zhuangzi* consists of thirty-three chapters divided into three sections—"Inner," "Outer," and "Miscellaneous." The first seven Inner chapters are generally believed to be the authentic writings of Zhuang Zhou, the putative author. Yet as in the case of the *Daodejing*, we have only a vague biographical account of Zhuang Zhou, and little of substance is known about him.

The *Zhuangzi* is overall a different kind of text from the *Daodejing*. Whereas the latter is terse and aphoristic in language, the former is effusive and vividly narrative. The *Daodejing* idealizes the feminine and regards the *Dao* as mother, but the *Zhuangzi* does not. The *Daodejing* gives much emphasis to politics and the techniques of rulership; the *Zhuangzi* is overtly adverse to politics. The *Zhuangzi* tells stories with a witty, playful, irreverent tone that is totally absent in the *Daodejing*. In terms of basic worldview and cosmological assumptions, however, the *Zhuangzi* shares much in common with the *Daodejing*, hence their grouping together by later historians and bibliographers as representatives of the "School of the *Dao*."

In the *Zhuangzi*, the *Dao* is not only the ineffable transcendent entity that gives rise to all things but also the immanent core that exists in all things, from the loftiest perfected beings to the lowliest broken tiles and excrement. It is therefore omnipresent, making all things ultimately equal. As such, the *Dao* transcends all polarities, dichotomies, and dualities that the human mind is inclined to create. Hence the use of the human cognitive and rational approach to apprehend the *Dao* is futile and unproductive, as it can only be realized intuitively through the abandonment of the intellect. The mind must be able to be free from all conventional distinctions and established views, hence the advocacy of "carefree wandering" (*xiaoyao yu*) in the *Zhuangzi*. In this connection the discussion of "fasting the mind/heart" (**xinzhai**) and "sitting and forgetting" (**zuowang**) becomes pertinent, as both practices dispense with rationality and deliberative cognition in order to arrive at the perfect intuitive understanding of the *Dao*.

Elements of Physical Invulnerability in the *Daodejing* and the *Zhuangzi*

Although both the *Daodejing* and the *Zhuangzi* are best known (in China and in the West) for their sophisticated philosophical discussions of the *Dao*, much less known is their commentary on the physical prowess of the Daoist practitioners. They hint at invulnerability to harm, longevity, and even immortality—the very goals of a Daoist religious movement that began no later than the second century C.E.

We next explore the impact the two have had on the content of Daoism as a religion. The following passages from both texts are highly suggestive:

EXCERPTS FROM THE *DAODEJING*

He who does not lose his proper place lasts long
He who dies but does not perish has longevity.

—*Daodejing, Chap. 33*

I have heard that people who are good at preserving their lives will not encounter wild bulls or tigers when traveling on land, and will not need to protect themselves with armor when in the army. Wild bulls will find nowhere to thrust their horns, tigers will have no place to sink their claws, and weapons will find no point to insert their cutting blades. And why is that? Because in them there is no room for death.

—*Daodejing, Chap. 50*

He who is richly endowed with *de* is comparable to a newborn baby: poisonous insects will not sting him, ferocious beasts will not seize him in their claws, and birds of prey will not snatch him with their talons.

—*Daodejing, Chap. 55*

EXCERPTS FROM THE *ZHUANGZI*

Far away on Mt. Guye there dwells a divine person (*shenren*) whose skin is like ice and snow, and who is gentle and shy like a young girl. He does not eat the five grains; but [only] inhales the wind and drinks the dew. He ascends the clouds, mounts flying dragons, and wanders beyond the four seas. His spirit is focused, thus he saves creatures from sickness and plagues, and guarantees bountiful harvests.

—*Zhuangzi, Chap. 1*

The ultimate person (*zhiren*) is spirit-like. Though the great marshes are set ablaze, they will not make him hot. Though the rivers and streams freeze up, they cannot chill him. Though violent thunder splits the mountains and howling gales churn the ocean, they will not frighten him. A man like this rides the clouds and mist, mounts the sun and moon, and goes beyond the four seas. Death and life have no effect on him, how much less will profit and loss?

—*Zhuangzi, Chap. 2*

The perfected individuals (*zhenren*) of old . . . could go up to high places without getting frightened, enter water without getting wet, and go into fire without feeling hot. Only those whose knowledge ascends the height of the Dao can be like this. . . . The perfected breathe with their heels, while the ordinary men breathe with their throat.

—*Zhuangzi, Chap. 6*

A Daoist immortal flying through the clouds, 1750. Portrayed is the sage mother of Dongling, who studied the Way and could cure illnesses. One day, amidst a throng wishing to thank her, she ascended to the clouds.

Blowing and breathing, exhaling the old and inhaling the new, [imitating the postures of] bear strides and bird stretches—these are all undertaken for the purpose of longevity. They are pursued with fondness by people who practice gymnastic calisthenics (*daoyin*) and body nourishments (*yangxing*) in hope of [attaining the longevity] of Patriarch Peng.

—*Zhuangzi, Chap. 15*

These passages on *Daoist* adepts describe their amazing magical power and physical invulnerability.

What these two texts suggest, at the very least, is that the numinous *Dao* (the holy) is accessible by potent (that is, healthy) individuals and that holiness and robust health are closely related. As described by the *Daodejing* and *Zhuangzi*, the early practitioners of the *Dao* were people who, through their use of various bodily techniques, acquired powers that enabled them to experience the divine. These techniques and powers would very much become the concern of later Daoists. In short, the *Daodejing* and the *Zhuangzi* can be perceived as "proto-Daoist" texts by virtue of their distinctive view of the *Dao* and their reference to various practices and powers that anticipate those of the later organized Daoist groups.

Immortality and Alchemy One later Daoist preoccupation is with the notion of **xian** (immortal or transcendent), long a folk religious fascination but articulated most eloquently in the *Baopuzi* (Master Who Embraces Simplicity), a text authored by

Ge Hong (283–343 C.E.). Central to this belief in *xian* is the conviction that physical transformation, invulnerability to disease, longevity, and ultimately immortality, can be acquired through proper diet, physical exercise, and drugs. People with the right recipe, formula, or prescription (**fangshi**) would teach these esoteric techniques and provide ready-made elixirs to those who had the financial resources and the necessary devotion to secure their services.

Inherent in the belief in immortality are the ancient Chinese assumptions about the human body and the measures that can be taken to keep it healthy and even immortal. The ancient Chinese believed that the human body is the microcosm that reflects the macrocosm of the cosmos. In other words, there is a direct correspondence and parallel between the human body and nature. All the myriad things in the universe are produced by the interaction of the vital energies (*qi*) of *yin* and *yang*. They also manifest the qualities of the five elemental phases (*wuxing*), follow the principle of alternation and constant return, while maintaining balance and harmony with one another. This belief was retained by Daoism and Chinese folk religion. According to this view, there are three central nodal points in the human body called **dantian** (locations for the production of pills of immortality)—in the head, the chest, and the abdomen—connected by meridian circuits through which the *qi* (energy) flows. And, because the body is the cosmos writ small, just as there are gods and deities inhabiting the physical world outside, there are also numerous spiritual beings residing in various organs of the human body.

Based on this whole series of assumptions, the techniques of **yangsheng** (nourishing life) are developed. First mentioned in the *Zhuangzi*, *yangsheng* has the goal of refining the body so that it can overcome its earthly limitations and be in perfect harmony with the *Dao*, making it last as long as the universe. It involves an entire spectrum of exercises, including deep meditation, controlled breathing, therapeutic gymnastics, dietary regimens, even sexual techniques. All these measures of nourishing life have been practiced by religious Daoists since the second century C.E. and are grouped under the general heading of **neidan** (internal alchemy).

While these *yangsheng* techniques aim at the regeneration and reinforcement of the human body by making use of what the body originally possesses, the *fangshi* also focus on the compounding and refining of elixirs with substances (herbal and mineral) from nature. References to "refining gold" (*lianjin*) and transmuting cinnabar (mercury sulphate) in some Han Dynasty texts indicate a growing practice of alchemy for the purpose of attaining longevity and immortality. This pursuit of alchemical manufacturing of *dan* with minerals and plants would eventually lead to the **waidan** (external alchemy) tradition in Daoism.

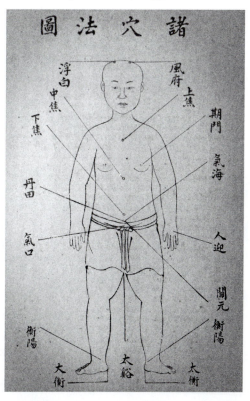

A Daoist view of the major nodal points in the human body through which the *qi* (energy) flows.

Figurine of Lord Guan as seen in many Chinese restaurants.

All the internal and external alchemical techniques discussed here are intended to produce a new body that grows within the old so that, in time, the old self will be replaced by the new in the same way cicadas and snakes regenerate themselves.

Daoist Deities   As the Daoist tradition matured, the most exalted god in the Daoist pantheon became the *Yuanshi tian-zun* (Celestial Venerable of Primordial Beginning), who is head of a trinity of Three Purities (*sanqing*). Below the *sanqing* are innumerable deities of both genders who fill up various ranks in a mind-boggling celestial bureaucracy that loosely corresponds to its human counterpart.

The lowliest among the spiritual bureaucrats is the local earth god (*tudi gong*), and the head of the celestial government is the Jade Emperor (*Yuhuang*). Many of them have divine origins, of course, but many also are former humans whose merits warrant their promotion to godly status. Some of the deities have national appeal, such as Lord Zhenwu [Perfect Martiality] of Mt. Wudang, whereas others are more local in influence, including the Stove god (*zaojun*) in each household. One ubiquitous Daoist deity, Lord Guan, is honored by business owners as their protector and benefactor. A human turned god, Lord Guan can be seen in the form of a heroic figure with a red face and a cascading black beard, sporting a long robe and holding a long blade. An altar or alcove containing a figurine of him can be found in most Chinese restaurants in North America, where he is worshipped as a patron deity.

Daoist deities not only reside in the heavens, on earth, in the underworld, and in the homes but also inside the human body. They are supposed to protect all the major internal organs from the decaying effect of unwholesome food and old age. The entire pantheon of Daoist deities can be accessed and appealed to through ritual performance for assistance in warding off evil, improving health, guaranteeing harmony in family and community, and attaining immortality.

Daoism and Women

Because of the feminine emphasis of the *Daodejing*, it is generally assumed that Daoism, unlike Confucianism, treats women fairly and kindly. Yet the situation is more complicated than it might appear at first thought. The positions and roles of women in organized Daoism have to be examined in the larger context of Chinese society, which until recent times has indeed been patriarchal and sexist. It is therefore not surprising that women only play limited roles even in Daoism.

And yet it is also undeniable that because of women's believed greater sensitivity to the spirits and their keener communication ability with the divine and invisible world, they do have access to roles and positions denied to most women in Chinese society at large. Women's special power to intercede with the deities often makes some of them more outstanding and influential practitioners of Daoism than men.

A Daoist movement known as the Celestial Masters (**Tianshi**; see more details in the section on the history of Daoism in this chapter) identified five classes of women suited to be Daoist practitioners: young unmarried women, women unable to marry because of their inauspicious horoscopes, women forced into marriage, rejected (divorced) wives, and widows. All these were vulnerable individuals to whom the Celestial Masters offered an escape and a way to assert their worth. In the Tang Dynasty (618–907 C.E.), women from aristocratic families became Daoist nuns in substantial numbers, either between marriages or as widows. There were also imperial princesses ordained as Daoist priestesses.

Xiwangmu (Queen Mother of the West) is one of the most prominent female Daoist deities. She rewards her devout followers with immortality by feasting them with magical peaches.

Equally noteworthy are a number of major Daoist goddesses who play key roles in the religion. Chief among them are Xiwangmu (Queen Mother of the West), best known for her granting of the power of immortality to the faithful, and Mazu, the virginal protectress of fishermen and merchants who is still very popular in southeast China and Taiwan today. Some women were actually founders of Daoist sects, most notably Wei Huacun (252–334 C.E.) of the Shangqing [Highest Clarity] tradition and Zu Shu (most active during 889–904 C.E.), who initiated the Qingwei [Pure Subtlety] tradition. Sun Bu'er (1119–1182 C.E.) was a famous female disciple of the founder of the Quanzhen [Complete Perfection] sect who became a senior leader in the movement with the power to teach and ordain other female practitioners. (We examine these other Daoist groups more closely later in this chapter.)

No comparable number of women can be identified as prominent Confucians. It is thus accurate to conclude that women generally fare better in Daoism than in Confucianism.

THE HISTORY OF CONFUCIANISM AND DAOISM

The earliest time in Chinese history for which we have both written records and archaeological evidences is the Shang Dynasty, whose traditional dates are 1600–1046 B.C.E. Representative of these records and evidences are the "oracle bone inscriptions," carved messages on smoothed-out oxen shoulder blade bones or tortoise shells that include questions put to (and supposed answers from) deceased members of the Shang royalty. The questions covered a wide spectrum of issues, from actions to be undertaken by the ruler (such as the decision to go to war) to intimate, personal matters of the imperial family (such as the gender of royal offspring about to be born). After the questions were put forth, heat was applied to a predrilled hole in the bone or shell, causing cracks to appear. Patterns formed by these cracks were read by the shaman-diviner, and

A Chinese oracle bone made of tortoise shell.

occasionally the Shang ruler himself, and were interpreted as answers to the original questions posed.

As indicated in the section on teachings in this chapter, the head of the Shang spiritual world was *Shangdi*, the ultimate benefactor of the royal house. Eventually, around the end of the second millennium B.C.E., the Shang dynasty was toppled by the Zhou. While retaining the ancestral focus of the Shang, as well as its belief in the religious underpinning of political authority, the Zhou founders nevertheless replaced *Shangdi* with *Tian* as the overarching spiritual authority. They exercised political power with the claim that it was a mandate they received from *Tian*, ostensibly because of their moral worthiness. Early Zhou society was reportedly well-ordered and harmonious, presided over by men of virtue. This impression was projected by the Zhou texts, collectively labeled as the Confucian Five Classics mentioned earlier in this chapter, which would serve as the prototypical source of the Confucian teachings.

The History of Confucianism

At the time of Confucius's birth, the entire political system and moral framework put in place by the early Zhou kings, as described in the previous section, was in disarray. Powerful feudal lords jockeyed for position to become the next *Tianzi*, the son of *Tian*, and to replace the current Zhou king. The more capable and ambitious among them actively sought the service of talented men outside the hereditary aristocratic circles, thereby creating upward social mobility for some among the commoners. Conversely, powerful lords could become commoners overnight as a result of their defeat by their rivals, creating a downward social spiral as well.

These critical social developments gave rise to the increasing prominence of a class of experts and specialists known as **shi** (men of service). Drawn from lower aristocratic or commoner backgrounds, they entered the employ of feudal lords and imperial rulers. The *shi* performed two major categories of duties: military and civil. The military men of service, the knights, were referred to as *wushi*, whereas their civilian counterparts, the scholars, were known as *rushi*, or simply **ru**. *Ru* were scribes and record keepers, masters of rituals and ceremonies, as well as diviners and religious professionals. To perform their duties well, *ru* had to acquire expertise in history, poetry, religious rites, divination, dance, and music.

Confucius was just such a *ru* who was born into a family of former aristocrats in the feudal domain of Lu (located in present-day Shandong province in North China). His father died when he was still an infant, so he had to do menial work as a young man to support himself, his sickly older brother, and his widowed mother. What enabled Confucius to lift himself up from poverty and anonymity was his desire for and success in scholarship. He apparently had an extraordinarily inquisitive mind and a voracious appetite for study, especially of the ancient texts of history, rituals, and poetry. By the age of thirty he was well known for his expertise as a *ru*. His service in government was limited to a number of minor posts, but his greatest accomplishment was in his vocation as a teacher. Confucius offered fresh insight into the human condition, creatively reinterpreting the belief system he inherited from the early Zhou. In addition, he communicated a forceful message of the need for improvement of individuals and society through moral cultivation and benevolent government. Aided by an intense and charismatic personality, Confucius became a popular private teacher with a huge following.

After age fifty, as he realized that the feudal lord of his native Lu did not value his service, Confucius left with a number of trusted disciples in tow and headed for other feudal domains. His hope was that other lords would embrace his ideas and would implement his political blueprint for restoring order to the world. For the next thirteen years he traveled all across Northern China, going from one feudal domain to another in search of opportunities to carry out his reform proposals. He was met with disappointment everywhere, at times suffering much indignity, deprivation, and even physical danger. In the twilight years of his life, he returned to his home state of Lu with his political ambition unfulfilled and devoted the remainder of his life to teaching, writing, and editing the ancient texts. Confucius died in his early seventies.

Confucius is believed to have put the major classical works into their final form. He supposedly edited the *Book of Odes* and the *Book of History*, wrote important commentaries on the *Book of Changes*, and contributed to the *Record of Rites,* as well as the no-longer-extant *Book of Music*. He also supposedly authored a book on the history of the late Zhou period from the vantage point of his native state of Lu, which is titled *Chunqiu (Spring and Autumn Annals)*. The work covers the years 722–481 B.C.E., a period that since has been known as the Spring and Autumn period in Chinese history.

Statue of Confucius at the entrance to the Confucian Academy in Beijing, China.

Toward the end of his long life, Confucius gave a telling summary and assessment of his intellectual development as recorded in the *Analects*, a work compiled by his followers that contains his celebrated sayings:

> At fifteen I set my mind on learning
> At thirty I had become established [as a *ru*]
> At forty I was free from doubts
> At fifty I knew the decree of *Tian* (*Tianming*)
> At sixty my ears became attuned [to what I heard from *Tian*]
> At seventy I could follow my heart's desires without transgressing what
> was right
>
> —*Analects 2:4*

This intellectual and spiritual autobiography of Confucius illustrates the pattern of his development from a scholar to a religious figure. His biography shows that he was a fully human figure with no claim to supernatural origin or power and was the consummate representative of the *ru* tradition and an exemplary teacher. Eventually, however, Confucius would be honored as a sage and the founder of China's most important philosophical and religious tradition.

Later Defenders of the Faith   The Chinese world after Confucius took a turn for the worse. Warfare among the feudal states became even more frequent and brutal. The centuries between Confucius's death in 479 and 221 B.C.E. are known as the Warring States period in Chinese history. Confucius's original vision of moral cultivation and benevolent government seemed impractical and quixotic. Internally, the Confucian tradition was rocked by self-doubt and resignation, as his *ru* followers became mere functionaries for the feudal lords, enjoying little influence or self-esteem. Externally, rival traditions such as Daoism and other more pragmatic schools competed for attention and attacked many of the Confucian ideas.

Into this picture came Mencius (371–289 B.C.E.?), the second most important figure in the Confucian tradition. As the most ardent defender of the faith, he articulated views that would be revered as definitive interpretations of what Confucius had outlined. We have already examined his contribution to the tradition in the section on the teachings of Confucianism in this chapter. His ideas would become orthodox for most future Confucians.

A younger contemporary of Mencius was Xun Qing (310–238 B.C.E.?), or Master Xun (Xunzi), who actually exerted far greater influence on the Confucian movement through the second century C.E. than Mencius did. Xun Qing's rationalism and pragmatic approach to rituals and learning had given a decisively secular and worldly bent to the Confucian tradition, resulting in a noticeable neglect of its religious nature. His view of human nature as evil also contradicted the Mencian version. Nevertheless, Xun Qing shared with Mencius an abiding faith in the transformative influence of moral cultivation and the perfectibility of humanity through self-effort. Eventually, however, Xun Qing was rejected by later Confucians as heterodox, and the text bearing his name was never recognized as a Confucian scripture.

Confucianism as Orthodoxy   When China was unified by the Qin (Ch'in) state in 221 B.C.E., the Confucian tradition was initially a target of state persecution. Its call for benevolent government and individual moral autonomy was rejected by the First Emperor of Qin as impractical and subversive. But the Qin Dynasty soon fell, replaced by the Han (206 B.C.E.–220 C.E.), a much more hospitable regime for Confucian teaching. By the middle of the second century B.C.E., the Confucian tradition finally surpassed all its competitors by becoming the state-designated orthodoxy, in recognition of its usefulness in fostering effective governance and enhancing social cohesiveness. Yet its orthodox status also necessitated fundamental changes in its orientation. From a teaching that called for high-minded personal moral cultivation and benevolent government, Confucianism in the Han Dynasty became a scholastic tradition and a tool for state control and patriarchal authoritarianism. In fulfilling that role, Confucius was showered with grandiose titles by subsequent generations of Chinese rulers who scrambled to outdo one another in their adoration of him, culminating in the breathtakingly exuberant title of "Ultimate Sage of Greatest Accomplishment, King of Manifest Culture" given to him by an emperor in 1308. "Temples" dedicated to Confucius were built in all the administrative and political centers throughout the empire. Nevertheless, these temples served more as memorials, such as those dedicated to Thomas Jefferson or Abraham Lincoln, than as places of worship, and Confucius himself remained by and large an exemplary human figure worthy of veneration, rather than a god promising salvation and demanding pious submission.

The Neo-Confucian Tradition   Though Confucianism served nominally as China's orthodoxy from the second century B.C.E. to the beginning of the twentieth century C.E., a span of over 2,000 years, it coexisted with Daoism and Buddhism during that entire period, and at times was even overshadowed by them. Since the twelfth century C.E., however, through a revitalization movement known in the West as Neo-Confucianism, it regained the initiative over its Daoist and Buddhist rivals and became the predominant religious tradition in China until the modern era. Indeed, as advocated by its most eloquent representative, the scholar Zhu Xi (1130–1200), its new scriptural corpus, the Four Books, composed of the *Analects*, the *Mencius*, the *Great Learning*, and the *Doctrine of the Mean*, would constitute the main curriculum upon which the civil service examination of late imperial China would be based. Between 1313 and 1905, all aspiring scholars and government officials in China had to study and were examined on their mastery of this set of canonical works, which provided the basis of their worldview and their outlook on life. To be sure, there would be other voices within the Neo-Confucian movement that challenged Zhu Xi's interpretations, notably that of Wang Yangming (1472–1529). They differed primarily in how best to attain the same goal of "inner sagely moral perfection and outer political ability and administrative skills" (**neisheng waiwang**). Personal moral perfection and universal transformation of the human community formed one continuum in their ultimate religious quest.

The Apricot Platform (Xingtan) is traditionally identified to be the location where Confucius lectured to his students.

Beginning in the fourteenth century, as China entered the late imperial period, the Confucian tradition became fossilized and rigid. The examinations were formulaic wordplays instead of genuine expressions of moral insight or sound administrative proposals. The entire Confucian tradition was turned into a mere tool of state control and social climbing. Political autocracy, patriarchal authoritarianism, and social exploitation were all carried out in its name.

Confucianism as Pan-Asiatic Tradition   Confucian texts had found their way beyond China no later than the turn of the Common Era, along with China's

Confucian influence in
East Asia.

outward expansion both culturally and territorially. But it was in the form of
Neo-Confucianism that this religious and philosophical tradition had exerted its most
significant impact on China's neighbors such as Korea, Japan, and Vietnam. Thanks
to the dynamic influence of Zhu Xi and his intellectual successors, Confucianism
became the dominant philosophy and state orthodoxy, beginning with the Yi Dynasty
in Korea (fourteenth century), the Tokugawa Shogunate in Japan (seventeenth century),
and the Nguyen Dynasty in Vietnam (nineteenth century). The social organizations,

bureaucratic cultures, and religious assumptions of these Asian neighbors of China echoed much that existed in China during her late imperial period (fourteenth to twentieth centuries).

Confucianism in the Modern World Confucianism entered a period of sharp decline in the modern age. This process began after the Opium War of 1839–1842, in which China was handily defeated by Great Britain. Other foreign powers quickly followed suit to demand enormous concessions from a weakened and disgraced China. For China's patriotic young generation of intellectual elite, this humiliating development exposed the shortcomings of their Confucian heritage. Confucianism was blamed for China's political, social, and economic backwardness. As a result, the New Culture Movement that began in the second decade of the twentieth century made Confucianism their main target of assault. "Down with Confucius and sons!" was now the popular call for rebellion against the tradition. The logic was that unless the roots of the Confucian tradition were eradicated completely, China would not survive the challenge of modernity. Indeed, the birth of the Chinese Communist movement was in part attributable to this rebellious mode of thinking. From the perspective of the radical revolutionaries, Confucianism was a reactionary ideology of the ruling elite in China's feudal past that should be cast into the dustbin of history.

But the obituary for Confucianism appears to have been written prematurely. Despite repeated and sometimes violent attempts to rid China of the harmful influence of Confucianism, the "anti-Confucius" campaign of the Cultural Revolution period (1966–1976) on mainland China being the most glaring example, the tradition has survived. As the opening vignette demonstrates, Confucianism as a religious tradition is still very much alive in contemporary China. The central importance of the family, the persistence of ancestral remembrance, and the value placed on education and self-improvement are evidence of the resilience of the Confucian ethos among many Chinese, and even East Asians in general. Some argue that the economic and industrial progress of the "Four Dragons" of Taiwan, South Korea, Hong Kong, and Singapore since the 1980s, and a similar development under way in China as well, might have been brought about by the Confucian heritage in these East Asian countries.

At the same time, an emergent group of "New Confucians," both inside and outside China, has been active as advocates for the revival of the Confucian teaching on philosophical and religious grounds. This group finds a new relevance for the Confucian tradition in the postmodern world on the ground that it expresses values of universal significance. These new defenders of the Confucian faith seek to rearticulate Confucianism for our time in the same way Confucians of the past had rearticulated it for theirs.

Equally notable is the new popularity enjoyed by Confucianism in China within the last decade, in part endorsed by the Chinese government. Academies devoted to the study of the Confucian tradition have been established, instruction on and the memorization of the *Analects* for school-age children are widely promoted, and even

TV programs dedicated to the explanation of the relevance of Confucian teaching to contemporary Chinese society are eagerly viewed by a growing audience. The Chinese government also provides partial funding for the establishment of "Confucius Institutes" in European and North American universities to encourage interest in Chinese and Confucian studies.

The History of Daoism

As we learned in the section on teachings in this chapter, Laozi and Zhuangzi, traditionally recognized as early founders of the Daoist tradition, were shadowy figures whose books bearing their names were actually anthologies containing divergent strands of thought. At best they could only be considered proto-Daoists. Laozi, historically believed to have been an older contemporary of Confucius, was a mysterious figure who was already an old man at the time of Confucius's birth (hence his name "Laozi," which literally can mean "old baby"). Late in his life he reportedly left China beyond her western borders, but not before he dictated to a follower what came to be known as the *Daodejing*. Zhuangzi, whose historicity was more accepted, was believed to have been a fourth-century B.C.E. figure whose wit and irreverence made his comments on the Dao some of the most well-known and celebrated ones. His dreaming of being a butterfly, and upon waking, his questioning of the validity of his human identity was of course the most famous example of his relativistic thinking. There were, as well, numerous other early commentators of the Dao who contributed to the formation of a "Daoist school" or "Daoist tradition" no later than the second century B.C.E.

The Deification of Laozi   A crucial development that led to the rise of Daoism as an organized religion was the divinization of Laozi. Sometime between the second century B.C.E. and the second century C.E., Laozi was revered as a human incarnation of the *Dao*. Remarkably, a belief arose that the *Dao* could now intervene in human affairs and directly and personally impart teaching to the faithful through its human form. As the *Dao* incarnate, Laozi was the object of worship, thereby making the *Dao*, for the first time, a human-like being that demanded and received religious devotion. In a text entitled *Laozi bianhua jing* (*Scripture of the Transformations of Laozi*), compiled around the middle of the second century C.E., the various incarnations of Laozi over time were recounted. One such incarnation was in the form of a messianic figure dedicated to the salvation of the world, and the title Laozi assumed in this case was *Taishang Laojun*, the Venerable Lord of the Most High.

Even more significantly, Laozi as *Taishang Laojun* could give instructions to selected individuals on the esoteric secrets of the *Dao* as part of his scheme to save the world. This deified and messianic Laozi thus turned the Daoist teaching into a divine revelation on salvation, which has since become a major tenet of organized Daoism. Once Laozi was venerated as the *Dao* incarnate, as well as a dispenser of redemptive instructions, Daoism became a salvational faith. A whole pantheon of deities, both in nature and within the human body, came to be worshiped as physical manifestations of the *Dao* and as agents of deliverance.

Beginning in the middle of the second century C.E., Daoism became an organized and large-scale movement among the common people. In the year 142 C.E., a man by the name of Zhang Ling (or Zhang Daoling) allegedly had a fateful encounter with the deified Laozi, who indicated to him that the world was in great trouble and that he was the one who would be taught the right knowledge and proper practice to save it. He was to adopt the title of **Tianshi** (Celestial Master; see the section on the teachings of Daoism in this chapter), and the teaching he was to transmit would be called *Zhengyi* (Orthodox Unity).

Zhang Ling later transferred the *Tianshi* title to his descendants down through the ages until the present day (in Taiwan). The movement would be known variously as "Celestial Master," "Orthodox Unity," or "Five Bushels of Rice," the last derived from the amount of contributions members were expected to make to the organization at their initiation. During the second half of the second century C.E., the movement acted as a theocratic shadow government, providing material aid and physical healing services to its membership, in addition to offering a vague hope of messianic salvation. A contemporary and parallel movement, alternatively known as "Great Peace" (*Taiping*) and "Yellow Turbans" (more accurately, Yellow Kerchiefs) (*Huangjin*), took the messianic message more seriously and rebelled against the Han court in an attempt to usher in a new age. This movement was ruthlessly suppressed, even though the dream of *taiping* would live on.

Later Daoist Historical Development The Celestial Masters made an arrangement with the government in 215 C.E. whereby it abandoned its theocratic base in southwestern China and migrated closer to the political center in the north. But soon the Han Dynasty fell, and the subsequent short-lived regimes failed to maintain their power in the face of devastating invasions by nomadic non-Chinese groups such as the Huns, forcing the political and cultural elite to flee south toward the Yangzi River basin. The Celestial Masters followed, and became popular there as well, setting up its headquarters on the Dragon and Tiger Mountain in Jiangxi province in southeast China. During the ensuing Period of Disunion, three centuries when China was politically divided between north and south, Daoism entered a most creative period.

First, both the *Daodejing* and the *Zhuangzi* were given new philosophical interpretations that downplayed, if not totally eliminated, the religious elements on meditative transformations and magical physical transmutations in the two texts. Then someone who was much more closely related to the Celestial Masters, a certain Ge Hong (283–343 C.E.), who styled himself the "Master Who Embraces Simplicity" (*Baopuzi*), vigorously asserted the possibility of attaining physical perfection in the form of immortality through various techniques involving alchemy.

But the most significant development in Daoism was in the area of textual revelations and ritual reforms. Responding both to the competition offered by a rapidly expanding Buddhism and to the need to distinguish itself from the "uncouth" and "coarse" practices of popular religion, Daoist leaders from aristocratic families created new texts and devised new rituals that they claimed were revealed to them through ecstatic encounters with an ever-growing number of Daoist deities.

In the south, the Shangqing (Highest Clarity) and the Lingbao (Numinous Treasure) set of texts and rituals began to emerge almost simultaneously in the fourth century C.E. While the former emphasized individual experiences of spiritual fulfillment through meditation and mental visualization, the latter focused on ritual precision and use of talismans for the purpose of universal salvation, though there was considerable overlapping between the two as well. In the north, similarly intense and creative activities also took place under the claim of new revelations from *Taishang Laojun*, the deified Laozi. A Tuoba (a people outside of the Great Wall) ruler, Emperor Taiwu of the Northern Wei Dynasty, was touted as the "Perfect Lord of Great Peace" (*Taiping zhenjun*) and declared that the ideal world had arrived.

Common among the various Daoist groups of this period was the belief in and anticipation of an impending cataclysmic disaster that would radically transform the existing world. There was an anxious yet exciting expectation of the imminent arrival of a savior-like figure who would protect the devout followers from harm and ensure them a safe journey to the world to come—a perfect world populated by the faithful alone. This eschatological (vision of the end of time) and apocalyptic (revelation of a secret divine design) feature of the Daoist movement resembles many millennial traditions in other cultures.

Because of the proliferation of revelatory texts and the diverse array of rituals, the Period of Disunion also witnessed the first attempts made to classify and standardize them. The Lingbao master Lu Xiujing (406–477 C.E.) was the first to propose the notion of the "three caverns" (*sandong*) to categorize the growing corpus of texts. This tripartite principle of organization was a conscious imitation of the *Tripitaka* (Three Baskets), the canonical corpus of Buddhist texts. Subsequent centuries and regimes would see the organization of the texts become more elaborate with the addition of "four supplements" (*sifu*). This form of classification would constitute the framework of the entire Daoist canon, known as the ***Daozang***, the most complete and monumental version of which was printed in 1445 C.E. in 480 sections, 1,120 titles, and over 5,300 volumes.

During China's medieval period, lasting from the seventh to the fourteenth centuries, organized Daoism enjoyed imperial patronage and became very much a part of the cultural life of the elite. Along with a very popular Buddhism and the nominal state ideology of Confucianism, it was one of the "three teachings" (*sanjiao*) of the realm. Its emphasis on nature and a free spirit informed much of the art and literature of the time. The breathtaking monochrome landscape paintings and cursive calligraphic art of the elite scholars reflected central Daoist values.

Several new orders also gained prominence during this time, the most influential among them being the *Quanzhen* Sect (Complete Perfection). Founded by a man named Wang Zhe (1113–1170 C.E.), this school of Daoism embraced elements from both Confucianism and Buddhism. From Confucianism it took moral values, and from Buddhism it adopted monasticism and clerical celibacy. In addition to the *Daodejing*, the Confucian *Classic of Filial Piety* and the Buddhist *Heart Sutra* were given the highest prominence by this tradition. The *Quanzhen* Sect was the most popular religious organization in Mongol Yuan China (1279–1368 C.E.), even overshadowing Buddhism. It is one of the only two Daoist groups that still exist today, the other being the Celestial Masters.

During the late imperial period in Chinese history (fourteenth to nineteenth centuries), Daoism was put on the defensive by the triumphant Neo-Confucians. Its clergy was tightly controlled by the state through the highly regulated issuance of ordination certificates. Though individual emperors might have supported Daoism, as evidenced by the printing of the complete *Daozang* in 1445, as a religious tradition it was overshadowed by Confucianism. Although the Confucian elite grudgingly acknowledged the "philosophic" brilliance of the *Daodejing* and the *Zhuangzi*, they regarded organized Daoist groups as nothing more than a degenerated form of pristine, original Daoism. Organized Daoism was marginalized as superstition, unworthy of elite attention. This contempt for Daoism continued beyond the imperial period, was intensified in the early twentieth century, and was adopted as official policy under the Communist regime since 1949.

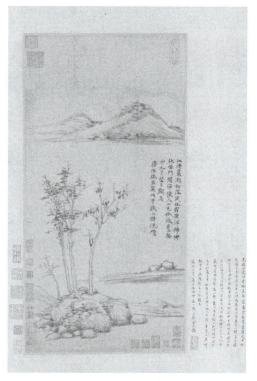

This painting, *Wind among the Trees on the Riverbank* by Ni Zan (1306–1374), is best known for the quietude and balance in nature it expresses. China, Yuan Dynasty (1271–1368), dated 1363.

Daoism as a Pan-Asiatic Tradition Like its Confucian counterpart, Daoism is not confined to the Chinese mainland. The proto-Daoist texts of *Laozi* and *Zhuangzi* had certainly reached Korea no later than the Goryeo Period (918–1392), even though Buddhism was the dominant faith of the time. By the ensuing Joseon Dynasty (1392–1897), when Confucianism was the state orthodoxy, Daoism in the form of shamanism, mountain worship, and immortality practices had become an integral part of Korean folk religion. Even today, the national flag of South Korea contains the Taegeuk symbol of yin-yang complementarity and four of the eight divinatory trigrams. In Japan, similarly, Daoism was never a dominant, independent tradition when compared with Confucianism and Buddhism. Rather, in its diffused form, it has combined with certain Buddhist groups and indigenous Shinto cults to form specific folk religious traditions since the Tokugawa period (1600–1868). Specifically, the Shūgendō (shamanistic mountain ascetics) and the Kōshin religious practice of controlling the decaying agents of the human body to prevent them from shortening human life span display unmistakable Daoist influences. In Southeast Asia as well, Daoism has found its way into the beliefs of the Xiantian Dao (Way of Prior Heaven) of Malaysia and the Caodai (High Power) tradition in Vietnam.

Daoist influence in East Asia.

Both are movements promising deliverance from the current age of decadence and corruption.

Daoism Today   Because of elite hostility and government neglect, if not active persecution, Daoism as a religious tradition has fared generally very poorly in the modern period. Although the intellectuals still recognized the philosophical ideas in the *Laozi* and the *Zhuangzi* as properly Daoist, they totally ignored the meditative exercises and amazing magical powers of the Daoist seekers of perfection discussed in the two texts, along with the entire corpus of the *Daozang*, the Daoist canon. Daoism was lumped with shamanic popular religion and viewed with disdain. The New Culture Movement of the 1910s and 1920s regarded both Daoism and Confucianism as unwelcome remnants of China's feudal past. The Cultural Revolution (1966–1976) that did so much damage to Confucianism also proved devastating to Daoism. Many historic Daoist shrines and sites were destroyed or sacrilegiously defaced, and all performances of Daoist rituals and liturgies were banned. For all intents and purposes, Daoism as an organized religion ceased to exist in mainland China. Yet the tradition survived amidst China's nebulous folk religion. It also continued to exist, if only barely, outside China among Chinese communities in Taiwan, Hong Kong, and Southeast Asia. Since the late 1970s, however, a Daoist revival of sorts has begun. Daoist ceremonies are once again openly ob-

This painting of the poet Li Bo (Li Bai, 701–762) shows him as a Daoist immortal.

Both Confucianism and Daoism have been embraced by political authorities to legitimize their rule and to impose order on society. How did they fare when compared with other major world religions?

served in China, and a new generation of Daoist priests has been trained to carry on the tradition and to rebuild the shrines. Academic study of Daoism, primarily by Japanese and French scholars at the beginning, and now joined by Americans and Chinese themselves, has created new understanding of the tradition both from the point of view of doctrines and practices. Some of the scholars have actually become ordained Daoist priests of either the Celestial Master or the Complete Perfection tradition to access more accurate and authoritative interpretations of Daoism. In recent decades, *qigong* exercises (meditation and respiration techniques designed to enhance the body's vital energy), martial arts, and food therapy are popular both in China and abroad. Though not strictly associated with organized Daoism, such phenomena are nevertheless in part based on and inspired by Daoist views on nature and the human body. Respective Daoist practices in breath circulation, gymnastics, and dietetics, discussed in more detail in the next section, attest to the continued relevance of Daoism in the modern world.

CONFUCIANISM AND DAOISM AS WAYS OF LIFE

The two Chinese religions discussed in this chapter are not just a collection of precepts and beliefs. More important, they are lived and practiced traditions. It is in the living and practicing of the two traditions that their true meaning and value can be gauged.

Confucian Rituals

From the very beginning, the Confucian tradition has put great emphasis on ritual as a crucial expression of humanity. As "moral behavior," ritual teaches people to conduct themselves with dignity and decorum, making them authentically human. As "holy rites," ritual enables them to communicate effectively with the spiritual powers and interact harmoniously with one another. It is in the latter, more overtly religious sense that Confucian ritual is addressed in this section.

In addition to the mundane rituals of familial and social interaction with other human beings in accordance with the prescribed rules outlined in the classic texts, the most important aspect of religious ritual in Confucianism in the premodern period was the sacrifice (*jisi*), or the making of offerings to the spirits, including ancestors, in the form of animals, other food and drink, even jade and silk. These sacrificial rituals were performed at different levels—the state, the community, and the family. The grandest of the rituals were, of course, conducted at the state level. And chief among the state rituals were those connected with sacrifices to *Tian* and *Di*—and to Confucius once his teaching was exalted to orthodoxy.

Sacrifice to *Tian* and *Di*   *Tian*, it should be recalled, had been the source of legitimate political power since the Zhou Dynasty. As son of *Tian* (*Tianzi*), the Chinese

The Temple of Tian (*Tiantan*), where the Chinese emperor prayed to *Tian* on behalf of his subjects and in his capacity as "Son of Tian," is now a popular park in Beijing.

The Hall of Praying for an Abundant Harvest (*Qi'nian dian*), Temple of Tian (*Tiantan*), Beijing. The whole complex was built in 1420 under the emperor Yongle and restored in 1530 and 1751. Here the emperor celebrated the sacrifice to *Tian* for a good harvest. The decorated ramp between the two stairways was reserved for the emperor's palanquin.

VOICES: An Interview with Jason Ch'ui-hsiao Tseng

Jason Ch'ui-hsiao Tseng is a Taiwanese man in his fifties with a master's degree from an American university. He engages in educational exchange for Chinese students wishing to study in the United States.

Do you consider yourself a Confucian or a Daoist?

I do not consider myself exclusively one or the other. Both have influenced me deeply and I regard their teachings as equally valid and complementary.

How is that possible, as their teachings often conflict with each other?

They are not in conflict. They merely represent the polar opposite of the other. They complete each other. For most Chinese, there is no necessity to choose one or the other. We think of them as the two sides of a coin—without both there is no coin. The two together constitute our native Chinese religious outlook. As a matter of fact, we also consider Buddhist teaching a third way of guiding our religious life. These teachings are generally not jealous of one another. They do not demand total exclusive devotion. They provide meaning to different aspects of our lives. There is religious pluralism for most Chinese.

How is that so?

We do not believe that one teaching alone corners the market. As a respectful son and an upright citizen, I embrace Confucian values. They teach me to put family and society ahead of myself and to value education as the most important undertaking to improve myself. In my views on how my body works, how my health can be maintained, how different ingredients should be used to achieve balance in my food, and how I can relate to the spirits in the invisible world, I follow the Daoist teaching. And Buddhism gives me hope for a good afterlife. Together they make me a complete person.

Jason Ch'ui-hsiao Tseng

ruler carried out *Tian*'s mandate (*Tianming*) to exercise his imperial prerogatives over the entire realm under *Tian* (*Tianxia*). The worship of *Tian* thus became the ruler's exclusive privilege and obligation. Later, with Confucianism imbued with *yin-yang* cosmological ideas in the Han Dynasty, *Tian*, the *yang* element, was paired up with *Di* (earth), the *yin* element, and worship of *Di* was added, though with much less pomp and ostentation.

In late imperial China, the worship of *Tian* and *Di* took place annually. On the day of the summer solstice, the emperor made sacrifice to *Tian* at the Temple of Tian (*tiantan*) located in the southern suburb of Beijing. Correspondingly, on the day of the winter solstice, worship of *Di* was conducted at the Temple of Di (*ditan*) located at the northern suburb of the capital. The rituals involved nine steps, including the purification of the participants, the performance of dance and music, the reading of prayer documents, and the offering of sacrifices.

Confucius serves as an object of veneration and commemoration. He is the "Utmost Sage and Late Teacher," as the tablet in front of his statue declares.

A far more elaborate rite known as "*feng* and *shan*" has only been performed a total of six times in all of Chinese history.[14] *Feng*, literally meaning "to seal," was the rite of worshipping *Tian* atop Mt. Tai, the "Sacred Eastern Peak" located near Confucius's native town of Qufu in modern Shandong province. *Shan*, literally meaning "to yield" or "to clear away," was the ritual of sacrificing to *Di* at the lesser peak of Liangfu at the foot of Mt. Tai. The ultimate purpose of the *feng* rite was to seal a new covenant between the ruler and the numinous Absolute that gave him his legitimacy to rule. Similarly, the *shan* performance was meant to establish a bond with the earth. Because of the huge expenses and elaborate arrangements involved, *feng* and *shan* were conducted consecutively on the same trip.

Sacrifice to Confucius   The state cult of Confucius began in the Han Dynasty with the designation of Confucianism as orthodoxy. The descendants of Confucius were first given a hereditary fief, and later the Master himself was given increasingly laudatory titles and ducal honors. Finally temples commemorating Confucius were ordered to be built in every county and major city throughout the empire. In time, wooden tablets commemorating some of his prominent students, as well as those of successive generations of Confucian worthies such as Mencius and Zhu Xi, were installed in these temples. Though the frequency and elaborateness of the sacrificial rites conducted at these temples varied with time and locale, the traditional birthday of Confucius (the twenty-seventh day of the ninth month) was generally observed. These rites involved dance and music accompanied by drums and bells, proclamations and didactic lectures given by local dignitaries and government officials, and offerings of incense and animals. It should be noted that Confucius's divinity was never claimed at these ceremonies, nor was his intervention sought in solving human problems. Rather, they were expressions of veneration and respect for a human cultural hero who had helped to define Chinese civilization.

The most magnificent Temple of Confucius, as can be expected, is located in his native county of Qufu, not far from Mt. Tai. Built and maintained at state expense, the Qufu Confucian Temple has a main building with a palatial design supported by dragon-decorated pillars, all meant to accord the Master the highest honor comparable to that of a ruler. Stone steles are engraved with the calligraphy or essays of various emperors in Chinese history, all lauding the moral and cultural accomplishments of the sage. This Confucian Temple in Qufu was a pilgrimage site for generations of scholars and aspiring literati and is still popular among tourists today.

Family Rituals   Commemorating and honoring of ancestors in China goes back to the very dawn of recorded Chinese history. But Confucianism lent further theoretical support to the practice with its discussion of *xiao* (filial piety). The Confucian teaching maintains that one's filial obligation to parents and ancestors is the core of one's humanity. Thus while the state monopolized the worship of *Tian/Di* and the educated elites controlled the sacrifice to Confucius, all people could participate in the family ritual of honoring parents and ancestors. Sacrifice to ancestors, in particular, is important because it gives the descendants a sense of belonging and continuity and thereby a religious appreciation of the chain of life that links them to their forebears.

In the *Family Rituals* (*Jiali*), compiled by the Neo-Confucian scholar Zhu Xi, detailed step-by-step liturgies are provided for ceremonies associated with ancestor worship. Chapters describe daily "looking in" on the ancestors; more elaborate semimonthly "visits," "reports" on major family events such as births, weddings, and deaths; and formal "offerings" on festival days and seasonal sacrifices. What follows is a summarized version of Zhu Xi's instructions for the rites of making seasonal offerings to the ancestors.[15]

Confucius's tombstone boldly declares that he is the "Ultimate Sage of Greatest Accomplishment, King of Manifest Culture."

In the preparatory phase, the date for the sacrifice is selected by divination performed in front of the ancestral shrine in the preceding month. Then, three days before the event, the designated leading man and woman will each lead family members of their respective gender to perform purification rituals in their designated quarters, men in the outer and women in the inner. The men also make the main hall sparkling clean and arrange the place settings for each generation properly. The women will set the incense burner and incense box, as well as prepare wine racks and containers, along with meat plates for the ancestors.

On the day of the event, when the sun is fully up, the wooden tablets containing the names of the different generations of ancestors, separated by gender, are moved to their proper places in the main hall. Then the spirits of the ancestors are greeted, and food is offered to them three times. The ancestors are entreated to eat the food and are given privacy to do so, with everyone from the presiding man on down exiting the main hall, and the door is closed. After a suitable interval, the master of ceremony coughs three times to announce his intention to reenter; then he opens the door, and everyone else comes back in. Tea is offered to the ancestors to supposedly cleanse their mouths. Then the presiding man receives the sacrificed food from the master of ceremony. With reverence the presiding man bows and prostrates himself to taste the food and drink the wine. Then the entire group takes leave of the ancestral spirits, returns their tablets back to their original locations, and clears away the offering tables. The presiding man supervises the division of the sacrificial food to be consumed by all the family members later that day. This brings an end to the ritual of the ancestral sacrifice. The intended effect of this ritual is apparent—to create familial cohesiveness and

VISUAL GUIDE
Daoism and Confucianism

This is an iconic image of Confucius as a learned scholar and an exemplar of human moral accomplishment. Traditionally the Chinese did not see religion as a separate realm of activity, hence the pursuit of scholarship and the enactment of moral behavior within the family and community were very much part of their religious experience.

Though not strictly Confucian, this yin-yang symbol surrounded by the eight trigrams does reflect the Chinese belief in the complementarity of opposites and the harmonious unity of the cosmos. More than any other visual symbol, it represents Chinese religiousness.

Family cohesion and respect for elders are central Confucian values. A daughter and her husband pay a visit to her parents on Chinese New Year's Day to renew her kinship tie with her natal family.

Statue of Laozi carved out of a huge rock in Fujian province, China. This legendary founder of Daoism symbolizes wisdom and irreverence for conventional thinking. He is understood as the yin to Confucius's yang, and the image of passive acceptance of what nature has ordained to Confucius's active attempt at improving society.

(continued)

to recognize the unseverable bond between the living and the deceased family members. You may notice that the opening scene of *qingming* observance at the beginning of this chapter has similar rituals.

Daoist Practices

As can be deduced from our discussion of Daoist beliefs, Daoism is essentially lived, not merely believed. Whether it is the amazing feats of the immortals and perfected beings in the *Daodejing* and the *Zhaungzi*, or whether it is the physical-spiritual regimens and alchemical techniques of the later Daoists, there is always an understanding and expectation that the beliefs need to be put into practice to be truly meaningful. Returning to the *Dao*, warding off physical deterioration, and attaining actual immortality involve a whole spectrum of undertakings and practices.

Daoist Communal Festivals and Liturgies

To ordinary believers—those who have no hope of going through the rigor and the expenses of pursuing immortality—the Daoist religion as practiced by the Celestial Master sect offers the promise of health, long life, even collective salvation. Membership in these organized movements during the tumultuous centuries after the collapse of the Han Dynasty meant a special sense of belonging to a select group destined to survive those trying times. Noteworthy in their beliefs was the idea of chosenness—that they constituted a special group of people who, because of their embrace of an apocalyptic ideology, were favored by the gods. Referred to as *zhongmin* (seed people), they confirmed their "elect" status through their participation in collective rituals called **zhai** (fasts). Lasting several days each, these fasts involved abstinence from food, public performance of penance for past moral transgressions, submission of written memorials to request pardon from the deities, and communal prayers for the salvation of the faithful.

The Fast of Mud and Soot (*tutan zhai*) in China's medieval period reflected the general tenor of *zhai* rituals. With hair disheveled and face smeared with soot, believers prostrated themselves like condemned criminals before a raised altar to ask for forgiveness from the gods. Moved by their emotions, many fell to the ground and rolled about amidst loud wailings. Such public acts of penance were performed to earn pardon and spiritual merit. Another liturgical ritual was the Fast of the Yellow Register (*Huanglu zhai*), during which the participants performed penitence for their ancestors going back seven or nine generations. The names of deceased ancestors, entered in registers, were read by the officiating priests and were then considered to have gained postmortem immortality. In this way the filial obligation of the faithful was ritually expressed.

Another communal ceremony, the ***jiao*** (offering), is popular even down to the present day. It is a public liturgy performed usually by the Daoist priests on behalf of the entire community to petition the gods to bestow good fortune, health, and prosperity on all. Sometimes labeled as a rite of cosmic renewal, the *jiao* brings together the community to participate collectively in a religious ritual that is loud, colorful, and dramatic. Depending on the needs of the community, a *jiao* is conducted at periodic intervals (ranging from once a year for the affluent communities to once every sixty years for the poor communities) or to give special thanks to the deities for having successfully protected the entire community by, for example, warding off an epidemic.

A *jiao* ceremony usually lasts several days. The dates are chosen for their astrological auspiciousness. Daoist priests are contracted to perform the ritual with efficacy and precision. Prior to the official dates of the ceremony, "memorials" are submitted by the priests to the celestial bureaucracy of the gods to give notice of the scheduled *jiao*. Then the location at which the liturgy takes place, usually both the inside and the outside of the largest local temple or shrine, is marked off by hoisted lanterns to signal the enclosure of the sacred space. Afterward the local deities are invited to take their honored seats within the enclosure; their statues or wooden tablets are carried there by community elders. The procession of the deities through the community is accompanied by lion or dragon dances, made even more boisterous with lots of firecrackers. Then the ritual proper begins in earnest.

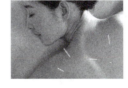

A group of Daoist priests perform a ritual service for a member of the community.

Reenacting the beginning of the cosmos in a ritual called *fendeng* (spreading the light), the chief Daoist priest, in full vestment, blows on a buffalo horn and rings his "thunder" bell, to the accompaniment of an entire music ensemble, and repeats the forty-second chapter of the *Laozi* by announcing that "the *Dao* gives birth to the One [Being, Existence]; the One brings forth the Two [*Yin* and *Yang*]; the Two give rise to the Three [*Tian*, *Di*, and Humans]; and the Three engender the Ten Thousand Things [world of multiplicity and diversity]." Entering a meditation-induced trance, he transforms his body into the body of the *Dao*. He takes prescribed steps that are dancelike, spins on himself, and sanctifies the ritual enclosure by requesting the dispatch of heavenly troops to guard the place. At the same time, to placate the wandering ghosts in the neighborhood and to warn them against intrusion into the sacred ground, he provides a feast for them while lecturing them on the reasons for their suffering.

At some point during the ceremony, the names of every member of the community will be posted on a roster and read aloud by the priests to signal their financial and spiritual support of this elaborate and expensive event, as well as to ensure that they will receive their share of the benediction of the gods. There is great interest among the community members in checking the posted name list to make sure that the names are written accurately and that they have not been inadvertently left out.

The climax of the ceremony occurs when the highest of the Daoist deities, the Three Purities and the Jade Emperor, are invited to take part in the ceremony. Piercing prepared talismans with his sword, the chief Daoist priest burns them with great dramatic effect to appeal to the august deities. Once the gods are properly seated, a blanket pardon of every immoral act committed by every member of the community between the last *jiao* and the present one is announced. In grateful response, the community performs a public charitable act of "releasing life"—setting cages of captured birds free and returning to a stream a bucket full of live fish. On the last night of the ceremony, a grand feast for all ghosts trapped in hell is hosted by the community. Once again, the Daoist priests exhort the ghosts to behave themselves and to refrain from wreaking havoc in the lives of the living. Balance is restored among the worlds of humans, gods, and ghosts. The rite concludes with the sending off of the celestial gods and the local deities and the distribution of food and buns to the spectators and the performance of operas for the entertainment of all.[16]

CONCLUSION

In this chapter we have invited you to explore the religious world of the Chinese through a study of their two native religious traditions—Confucianism and Daoism. We have highlighted the religious nature of both traditions. In the case of Confucianism, we have established that it is not just a teaching of ethics and good government but is in fact informed by a deep religious faith in a numinous Absolute—*Tian*. This faith, moreover, mandates dedicated human effort to transform the individual and the world. We have also documented the historical unfolding of this tradition over the course of more than two thousand years. At the same time, we have also identified the ritual dimensions of this tradition, from the ornate and solemn state observations of the past to the simple familial ceremonies that are still practiced today.

As for Daoism, we have clarified that it is not confined to the metaphysical discussions of the *Daodejing* and the *Zhuangzi*, but that it is richly informed by an elaborate belief in the cosmological importance of the human body, a salvational message of communal redemption, and an abiding yearning for physical transformation and perfection. Moreover, we have examined the historical progression of this tradition as it meandered through the different periods in China. We have also documented the colorful ritual performance of Daoism in the community.

Both Confucianism and Daoism (along with a Chinese version of Buddhism and a syncretized amalgamation of the three teachings in the form of folk religion) have contributed to the shaping of the Chinese religious mindset. Both have experienced ups and downs in their respective history, at times being the dominant ideology of the realm and at times being eclipsed by other traditions in influence. Nevertheless, both have maintained their central importance to the Chinese people, at no time risking irrelevance or extinction. Despite suffering a brutal critique and rejection in the twentieth century by the modern Chinese intellectual elite in the name of rationalism and egalitarianism, both have remained resilient among the common people. In fact, there are signs of their revival and rejuvenation at the dawn of the twenty-first century. Confucian values continue to inform Chinese familial ethics and social and political behavior, and Daoist concerns for the well-being of the human body and harmonious

Confucianism and Daoism have together shaped personal conduct and social behavior in China. How do the Chinese allow themselves to be guided by two very distinct religious traditions in their daily lives without much sense of tension and conflict?

relationship with the spiritual world shape contemporary Chinese attitudes toward health, medicine, cuisine, and the environment.

Most important, we have attempted to justify the inclusion of both Confucianism and Daoism in the study of world religions. Confucianism treats the fulfillment of the human potential as an ultimate concern. The tenacity with which Confucianism exhorts people to strive for human perfection in our mundane lives as a form of divine calling—thereby making the secular sacred—demonstrates an interesting type of religiosity. Its assertion of human coequality with the divine offers an intriguing contrast with other religious traditions as well. Daoism is similarly a significant world religion. Its perception of the divine Absolute as a life-generating, feminine entity; its call for a harmonious coexistence between humans and nature; its emphasis on healthy improvement of the human body as a religious mission; and its promotion of communal cohesiveness through ritual participation make it all the more relevant in a postindustrial world.

SEEKING ANSWERS

What Is Ultimate Reality?

Confucianism and Daoism share the same cosmological myth, inherited from ancient China. The natural world is not in a fallen state. There is no almighty creator, nor is there a demonic counterpart. There is no definite beginning of the world, and there is no predicted end. Instead, the world unfolds cyclically and operates like a pendulum, arcing between two extremes and alternating between two polar but complementing opposites. Human beings are not caught in a tug of war between good and evil, and the side they choose does not result in a permanent fate in paradise or hell. Emphasis is placed on balance, coexistence, and harmony. For the Confucians, ultimate reality is *Tian* (Neo-Confucians sometimes use the term *Taiji*, Supreme Ultimate). *Tian* is the procreator of the cosmos and all the myriad things in it. Moreover, *Tian* has a special relationship with humans and communicates with chosen individuals its grand design for humanity. This communication does not occur through dramatic and ecstatic encounters such as that between god and the prophets in Abrahamic traditions. Instead, *Tian*'s message is discerned by perceptive and insightful human representatives through their keen observation of nature and diligent study of human affairs as recorded in history and enacted in the present. It is in this sense that Confucianism is not a revelatory religion in the conventional sense. In contrast, Daoism, in its organized form, is a revelatory religion. Its ultimate reality is the *Dao*, the "mother of the universe." Originally formless and undifferentiated, it later takes on human and divine forms, giving instructions and revealing texts to the faithful. Daoism can also be salvational in its message, complete with prescriptions for repentance and thanksgiving.

(continued)

SEEKING ANSWERS *(continued)*

How Should We Live in This World?

Both Confucianism and Daoism inherit the ancient Chinese religious view regarding the human condition: human beings are, like everything else in the cosmos, the product of the interaction between *yin* and *yang*. They have a corporeal aspect (the body) and an incorporeal aspect (the "soul"), consisting of *hun* and *po*. There is no notion of any alienation from or disobedience of an almighty god, thus a total absence of sin. However, this does not mean that human beings are already perfect and need no improvement from their current state. There is still a yawning gap between human beings as they are and human beings as they should or can become. For the Confucians, the right way to live is to live ethically, in accordance with the moral dictates of *Tian*. Humans alone have the responsibility to model and exemplify *Tian*'s moral imperative, thereby making themselves partners in creating harmony and prosperity throughout the cosmos. In concentric circles extending outward from the individual, moral behavior will transform the family, the community, and the world at large. "Do not do unto others what you do not want done to you" is the minimal moral guide for correct living in Confucianism. For the Daoists, the right way to live is to live healthily. To be sure, ethical behavior is part of desirable living, but Daoists also emphasize the human body as a microcosm reflecting perfectly the macrocosm of the cosmos. Thus taking care of one's body through both internal and external "alchemical" means is a way of living life properly in accord with the Dao. Similarly focusing on the intimate connection between the individual, the community, and the cosmos, Daoists prescribe diet, exercise, and preservation of health and energy as a way of approaching the holy.

What Is Our Ultimate Purpose?

Confucians and Daoists differ in their answers to this question. For the Confucians, humans are potentially perfect and inclined toward the good. Yet this potentiality and inclination need to be rigorously nurtured and developed through scholastic learning, moral introspection, and ethical behavior. Learning to be authentically human, to enact the "way" of *Tian*, is the way to improve the human condition and to perfect it. The highest achievement of human endeavor is to become the coequal of the divine ultimate—*Tian*.

Daoists regard humans on the same level as all the myriad things—they are all concrete expressions of the *Dao*, the numinous Absolute. Through their ignorance or negligence, however, humans dissipate their primordial endowment of the vital energy, the *qi*, resulting in their vulnerability to disease and death. Consequently, the Daoist prescription for improving the human condition is to engage in exercises and rituals designed to replenish the body and the spirit, making it once again as immortal as the *Dao*. Confucians and Daoists also diverge in their beliefs about what happens after we leave this life. Confucius himself

(continued)

SEEKING ANSWERS (continued)

famously brushed aside a student's inquiry on death. He just did not consider it an issue worthy of exploration. His priority was to pay exclusive attention to life and how to improve it. This "prejudice" has affected all subsequent Confucians, none of whom showed any strong interest in addressing death or its religious meaning. Even the Confucian practice of ancestor worship and respecting the dead can be explained as a way of bypassing the issue, as dead ancestors are treated very much as living members of the lineage and the family. Daoists, on the other hand, confront the topic of mortality by emphasizing the possibility and the desirability of immortality. Even with the appearance of death as inevitable, Daoists explain it as a stage of transformation to a higher plane of existence, a way of attaining true immortality. Thus the deeper meaning of death is equally ignored by Daoists.

REVIEW QUESTIONS

For Review

1. Why should the term "Confucianism" be used with caution? In what way may it be a misnomer?
2. How do Confucianism and Daoism define such terms as *Tian*, *Dao*, and *de* differently?
3. Why is Daoism more than the teachings of the *Laozi* and the *Zhuangzi*?
4. Why is Confucianism a religious tradition despite its lack of concern for the afterlife?

For Further Reflection

1. In what ways do Confucianism and Daoism complement each other, and in what ways do they oppose each other?
2. Compare and contrast the Confucian notion of *Tian* with the Christian concept of God.
3. Compare and contrast the Daoist notion of *Dao* with the Hindu concept of Brahman.
4. Having examined Confucianism and Daoism, have you arrived at any conclusion regarding Chinese religiosity? How does it differ from that of other religious traditions?

GLOSSARY

dantian (dahn'-tee'ən) "Fields for the refinement of the immortal pill"; major nodal points in the human body where the "pill" of immortality can be refined through alchemical means.

dao (dow) A fundamental concept in Chinese religion, literally meaning the "path" or the "way." In Confucianism, it specifically refers to the entire ideal human order ordained by the numinous Absolute, *Tian*. In Daoism, it is the primary source of the cosmos, the very ground of all beings.

Daodejing (dow'-duh-jing) Basic Daoist scripture, lit. "The Scripture of the Way and Its Potent Manifestation"; also known as the Book of *Laozi*, the name of its purported author.

(continued)

GLOSSARY (continued)

Daozang (dow' zahng) Literally "Treasury of the Dao," this is the Daoist Canon that contains the entire corpus of Daoist texts. The most complete version, still in use today, was first published in 1445.

de (duh) Another fundamental concept in Chinese religions, meaning "virtue" or "potency." In Confucianism, it is the charismatic power of the ruler or the man of virtue, while in Daoism it means the concrete manifestation of the *dao*.

fangshi (fahng-shər) "Magicians" who allegedly possessed the recipe for immortality.

Five Classics The five canonical works of Confucianism designated in the Han Dynasty. They are *Book of Odes*, *Book of History*, *Book of Changes*, *Record of Rites*, and *Spring and Autumn Annals*.

Four Books The four texts identified by the Neo-Confucian Zhu Xi as fundamental in understanding the Confucian teaching. Between 1313 and 1905, they made up the curriculum for the civil service examination. They are *Analects*, *Mencius*, *Great Learning*, and *Doctrine of the Mean*.

gui (gwei) Ghosts and demons, malevolent spirits.

jiao (jee'au) Daoist communal sacrificial offerings to signal cosmic renewal and collective cohesion.

junzi (ju'un zee) The personality ideal in Confucianism; the noble person.

li (lee) Etiquette and proper manners; rituals and holy rites.

ming (*see* ***Tianming***)

neidan (nay'-dahn) Daoist "internal" alchemy designed to attain immortality through meditation, breath control, gymnastics, diet, and massage.

neisheng waiwang (nay'-sheng' wī'-wahng) Neo-Confucian ideal of "inner sagely moral perfection and outer political skills."

qi (chee) Breath, force, power, material energy.

ren (rən) Human-heartedness, benevolence; the unique moral inclination of humans.

ru (rōō) Scribes and ritual performers of the Zhou period; later used exclusively to refer to Confucians.

Shangdi (shahng'-dee) The August Lord on High of the Shang period.

shen (shən) Gods and deities; benevolent spirits.

shengren (shəng rən) (or ***sheng***) The Confucian sage, the epitome of humanity.

shi (shər) Men of service; lower-ranking civil and military officials in the Zhou period.

Tian (tee'ən) The transcendent, numinous entity in ancient Chinese religion; the conscious Will that regulates the cosmos and intervenes in human affairs; conventionally translated as "Heaven."

Tianming The mandate or command of *Tian* that confers political legitimacy to the ruler; also understood by Confucians as the calling to morally improve oneself and to transform the world.

Tianshi (tee'ən shər) "Celestial Master"; reference to a Daoist salvational figure, as well as an organized movement.

waidan (wī dahn) Daoist "external" alchemy involving refining of "pills" with herbs and minerals for ingestion so that immortality can be attained.

wuwei (wōō way) Daoist notion of action without intention; actionless action.

wuxing (wōō shing) The five elemental phases of metal, wood, water, fire, and soil that mutually support and overcome one another.

xian (shee'ən) Daoist immortals and perfected individuals.

xiao (shee'au) Filial piety; respect and care for parents and ancestors.

xinzhai (shin jī) "Fasting of the Mind" in the *Zhuangzi*.

yang (young) Lit. the south-facing side of a mountain, representing the energy that is bright, warm, dry, and masculine.

(continued)

GLOSSARY (*continued*)

yangsheng (young shəng) Daoist techniques of nourishing life and attaining immortality.

yin Lit. the north-facing side of a mountain, representing the energy that is dark, cold, wet, and feminine.

zhai (jī) Daoist "fasts" designed to seek redemption of transgressions by the gods.

ziran (zee'-rahn) Daoist notion of natural spontaneity.

zuowang (zoh'-wahng) "Sitting and Forgetting" in the *Zhuangzi*.

SUGGESTIONS FOR FURTHER READING

de Bary, William Theodore. *The Trouble with Confucianism*. Cambridge, MA: Harvard University Press, 1991. A thought-provoking discussion of the "prophetic voice" in Confucianism.

Fingarette, Herbert. *Confucius: The Secular as Sacred*. New York: Harper Torchbooks, 1972. A creative interpretation of the Confucian notion of *li* as holy rites.

Gardner, Daniel K., trans. *The Four Books: The Basic Teachings of the Later Confucian Tradition*. Indianapolis, IN: Hackett Publishing, 2007. A handy translation of important excerpts from the scriptural corpus of Confucianism.

Gardner, Daniel K. *Confucianism: A Very Short Introduction*. New York: Oxford University Press, 2014. A pocket-size introduction to the Confucian tradition for beginners.

Kirkland, Russell. *Taoism: The Enduring Tradition*. London: Routledge, 2004. An impassioned monograph by a specialist to correct many of the misconceptions regarding Daoism and its history.

Kohn, Livia, ed. *Daoism Handbook*. Leiden, Netherlands: Brill, 2000. A magisterial and encyclopedic collection of essays on various aspects of Daoism, ranging from history to schools to texts.

Sun, Anna. *Confucianism as a World Religion*. Princeton, NJ: Princeton University Press, 2013. An authoritative monograph on the issue of Confucianism's religious content and labeling.

Schipper, Kristofer. *The Taoist Body*. Berkeley: University of California Press, 1993. An authoritative discourse by an ordained Daoist priest on the rituals and practices of Daoism as they relate to the texts and teachings.

Taylor, Rodney L. *The Religious Dimensions of Confucianism*. Albany: State University of New York Press, 1986. A convenient collection of mostly previously published essays by the author to argue for the religiousness of Confucianism.

Yao, Xinzhong. *An Introduction to Confucianism*. Cambridge, UK: Cambridge University Press, 2000. An authoritative basic text on the entire Confucian tradition.

ONLINE RESOURCES

Research Centre for Confucian Studies

cuhk.edu.hk/rih/confucian

This useful website for Confucian studies is maintained by the Research Center for Confucian Studies, Chinese University of Hong Kong. It contains a rich resource guide for Confucian studies.

The Daoist Foundation

daoistfoundation.org

The Daoist Foundation was created by two American academics who, having studied and practiced Daoism for many years, "are committed to fostering the flourishing of authentic and tradition-based Daoist practice, community, and culture with attentiveness to the needs and concerns of Western students."

Center for Daoist Studies

daoistcenter.org

This useful website is the education and research branch of the Daoist Foundation.

SHINTO

IT IS THE LAST DAY of the three-day Sanja Festival in Asakusa, a historic precinct in Tokyo. The climax of the festival is the wild parading of ***mikoshi***, portable shrines carrying the "essence" of the patron deities of the various neighborhoods and merchant groups.[1] As one of the most popular annual festivals in Tokyo, the Sanja Festival attracts upward of half a million spectators and participants during the three-day festivities.

At 5 A.M. on the third Sunday in May, Satoshi Tanaka, a young grocery clerk in his twenties, is waiting expectantly outside the Asakusa Shrine. Along with hundreds of other young men (and some brave women), he has signed up months in advance to form teams of shrine carriers sponsored by local merchants and civic groups. Though ordinarily preferring to sleep late, Satoshi finds himself in a state of excited anticipation and alertness this morning. Dressed in colorful shirts and shorts with matching headbands, he waits with others to receive their purification by the Shinto priests so that he will be considered spiritually clean and ready for the sacred task ahead. Even though he does not see himself as a seriously religious person, Satoshi feels perfectly comfortable in being a shrine carrier at this Shinto festival. It is his way of interacting with his community and with the deities he believes are present.

The job of these carriers is to carry the *mikoshi* through the streets of Asakusa so that all in attendance can share a moment of intimacy with the deities temporarily housed in these portable shrines. These ornately

Throngs of portable shrine carriers with their respective mikoshi outside the Asakusa Shrine in Tokyo.

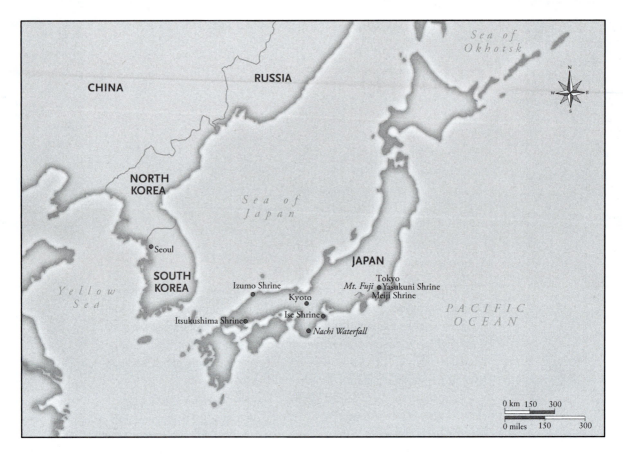

Significant sites in the history of Shinto.

decorated *mikoshi* rest on poles that are carried on the shoulders of the carriers. Shouting and grunting in unison, to the accompaniment of much drumming, cymbal clanging, and loud cheers from the crowd, the carriers attempt to move the portable shrines along. But because no one among them is in total control of the direction of the *mikoshi*, all the carriers move back and forth or sideways more or less blindly. The movement of the portable shrines can thus be wild and unpredictable, subject to the unconscious collective will of the entire group of carriers (or, supposedly, that of the deity inside). This cumbersome and potentially dangerous parade lumbers down narrow streets and broad boulevards amidst large crowds.

Quite frequently one shrine will cross paths with another, resulting in great commotion and competition for attention from the throngs of spectators. Sweating profusely and hoarse from too much shouting and chanting, individual shrine carriers drop out and are quickly replaced without disrupting the progress of the shrines. Thirsty and hungry, the temporarily retired carriers sit or lie on the ground in total exhaustion. Meanwhile, the spectators watch, take pictures, applaud, cheer, visit the main shrine, purchase the sundry food, drink, and souvenirs offered by enterprising street vendors, and make a day of it. ☼

The preceding scene is typical of a *matsuri*, a Shinto festival in contemporary Japan that helps to create religious awareness and social solidarity within the entire community. The *matsuri* is both a religious and a social occasion. Though the oldest surviving religion in Japan, Shinto has, by and large, coexisted with Buddhism and Confucianism since the sixth century C.E. The two latter traditions were introduced into the country from China by way of Korea. Although there has been rivalry and competition among the three religions over the centuries, there has also been accommodation and mutual acceptance. There is an observation about Japanese religious behavior that describes perfectly the eclectic attitude of the Japanese. It says that the Japanese are born and wed in Shinto, die Buddhist, and live in accordance with Confucian ethical principles. In other words, most Japanese do not see the three religions as mutually exclusive or incompatible. Rather, they regard them as mutually reinforcing and relevant in separate aspects and stages of their lives. In this chapter, we invite you into the life of the Shinto believers as they practice their religion in the context of recognizing, and sometimes actually embracing, the other faiths. We do so by discussing its beliefs, history, and ritual practices. As Shinto is practiced almost exclusively in Japan, this chapter does not include a map showing global distribution of Shinto adherents.

TIMELINE
Shinto

10,000–300 B.C.E.* Jōmon period.

300 B.C.E.–300 C.E.* Yayoi period.

300–500 C.E.* Kofun period.

538 Introduction of Buddhism and Confucianism, possibly also Daoism, to Japan.

593 Prince Shōtoku becomes regent.

712 *Kojiki* (Record of Ancient Matters) completed.

720 *Nihon-shoki* or *Nihongi* (Chronicles of Japan) completed.

794 Heian (present-day Kyoto) becomes the permanent capital.

1185 Beginning of samurai rule in Japan.

1339 Kitabatake Chikafusa publishes the *Jinnō shōtōki*.

From 1750s* Rise of *Kokugaku* (National Learning, Neo-Shinto).

From 1780s* Birth of founders of New Religions.

1868 Meiji Restoration begins creation of State Shinto.

1937 Beginning of Pacific War, fought in the name of Emperor Hirohito.

1945 Japan surrenders to Allies, Shinto separated from state.

Note: Asterisks indicate contested or approximate dates.

THE TEACHINGS OF SHINTO

The term **Shinto** is an elegant reference to the longest existing religion in Japan. "*Shin*" is the Japanized pronunciation of the Chinese word "*shen*," which refers to gods and deities (see Chapter 6). "*To*," alternatively "*dō*," is the Japanese way of pronouncing the Chinese word "*dao*," which suggests the "way." Hence Shinto literally means "the way of the gods." As a matter of fact, the term Shinto did not come into existence until the Japanese used it to distinguish their preexisting religion from Buddhism, which, when first introduced into the country in the middle of the sixth century C.E., was known as "*Butsudō*," "the way of the Buddha." In more colloquial form, Shinto is known as *kami-no-michi*, "the way of the **kami**," as the core of Shinto is the belief in the existence and power of *kami*, a broad term that suggests a whole range of meanings.

The Meaning of *Kami*

The complexity of the word *kami* is best illustrated by the great eighteenth-century Japanese scholar Motoori Norinaga (1730–1801). As an articulate advocate for the revival of Shinto in a Japan dominated by Confucian orthodoxy and Buddhist piety, Motoori points out the diverse meaning of the term *kami*:

> I do not yet understand the meaning of the term *kami*. Speaking in general, however, it may be said that *kami* signifies, in the first place, the deities of heaven and earth that appear in the ancient records and also the spirits of the shrines where they are worshiped. It is hardly necessary to say that it includes human beings. It also includes such objects as birds, beasts, trees, plants, seas, mountains, and so forth. In ancient usage, whatsoever was outside the ordinary, possessed superior power, or was awe-inspiring, was called *kami*.[2]

Put simply, then, *kami* refers to anything that is out of the ordinary, awe-inspiring, mysterious, powerful, marvelous, and beyond human control or comprehension. The awe and marvel accorded the *kami* seem to date back to the earliest times in Japanese history. A closer examination of the Shinto beliefs and practices will bear this out.

Belief is the least precise aspect of Shinto, as this religion has no identifiable founder, nor does it have a sacred book similar to the Bible. Our discussion of Shinto beliefs cannot then rely on a professed creed or doctrine. Rather, it is based on a set of highly revered texts, dating back to the eighth and ninth centuries C.E. The ***Kojiki*** (*Record of Ancient Matters*, completed in 712 C.E.) and the ***Nihon shoki*** (alternatively known as *Nihongi, Chronicles of [the Land Where] the Sun Originates*, compiled in 720 C.E.) are the two authoritative texts for the study of ancient Shinto mythologies and beliefs. The following narrative is primarily based on the former.

Creation Myth in the *Kojiki*

The *Kojiki* begins with several generations of invisible divinities at the beginning of time, all of whom have titles that end with the word *kami*, until the primordial pair, **Izanagi** and his wife **Izanami**, appear. The couple is credited with bringing the world out of its original chaos. Standing on the Heavenly Floating Bridge, they lower a jeweled spear to stir the ocean below. When they lift up the spear, the brine dripping down from its tip forms an island. In like manner, "the grand eight islands" of the Japanese archipelago are created. The divine couple then descends to take up residence there, and through their sexual union they produce the various nature deities.

Izanami is burned to death while giving birth to her last child, the fire god. Izanagi follows his wife to Yomi, the underworld of the dead, where, upon seeing her putrefied and decomposing body, he is horrified and beats a hasty retreat. After his return to the world of the living, Izanagi washes himself in a stream. From his eyes are born the solar goddess **Amaterasu**-no-Ōmikami (The Great August Kami who Shines in the Sky)[3] and the lunar god Tsukiyomi. From Izanagi's nose comes the violent and ill-tempered storm god Susa-no-o.[4]

When the *Kojiki* continues, the focus shifts to the relationship between Amaterasu and her brother Susa-no-o. Petulant and mischievous, Susa-no-o gives much grief to his sister. He ravages her heavenly domain, destroys her rice fields, and desecrates her house. Annoyed and frightened, Amaterasu retreats into a cave, thereby plunging the world into darkness. The other deities try to lure her back out with all sorts of tricks, but to no avail, until a goddess by the name of Uzume performs a lewd dance that causes so much raucous laughter among the gods that the curious Amaterasu is finally enticed to emerge from her hiding. (This is an ingenious Shinto attempt at explaining solar eclipse.) Susa-no-o is forced to apologize to his sister and is banished to Izumo, a region facing the Japan Sea (alternatively referred to as the East Sea) on the other side of the main island from Ise, the future home of Amaterasu's grand shrine. In Izumo Susa-no-o settles down and locates a sword, which he presents to Amaterasu as a token of his apology and goodwill. The sword will later become one of the "three imperial regalia" Amaterasu bestows on her descendants who occupy the Japanese throne.

The final cycle of the narrative in the *Kojiki* deals with the successors of Susa-no-o and the descendants of Amaterasu. Ninigi, grandson of Amaterasu, is instructed by her to rule all of Japan. But his mission is thwarted by Susa-no-o's successors in Izumo, who refuse to yield to the Amaterasu line until she promises to honor her young brother by building him a grand shrine. After Izumo's accommodation with the Sun Goddess group, the descendants of all the other deities then fall in line, and Ninigi's own grandson, the Emperor Jimmu, is the first human ruler to claim imperial authority over all of Japan. He is provided with the three imperial regalia of the sword, the mirror, and the curved jewel as symbols of his power, which he is believed to have exercised in the Yamato region near present-day Nara. According to tradition, this momentous event took place in 660 B.C.E., and the imperial line has supposedly continued uninterrupted to the present time.

From the *Kojiki* story just outlined, major themes of Shinto belief can be identified: the divine creation of Japan, a concern with fertility and purification, the importance of the feminine, an absence of ethical teachings, a corresponding lack of absolute good or radical evil, and a profound intertwining of divinity with imperial power.

Japan as a Divine Creation The core belief of Shinto centers on the *kami* and Japan's unique relationship with them. Representative of the Shinto notion of the sacred or the holy, *kami* are mysterious and tremendous powers in nature and in the human world, powers that have been the object

The Meoto-iwa (Husband and Wife rocks) in Mie Prefecture is an iconic landmark in Japan that symbolizes the union between Izanagi and Izanami.

of worship in Japan since prehistoric times. Most *kami* are believed to be the source of blessing and protection, hence worship of them is understood either as thanksgiving or as pleading for more divine gifts. But some *kami* are ill-tempered and even ill-intentioned, so worship of them is a necessary and prudent act for preventing disaster.

Kami are most evident in nature. Illustrious objects in the sky such as the sun and the moon, majestic mountains such as Fuji, serene waterfalls such as the Nachi, and strange-shaped rocks are all regarded as *kami*.

Furthermore, the *Kojiki* story of creation reflects a fundamental Japanese senti-ment that their island nation was created by the *kami* as a paradise on earth. Nature, then, with its awesome power and captivating beauty, is the very expression of divine presence. Human beings, who themselves are also descendants of divinity, have the duty to respond in celebration and adoration to the gifts and blessings of the *kami*. The *kami* among humans—the ancestors of clans and communities, the heroes and powerful individuals, the emperors and some of their high officials, all exemplify godly quali-ties. They therefore equally deserve veneration and worship.

In the prehistoric or quasi-historic periods prior to the fifth or sixth century C.E., when Japan had no centralized imperial rule or institutionalized governmental struc-ture, only clans and communities existed. With the ascendancy of the Yamato clan that claimed descent from the Sun Goddess Amaterasu, the chiefs and heads of the various clans and communities surrendered their power to the Yamato ruler in return for recognition and position in the divine/political power structure. The result was the entire country of Japan forming a network of *kami* with strong local identities that were loosely linked to the worship of the emperor as a deity.

Fertility and Purification   Early Shinto is centrally concerned with fertility. In the *Kojiki* cosmogonic (explanation of how the cosmos came about) myth, the main func-tion of the primeval pair of *kami* is to "fertilize" the land and to procreate the other gods. Much emphasis is placed on the sexual union between Izanagi and Izanami in the population of the world, especially Japan, with plants, animals, and people. This procreative power of the original divine couple continues even after the death of the wife, when Izanagi, on his own, manages to bring forth more deities through ritual washing. At the same time, this mythic story highlights the Shinto fear of contamina-tion and defilement, as well as its emphasis on purification. Despite the love that he has for his wife, Izanagi is so horrified and repulsed by Izanami's decomposing form after her death that he abandons her in the netherworld and hurries back to the world of the living. Death, disease, and blood are thus seen as polluting; persons connected to those things are considered spiritually impure and must be ritually purified before they can approach the *kami*. The arrangement of the typical Shinto shrine and the main ritual responsibility of the Shinto priests illustrate well this vital aspect of Shinto belief, as we shall see later in this chapter.

The Feminine in Shinto   It is highly noteworthy that in the Shinto myth, the sun, the most illustrious object in the sky, is portrayed as female, this despite the later patriarchal (male-dominated) nature of Japanese society. It is equally significant that the Sun Goddess Amaterasu is also the ancestress of the Japanese royal family and that, at least up through the tenth century C.E., it was not uncommon for the imperial ruler to be a woman. Also prominent in early Shinto is the role of the shamanic figure, often a female. The ecstatic dance of the goddess Uzume to lure Amaterasu out of hiding, thereby saving the world from perpetual darkness caused by solar eclipse, is indicative of the power of the female shamanic dancer. In addition, both the *Kojiki* and the *Nihongi* mention the mother of Emperor Jimmu, the first human ruler of Japan, whose name is Tama-yori-hime. This name suggests her role as a female shaman, as it literally means "a princess (*hime*) in whom dwells (*yori*) the spirit (*tama*) of the *kami*." Equally noteworthy is the account of Emperor Sujin in the *Nihongi*, whose rule is assisted by two female diviners, one being his own aunt, and the other a charismatic commoner named Ōtataneko, the favorite woman shaman of the deity of the Yamato region. It is the latter who is credited with the peace and prosperity of Sujin's reign, as she is known for her capacity to commune with the *kami* and be possessed by them.

The high prestige of female shamans in ancient Japan is further attested by the story of Empress Jingō, also recorded in the *Nihongi*. Jingō is a capable shamanic diviner for her husband, Emperor Chūai, who, after his death, personally leads an armada to invade Korea because of the oracle of assured victory she receives from the gods. It is the extension of Japanese political control over Korea that paves the way for the powerful reign of her son, Emperor Ōjin. Scholars today speculate that Empress Jingō's legendary account is modeled after the story of Himiko in Chinese historical records dating back to the fourth century C.E. They describe a female shamanic ruler of a region called Yamatai (suspected to be a variation of Yamato) in the country of Wa (Japan) whose bewitching control over the people is the source of her power. One possible interpretation of the term Himiko is "*miko* of the Sun (*hi*)." At the same time, **miko** to this day refers to unmarried women attendants at Shinto shrines who possess shamanic power to communicate with the *kami* through dance and other ritual performances. Himiko's central role as medium for the Sun Goddess can thus be imagined. Jingō's possible association with Himiko only highlights the critical importance of female diviners in ancient Shinto.

Ethics, Good, and Evil   Conspicuously absent in early Shinto belief is any reference to ethics. Although much emphasis is placed on fertility and purity, *Kojiki*'s cosmogonic story does not address the issue of morality at all. The fire god, though causing the death of his mother Izanami, is not depicted as a villain. Izanagi, though abandoning his wife in the eternally dark and terrifying underworld, is not blamed for being a heartless spouse. Susa-no-o, though causing much distress to his sister Amaterasu with his destructive and willful behavior, is not portrayed as an evil culprit. Likewise, the explicitly lewd behavior of the *kami* in drawing Amaterasu out of her hiding is not seen as immoral. In other words, the early Shinto account of creation and the relationship between the gods gives no emphasis on proper ethical conduct. There is no supreme god giving moral instructions and laws. Nor is there any hint of a cosmic struggle between good and evil. Whether in the primeval divine realm of the gods, in the natural world, or within the human community that comes into being afterward, there is no existence in Shinto beliefs of a radical evil entity that is bent on subverting the will and the handiwork of a benevolent creator god. Divine and human actions are judged only as fertile or unproductive, pure or impure, desirable or undesirable. Wayward behavior can be remedied and impurities can be removed. What are most offensive to the gods are not sin and guilt, but pollution and defilement.

The notable absence of ethical concerns in early Shinto myth by no means signals that the Japanese are not governed by moral principles in their behavior. What it does mean is that Japanese ethics came from other sources, primarily Buddhism and Confucianism. The introduction of these two alien traditions in the history of Shinto is discussed later.

State Shinto   One controversial issue in Shinto that must be addressed is the religion's tie to the imperial state and to the worship of the emperor. As early Shinto texts make clear, the divine origin of the imperial family and of the reigning emperor had been asserted right from the beginning. As descendant of the Sun Goddess Amaterasu, the Japanese ruler (both male and, not infrequently, female—at least up to the tenth century C.E.) traditionally wielded both political and religious power. As a matter of fact, government affairs and government in general were originally referred to as *matsurigoto*, "matters relating to festivals." Meanwhile, the principle of **saisei-itchi**, "the unity of the religious and the political," theoretically guided government operations. Sentiments showing strong advocacy of Japan's special position and the emperors' sacred nature based on Shinto beliefs were expressed by nationalists and royalists from the fourteenth century on. In a work entitled *Jinnō shōtōki* (*Direct Succession of Gods and Sovereigns*), published in 1339 by Kitabatake Chikafusa (1293–1354), the superiority of Japan and the divine status of the emperors were forcefully asserted: "Great Japan is the divine land (*shinkoku*). The heavenly progenitor founded it, and the Sun Goddess bequeathed it to her descendants to rule eternally. Only in our country is this true; there are no similar examples in other countries."[5] But it was during the eighteenth and nineteenth centuries C.E., when an intense Shinto revivalist movement took hold in Japan, that such sentiments came to be even more extravagantly expressed. Known as National Learning (*Kokugaku*), this movement aimed at preserving the very essence of Japanese culture by ridding the country of all foreign elements, including Confucian and Buddhist influences. These concepts were advanced in the National Learning writings of Motoori Norinaga (1730–1801) and Hirata Atsutane (1776–1843).

> Our country's Imperial Line, which casts its light over this world, represents the descendants of the Sky-Shining Goddess [Amaterasu]. And in accordance with that Goddess' mandate of reigning "forever and ever, coeval with Heaven and Earth," the Imperial Line is destined to

rule the nation for eons until the end of time and as long as the universe exists. That is the very basis of our Way. That our history has not deviated from the instructions of the divine mandate bears testimony to the infallibility of our ancient tradition. It can also be seen why foreign countries cannot match ours and what is meant by the special dispensation of our country.

—Motoori Norinaga

[A]s a special mark of favor from the heavenly gods, they gave birth to our country, and thus there is so immense a difference between Japan and all the other countries of the world as to defy comparison. Ours is a splendid and blessed country, the Land of the Gods beyond any doubt, and we, down to the most humble man and woman, are the descendants of the gods. . . . Japanese differ completely from and are superior to the peoples of China, India . . . and all other countries of the world, and for us to have called our country the Land of the Gods was not mere vanity. . . . This is a matter of universal belief and is quite beyond dispute.[6]

—Hirata Atsutane

These chauvinistic sentiments, buttressed by a revived nationalistic Shinto, became a prime motivating force that eventually brought down the last feudal military government and ushered in an imperial Restoration in 1868. With the help of Shinto nationalism and deep respect for the imperial line, the fifteen-year-old Meiji emperor emerged from the shadow of centuries of domination of the royal family by military commanders to reclaim his divine right to rule. A "State Shinto" was implemented to promote the worship of the emperor as a living *kami*, at once sacred and inviolable, and to propagate a form of ethnocentric nationalism. It was this State Shinto that was responsible for the cult of emperor worship and the rise of ultra-nationalism in Japan in the twentieth century, a subject to which we return in the section on the history of Shinto later in the chapter.

How has Shinto managed to maintain its independent identity in light of the overwhelming influence of Buddhism and Confucianism in Japan since the beginning of its recorded history?

VOICES: An Interview with Watanabe Minoru

Mr. Watanabe Minoru is a Shinto priest in his fifties at a shrine in the Nerima district of Tokyo.

Why did you want to become a Shinto priest?

My family has been in charge of a shrine at my native city of Shizuoka for generations. Both my grandfather and father were chief priests there. So, ever since my childhood, I have been expected to carry on this family profession also.

Did you have to go to a special school in order to be a Shinto priest?

> After high school, I attended the Kokugakuin University in Tokyo to learn all about being a Shinto priest. The university is pretty much like all other universities, except that it is one of the two main training centers for Shinto priests, the other being Kōgakkan in Mie prefecture, near Ise. In addition to Shinto culture and practices, the university offers numerous other disciplines, including economics and law. I led a typical college student's life. I was even president of the judo club during my senior year.

What does it mean to be a Shinto priest?

> To me, being a Shinto priest is more than knowing all the Shinto teachings and ritual performances. Most important, it is to serve as "cement" for the community by bringing all the neighbors together through year-round shrine activities. The shrine should be a place where people can come and interact with the *kami* and one another on all sorts of occasions and for all kinds of needs whenever they want to. It is a fundamental aspect of Shinto to have a sense that *kami* is so close to us that we can communicate with it whenever we need guidance and protection. Respect of the *kami* and closeness to it either as an individual or as a community form the very basis of our Japanese cultural identity. As a Shinto priest I consider it my solemn duty to preserve this identity and to invite people to appreciate and respect this identity.

THE HISTORY OF SHINTO

The long history of the Shinto tradition can be divided roughly into three periods: ancient, medieval, and modern. The ancient period lasted from prehistoric times to the unification of the country by the Yamato leaders sometime prior to the sixth century C.E. We have already discussed the major tenets of this ancient Shinto as revealed in the classical works of the *Kojiki* and the *Nihongi*, compiled in the eighth century C.E.

Medieval Shinto

By the time the *Kojiki* and *Nihongi* had been compiled, Shinto had actually begun its second (medieval) stage of development. This stage was marked by the new religious and political challenge from the continental culture of China by way of Korea. In the year 538 C.E., Confucianism and Buddhism were formally introduced into Japan by the Yamato leaders, who had consolidated their power over all other rival clans. This was an accomplishment confirmed by the mythological accounts that describe the submission of the various *kami* (who were believed to be the founding ancestors of these clans) to Amaterasu, the ancestress of the Yamato rulers.

Confucianism and Buddhism gave a great jolt to the established Shinto faith, addressing issues it had ignored or had no interest in. Confucianism (see Chapter 6) provided an ethical framework for state, society, and family, and Buddhism (see Chapter 3) gave special attention to the issues of suffering and death. The clearest evidence of the influence of the two alien traditions can be seen in the "Seventeen Articles Constitution" promulgated in 604 C.E. by Prince Shōtoku, regent to his aunt the Empress Suiko.

More a vision statement than a constitution in the modern sense, the document clearly acknowledges the strengths of Confucianism and Buddhism in giving guidance to harmonious living and purpose in life. Article One declares the primacy of Confucian harmony as the operating principle of both state and society, while Article Two professes hearty adherence to the Buddhist Three Treasures: the Buddha, his teachings (the *dharma*), and the community of monks he created, the *Sangha*.

In the face of strong challenge from such potent rivals, the reaction of Shinto practitioners was accommodation and adaptation. With no clear inherent ethical orientation (as noted earlier), Shinto adopted Confucian moral principles with little resistance. With respect to Buddhism, the Shinto reaction was more complicated. The Buddha was initially vehemently rejected as a foreign *kami* with no relevance to Japan. In time, however, when Buddhism began to be fully embraced by the Japanese court during the Nara period (710–784 C.E.), Shinto *kami* became guardians and protectors of the newly arrived Buddha and his various manifestations. Sometime later, Buddhas and *bodhisattvas* in turn became saviors of the *kami!* It was common for Buddhist scriptures to be recited before the altar of *kami*, and conversely Buddhist monks were in charge of Shinto shrines. At the end, though, the accommodation between Shinto and Buddhism became nearly a total merger, when Shinto *kami* were worshiped as Buddha or *bodhisattva* and the alien Buddhist deities were likewise regarded as Japanese *kami*. Using the Tōdaiji temple in Nara as an example, the Vairocana Buddha housed there is known as Dainichi, the "Great Sun," a conscious effort to equate and identify with Amaterasu the Sun Goddess. By the Heian period (794–1191), a perfect amalgamation of Shinto and Buddhism was complete.

One interesting form of this Shinto-Buddhist merger at the folk level was the emergence of a lay Buddhist and occult Shinto group known as Shūgendō ("The Way of Cultivating Magical Power"). Practitioners of this faith usually underwent austere training in the mountains to acquire mysterious powers of healing, divination, and exorcism. Commonly referred to as *yamabushi* ("those who sleep in the mountains"), Shūgendō members were ascetics with no formal affiliation with either established Shinto or Buddhism but were revered as shamanic healers and exorcists, as well as guides for pilgrims making their way to remote sacred sites.

The convergence of Shinto and Buddhism (and Confucianism, for that matter) in Japan has been credited with the formulation of the *samurai* ("sword-wielding warriors") code of conduct in premodern Japan. Known alternatively as *Bushidō* ("Way of the warrior"), this *samurai* ethic emphasizes purity of the heart and soul, contempt for pain and death, and undying loyalty to the feudal lord. It aims to combine the best elements of Shinto, Buddhism, and Confucianism within Japan's cultural heritage.

The Modern Period

The modern period of Shinto history began with its attempt at recovering its pristine past and its claim of superiority over the non-native traditions. Stirrings of this sentiment can be detected after the unsuccessful Mongol invasions of Japan in 1274 and 1281. The near disasters aroused in the Japanese a strong sense of national consciousness, resulting in their reevaluation of their native beliefs and those coming from abroad. The aforementioned nationalistic sentiment of Kitabatake Chikafusa, whose writing insisted that Japan was superior to all other countries because of its single line of emperors descended from the gods, reflected this trend in the political realm.

With the rise of the *Kokugaku* (National Learning) movement in the eighteenth century, a call was made for the return of Japan to the pristine beliefs and practices of ancient times before the introduction of "inferior" alien traditions such as Buddhism and Confucianism had contaminated Japanese culture. Meanwhile, with reinvigorated effort, the priests of the Grand Shrine at Ise actively promoted pilgrimage to the shrine by groups from all over Japan. This helped create a sense of national unity, binding all Japanese together under one common Shinto faith.

State Shinto   All these developments paved the way for the establishment of State Shinto after the Restoration of the Meiji Emperor in 1868. In 1870, the Meiji government proclaimed that "the Way of the *Kami*" would be the guiding principle of the nation. Reversing the previous Tokugawa military regime's practice of requiring all households to register in Buddhist temples, the new government mandated every household to enroll in the shrine of the local *kami*. The government also actively encouraged Shinto funeral rites in a deliberate effort to deprive Buddhism of its monopoly in conducting funeral services. Indeed, Buddhism was forcefully separated from Shinto, and Buddhist monks who had been affiliated with Shinto shrines were ordered to return to secular life.

But it was the Meiji government's promotion of the emperor cult that constituted the core of State Shinto. The emperor was venerated as a "living *kami*"—a god in flesh and blood. During the Meiji reign, a special shrine was built in Tokyo (formerly known as Edo), the seat of power of the just-toppled Tokugawa shogunate, which had become the new capital. The shrine, named Yasukuni Jinja ("Shrine for the Pacification of the Nation"), was dedicated to those who had sacrificed their lives for the royalist cause in toppling the last feudal regime and the restoration of imperial authority in 1868. All of them had been elevated to *kami* status, as would others who were subsequently enshrined there after each of Japan's foreign wars in the twentieth century, including the Russo-Japanese War of 1904–1905 and World War II. Because of its close association with State Shinto and the emperor cult, both of which have been blamed for Japan's imperialistic expansion in Asia (the colonization of Taiwan and Korea in 1895 and 1910, respectively; the occupation of Manchuria in the 1930s; and the outright invasion of China and Southeast Asia during the Pacific Wars of 1937–1945), the Yasukuni Shrine has become a controversial symbol. That it also houses the remains of some of the most notorious government leaders and commanders at the end of World War II makes matters even more sensitive. Japan's neighbors (China and Korea, in particular), who were victims of Japan's ultra-nationalistic aggression in the first half of the twentieth century, invariably file official complaints whenever prominent Japanese political figures (such as the prime minister) pay formal visits to the Yasukuni Shrine.

State Shinto has also been blamed for the fanatical nationalism among many Japanese, particularly among the rank and file of the military, during World War II. Japanese soldiers ravaged much of Asia in the name of their imperial ruler, Emperor Hirohito (r. 1926–1989). They considered their foreign aggression a divine mission, to be carried out without remorse or hesitation. Even when Japanese defeat appeared inevitable by the early 1940s, the military commanders sent suicide pilots to plunge their planes into Allied battle ships in a desperate attempt to reverse the fortune of the war. Calling the pilots *kamikaze* ("divine wind"), they tried to evoke the memory of the Japanese defeat of the invading Mongol troops in 1274 and 1281 thanks to the alleged assistance of the divine storm (*kaze*) sent by the *kami* to protect the nation. State Shinto's hold on Japan during those war years was unmistakable.

But the best illustration of the emperor cult in State Shinto was the building of the Meiji Shrine that began in 1915 and was completed in 1920. Constructed to enshrine the *kami* spirits of the Meiji emperor and his wife, the shrine was a tremendous undertaking, funded by the government. Located in the heart of Tokyo, the Meiji Shrine covers close to 200 acres of prime real estate, surrounded by elaborate gardens and wooded areas. It remains to this day a popular site for New Year's celebrations and other festivals.

Sect Shinto The Modern period of Shinto also saw the rise of Sect Shinto and other new religions. A combination of Shinto, Confucianism, Buddhism, Shūgendō, and folk beliefs, Sect Shinto arose at the end of the Tokugawa period and became popular throughout the Meiji period. Thirteen such sects have gained official recognition. Grouped with other eclectic religious organizations that arose in the 1920s and 1930s under the general category of "New Religions," they include such influential sects as Tenrikyō ("Teaching of Heavenly Principles"), Konkōkyō ("Teaching of Golden Light"), and Kurozumikyō ("Teaching of the founder, Kurozumi Munetada" [1780–1850]).

Although different in doctrine and practice, these religious groups share a number of common features. Their founders were charismatic individuals steeped in the shamanic tradition of Shinto, the esoteric teachings of Buddhism, and a whole host of other folk beliefs. A noticeable number of them were women. Mostly of farming origin, they appealed to the anxiety and unease experienced by the lower classes during a time of rapid social change and political upheaval, as was the case in much of modern Japanese history. Explaining that calamity and disaster emanate from disturbances in people's spiritual state, they offered their shamanic powers to bring peace, harmony, health, and prosperity to their followers. The emphasis on worldly benefits was often accompanied by the promise of the impending arrival of a new age and a new world. To impress the faithful and the larger society around them, they have built imposing headquarters and even whole cities of great beauty. Their teachings generally stress clean living, hard work, moral conduct, familial cohesion, and social solidarity. The sectarian nature of these groups has made their believers more fervent than members of the established traditions of Shinto and Buddhism.

Shinto in Japan Today

Japan's defeat at the end of World War II in 1945 fundamentally changed the religious landscape of the country. The State Shinto that sponsored the cult of the emperor and government support of the shrines was, in theory at least, abolished. The divinity of the Japanese emperor was officially disavowed. Yet the imperial family continues to enjoy great affection from the majority of the Japanese people. Public reference to members of the emperor's family, even children, has to be couched in honorific language, and great throngs of people visit the grounds of the Imperial Palace on New Year's Day to greet the imperial family. The emperor opens each session of the parliament as the constitutional monarch and officially receives each new prime minister upon his assumption of office (a female prime minister is yet to be elected in Japan). Members of the imperial household, particularly the Crown Prince, visit the Grand Shrine at Ise periodically to signal their claimed lineage tie to the Sun Goddess Amaterasu.

Meanwhile, Sect Shinto in the form of the many new religions discussed previously has flourished. With their charismatic leaders and their emphasis on this-worldly benefits, the various Shinto-inspired groups attract large followings by serving the practical needs of the faithful. Local, regional, and even national shrines are maintained largely with nonofficial sources of funding, providing quiet locations of escape from the hustle and bustle of urban living and scenic sanctuaries where people can commune with the numinous forces in nature. Shinto values continue to give the Japanese people their sense of identity and aesthetics, as well as solace and comfort after disasters. In the aftermath of the 9.0 earthquake and its subsequent nuclear leak and devastating tsunami that wreaked so much havoc in northeastern Japan in March 2011, Shinto beliefs about life renewal and rejuvenation, as well as its emphasis on purification and decontamination, have provided the Japanese people with the purpose and resolve to carry out a massive program of reconstruction and revival of the stricken areas. Shinto remains at the core of Japanese culture. As the opening vignette illustrates, it is the ritual and social functions of Shinto that continue to provide solidarity for the Japanese people and justify the relevance of this religion for the Japanese nation.

Given that religious justification of political rule is a common phenomenon in world history, in what ways is Shinto's justification of the Japanese imperial system unique?

SHINTO AS A WAY OF LIFE

Far more important to Shinto than beliefs are ceremonies and ritual practices. Some scholars even argue that Shinto beliefs are "more acted out than thought out."[7] It is often the case that many Japanese perform some of the Shinto rituals and daily habits without full knowledge or consciousness of their doctrinal and theoretical underpinnings. It is certainly the rituals, both public and private, that enable Shinto practitioners to directly experience the presence of the divine *kami* and to recognize their bond with the *kami*, as well as with one another. The young shrine carrier Satoshi Tanaka, whom we met at the beginning of this chapter, is representative of this Shinto mindset. Though he does not consider himself a deeply religious man, he finds fun and meaning in his participation in the Sanja Festival. Let us examine how the Shinto beliefs discussed in the previous section of this chapter are lived and acted out in the daily lives, as well as the ceremonial occasions, of the believers.

Fertility Rites

A major emphasis of Shinto is fertility. In villages throughout Japan, one can still find phallic symbols and representations of the female sex organ on display and worshipped. The Shinto ritual calendar to this day gives prominence to ceremonies revolving around fertility and productivity. In early spring, the *kinensai* (festival for praying for good harvest) is celebrated when the fertility-dispensing *kami* are believed to be physically present in their shrines. Processions of worshippers greet these deities, carry them into the fields on portable palanquins, and dance to celebrate their divine powers while rice seedlings are being planted or transplanted. In the fall, the *niiname matsuri* (harvest festival), the largest event of the ritual year, is observed, when the *kami* are honored and thanked for the bounteous crops with joyous and boisterous celebrations.

The harvest festival is also closely linked with the Shinto belief in divine kingship. The Japanese emperor, the *tennō* ("august heavenly ruler"), had until 1945 both religious and political responsibilities, as he was regarded as a direct descendant of the Sun Goddess Amaterasu and thereby entrusted to rule over the land. One such religious responsibility was the guarantee of fertility of the soil and bountiful harvest. This is consummated ritually each fall at the *niiname* festival, presided over by the emperor as high priest. The most spectacular expression of this magical power of the Japanese ruler is the *daijosai* ("the great food festival"), which is performed by a new emperor the year after his ascension to the throne. In an elaborate and ancient ritual, rice and wine from specially cultivated fields are presented by the new ruler to the deities in the middle of the night, a gesture that consecrates the emperor's religious power and political legitimacy. This rite, still performed as the climax of a royal accession in modern Japan, marks the very distinctive religious foundation of the Japanese imperial institution.

Women in Shinto

As we have seen in an earlier discussion of the feminine in Shinto, its mythology includes many powerful female figures and forces. It should also be noted that, though small in number and usually more junior in rank, Shinto priestesses constitute an integral part of the Shinto clergy and can be found in many of the larger shrines all over Japan. They participate fully in all the Shinto rites performed by their male counterparts, though serving as chief ritualist remains rare. Yet it is also true that the most supreme religious figure at the Grand Shrine of Ise, the home of the Sun Goddess Amaterasu, is the *saishu*, the female priestess who is usually a relative of the imperial family and is ranked above even the chief priest there!

The role of the *miko* (unmarried female shrine attendants) cannot be overlooked. Practically all Shinto shrines have *miko* performing a variety of important, though subordinate, functions. Because of the persistent belief in the shamanic power of these young women to communicate with the *kami*, they are entrusted to perform the sacred dance of *kagura* (music of the *kami*) at festivals and other ritual occasions as an indispensable complement to the prayers and purifying acts of the priests. In addition, they serve as secretaries in shrine offices, sell amulets and other trinkets at shrine gift shops, and generally interact with the public by providing a feminine touch on behalf of the shrine.

Last but not least, a noticeable number of the founders of Japan's New Religions are women. These new religious groups are heavily indebted to Shinto beliefs and motifs, even though they also borrow substantially from other traditions, such as Buddhism and Daoism. As a religious tradition, Shinto recognizes the considerable power and potency of women.

Rites of Purification, Presentation, Petition, and Participation

The Shinto ritual event generally involves a four-step sequence of purification, presentation, petition, and participation. The first three steps are performed by priests, and the last one involves the "congregation" in attendance. The rationale for the sequence is first to make the participants (both clergy and laity) physically and spiritually clean for their encounter with the *kami*. The second step is to present food offerings to the *kami* in an attempt to show respect and good will and to pave the way for the next act. This is to formally plead with the *kami*, through beautiful and correct words intoned with reverence and awe by the chief priest, for the concrete benefits being sought. Finally, the last sequence of the ritual is to have the entire worshipping audience fully participate in the ceremony through the watching of performances, sharing of ritual drinks, and the gift of shrine souvenirs.

Entry of the bridal procession at a Shinto wedding, walking through the shrine gate, led by *mikos*. Yasaka Shrine, Maruyama Park, Kyoto, Japan.

The Japanese word for the purification ritual performed by the Shinto priest is **harae**, the purpose of which is to please and soothe the *kami*. The ceremony is deemed necessary to prepare the faithful for their encounter with the deity or to remove the defilement that results from any contact with pollutants. All sorts of occasions call for the performance of *harae*, which may take place at the shrine; otherwise, the priest may go to the place where it is needed. It is common to call in the Shinto priest to perform the *harae* before moving into a new home, occupying a new office building, opening a new highway, or even driving a new car. The priest, dressed in sacramental vestments, waves an *onusa* (the wand of stripped paper or an evergreen branch) over the person(s) or the object(s) to be purified, first on the left, then the right, and finally back to the left. Ritual bathing is another form of purification. In a practice known as **misogi**, Shinto believers purify themselves by standing under a waterfall or immersing themselves in ocean water. As is well known, the Japanese are a meticulously clean people who enjoy long and frequent baths during which they scrupulously clean and scrub themselves. This national trait certainly has Shinto roots.

Salt also plays an important role in the *harae*. Its snow-like appearance symbolizes purity, and its potency as a purifying agent is widely accepted in Japan. The Shinto priest often sprinkles salt over the place, the people, or the object to be purified. Sumo wrestlers, whose characteristic Japanese spectator sport has strong Shinto connections, are purified with salt before each match. This belief in salt as spiritual purifier also makes its way into many aspects of Japanese life. After attending a funeral service, people sprinkle salt in the doorway before reentering their homes so as not to carry the defilement of death inside. Shop owners also put small mounds of salt on either side of their storefronts to ward off evil spirits. The Shinto concern with purification is evident in these examples.

The presentation component involves the offering of rice, fish, fruit, rice wine, water, and salt to the *kami*. It should be pointed out that there is absolutely no blood sacrifice in the offerings, as blood is considered repulsive and polluting in Shinto. (For the same reason, menstruating priestesses cannot participate in the *harae* ritual, thus making them less available and qualified to officiate at Shinto rites.) The petition takes the form of the priest reverently reciting the **norito** (prayers or "words spoken to the *kami*"), which is usually written in advance in very elegant and flowery language and read aloud with a rhythmical cadence, ending with a vowel that slides down an octave in pitch with the volume tapering off slowly. The worshippers' participation in the ritual event includes receiving purification by the priest, watching the dance of the *miko*, listening to the performance of the musicians, and, when over, taking small sips of rice wine called *omiki*, as well as bringing home leafy sprigs of the native Japanese *sakaki* tree to complete their encounter with the divine. All of these activities are designed to create bonding between the worshippers and their *kami*, as well as among themselves.

The Shrine The Shinto shrine is generally the location where Shinto rituals are carried out. It is referred to as the **jinja**, the "dwelling place of the *kami*." It is here that the *kami* can be approached and worshipped. In early Shinto and in some remote, isolated sacred locations today, the *jinja* can be a tree, a waterfall, or an extraordinarily shaped rock, which local people believe to be a source of spiritual power. These *kami* dwellings are filled with awe-inspiring mystery and great natural beauty. They are often marked with nothing more than a pile of rocks, or sometimes an ornamental rope to suggest the approach to sacred space. Most *jinja*, however, are enclosed areas with a few simple structures. Entry into them requires a purified body and, ideally, a purified mind, as godliness in Shinto is synonymous with cleanliness. Thus the shrine is a holy space, of which the visitor is immediately reminded by two guardian stone lions, one on each side of the entry approach. (In the case of the shrines of the grain goddess Inari, the stone lions are replaced by foxes, which are believed to be her preferred messengers.) The entry path then passes under the distinctive Shinto crossbar gateway, known as the **torii**, whose literal meaning is "bird dwelling," probably reflecting the earliest function of it as a roost for sacred birds.

In its most characteristic form, the *torii* of today is painted red and consists of two upright posts joined by one or two crossbeams, with the upper crossbeam gently curved in the middle toward the ground. This use of red paint and the curved line in the upper crossbeam indicates both Chinese and Buddhist influence and would not have been found in the early days of Shinto. The *torii* is not meant merely to be a decorative gateway. It is a magical protective device that guards the shrine against all impurities and contaminants. Sometimes visitors have to pass under multiple *torii*, and on occasion an extended series of them are set so close together that they form a veritable tunnel.

There is an ancient belief that every part of the island of Itsukushima is so sacred that even the hills and surrounding waters are gods. When the tide is high, the main sanctuary and other structures appear to be floating. The shaded sanctuary's stage is used for events such as Noh performances.

Once inside the shrine grounds, all visitors perform a simple purification ritual by approaching a basin or trough of purified water called **temizuya** (usually a natural stone basin filled with clear water from the mouth of a sculpted dragon) and, using a bamboo dipper, taking a ladleful of water to rinse their mouth and hands. They are now ready for communion with the *kami*. The *jinja* generally has two buildings—the *haiden* and the *honden*. The former, the "worship sanctuary," is the more public of the two. As its name implies, the *haiden* is where the faithful can approach and worship the *kami*. One very noticeable feature of the *haiden* is the **shimenawa**, a huge rope made of rice straw that marks the boundaries of the building that has been purified or an area in which the kami might be present. Strips of paper called *shide* are hung from the rope.

Worshippers stand in front of the building, clap their hands twice, and ring a suspended bell to attract the attention of the deity. Then they bow their heads and, with hands clasped and sometimes eyes closed, silently utter their prayer of requests or thanksgiving. Occasionally they also deposit offerings into a money chest. The *haiden* is also the place where the priests conduct their ordinary ceremonies on specific occasions on behalf of the community or the state but sometimes also purely private matters for individuals or small groups.

In the courtyard facing the *haiden*, visitors display their interaction with the *kami* through two specific objects: the **ema**, wooden tablets on

The Fushimi Inari-taisha Shrine in Kyoto, Japan, is dedicated to the god of rice and sake. Here, a tunnel of *torii* arches is guarded by a pair of foxes.

which are written their pleadings with the *kami* for success in marriage, childbirth, investment, and entrance examinations; and the **omikuji**, paper fortunes wrapped around tree branches as a form of divination to gauge the future outcome of an undertaking.

Beyond the *haiden* and more hidden from public view is the *honden* ("main sanctuary"), the place where the *kami* resides. It is generally raised higher than any other structure on the premises and has steep access stairs in front and at the sides. Only priests can enter this building, for it is regarded as the shelter of the **shintai**, the "body of the deity" that is the very physical embodiment of the *kami*. This *shintai* is the kernel of sacredness, the symbolic representation of the *kami* honored at the shrine. In and of itself the *shintai* has little intrinsic value. It may be a stone, a scroll, a mirror, a sword, or a small statue. Yet it is regarded with such awe and reverence that even the priests are prohibited from gazing upon it or handling it except on special occasions. As the soul of Shinto holiness and cleanliness, the *shintai* is both inviolably sacred and pure.

The Grand Shrine at Ise, the main sanctuary of the Sun Goddess Amaterasu and official shrine of the imperial family, deserves special mention in connection with this Shinto concern for purity and cleanliness. Though originally built more than thirteen centuries ago, it is completely torn down and rebuilt every twenty years for the purpose of regular purification and renewal. According to tradition, this practice was inaugurated in 690 C.E. by Emperor Jitō. The design, however, is meticulously copied each time. The shrine we see today is supposedly an exact replica of the original one, and it was freshly built in 2013.

The carpenters for the Ise Shrine come from families that have been hereditarily entrusted to undertake the task. Only natural cypress wood is used for the main structures, and only hand tools are allowed to work on the wood. There are no metal braces or nails used in construction, and the different parts of the shrine are held together by complex and intricate wooden joints. The cypress wood is carefully selected years in advance of the rebuilding and is paraded through different communities throughout

Top: The *shimenawa* marks off a sacred space at a Shinto shrine. Bottom: These prayer plaques express the hopes, aspirations, and requests for blessing of the shrine visitors.

The inner shrine of Amaterasu at Ise.

Shrine visit is a regular practice of most Japanese, even though many of them do not regard it as an overt or deliberate religious act. How does it reflect Shinto's intertwining relationship with the Japanese way of life?

Japan to drum up support for and interest in the shrine rebuilding project. Thus the Ise Shrine is simultaneously the oldest and the newest, as well as the purest, shrine in Japan.

Religious Observances throughout the Year

Because of the diversity in Japanese religion, the yearly round of customary ritual observances (*nenjū gyōji*) is correspondingly diverse in religious orientation. Excluding the various local festivals that pay tribute to particular Shinto *kami* and Buddhist feasts that honor the Buddha and specific *bodhisattvas*, the following are the most popularly observed annual ritual occasions.

New Year (*Oshōgatsu*)   People prepare for the New Year each January 1 by cleaning their houses thoroughly in an attempt to get rid of both physical and spiritual dirt. On New Year's Eve near midnight, they visit one of the major Shinto shrines such as the Meiji Shrine in Tokyo or a prominent Buddhist temple such as the Honganji in Kyoto to welcome in the New Year. Beginning on New Year's Day, they visit friends and relatives to offer their greetings and renew their relationship.

The Turn of the Seasons (*Setsubun*)   This festival is observed on February 3, the last day of the winter season. A special purification ritual is performed by the entire family, which involves the throwing of roasted beans from the house into the yard, yelling *Oni wa soto!* (Demons get out!) and, from the yard into the house, calling out *Fuku wa uchi!* (Fortunes come in!). Shinto shrines in the community do the same, though on a much larger scale.

Doll Festival (*Hina Matsuri*) March 3 is devoted to the celebration of girls and daughters in the household. A notable feature of the observance of this special day is the prominent display of tiers of dolls with elaborate costumes that represent the styles of the court ladies of the ancient imperial period. These dolls are expensively made and are seen as a reflection of the family's financial standing.

Boys' Day (*Tango no Sekku*) This counterpart of the Doll Festival is celebrated on May 5. Dedicated to celebrating the healthy growth of boys, this day refers to the annual festival (*sekku*) held on the day of the horse (*go*) at the beginning (*tan*) of May. It also involves the display of figurines of armored fighters and the flying of carp-shaped paper or fabric streamers on a tall pole.

Star Festival (*Tanabata*) This festival was introduced from China to commemorate the romantic story of two stars, Vega and Altair, personified respectively as a young weaver maiden and her lover the cowherd, who are allowed this one-time-a-year rendezvous in the heavens. Observed on July 7, it is a festival for young lovers and for unmarried girls who want to improve their chances of marriage by honing their skills in weaving, sewing, and embroidery or any arts and crafts requiring manual dexterity.

Ghost Festival (*Obon*) Unlike the other festivals listed here, the Ghost Festival's date each year is not determined by the solar calendar. Instead, it falls on the fourteenth day of the seventh month in the lunar calendar. This is the Japanese

VISUAL GUIDE
Shinto

This image contains three major aspects of Japanese religiosity—the sun, the Shinto torii, and cherry blossoms. The sun is the chief deity responsible for the rise of the Japanese state, the torii (lit. "bird perch," hence the bird atop the arch) marks off the sacred space of the Shinto shrine ground, and cherry blossoms convey the Japanese sense of fragile beauty and transience.

Mt. Fuji is probably the most recognized mountain in the world, with its perfect cone shape and white top for a good part of the year. It is also believed by the Japanese to be a kami—a deity with awesome power. Framed by blooming cherry blossoms in early spring, it offers a breathtaking sight.

The *shimenawa* in front of a Shinto shrine. A giant rope made of rice stalk, the *shimenawa* marks off the sacred space within the shrine complex. Worshippers believe that beyond the line resides the spirit of the *kami*.

The Nachi Waterfall in Kumano, Japan. Like Mt. Fuji, the Nachi Fall is an iconic Shinto symbol long revered in Japan. Also considered a *kami*, it is a popular site for Shinto pilgrims who appreciate not only its magic power but also its scenic beauty.

A Shinto priest at the Itsukushima Shrine in Miyajima, Japan. The priest acts as bridge between the worshippers and the *kami* housed at the shrine. He makes presentation to the deity on behalf of the community, purifies the shrine visitors with prescribed rituals, and presides over community events.

version of the *Yülanpen*, a Chinese Buddhist festival. *Bon* is the Japanese pronunciation of the Chinese word *pen* (bowl of offerings), and *o* is the honorific. This is the festival to welcome the ancestral spirits to return home with food and offerings. Families clean the graves of their ancestors and wash the headstones. On the previous evening, people build a small fire outside the gate of their homes to greet the returning spirits. Sometimes Buddhist monks are invited to the house to recite *sutras* to soothe the souls of the deceased and comfort the living. Over the next two days, people participate in communal folk dances called *bon odori* to please the spirits and to enhance communal solidarity.

Harvest Festival (*Niiname-sai*) This giving of thanks by the community for rice harvest occurs on November 23. In modern Japan, it is renamed "Labor Thanksgiving Day" (*Kinro kansha no hi*) and designated a national holiday. Celebrating the harvest with the people, the Japanese emperor traditionally would taste the newly ripened rice and would offer it to the *kami* on behalf of his subjects. The festival also links all local shrines to the imperial court, as the emperor is believed to be the representative of the people to thank the *kami* for providing fertility and bountifulness.

CONCLUSION

We have established in this chapter that Shinto is the longest surviving and most distinctive religious tradition in Japan. It pervades much of Japanese life and informs much of Japanese behavior. It also provides a sense of identity and unity to the Japanese people. Shinto belief in the ubiquitous presence of the *kami*, both in nature and in human society, makes the Japanese view nature and human community with awe and respect. Though lacking an ethical code and detailed understanding of the afterlife, Shinto is complemented by Confucianism and Buddhism to allow the Japanese the full experience of a religious life.

SEEKING ANSWERS

What Is Ultimate Reality?

According to Shinto, the world is a sanctified place divinely created and ordained by the *kami*. The *kami* reveal themselves in living and nonliving things, in nature and in the human world. They are responsible for the fertility of the world, and they prefer purity and cleanliness. Humans, some of whom are *kami* themselves, must pay constant attention to their relationship with the *kami*, for that is the only way that life can be fulfilled. Because the world is the creation of the *kami*, humanity is obligated to maintain the world's sanctity by acting as its guardian and caretaker. Shinto believers are

(continued)

SEEKING ANSWERS (continued)

extremely sentimental about nature and are easily moved by its beauty. Many Japanese literary compositions express this Shinto affirmation of the divine and sanctified nature of the world.

How Should We Live in This World?

Original Shinto gives little emphasis on morality or ethical living. There is no revealed moral code. Instead, it teaches right living primarily as fertile and pure living. The human condition is defined more in terms of purity and defilement. Death, blood, improper food, or improper behaviors are sources of contamination that make humans unfit to interact with the *kami*. However, these are temporary conditions. Constant attention to maintaining cleanliness and purity will ensure favor from the deities. As a result, rituals of purification and sanctification are meticulously performed by Shinto believers to seek good interaction with the *kami*.

What Is Our Ultimate Purpose?

Unlike many other religions, Shinto does not perceive the human condition as a fallen state or intrinsically flawed by sin. Humans are therefore not evil by nature; thus there is no need for improvement or transcendence. Conversely, Shinto has no belief in an almighty benevolent God who has made humans in an initial state of perfection. Humans are therefore not good by nature, either. Instead, humans are very much a part of nature, striving to live in harmony with it through interaction with its various spiritual manifestations, the *kami*.

REVIEW QUESTIONS

For Review

1. What is the Shinto version of creation?
2. Why is the concept of *kami* so central to Shinto beliefs?
3. How does Shinto view death?

For Further Reflection

1. If Shinto does not address ethics in its original outlook, what is the source of morality for the Japanese?

2. Discuss the role played by women in Shinto.
3. What role does Shinto play in bolstering the nationalistic sentiments of the Japanese people?
4. Although there are rivalry and competition among the three major religions in Japan, there has been a conspicuous absence of religious wars based on doctrinal or theological differences. Please explain.

GLOSSARY

Amaterasu (ah-mah'-te-rah'-soo) "Deity that shines in the sky," the Sun Goddess in Shinto. Enshrined at Ise, Amaterasu is the *kami* of the imperial family. As the Sun Goddess, she is the most august of all deities. Her descendants are considered the only rightful rulers of Japan.

ema (∂-mah') Wooden tablets expressing pleadings to *kami* for success in life.

harae (hah-rah'-∂) Shinto purification.

Izanagi (ee-zanah'-gee) The male *kami* who is the procreator of the Japanese islands.

Izanami (ee-za-nah'-mee) The female *kami* who is the procreator of the Japanese islands.

jinja (jin'-ja) Shinto shrine.

kami (kah-mee) Shinto deity and spirit with awe-inspiring power.

Kojiki (koh'-jee-kee) *Record of Ancient Matters*, compiled in the eighth century C.E.

matsuri (mah-tsu'ree) Shinto religious festival.

miko (mee'-koh) Unmarried female Shinto shrine attendants.

mikoshi (mee-koh'-shee) Portable shrine temporarily housing a Shinto deity.

misogi (mee-soh'-gee) Shinto ritual of purification with water.

Nihon shoki (nee-hohn shoh-kee) *Chronicles of [the Land Where] the Sun Originates*.

norito (noh-ree'-toh) Invocational prayer offered by Shinto priests to the *kami*.

omikuji (oh'-mee-koo-jee) Paper fortunes wrapped around tree branches at shrines.

saisei-itchi (sai-sei ik'-kee) Unity of the religious and the political realms.

shimenawa (shee-m∂' nah-wa) Huge rope hung in front of the worship sanctuary of a shrine.

shintai (shin-tai) The "body" of a *kami* housed in a shrine or temporarily in a *mikoshi*.

Shinto (shin-toh) The Way of the Gods. Traditional Japanese religion that acknowledges the power of the *kami*.

temizuya (te mee' zoo-ya) Purification fountain at a shrine.

torii (toh- ree' ee) Cross-bar gateway leading up to the Shinto shrine.

SUGGESTIONS FOR FURTHER READING

Ashkenazi, Michael. *Matsuri: Festivals of a Japanese Town*. Honolulu: University of Hawaii Press, 1993. An anthropological and sociological description of Shinto in practice at Yuzawa, a town in Japan's northern region.

Bellah, Robert N. *Tokugawa Religion: The Cultural Roots of Modern Japan*. New York: Free Press, 1985. A classic sociological study of the religious roots of modern Japan, with an in-depth look at possible parallels to the Protestant ethic.

De Bary, William Theodore, et al., eds. *Sources of Japanese Tradition*. 2nd ed. 2 vols. New York: Columbia University Press, 2001, 2005. Though not exclusively focused on religious writings, this two-volume anthology is a gold mine of information for the study of Japanese religion.

Earhart, H. Byron. *Religion in the Japanese Experience: Sources and Interpretations*. 2nd ed. Belmont, CA: Wadsworth, 1997. An informative collection of source materials on Japanese religion, arranged topically and with insightful comments.

Ellwood, Robert, and Richard Pilgrim. *Japanese Religion: A Cultural Perspective*. Englewood Cliffs, NJ: Prentice Hall, 1985. A concise volume for the cultural study of Japanese religion.

Kasahara, Kazuo, ed. *A History of Japanese Religion.* Tokyo: Kosei, 2002. An English translation of a two-volume work in Japanese that contains chapters written by scholars on different stages in the historical development of Japanese religion.

Kitagawa, Joseph M. *Religion in Japanese History.* New York: Columbia University Press, 1990. A detailed historical narrative of the development of Japanese religions.

Nelson, John K. *A Year in the Life of a Shinto Shrine.* Seattle: University of Washington Press, 1996. An ethnographical description of the ritual cycle at the Suwa Shrine in Nagasaki.

Ono, Sokyo. *Shinto: The Kami Way.* Tokyo: Charles E. Tuttle, 1962. This remains a very convenient single volume on Shinto.

ONLINE RESOURCES

Encyclopedia of Shinto

eos.kokugakuin.ac.jp

This useful, English-language resource is maintained by the Kokugakuin University in Japan. In addition to the *Encyclopedia of Shinto*, it includes various images and video clips of Shinto objects and rituals.

Tsubaki Grand Shrine of America

tsubakishrine.com

The Tsubaki Grand Shrine, located near Seattle, is the North American branch of one of the most ancient Shinto shrines in Japan. This English-language website provides information about Shinto, as well as a schedule of observances at the Tsubaki shrine.

NOTES

Chapter 1

1. See especially Tomoko Masuzawa, *The Invention of World Religions: Or, How European Universalism Was Preserved in the Language of Pluralism* (Chicago: University of Chicago Press, 2005).

2. See especially Immanuel Kant, *Religion within the Limits of Reason Alone*, trans. Theodore M. Greene and Hoyt H. Hudson (New York: Harper & Row, 1960).

3. Émile Durkheim, *Elementary Forms of the Religious Life*, trans. J. W. Swain (1912; repr., New York: Free Press, 1965), 62.

4. William James, *The Varieties of Religious Experience* (1902; repr., London: Penguin Books, 1985), 31.

5. Paul Tillich, *Theology of Culture*, ed. Robert C. Kimball (New York: Oxford University Press, 1959), 7–8.

6. Jonathan Z. Smith, ed., *HarperCollins Dictionary of Religion* (New York: HarperCollins, 1995), 893.

7. Bruce Lincoln, *Holy Terrors: Thinking about Religion after September 11* (Chicago: University of Chicago Press, 2003), 5–7.

8. Peter Berger, *The Sacred Canopy* (New York: Doubleday, 1967), 175.

9. Sigmund Freud, *The Future of an Illusion*, trans. James Strachey (1927; repr., New York: W. W. Norton & Company, 1961), 55.

10. Karl Marx, "Contribution to the Critique of Hegel's Philosophy of Right," in *On Religion* (Chico, CA: Scholars Press, 1964), 41–42.

11. The term "transtheistic" is used of Jainism by Heinrich Zimmer, *Philosophies of India,* ed. Joseph Campbell (Princeton, NJ: Princeton University Press, 1951), 182.

12. Mircea Eliade, *The Sacred and the Profane: The Nature of Religion*, trans. Willard Trask (London: Harcourt Brace & Company, 1959), 11.

13. Matthew 7:12.

14. *Tremendum* literally means "causing to tremble." The English term "awesome" conveys this meaning.

15. See especially Smart's *Dimensions of the Sacred: An Anatomy of the World's Beliefs* (Berkeley: University of California Press, 1999) and his earlier and very popular *Worldviews: Crosscultural Explanations of Human Belief* (New York: Scribner's, 1983), which details six of the dimensions (Smart later separated out the material dimension as a seventh).

16. Barna Group, "Number of Female Senior Pastors in Protestant Churches Doubles in Past Decade," September 14, 2009, https://www.barna.org/barna-update/leadership/304-number-of-female-senior-pastors-in-protestant-churches-doubles-in-past-decade.

17. Rice University Office of Public Affairs, "Misconceptions of Science and Religion Found in New Study," news release, February 16, 2004, http://rplp.rice.edu/uploadedFiles/RPLP/Ecklund_MediaRelease_2014_0218.pdf.

18. This analogy is drawn from Wilfred Cantwell Smith, *The Meaning and End of Religion* (San Francisco: Harper & Row, 1964), 7.

Chapter 2

1. *Brhadaranyaka Upanishad* 3.9.1–2. In Sarvepalli Radhakrishnan and Charles A. Moore, *A Sourcebook in Indian Philosophy* (Princeton, NJ: Princeton University Press, 1957), 85.

2. Sarvepalli Radhakrishnan and Charles A. Moore, *A Sourcebook in Indian Philosophy* (Princeton, NJ: Princeton University Press, 1957), 77.

3. *Bhagavad Gita* 4:6–8. In Laurie L. Patton, trans., *The Bhagavad Gita* (London: Penguin Books, 2008), 50–51.

4. David M. Knipe, *Hinduism: Experiments in the Sacred* (New York: HarperCollins, 1991), 44–45. The passage appears repeatedly in the *Chandogya Upanishad* 6.9–6.13.

5. *Bhagavad Gita* 2.71. In Radhakrishnan and Moore, *Sourcebook in Indian Philosophy*, 112.

6. *Bhagavad Gita* 5.11–12. In Barbara Stoler Miller, trans., *The Bhagavad-Gita: Krishna's Counsel in Time of War* (New York: Bantam Books, 1986), 60.

7. *Bhagavad Gita* 12.6–8. In Miller, *Bhagavad-Gita,* 110.

8. *Bhagavad Gita* 4.38–39. In Radhakrishnan and Moore, *Sourcebook in Indian Philosophy*, 118–119.

9. *Laws of Manu* II.36. In Radhakrishnan and Moore, *Sourcebook in Indian Philosophy*, 177.

10. An oft-quoted line from Major-General Charles Stuart's (1758–1828) *Vindication of the Hindoos*, which was published in 1808.

11. Diana Eck, *Darsan: Seeing the Divine Image in India* (New York: Columbia University Press, 1998).

12. *Laws of Manu* III.56. In Radhakrishnan and Moore, *Sourcebook in Indian Philosophy*, 189.

Chapter 3

1. "The Global Religious Landscape," December 18, 2012, Pew Research Religion and Public Life Project, www.pewforum.org/2012/12/18/global-religious-landscape-exec/.

2. This term is used of Jainism by Heinrich Zimmer, *Philosophies of India*, ed. Joseph Campbell (Princeton, NJ: Princeton University Press, 1951), 182.

3. Henry Clarke Warren, *Buddhism in Translations* (New York: Atheneum, 1984), 109.

4. Richard H. Robinson and Willard L. Johnson, *The Buddhist Religion: A Historical Introduction*, 3rd ed. (Belmont, CA: Wadsworth, 1982), 40.

5. Juan Mascaró, trans. *The Dhammapada: The Path of Perfection* (London and New York: Penguin Books, 1973), 35.

6. Stephen Beyer, *The Cult of Tara: Magic and Ritual in Tibet* (Berkeley: University of California Press, 1973), 92.

7. "Flash Animated Philosophy from South Park Creators," coldhardflash.com/2007/07/flash-animated-philosophy-from-south.html.

8. Anne Bancroft, *Zen: Direct Pointing to Reality* (New York: Thames and Hudson, 1979), 5.

9. See, for instance, Bernard Faure, "Buddhism and Violence," December 6, 2003, sangam.org/articles/view/?id=118.

Chapter 4

1. *Acarangasutra* 1.4.1.1–2, trans. Hermann Jacobi. In *Sacred Books of the East,* vol. 20, ed. Friedrich Max Müller (Oxford: Oxford University Press, 1884).

2. Yogendra Jain, *Jain Way of Life: A Guide to Compassionate, Healthy, and Happy Living* (Boston: Federation of Jain Associations of North America, 2007), i.

3. *Tattvarthadhigama Sutra*, Chapter II, 22–23, trans. J. L. Jaini. In *A Sourcebook in Indian Philosophy,* ed. Sarvepalli Radhakrishnan and Charles A. Moore (Princeton, NJ: Princeton University Press, 1957), 254.

4. This term is used of Jainism by Heinrich Zimmer, *Philosophies of India*, ed. Joseph Campbell (Princeton, NJ: Princeton University Press, 1951), 182.

5. Paul Dundas, *The Jains* (New York: Routledge, 1992), 47; the text referenced here is the *Sthānanga* 171.

6. *Avashyakasutra* 32; cited in Dundas, *The Jains*, 171.

7. Dundas, *The Jains*, 55–56; the text referenced here is the *Kalpasutra*.

8. Padmanabh S. Jaini, *The Jaina Path of Purification* (Berkeley: University of California Press, 1979), 196–197.

Chapter 5

1. Gurinder Singh Mann, *Sikhism* (Upper Saddle River, NJ: Prentice Hall), 14.

2. Hew McLeod, *Sikhism* (London: Penguin, 1997), 219.

3. Adapted from a quotation in W. Owen Cole and Piara Singh Sambhi, *The Sikhs: Their Religious Beliefs and Practices* (London: Routledge & Kegan Paul, 1978), 9.

4. Quoted in ibid., 10.

5. Quoted in Khushwant Singh, "Sikhism," *Encyclopedia of Religion* (New York: Simon & Schuster Macmillan, 1995), 13:316.

6. Quoted in ibid., 316.

7. From *Puratan Janam-sakhi*, cited in W. H. McLeod, ed. and trans., *Textual Sources for the Study of Sikhism* (Totowa, NJ: Barnes & Noble Books, 1984), 25.

8. Khushwant Singh, "Sikhism," 319.

9. Cited in McLeod, *Sikhism*, 271.

10. Cited in ibid., 272.

11. Ibid., 98.

12. Gopal Singh, *A History of the Sikh People* (New Delhi, India: World Sikh University Press, 1979), 263–264.

13. Teja Singh and Ganda Singh, *A Short History of the Sikhs: Volume One (1469–1765)*, 3rd ed. (Patiala, India: Punjabi University, 1999), 67.

14. Mann, *Sikhism*, 14.

15. Ibid.

16. Cited in W. H. McLeod, *Textual Sources*, 79–80.

17. Cited in Hew McLeod, *Sikhism*, 216.

18. *Āsā ki Vār* 19:2, Adi Granth, 473. Cited in W. H. McLeod, *Textual Sources*, 109.

19. Mann, *Sikhism*, 106.

Chapter 6

1. All Chinese names in this chapter are indicated in the conventional Chinese manner, namely, the family name comes first, followed by the given name. All romanization of Chinese terms and names adheres to the official Chinese pinyin system. Terms and names with an established familiar spelling in the West, such as Taoism (instead of the official pinyin rendition of Daoism) are provided in parentheses at their first occurrence.

2. See Joseph Needham, ed., *Science and Civilization in China* (Cambridge, UK: Cambridge University Press, 1956), 2:55ff.

3. This term is not found in the *Book of Changes* itself but is in fact a later Daoist rendition of the idea of the primordial one.

4. Refer to the highly suggestive article of David N. Keightley, "The Religious Commitment: Shang Theology and the Genesis of Chinese Political Culture," *History of Religions* 17, nos. 3–4 (Feb.–May 1978): 211–225.

5. Also translated as *Book of Songs* or *Book of Poetry*.

6. Also known as the *Book of Documents*.

7. The masculine pronoun is used advisedly throughout the entire discussion of Confucian teachings. Confucius and his intellectual followers after him, like many in the premodern age worldwide, did not seriously entertain the possibility that women could participate meaningfully in the exercise of virtue, pursuit of scholarship, and service in government. The masculine pronoun is adopted not as an endorsement of that view but as a faithful reflection of the Confucian assumption.

8. William Theodore de Bary, *Neo-Confucian Orthodoxy and the Learning of the Mind-and-Heart* (New York: Columbia University Press, 1981), 9.

9. See Tu Wei-ming, "Li as a Process of Humanization," in *Philosophy East and West* 22, no. 2 (April 1972): 187–201.

10. See Herbert Fingarette's *Confucius: The Secular as Sacred* (New York: Harper Torchbooks, 1972), 7.

11. See Xinzhong Yao, *An Introduction to Confucianism* (Cambridge, UK: Cambridge University Press, 2000), 46.

12. See the highly nuanced discussion of the topic by Li-Hsiang Lisa Rosenlee, in her *Confucianism and Women: A Philosophical Interpretation* (Albany: State University of New York Press, 2006). See also Chenyang Li, ed., *The Sage and the Second Sex: Confucianism, Ethics, and Gender* (Chicago: Open Court, 2000). Deborah Achtenberg's "Aristotelian Resources in Feminist Thinking," in *Feminism and Ancient Philosophy*, ed. Julie K. Ward (London: Routledge, 1996), 97, is also very suggestive.

13. Many Chinese books carry the name of their supposed author as their title. To distinguish between the text and its reputed author, the former will be indicated in italics.

14. This discussion of *feng* and *shan* rites is based on Stephen Bokenkamp's "Record of the Feng and Shan Sacrifices," in *Religions of China in Practice,* ed. Donald S. Lopez Jr. (Princeton, NJ: Princeton University Press, 1996), 251–260.

15. Summary based on Patricia Buckley Ebrey, ed., *Chinese Civilization: A Sourcebook*, 2nd ed. (New York: Free Press, 1993), 157–163.

16. This summary of the *jiao* liturgy is based on a composite description of two separate ceremonies conducted, respectively, in 1994 and 2005 in Hong Kong. A DVD depicting the rites and explaining their religious meaning was produced in 2009 by the Center for the Study of Daoist Culture of the Department of Culture and Religion, Chinese University of Hong Kong.

Chapter 7

1. This "body" is known as the *shintai*, the physical embodiment of the deity, which is believed to contain the spirit and magical power of the deity. It is discussed in greater detail in the section on the teachings of Shinto.

2. Quoted in H. Byron Earhart, *Religion in the Japanese Experience: Sources and Interpretations*, 2nd ed. (Belmont, CA: Wadsworth, 1997), 10.

3. That the Japanese should regard the sun as female is most noteworthy. That this female sun goddess should serve as the primordial ancestor of the imperial line, as is discussed later, is even more significant, for it is incongruent with the later patriarchal orientation of the country.

4. The *Nihongi* has a slightly different version of this episode. It asserts that the three deities are the product of the union between Izanagi and Izanami.

5. Quoted in William Theodore de Bary et al., eds., *Sources of Japanese Tradition* (New York: Columbia University Press, 2001), 1:259.

6. Quoted in de Bary et al., eds., *Sources of Japanese Tradition* (New York: Columbia University Press, 2005), 2:498, 512.

7. See Evan Zuesse, *Ritual Cosmos* (Athens: Ohio University Press, 1979), 402.

GLOSSARY

Adi Granth (ah'dee gruhnth; Punjabi, "first book") Sikhism's most important sacred text and, since the death of Guru Gobind Singh in 1708, Sikhism's primary earthly authority; traditionally known as Sri Guru Granth Sahib.

ahimsa (ah-him'suh; Sanskrit, "nonviolence," "not desiring to harm") Both the avoidance of violence toward other life forms and an active sense of compassion toward them; a basic principle of Jainism, Hinduism, and Buddhism.

ajiva (uh-jee'vuh; Sanskrit, "nonsoul") Nonliving components of the Jain universe: space, time, motion, rest, and all forms of matter.

Amaterasu (ah-mah'-te-rah'-soo) "Deity that shines in the sky," the Sun Goddess in Shinto. Enshrined at Ise, Amaterasu is the *kami* of the imperial family. As the Sun Goddess, she is the most august of all deities. Her descendants are considered the only rightful rulers of Japan.

amrit (ahm-reet; Punjabi, "immortalizing fluid") A special drink made from water and sugar crystals, used in the Khalsa initiation ceremony.

anatman (un-aat-mun; Sanskrit) The doctrine that there is no independent, eternal self or soul underlying personal existence.

arati (aah-ra-tee) Worship with light, involving the waving of a lamp in front of the deity.

arhat (ar'hut) In Theravada Buddhism, one who has attained enlightenment.

atheism Perspective that denies the existence of God or gods.

atman (aat-mun; Sanskrit) The eternal self or soul that is successively reincarnated until released from *samsara* through *moksha*.

avatar (ah-vah-taahr; from Sanskrit *avatara*) A "descent" of God (usually Vishnu) to earth in a physical form with the specific goal of aiding the world.

bhakti marga (bhah-k-tee mar-guh; Sanskrit) The path of devotion.

bodhichitta (bow-dhi-chit-ta; Sanskrit, "the awakening mind or heart") In Mahayana Buddhism, the wise and compassionate intention to attain Buddhahood for the sake of all other sentient beings.

bodhisattva (bow-dhi-sut-tva; Sanskrit, "enlightenment being") One who is on the verge of enlightenment. In Mahayana Buddhism, a bodhisattva is one who has taken a "bodhisattva vow" to remain in samsara in order to work for the enlightenment of all sentient beings.

Brahman (braah-mun; Sanskrit, "expansive") For monistic Hinduism, the supreme, unitary reality, the ground of all Being; for dualistic Hinduism, *Brahman* can refer to the supreme God (e.g., Vishnu).

brahmin (braah-mun; Sanskrit) A member of the priestly class of the *varna* or caste system.

Buddha (bood-dha; Sanskrit, "the Awakened One") A fully enlightened being.

Chan/Zen (Chinese/Japanese) Respectively, the Chinese and Japanese names for the "meditation" school of Buddhism that values meditative experience far and above doctrine.

cosmology Understanding of the nature of the world that typically explains its origin and how it is ordered.

dalit (daah-lit; Sanskrit, "oppressed"; Marathi, "broken") Self-designation of people who had traditionally been classified as untouchables or outcastes.

dana (dah'nuh; Sanskrit, Pali, "giving") Ritual of giving.

dantian (dahn'-tee'ən) "Fields for the refinement of the immortal pill"; major nodal points in the human body where the "pill" of immortality can be refined through alchemical means.

dao (dow) A fundamental concept in Chinese religion, literally meaning the "path" or the "way." In Confucianism, it specifically refers to the entire ideal human order ordained by the numinous Absolute, *Tian*. In

Daoism, it is the primary source of the cosmos, the very ground of all beings.

Daodejing (dow'-duh-jing) Basic Daoist scripture, lit. "The Scripture of the Way and Its Potent Manifestation"; also known as the Book of *Laozi*, the name of its purported author.

Daozang (dow' zahng) Literally "Treasury of the Dao," this is the Daoist Canon that contains the entire corpus of Daoist texts. The most complete version, still in use today, was first published in 1445.

darshan (dur-shaan; Sanskrit, "to see") Worship through simultaneously seeing and being seen by a deity in the presence of its image.

de (duh) Another fundamental concept in Chinese religions, meaning "virtue" or "potency." In Confucianism, it is the charismatic power of the ruler or the man of virtue, while in Daoism it means the concrete manifestation of the *dao*.

***dharma*/Dharma** (dhur-mah; Sanskrit) Duty, righteousness, "religion"; basis for living in a way that upholds cosmic and social order. In the Buddhist context, Dharma refers both to Buddhist teaching and Buddhism as a religion.

Digambara (dig-ahm'buh-ruh; Sanskrit, "those whose garment is the sky") The second largest Jain sect, whose monks go about naked so as to help abolish any ties to society; generally more conservative than the Shvetambara sect.

dukkha (doo-kah; Pali, "suffering") Usually translated as "suffering," it can also be understood as the anxiety, unease, and dissatisfaction caused by desire.

ema (ə-mah') Wooden tablets expressing pleadings to *kami* for success in life.

empathy The capacity for seeing things from another's perspective, and an important methodological approach for studying religions.

fangshi (fahng-shər) "Magicians" who allegedly possessed the recipe for immortality.

Five Classics The five canonical works of Confucianism designated in the Han Dynasty. They are *Book of Odes*, *Book of History*, *Book of Changes*, *Record of Rites*, and *Spring and Autumn Annals*.

Four Books The four texts identified by the Neo-Confucian Zhu Xi as fundamental in understanding the Confucian teaching. Between 1313 and 1905, they made up the curriculum for the civil service examination. They are *Analects*, *Mencius*, *Great Learning*, and *Doctrine of the Mean*.

Four Noble Truths The four truths that form the basis of the Dharma: Suffering is inherent in human life, suffering is caused by desire, there can be an end to desire, the way to end desire is the Noble Eightfold Path.

globalization The linking and intermixing of cultures; any process that moves a society toward an internationalization of religious discourse.

gui (gwei) Ghosts and demons, malevolent spirits.

gurdwara (goor'dwah-ruh; Punjabi, "doorway of the Guru" or "by means of the Guru's [grace]") A building for Sikh worship that houses a copy of the Adi Granth; the central structure of any Sikh community.

Guru (goo'roo; Sanskrit, "venerable person") A spiritual teacher and revealer of truth, common to Hinduism, Sikhism, and some forms of Buddhism. When the word *Guru* is capitalized, it refers to the ten historical leaders of Sikhism, to the sacred text (Sri Guru Granth Sahib, or Adi Granth), and to God (often as True Guru).

harae (hah-rah'-ə) Shinto purification.

haumai (how'may; Punjabi, "self-reliance," "pride," or "egoism") The human inclination toward being self-centered rather than God-centered, which increases the distance between the individual and God.

henotheism The belief that acknowledges a plurality of gods but elevates one of them to special status.

hindutva (hin-doot-vah; Sanskrit, "Hindu-ness") A modern term that encompasses the ideology of Hindu nationalism.

hukam (huh'kahm; Punjabi, "order") The divine order of the universe.

Impermanence According to the Buddha's doctrine of Impermanence, all phenomena are in a constant state of change.

Interdependent Origination (Sanskrit: *pratitya-samutpada*, "arising on the ground of a preceding cause") The doctrine that reality is a complex of interrelated and interdependent phenomena in which nothing exists independently; instead, the origination of all things depends on other things.

Izanagi (ee-zanah'-gee) The male *kami* who is the procreator of the Japanese islands.

Izanami (ee-za-nah'-mee) The female *kami* who is the procreator of the Japanese islands.

jati (jaah-tee; Sanskrit, "birth group") One of thousands of endogamous groups or subcastes, each equal in social and ritual status.

jiao (jee'au) Daoist communal sacrificial offerings to signal cosmic renewal and collective cohesion.

jina (ji'nuh; Sanskrit, "conqueror") Jain title for one who has "conquered" *samsara;* synonymous with *tirthankara.*

jinja (jin'-ja) Shinto shrine.

jiva (jee'vuh; Sanskrit, "soul") The finite and eternal soul; also the category of living, as opposed to non-living, entities of the universe.

jnana marga (nyah-nah mar-guh; Sanskrit) The path of knowledge.

junzi (ju'un zee) The personality ideal in Confucianism; the noble person.

kami (kah-mee) Shinto deity and spirit with awe-inspiring power.

karma (Sanskrit, "action") "Action" and the consequences of action; determines the nature of one's reincarnation; in Jainism, all activity is believed to involve various forms of matter that weigh down the soul (*jiva*) and thus hinder the quest for liberation.

karma marga (kur-mah mar-guh; Sanskrit) The path of ethical and ritual works, or "action."

kevala (kay'vuh-luh; shortened form of Sanskrit *kevalajnana,* "isolated knowledge" or "absolute knowledge") The perfect and complete knowledge or omniscience that is Jain enlightenment; marks the point at which one is free from the damaging effects of karma and is liberated from *samsara.*

Khalsa (khal'sah; Punjabi, "pure ones") An order within Sikhism to which the majority of Sikhs belong, founded by Guru Gobind Singh in 1699.

Kojiki (koh'-jee-kee) *Record of Ancient Matters,* compiled in the eighth century C.E.

kshatriya (kshut-ree-yuh; Sanskrit) A member of the warrior and administrator class of the *varna* or caste system.

lama (laah-mah; Tibetan) In Tibet, a teacher of the Dharma.

li (lee) Etiquette and proper manners; rituals and holy rites.

loka (loh'kah; Sanskrit, "world") The Jain universe, often depicted as having the shape of a giant man.

Mahayana (muh-haah-yaah-na; Sanskrit, "great vehicle") Also known as the "Great Vehicle," Mahayana is the form of Buddhism most prominent in China, Japan, Mongolia, Tibet, and Korea.

mandala (muhn-daah-la; Sanskrit "circle") Typically, a circular diagram representing the entire universe. Often used as an aid in meditation.

mantra (mun-trah; Sanskrit) A sacred sound or syllable used as a focus for meditation, as an invocation of a deity, or as a protective spell; a ritual formula recited to produce a spiritual effect.

matsuri (mah-tsu'ree) Shinto religious festival.

maya (my-yah: Sanskrit, "magic" or "illusion") In the *Vedas,* the magical power the gods used to create this world; in *Vedanta* philosophy, illusion that veils the mind.

Middle Way The Buddha's principle of the path between extremes of asceticism and self-indulgence that leads to enlightenment.

miko (mee'-koh) Unmarried female Shinto shrine attendants.

mikoshi (mee-koh'-shee) Portable shrine temporarily housing a Shinto deity.

ming (*see* **Tianming**)

misogi (mee-soh'-gee) Shinto ritual of purification with water.

modernization The general process through which societies transform economically, socially, and culturally to become more industrial, urban, and secular; any transformation of societies and cultures that leads to the abandonment of traditional religious values.

moksha (mohk-shah; Sanskrit, "release") Liberation, the final release from *samsara.*

monism The belief that all reality is ultimately one.

monotheism The belief in only one god.

mukti (mook'tee; Punjabi, "liberation") Spiritual liberation bringing on the eternal and infinitely blissful state of being in the presence of God; sometimes the Sanskrit term *moksha* is used instead.

Mul Mantra The summary of Sikh doctrine that comprises the opening lines of the *Japji,* Guru Nanak's composition that in turn comprises the opening section of the Adi Granth.

multiculturalism The coexistence of different peoples and their cultural ways in one time and place.

mysterium tremendum* and *fascinans The contrasting feelings of awe-inspiring mystery and of overwhelming attraction that are said by Rudolf Otto to characterize the numinous experience.

mystical experience A general category of religious experience characterized in various ways, for example, as the uniting with the divine through inward contemplation or as the dissolution of the sense of individual selfhood.

myth A story or narrative, originally conveyed orally, that sets forth basic truths of a religious tradition; myths often involve events of primordial time that describe the origin of things.

Native American Church A church founded in early twentieth century based on peyote religion.

neidan (nay'-dahn) Daoist "internal" alchemy designed to attain immortality through meditation, breath control, gymnastics, diet, and massage.

neisheng waiwang (nay'-sheng' wī'-wahng) Neo-Confucian ideal of "inner sagely moral perfection and outer political skills."

Nihon shoki (nee-hohn shoh-kee) *Chronicles of [the Land Where] the Sun Originates.*

nirvana (nihr-vaah-nah; Sanskrit, an "extinguishing" or "blowing out") The ultimate goal of Buddhist practice, nirvana is the extinguishing of desire and the suffering it causes.

Noble Eightfold Path The Buddha's prescription for a way of life that leads to enlightenment. Based on the principle of the Middle Way, it is also defined by eight virtues.

nontheistic Term denoting a religion that does not maintain belief in God or gods.

norito (noh-ree'-toh) Invocational prayer offered by Shinto priests to the *kami*.

No-Self The doctrine that there is no independent, eternal self or soul underlying personal existence. See also ***anatman***.

numinous experience Rudolf Otto's term for describing an encounter with "the Holy"; it is characterized by the powerful and contending forces, *mysterium tremendum* and *fascinans*.

Odu (oh-doo; Yoruba) The original prophets in Yoruba religion.

OM (oh-m; from Sanskrit letters A, U, M) The primordial sound through which the universe is manifested.

omikuji (oh'-mee-koo-jee) Paper fortunes wrapped around tree branches at shrines.

Pali Canon Also known as the ***Tripitaka*** (Sanskrit, "Three Baskets"), the Pali Canon is the first canon of Buddhist texts. It consists of three "baskets" or sections of sutras.

Panth (puhnth; Punjabi, Hindi, "path") The Sikh community. In lower case, *panth* ("path") is a term applied to any number of Indian (primarily Hindu) religious traditions.

pantheism The belief that the divine reality is identical to nature or the material world.

parinirvana (pah-ree nihr-vaah-nah; Sanskrit, "supreme release") The full entry into nirvana that occurs at the death of one who has achieved nirvana in his or her lifetime.

polytheism The belief in many gods.

puja (poo-jah; Sanskrit, "worship") Generally, worship; usually the offering before an image of the deity of fruit, incense, or flowers.

Purana (pooh-raa-nah; Sanskrit, "ancient") A compendium of myth, usually with a sectarian emphasis.

qi (chee) Breath, force, power, material energy.

Rahit (rah-hit'; Punjabi) The *rahit-nama*, a collection of scripture that specifies ideals of belief and conduct for members of the Khalsa and, by extension, for Sikhism generally; the current authoritative version, the *Sikh Rahit Maryada*, was approved in 1950.

ren (rən) Human-heartedness, benevolence; the unique moral inclination of humans.

revealed ethics Truth regarding right behavior believed to be divinely established and intentionally made known to human beings.

revelation The expression of the divine will, commonly recorded in sacred texts.

ritual Formal worship practice.

ru (rōō) Scribes and ritual performers of the Zhou period; later used exclusively to refer to Confucians.

saisei-itchi (sai-sei ik'-kee) Unity of the religious and the political realms.

samsara (sum-saah-ra; Sanskrit, "continuous flow") The continuing cycle of birth, death, and rebirth; also, the this-worldly realm in which the cycle recurs.

Sangha (suhn-ghaah; Sanskrit, "community") The worldwide community of Buddhists. Alternatively, the order of Buddhist monks or the membership of a particular Buddhist congregation.

sannyasi (sun-nyaah-see; Sanskrit) Renouncer in the fourth stage (*ashrama*) of life.

secularization The general turning away from traditional religious authority and institutions; any tendency in modern society that devalues religious worldviews or seeks to substitute scientific theories for religious beliefs.

Shaiva (shay-vah; Sanskrit) A devotee of Shiva.

Shakta (shah-k-tah; Sanskrit) A devotee of the Great Goddess, Devi.

Shangdi (shahng'-dee) The August Lord on High of the Shang period.

shen (shən) Gods and deities; benevolent spirits.

shengren (shəng rən) (or *sheng*) The Confucian sage, the epitome of humanity.

shi (shər) Men of service; lower-ranking civil and military officials in the Zhou period.

shimenawa (shee-mə' nah-wa) Huge rope hung in front of the worship sanctuary of a shrine.

shintai (shin-tai) The "body" of a *kami* housed in a shrine or temporarily in a *mikoshi*.

Shinto (shin-toh) The Way of the Gods. Traditional Japanese religion that acknowledges the power of the *kami*.

shruti (shroo-tee; Sanskrit, "that which is heard") Term denoting the category of Vedic literature, accepted by orthodox Hindus as revealed truth.

shudra (shoo-druh; Sanskrit) A member of the servant class of the *varna* or caste system.

Shvetambara (shvayt-ahm'buh-ruh; Sanskrit, "those whose garment is white") The largest Jain sect, whose monks and nuns wear white robes; generally more liberal than the Digambara sect.

skandhas (skuhn-dhaah; Sanskrit, "heaps" or "bundles") The five components (body, perceptions, feelings, innate tendencies, and thought) that give rise to a sense of self.

smriti (smree-tee; Sanskrit, "tradition") Term denoting the vast category of Hindu sacred texts that is not *shruti*.

stupa (stooh-puh; Sanskrit, "heap") A reliquary mound in which the relics of the Buddha or a Buddhist saint are buried and venerated.

sutra (sooh-trah; Sanskrit, "a thread") Verses of text or scripture.

temizuya (te mee' zoo-ya) Purification fountain at a shrine.

theistic Term denoting a religion that maintains belief in God or gods.

Theravada (thair-ah-vaah-duh; Pali, "the Way of the Elders") The form of Buddhism that is most prominent in Sri Lanka, Cambodia, Laos, and Vietnam.

Three Marks of Existence The Buddha's teachings on impermanence, suffering, and the nonexistence of an eternal unchanging self or soul.

Tian (teeən) The transcendent, numinous entity in ancient Chinese religion; the conscious Will that regulates the cosmos and intervenes in human affairs; conventionally translated as "Heaven."

Tianming The mandate or command of *Tian* that confers political legitimacy to the ruler; also understood by Confucians as the calling to morally improve oneself and to transform the world.

Tianshi (tee'ən shər) "Celestial Master"; reference to a Daoist salvational figure, as well as an organized movement.

tirthankaras (teert-hahn'kuhr-uhs; Sanskrit, "makers of the river crossing") The Jain spiritual heroes, such as Parshva and Mahavira, who have shown the way to salvation; synonymous with *jinas*.

torii (toh- ree' ee) Cross-bar gateway leading up to the Shinto shrine.

transtheistic Term denoting a theological perspective that acknowledges the existence of gods while denying that the gods are vital with regard to the most crucial religious issues, such as the quest for salvation.

Tripitaka (see Pali Canon)

Upanishad (ooh-pah-nee-shud; Sanskrit, "sitting down near [a teacher]") A philosophical text from the later period of Vedic literature, also called *Vedanta* ("end of the *Vedas*").

upaya (ooh-paah-ya; Sanskrit, "expedient means") "Skillful Means" was developed into a form of Buddhist practice that encourages imaginatively applying wisdom to whatever circumstances one is in to assist in easing suffering or cultivating insight.

urbanization The shift of population centers from rural, agricultural settings to cities.

Vaishnava (vie-sh-na-vah; Sanskrit) A devotee of Vishnu and his *avatars*.

vaishya (vie-sh-yuh; Sanskrit) A member of the producer (farmer and merchant) class of the *varna* or caste system.

Vajrayana (vaah-jiraah-yaah-nah; Sanskrit, "Diamond Vehicle" or "Thunderbolt Vehicle") Often described as a form of *Mahayana*, *Vajrayana* is the most prominent form of Buddhism in Tibet and Nepal. It incorporates both Mahayana and tantric ideas and practices.

varna (vaar-nah; Sanskrit, "color") Caste or class; the four main classes form the basis of the traditional hierarchical organization of Hindu society.

Vedanta (veh-daan-tah; Sanskrit, "end of the *Vedas*") Synonym for *Upanishads*; prominent Hindu philosophical school.

Vedas (veh-duhs; from Sanskrit *veda*, "knowledge") Broadly, all Vedic literature; narrowly, four ancient collections (*samhitas*) of hymns and other religious material.

waidan (wī dahn) Daoist "external" alchemy involving refining of "pills" with herbs and minerals for ingestion so that immortality can be attained.

wuwei (wōō way) Daoist notion of action without intention; actionless action.

wuxing (wōō shing) The five elemental phases of metal, wood, water, fire, and soil that mutually support and overcome one another.

xian (shee'ən) Daoist immortals and perfected individuals.

xiao (shee'au) Filial piety; respect and care for parents and ancestors.

xinzhai (shin jī) "Fasting of the Mind" in the *Zhuangzi*.

yang (young) Lit. the south-facing side of a mountain, representing the energy that is bright, warm, dry, and masculine.

yangsheng (young shəng) Daoist techniques of nourishing life and attaining immortality.

yin Lit. the north-facing side of a mountain, representing the energy that is dark, cold, wet, and feminine.

yoga (yoh-gah; Sanskrit, "yoking" or "uniting") Generally, uniting of the self with God; sometimes used as an alternative to *marga* when referring to the three main paths to liberation; also (normally capitalized: Yoga) one of the six philosophical schools, focusing on moral, physical, and spiritual practices leading to liberation.

zhai (jī) Daoist "fasts" designed to seek redemption of transgressions by the gods.

ziran (zee'-rahn) Daoist notion of natural spontaneity.

zuowang (zoh'-wahng) "Sitting and Forgetting" in the *Zhuangzi*.

CREDITS

INDEX

Page numbers in *italics* indicate
photographs/illustrations.